POKER BRAT
PHIL HELLMUTH'S AUTOBIOGRAPHY

To chart,

I have enjoyed
knowing you and
following your
life, keep crushing!!

Good luck,

Phil J
in SF.

D+B

POKER

First published in 2017 by D&B Publishing
Copyright © 2017 Phil Hellmuth

The right of Phil Hellmuth to be identified as the author
of this work has been asserted in accordance with the
Copyrights, Designs and Patents Act 1988.

British Library Cataloguing-in-Publication Data
A catalogue record for this book is available from the British Library.

ISBN: 978 1 909457 74 4

WSOP Entrance photography by Eric Harkins &
Rob Gracie/pokerphotoarchive.com

Jay Z and Phil Hellmuth photo courtesy
of Kyle Terada-USA TODAY Sports

Cover and book design by Horacio Monteverde.

Printed and bound by Versa Press in the US.

D+B

POKER

All sales enquiries should be directed to D&B Publishing:
info@dandbpoker.com

Dedication

To my oldest son Phillip III, you have strength and integrity, and I'm proud of you. To my parents Lynn and Phil, thanks for teaching me honor and ethics and to believe I can do it...

Contents

Foreword

by Daniel Negreanu

For years Phil Hellmuth has been the most polarizing figure in all of poker. Knowing the man, I also think he might be the most misunderstood. Love him or hate him, there is no denying the fact that when Phil is playing on television, people watch. He wears the passion that he plays with on his sleeve for all the world to see. You get to endure every bad beat and tongue lashing his opponents may receive, as well as the child-like joy he emanates when he is victorious.

Phil cares so deeply about the game of poker that when you see him on a tirade after a bad beat, you are seeing his genuine feelings in that moment. These are feelings that I am sure we can all relate to when the river card dashes our hopes. Phil doesn't hold back and watching him play is reality TV at its best.

I say that Phil might be the most misunderstood figure in poker because the "haters", who don't know the man behind the brat-like tirades, don't get to see the kind, honest, joyous, family man that he is away from the table. I'll be the first to say that I think sometimes he crosses the line with his behavior at the table, but I also know his intentions aren't malicious. Nobody wants to win more than Phil. He puts his heart out there in every tournament and fights for every chip.

He is an asset to the poker community and, by reading this book, you will learn more about Mr. Hellmuth than the title "Poker Brat" suggests. What has made him successful all these years? What drives him? How is he able to stay positive and confident in such a profession that is so often stressful? This is a fascinating look into the mind of one of poker's biggest stars.

Please Help Me, Mom!

In April 1987, as I wandered aimlessly between the slot machines and the craps tables at the Riviera Hotel and Casino, the gravity of my predicament began to sink in. The poker had gone badly for me in Las Vegas. I had no money on my person – I had $800 left to my name hidden in my parents' house in Madison, Wisconsin – no credit cards, no friends in town to borrow money from, no way home, no way to pay my overdue hotel bill and, worst of all, I was hungry. After wandering around for an hour examining my limited options (I even searched the Riviera Casino floor for chips!), I came to see that the only way out was to call my parents and beg them to buy a plane ticket home for me. I knew that my father would tell me, "Good luck hitchhiking home." But perhaps my mom (I pray that she's home!) could be persuaded to help me out. After all, I did have the money to pay her back the moment I reached home.

I'm Dropping out of School

Only five months before I found myself in this sorry state of affairs, I had called my parents and said, "I'm dropping out of college [at the University of Wisconsin] to play poker professionally." Can you imagine my father's response? This is a man who has more degrees than seems possible: a JD (law degree), a PhD, and a Masters in Business Administration (MBA) for good measure! Add to that the fact that I'm the oldest of five, the oldest son. Can you imagine how he reacted to my dropping out of university to play poker professionally? I was the son who had to go to college, who had to get good grades. I was the son he had tried desperately to mold and shape, so that I would set a good example for my younger brother and my three younger sisters. My dad is so deeply into education that he spent his whole working life working at the University of Wisconsin (UW).

So I made my way back to my hotel room, dreading the phone call that I needed to make, while trying to think of another way out. There wasn't one. Finally, I picked up the phone. After my first attempt to call failed, I realized that I would have to call "collect," because my "cash only" outside phone line had been cut off by the hotel.

Operator: "Sir, will you accept the charges and take a collect call from P.J.?"

After a brief hesitation, my father said, "Yes (oh great, Dad answered the phone!), I accept the charges."

"Hi, Dad, things aren't going so well here in Las Vegas."

"Has it ever gone well for you there, even one time?"

Trying not to let my voice crack, I said, "Dad, I need your help. I'm stuck here in Las Vegas with no money and no way to get home, and I'm hungry. I can't believe I did this to myself, but I lost all my money."

"You might want to talk to your mother, bye..."

Mom, "Hi, P.J., what's going on?"

"Mom, I lost all my money, I'm hungry, and I need you to call the airlines and buy a plane ticket home for me on your credit card for $180. I have $800 at home and I'll pay you back as soon as I get home."

A long pause...

"OK, P.J., listen carefully, I'm going to help you out this one time. But I will never ever help you out again. I love you, but we have four other younger children, and we need to save our money for them. Do you understand?"

"Yes, Mom, thank you."

As I slunk out of the Riviera hotel, unable to pay my bill and ferociously hungry, I felt awful. As I arrived at the airport I realized that I couldn't even pay the cab driver full fare! The cab driver smiled at me out of pity, and told me to keep my last 47 cents.

Too Many Peanuts

So how was this professional poker thing working out? I was at war with my father over my new choice of "career," I had just used the only "get out of jail free card" that my mom would ever give me, I had carelessly lost all the money on my person, and I had left myself stranded in Las Vegas with no way home. Here's how it was working out: I ate so many peanuts on the flight home that I hated peanuts for the next ten years!

2

Every Rose has its Thorn, Part 1

How have a managed to become the "poker brat"? Why do I throw tantrums when I lose? Worse, why do I berate other players when they beat me in big pots? It's about battling a lifetime of self-esteem issues!

But how is it possible that I would suffer from low self-esteem? I have never cheated on my wife in 25 years of marriage, I have been a father; I have perfect health, I don't do drugs (not even aspirin!), and I don't drink heavily; I am honorable and honest to the nth degree, and I haven't been broke since 1987; and I have earned a good measure of fortune and fame, I own every important record at the World Series of Poker (WSOP), and these days I have become a global poker icon. In a nutshell, I have solid reasons for feeling comfortable about myself, but I've suffered from low self-esteem because of how things went during my first 21 years on the planet.

Not Much Going On

My early life, from the time I was born, on July 16, 1964, until I reached 21, was pretty much a washout. I suffered from bad grades, owing probably to some form of Attention Deficit Disorder (ADD), a shortage of friends, a lack of social skills, warts that made my hands so grotesque that I was driven to hide them from plain view whenever I was in public. Not to mention a serious case of acne on my face, and problems with parental support. Rebellion against my parents took the form of petty shoplifting until I turned 16 years old. Because of this sea of troubles, which I will talk about in this chapter, when I did at last have some success in poker (Chapter 4), I dealt with it horribly! Considering the general ineffectiveness of my earlier life, how well was I likely to cope with major poker successes? Not well!

Deep in my mind somewhere are memories of being distinctly unpopular in high school, memories of having done poorly academically in both grade school and high school (a big issue in our family that my father hammered home constantly), and memories of letting my father down with both my general behavior and my athletic efforts. He expected me to do well academically; I didn't. He expected me to be a competitive swimmer; I wasn't. He expected me to work hard at school and whatever else I attempted; I didn't. Both of my parents thought I was undisciplined (they were right), and we fought constantly about most everything as I grew up. Since I seemingly let down both of my parents, I had no long-lasting friends, and I did poorly in school; my self-assessment was always low. In order to survive with such a low opinion of myself, I began consciously to fashion an ego.

Mom and Dad

When I was very young, my parents, Phil and Lynn, lived in Madison, Wisconsin, on West Washington Avenue, just a few blocks from the capital of the state of Wisconsin. The neighborhood wasn't especially nice, but the Capitol building itself is beautiful. So at least we had a nice view. My father had already completed his JD (law degree) at Marquette Law School – in Milwaukee, Wisconsin – where he courted and married my mother, Lynn. Mom was a student at Marquette, completing her degree in teaching, when she met my father. It must have been a pretty good match, because 50 years and five children later, they are still together, and now they have nine grandchildren. By the time I entered the world, my father (Phil, Sr) had finished up all the work required to receive his MBA and went to work for the UW, in the Letters and Science Department, where he would remain for the next 20 years.

After that year at West Washington Avenue, we moved to a small green house located at 915 Van Buren Street, in a beautiful neighborhood on the near west side of Madison. Twenty yards away from us, Van Buren Street collided with the fabulous Vilas Park and Zoo, which was a good three miles in circumference. If you turned right from Van Buren Street onto Vilas Avenue where it too intersected with the park, then two blocks later you would run into Edgewood grade school, high school, and college, a Catholic facility itself roughly three miles in circumference. Vilas Park offered tennis courts, basketball courts, a lagoon, open fields where we played football and soccer, tons of swing sets and playground space, and a medium-sized zoo. Right next door to Vilas Park, Edgewood provided tons of woods and open spaces for us children to explore.

Great Neighborhood

With so much open space surrounding us, our neighborhood was a wonderful place for anyone to grow up in. In the summers, my friends and I would play football, tennis, and basketball in Vilas Park, as well as explore the extensive woods of Edgewood. In the winters, I spent what seemed hours every day skating and playing hockey at a facility that we called the "VHL" (Vilas hockey league). My friends and I were always on the move, biking through the neighborhood, challenging the other neighborhood kids to games of "kick the can," "flashlight tag," hockey, and tons of other games.

Not Enough Attention

By the time I was seven years old, I had a six-year-old brother named Dave, a developmentally challenged five-year-old sister named Ann, a two-year-old sister named Kerry, and the youngest of the brood, my sister Molly, who was then a newborn.

With so many younger siblings, and a busy father (now working full time, swimming for an hour every morning, and working on a PhD as well), I wasn't getting the attention that I craved. I guess it was only natural that the younger kids would receive the lion's share of the attention, but that shouldn't have made the older children (especially me) feel the lack of attention any less! And to be honest, I had a hard time over the years competing with my brothers and sisters in the enterprises that my parents put the highest premium on: school grades and swimming. Since I couldn't get the attention I craved through any positive endeavors, apparently I sought their attention in negative ways. I excelled at seeking out things like teasing my younger brothers or sisters until they begged my parents to intervene; or failing to see to the few little chores that my mom and dad asked me to handle, like taking out the garbage, all of which forced them to get angry with me. Oh, and getting into trouble with the nuns during Catholic grade school was another fine way to guarantee attention.

In 1970, when I was six years old, we moved to a bigger house, at 2005 Jefferson Street, a mere two blocks from our Van Buren Street house. Up to that point I had been going to Edgewood grade school. In my kindergarten through third grade years at Edgewood my best friend was a kid from the near east side of town named Chris Farley. The world now knows Farley from his *Saturday Night Live* days, and from movies like *The Great White Ninja* and *Tommy Boy*. More on Chris later.

I Can Control Reality!

Way back in those kindergarten days I had come to believe that I had discovered some secret "slant system" that would enable me to gain whatever I wanted in life. Keep in mind that I was at the tender age when most of us believe in magic (and Santa Claus and the Easter Bunny). It was a simple system. I would simply say out loud, "I want X to happen." If it didn't happen, then I would say, "I do not want X to happen." And if that didn't work, then I would say, "I want X to happen, I do not want X to happen." So I would be asking for what I really wanted from a positive slant, then from a negative slant, and finally from a neutral slant. According to my theory, every day a new slant was in power, or worked. So on Thursday May 1st, the positive slant worked. On Friday May 2nd, the neutral slant or negative slant worked (I wish I could remember the order!). On Saturday May 3rd, the remaining slant worked, and then on Sunday May 4th, the positive slant worked again. It was a three-day cycle, and I just had to keep a close track of the days. Of course, if I lost track and really wanted something badly enough, then I could just ask for it in all three slants, but I had to make three separate and clear statements.

I called upon this powerful "slant system" more than a few times, but not too often: I mean, how often can you use it when you're that young? Once, we had a drawing at school (why, I can't remember), to determine the king of the class, the queen of the class, and the prince of the class. Right before we drew for king, I used the "I want" slant, but I wasn't drawn. Then they drew for queen and I used the "I do not want" slant, but again I wasn't drawn – I figured they wouldn't use a guy for that anyway, but I was trying to find whatever day was in power. Then I used the neutral slant, and I was drawn as prince. The next year, when we finally had another class drawing, I was drawn as king. And still another time, when I was mad at my father about something or other, I used the slant system to cause a box to fall out of the back of our station wagon, when the station wagon was on the move 30 yards away from where I stood!

Given that I had this incredible power, the trick was to learn how best to use it. I reasoned that I could ask for great things to come my way later on in life, and that this was the best way to use my powers. So, at the tender age of six, I began figuring out exactly what I wanted later on in my life, but not really having a clue. I waited to use the slant system to manifest my future until I knew exactly what I wanted. Then one day, when I was seven years old, I became conscious of the fact that I might not always be in control of this secret system. Would it always work for me? What if I forgot how to use it? What if it simply stopped working? I decided right then and there to use the power of the system to set up my future. Why wait and risk never being able to use this power again?

I remember clearly that it took a real effort to follow through on this reasoning and use the slant system to influence my future. The act of shaping my future was frightening, like being in a dream where you're always running away from, but never quite escaping from, the bad guy. Finally, a day arrived where I felt I had to use the slant system that day, or I would never use it for my future! Fully resolved to use the system that day to manifest my future, I asked for four things: to be attractive to women, to be rich, to be happy, and to be famous. The powerful sense of accomplishment that I felt after I finally used the slant system to influence my future was amazing! Even for, or maybe especially for, a seven-year-old. (I must say that I have received many of the blessings that that little boy asked for.)

So maybe the whole slant system is hogwash: the product of an overactive imagination, or the invention of a young boy who still believed in Santa Claus! But there are a few positives that I can talk about here. First, I did truly believe that I had set things in motion to achieve future happiness, future fortune, and future fame, and perhaps that counts for something. My mother Lynn would swear to you that if you believe 100% that something will happen, then it will happen. Second, it was the beginning of my thinking outside of the box while trying to construct ways to influence my present – and future – situation. (I will be talking about what I've discovered and what has worked for me along the way.)

Chris Farley

I remember telling Chris Farley about the slant system in kindergarten. He was the only one that I ever spoke to about it for the next 25 years, until I told my wife and my own children (and now countless numbers of you!). My wife, Kathy, probably wanted to tell me that I'm delusional, but instead she reminded me that young children often do believe in magic. Kathy is gentle with me when it comes to theories about accomplishing things, having seen me pull off some serious accomplishments. She knew about some of the goals that I had written down before I met her, goals that others thought undoable, or unattainable. (One written goal that I had when I first met Kathy in 1989 was to write a New York Times best-selling book, which I finally did accomplish in 2004 with my first book, a poker strategy book titled Play Poker Like the Pros.)

Chris Farley was a little bit overweight even back in grade school, and he was super funny even then! His grandmother lived two blocks from me, and I could hang out with him at her place a lot after school. Even though Farley lived across town in Maple Bluff, I hung out with him more than with anyone else in my class at Edgewood. He was my best friend until about second grade, but around that time I fell into a groove with a bunch of kids who lived within a block of me. My close friends back then were Mike and John Huggett, and Richard Grassy. We spent a lot of time hanging out at the Huggetts' place with Mike and John, and their three older brothers, Brad (the neighborhood bully), Mark (the math guy), and Jeff (the oldest). Five boys in one family! My first poker experience was at the Huggetts', and it included playing with Mark. After fourth grade I transferred to another Catholic school called Blessed Sacrament grade school and lost touch with Farley.

In third grade I saw a path to fortune and fame that I liked: acting. Weren't all successful actors rich and famous? One day I convinced my mother to let me try out for a television production. Somehow, with zero experience, I won a part in a small production that was being filmed on the campus of the UW. I was encouraged! I found something I was good at, and this led to my participating in the biggest play in Madison, Wisconsin: "A Christmas Carol." For three or four years I played the child who answers Ebenezer Scrooge's call, "Boy, is the prize turkey in the window still available?"

Me (boy), "Why, yes sir, I believe it is, sir."

Then Scrooge would throw a purse full of coins down to me and say, "Go buy it for me. Hurry up then!" After a few years, my acting career came to an abrupt halt when my mother got sick of driving me across town for all of my rehearsals. (But television wasn't done with me. Not by a long shot!)

Catholic School

Grade school at Blessed Sacrament was a tough deal for me. For starters, I had to walk more than a mile to school every day. And I had that ADD thing, which contributed to the fact that I had horrible marks in my classes. ADD is a major problem for any kid, but especially for one in a Catholic school. The nuns didn't take kindly to failure! These days, ADD would be diagnosed early on and treated. Back then, having ADD made your life incredibly difficult. There was the strain of my father demanding that I achieve good grades, balanced brutally with the fact that with ADD you are unable to pay attention to what the teacher says, you forget to bring in your assignments, you forget even that you had assignments in the first place, and it all produces a certain level of distraction that borders sometimes on madness. And the nuns were tough and unyielding, especially when your marks were as poor as mine were. Still, the nuns were fair, and this much I respected.

In grade school I was always one of the youngest kids, and believe it or not (I'm over 6' 5" now!), one of the shortest. I'm guessing that my being relatively young also had a lot to do with the way I performed in school back then. From ADD to being the youngest in my class, I was set up to struggle and fail, and there wasn't much that I could do about it.

The one great thing about going to Blessed Sacrament was that my old neighborhood friend Richard Grassy was now in my class. At Edgewood, other than Chris Farley, who had grown apart from me by fourth grade, I basically had no friends. Most of the kids at Edgewood lived miles from the school, and it was tough to arrange "play dates." As it turned out, my parents had withdrawn me from Edgewood and sent me to Blessed Sacrament for financial reasons. I don't think they could afford to send four kids to Edgewood. At least I now had a good friend from the neighborhood attending the same school that I was.

But at Blessed Sacrament I continued my trend and got into quite a bit of trouble. I was always missing assignments, showing up late for class, or talking in class, and I seldom paid attention in class. Still, I was not a bad kid. I didn't pull the fire alarm, beat up on the other kids, or swear at the nuns behind their backs, like a lot of the other kids did.

Mom's Powerful Message

It was when I was in fifth grade, and we were at 2005 Jefferson Street, that a small notebook card appeared on our bathroom mirror. The card, taped to the mirror, said:

You are what you think;
You become what you think;
What you think becomes reality.

My brothers, my sisters, and I were forced to read this sign every day for the next ten years. There was only one bathroom on our second floor – for four bedrooms – and all seven of us lived on that floor. Through showers, baths, teeth brushings, hand washings, and face scrubbings, that sign hung in there, and just when it was turning yellow and starting to rot, my mother would replace it with a fresh white one. To me, this saying means that you can forge your own reality, beginning with your own thoughts. You want to be a good writer? Then begin to think that you will become a good writer, and it will begin to happen. This little white sign, with the yellow edges, has had a profound influence on my life. Until I left my parents' house for college, I had read this sign every day for years, and I began to believe that I could use my thoughts to create some great successes for myself.

Go Ann!

Do you think that someone is limited in what they can achieve in life by their intelligence, or their athletic ability? Sure, not everyone can "Be like Mike" (Michael Jordan) or Tiger Woods, but let me share with you a little story about my sister Ann Michel Hellmuth. Ann was diagnosed with a learning disorder early on in life. She had to go to special needs schools, take special needs classes, and endure people calling her names like "Stupid" or "Retarded." In high school, Ann joined Special Olympics, and she went on to win three gold medals in swimming at the World Special Olympics held in North Carolina in 1998. As word of her success spread, she joined the Wisconsin Special Olympics Council, gave speeches to thousands of her peers, and even completed her college-level classes at Madison Area Technical College with straight As. She has held down the same job for 20 years; she takes care of kids at a day care center in Madison.

In 2002, Ann entered a qualifying speed skating race in Wisconsin for the worldwide Special Olympics event to be held in Alaska later that year. Ann finished second, and was eliminated, but the woman who won the race was so nasty to the other athletes, making several of them cry, that the organizers gave the nod to Ann. So off to Alaska went Ann, with my parents in tow. She barely qualified for the eight-person final by edging out another girl at the tape. In the final, it was understood by the other athletes and by observers that Ann had no chance to win. After all, she was ranked number 8 out of eight, and the other girls were much faster than she was. Still, Ann would never give up because she is a champion (you are what you think). Two laps in, with two more to be completed, Ann was in fifth place. Then the leader fell. "OK," Ann thought with guarded optimism, "I'm on my feet, I'm in fourth place, and I still have a chance!" Suddenly, the new first-place and second-place skaters tangled skates and fell. With one lap to go, the girl in front of Ann also fell, and all Ann had to do was finish the race to win the gold medal (you become what you think). Would Ann feel the pressure and fall like the other girls had? No, she finished strong! And that's how my little sister, who was not even the best Special Olympics skater in the state of Wisconsin, won the gold at the International Special Olympics in Alaska in 2002!

So don't tell me about your weaknesses, and don't tell me that you cannot do it. Tell me about your strengths, and tell me that you can do it! You are what you think; you become what you think; what you think becomes reality. Living by these words alone can help shape your life, and profoundly influence your legacy. I believe that I'm a great poker player; I became a great poker player; and now the world knows that I'm a great poker player.

Madison West High School

My next stop was West High (Madison West High School), and the great news for me there was that all of my neighborhood friends would be attending. There were over 500 kids in my freshman class. But on the basis of my middle school marks, Blessed Sacrament school had recommended that I attend "special classes" at West High. Thus, one of the history classes that I was signed up for in my freshman year was allegedly for "smart kids who struggle." In fact it turned out to be filled with a bunch of kids who were not very bright. To me it seemed like a remedial class, and even though my grades had been poor, I felt like I didn't belong there. Immediately, I asked to be transferred into a regular class, and I think that even my parents were shocked to discover the school's deception.

High School Pain!

Attending high school was nonetheless the worst experience of my life! My freshman year was a disaster as far as the most important things for a high school kid went. I had no girlfriend, I had bad grades, and my friends were on again, off again, probably because I was so insecure and sensitive about the warts on my hands. Sadly, I had learned to hide the backs of my hands at all times during school, because I had the worst case of warts on my hands that I have ever seen, or even that I have ever heard of. Literally, the back of every finger on both hands was covered with warts. To say that my hands were unsightly would be being kind. I learned how to write with the back of my right hand (the *back* of my right hand!) held down touching the school desk, and the back of my left hand holding down the paper. Take a second and try writing with your right hand and all of your fingers face up! It causes your thumb to be in pain after a few minutes, and it's hard to write anything legibly that way.

I was always hyperconscious of where my hands were during the school day. When I opened my locker, I was worried about people seeing my hands, so I would open the locker with my hands turned face up. When I walked up and down the halls at school, I held my hands at an angle (face up) so that no one could see the backs, or I kept them inside my long-sleeved shirt or jacket, or held them under my armpits. Riding my bike to school presented a special challenge! I learned to ride my bike "no hands" while I stowed my hands under my armpits. And, I raced out of Madison West at the first possible opportunity.

Somewhere along the way, my parents took me to see the family pediatrician, where I was told that if I had my warts removed, I would have permanent scars on both hands. After a year of this extreme awkwardness, I felt like I couldn't stand it anymore, so I had just one removed; and unfortunately it did leave a small scar.

But, beginning my sophomore year, my doctor informed me that the warts would probably go away soon on their own, if I could just wait it out. In time they did, but not until the end of that year. Can you imagine enduring two years of high school under those conditions? Constantly hiding your hands from everyone, every minute of every day? It's no wonder that I didn't make any friends my freshman year, or even hang out much with my old friends; I simply didn't want anyone close enough to me to see my hands. I've described my miserable existence in the first year and a half of high school in just a page or two, but the effect it had on me was profound. I couldn't show my hands to anyone, I avoided people, and I couldn't even consider having a girlfriend. The effect of this misery was to drive my self-esteem down a long way. I felt horrible about myself.

Juvenile Delinquent PH

It was during my freshman year that I began turning to the dark side. I smoked pot, but only four or five times. Mainly, I stole things, mostly gum or candy, but sometimes bikes, or bike parts. I was actually really good at stealing things! I had some discipline, I had some balls, and I was extremely wily. I knew that if I hadn't left a store with something new in my possession, then I hadn't stolen anything. So if I had four packs of gum in my jacket, I would watch the whole scene closely as I walked out of the store. Sometimes, I would even walk right to the door, and then turn around as if I had forgotten something.

I'm not proud of this period in my life. My coup de grace was when I imagined myself to be the villain in the latest James Bond movie. If I was going to be bad, then I was going to be *bad*. Gold prices had been really high that year, and I always liked to think big, so one day I walked into a jewelry store. Somehow I managed to steal a $1,200 gold necklace. When I made it out of the store, expecting to feel like a conquering hero, there was no thrill at all. I felt only remorse, and a great deal of it at that. I got what I deserved, more or less. What I richly deserved was to get caught! Instead, I took that necklace and sold it for $120, only to have the guy I sold it to, a week later, accuse me of writing in an extra zero on the price tag. He basically threatened to turn me in, unless I returned $100 to him. Whatever, a part of me felt better about what I had done, because in the end I had made just $20.

Rewarded for Good Behavior

One day in October of my sophomore year, my friends came by with a plan of stealing bike parts, and I refused to join them. I was 16 years old, and stealing something seemed childish, and turned my stomach. I was more than happy to end that dark period of my life. Strangely, they were caught by the police that very night, and in a devious and very deliberate effort, one of them said that his name was Phil Hellmuth. (I had probably used his name once or twice, but always for something harmless, not theft!) When the police came knocking at our door that night, my father answered and verified that I had been with him all evening, watching television, and that the thieves may have been the friends who had stopped by our house earlier that night (my father is no dummy!). How sweet for me: my friends used my name to get me in trouble, but ended up getting busted themselves without my having to say a word! I felt like the universe was sending me a message that night, a sort of confirmation that it was time to live life right, the way my parents had raised me; it was time to live with honor and ethics. And true to my word, I was never involved in any sort of shenanigans again, ever. I am as proud of my perfect reputation in poker as I am of all the bracelets I have won. Ask around the poker world, and you will find that I have a perfect reputation – and believe me, us poker players remember everything! Once caught cheating or even stiffing someone, and the poker world remembers forever.

Hello Laura Wood!

Earlier in my sophomore year I had met a freshman girl who was one of the best-looking girls at Madison West, and she lived only one block away from me. Laura Wood had blond hair and blue eyes, and she was beautiful. Laura's friend Cathy was the one who was interested in me at that point, but I wasn't interested in her. Perhaps because of our close proximity, Laura and I were close friends all year long, and I spent literally four hours a day with her. It seemed that I had walked her home from school every single day. Then we would just hang out at her house, eating and talking. At night we would play neighborhood games together like Kick the Can or Flashlight Tag. My social group shifted dramatically that year. I abandoned the little time I had spent hanging out with the Huggetts and Richard Grassy, and spent major time hanging out with Laura and her friends. Because of Laura, I have good memories from the end of my sophomore year, even though I was still hiding my hands from everyone, everywhere I went. And hallelujah! Over the summer between my sophomore and junior years, the warts suddenly disappeared!

My First Kiss

Early in my junior year, Laura and I began actually to date. Laura was my first love, even though we never did have sex. In short order, I went from having a physical affliction to dating one of the most desirable girls in school. It was the first time in my life that I had the good fortune to deal with sudden success, while simultaneously dealing with super low self-esteem. Let's face it, if you're keeping time with one of the most beautiful girls in high school, life is good! And you certainly feel successful.

The reason that Laura and I transitioned from friends to a couple came about because I was about to start dating another girl (she too was beautiful). This new girl and I were hitting it off one Friday night at a West High School mixer (dance), and as we did I noticed that Laura was really upset for some mysterious reason. A few nights later (Tuesday), I was on my way to taking the new girl out for our first date, and I stopped by Laura's house on the way over to pick up my new date. Laura was my best friend, and I was hoping she would give me thumbs up on my clothing choices, thumbs up on the way I combed my hair, and I was also there to ask her advice about the impending date. While Laura was combing my hair, our eyes just sort of locked, and our first kiss was very natural. Kind of like, "Of course we kissed each other. What took us so long?" I had been harboring huge feelings for Laura for over a year.

I canceled my other date (the first scheduled date of my life!), and Laura and I went on to have our first date that very night. I suppose this was the first time that I began to feel my ego developing. I had felt like a loser for years, and suddenly I was going out with one of the dream girls at my high school. Junior year was the happiest time of my young life, at least for the first half of the year.

All About Laura

My whole social life was now completely encompassed by Laura and her friends. She and I continued to walk home from school together every day, and we hung out constantly. I had been developing a false ego during my freshman year, an ego based on nothing. My life had seemed so bad that I had to have something to keep me moving forward and feeling good about myself. Fast forward to my heady days of dating Laura and this shaky ego was still there, but now I had an actual reason for a healthy one to exist. Now I was a confused boy who had gone from total loser status to big winner status overnight. I had moved from the outhouse to the penthouse, and I simply did not know how to handle myself (a recurring theme in my life, as we will see). I was acting way too cocky at school, and that made me an easy target (I still am an easy target!).

Broken Heart, Massive Pain!

But sometime in November during my junior year, Laura broke up with me (dumped me!). Maybe she broke up with me because I became way too cocky? Perhaps she broke up with me because I had so much trouble dealing with my new-found success as I tried to balance it with my low self-esteem. Perhaps she liked the modest version of me, and not the egotistical version? In any case, I cried every day for two weeks. I was in love with Laura. I was feeling the full effects of my first broken heart! Who knew that the pain would be so intense, and would last so long? To have someone in your life, someone you had spent many hours a day with for 18 months (whether as a couple or as friends) and then "poof," they're out of your life. Man, was that tough to handle. Not only that, but I had lost the whole social group she was a part of.

Now I had no one to hang out with on Friday or Saturday nights. I had driven my old friends away when I began hanging out with Laura's group, and I simply hadn't hung out much with my old friends over the first two-and-a-half years of high school. Forced to the social sidelines by November of my junior year, I came to believe that there was nothing worse than watching television (*Dallas* and *Falcon Crest*) with your parents and your younger sisters on Friday nights when you are in high school, and your friends are presumably out having fun. Even my younger brother was out having fun! Things were pretty bad; I was heartbroken, I was lonely, and I still had bad grades. But at least the warts were gone.

Hitting the Bottle, Hard

During that tough two-week recovery from having my heart broken (and it doesn't really end for anyone after merely two weeks, does it?), I hit the bottle hard one night when I was by myself. I found a bottle of brandy in the kitchen cupboard and got into it on an empty stomach – a bad plan. I don't know how much I drank that night, but it turned out to be way more than I could handle. It started innocently enough with two shots of brandy, straight up. It ended when my father came over to our neighbor's house and carried me home. Witnesses later told me that I had stopped by Laura's house and demanded that she come outside. I heard that her father was gentle, but firm with me. I was not going to see Laura this night! Allegedly I was then found wallowing around on the neighbor's lawn (mostly on the ground), and they immediately called my parents. All I know is that I woke up the next morning in my own bed with the worst hangover of my life!

Dreams Validated by World Famous Psychic?

The good feelings of self that I had begun to build for myself out of desperation were still there, and now I had some ammunition. Hadn't one of the most beautiful girls at my high school wanted to spend time with me, and then go out with me? But I had become cocky with no good reason to be cocky. About that time, my mother invited a world famous psychic, a woman named Rose Gladden, to our house (Madison hosted a big psychic convention every year) for dinner. I spent a few hours talking with Rose and eventually convinced her (I'm sure I was pushing her when she just wanted to relax) to "read my future."

In any case, Rose took my hand and held it tightly between her two hands, and something weird happened. Rose lost all expression on her face, then started shaking a bit, and finally began turning blue! These apparent physical changes – along with Rose's worldwide fame – convinced me that she may have actually been reading my future. Whatever was going on, it wasn't like anything I had ever seen! Rose told me that I would be "rich and infamous throughout the world." I made note of the word "infamous," and asked her about it, but she would tell me no more. Talk about fodder for an ego! A world famous psychic tells me that I will be rich, and more or less famous (my translation). That in itself was amazing, but then I listened to some of the predictions she had made for other people, and they were fairly plain and ordinary. If I was the only one she predicted fame and fortune for, then that might be statistically significant!

So, I would be rich and famous someday? I clung to that possibility, for hadn't I put myself on that path when I was in kindergarten, when I used my slant system to manifest future fortune and fame? It all calls to mind a song by the group Poison with their lyric "Just give me something to believe in." From then on, I believed that I would be great at something, and I wasn't going to let anything knock me off that path.

Dad and I Scream, Look Out!

The second half of my junior year of high school was fairly nightmarish. My grades continued to be bad, I continued to watch TV with my family most Friday and Saturday nights, and my parents' disapproval (chiefly about my poor grades) rained down on me daily. Sometime during my junior year, my fights with my father were so bad that they were disrupting the entire household. We would scream at each other, going toe-to-toe (it was never physical, just loud!), and the rest of the family literally ran for cover. Almost every single day as dinner wound down, my dad and I would square off. My mother would take my sisters and run them into the kitchen as our scream-fest continued unchecked.

Mom has my Back!

Eventually, my mother suggested that we all go see a family therapist. I knew that my parents had no such problems with my brother and sisters (they had good grades, they did their chores on time, and they didn't rock the boat), so seeing a family psychologist was really all about me. As regards my brother and sisters getting along well with my parents, I think they saw what an emotional toll it took on me to fight my parents' system, and decided to conform to the system, rather than spending their time relentlessly fighting it. After all, conforming was certainly easier than screaming and yelling back and forth every day.

I think that I had loosened up the system when I crashed through it. It seems like the oldest kid in the family always more or less paves the way, oftentimes with blood.

In any case, at our very first meeting with the psychologist, I made it clear to him that I was going to do some great things with my life. To that, the psychologist replied, "Phil, you better come down to reality, your record tells me that you won't do anything great with your life. You have poor grades, a bad attitude, and no real prospects."

Immediately, my mother jumped up off the couch (god bless her!) and said, "Are you crazy, don't tell him that." So ended the family visits with the psychologist! My mom is the "You are what you think; you become what you think; what you think becomes reality" woman, and the psychologist's negative approach simply wouldn't do. I'm proud of my mom: she has backbone and a positive attitude, and she fought for her son's right to seek greatness! The experience left me with a little more fodder for my emerging ego.

Dad and Me

My father had good reasons to fight with me. He was never abusive or mean spirited, and there was never any physical violence. Perhaps he was a little too loud. And we have had an exceptionally warm relationship in the years since he accepted my choice of careers, in 1989. I believe that back in the day he was a bit too overbearing when it came to my grade point average, but oftentimes when he would ask me to take out the garbage or wash the dishes, I either wouldn't do it or wouldn't do it in a timely manner.

I believe that my father may have been a bit overbearing in regard to my grades because his father had been the same with him. My grandfather, George Hellmuth, was a famous and highly regarded heart surgeon. (He won the American Heart Association's highest honor in 1973 for his contributions to research on cholesterol in eggs.) George expected my father to get straight As, and to become a doctor, but my father wasn't up to the "straight As" task. Dad did eventually wind up getting tons of secondary degrees. And with that many letters after your name, you too would probably hope that your kids would do well academically. Some of our fights were over lesser issues, such as my curfew time, or how I should be spending my time. We were both strong-willed, and neither one of us would back down.

3

Every Rose has its Thorn, Part 2

Over the summer between my junior and senior years of high school, my father set up a meeting with a powerful dean at the UW, named Jack Cipperly. I told Dean Cipperly that I had never really applied myself in school (which was true), and that that was why I was running a 2.78 grade point average (GPA) in high school. Dean Cipperly told me that if I took a tough curriculum my senior year of high school, and did well with it, then he would help me slide through a little-known back door at the UW called "special student status." Although anyone could go to the UW using this loophole, knowing the people who knew that the backdoor even existed certainly helped my cause! Like most of us, nothing motivates me better than desperation, and I worked harder than I ever had in high school, and I managed to pull out a decent enough GPA (roughly a 3.1 with tough classes like physics) the first semester of my senior year to satisfy Dean Cipperly. And so, somehow, I squeaked into the UW, which at the time was a top-ten school in the country academically.

Senior Year – Rough

My senior year proved to be another lonely year for me. But one good thing about that year, apart from hitting the books, was that I took a job on Friday and Saturday nights bussing tables and washing dishes at Crandall's Restaurant on Capital Square. At least I didn't have to watch TV on Friday nights anymore. And it turned out that the employees at Crandall's went out together to the bar next door after work ended. So I had found a small semblance of a social life during my senior year of high school. And the discipline it required of me was a good thing too!

Great Memories of Holidays With the Hellmuths

One thing that was always just right for me and my family was holidays at the Hellmuth's! From the time I can remember Christmas was hosted at my parents' house – my wife and I still celebrate Christmas Eve at my parents' house in Madison with all of my brothers and sisters – and we had tons of relatives come by and stack up the Christmas presents floor-to-ceiling. My parents always did holidays right, with family, friends, tradition, presents, and food. For 46 years I have had oyster stew and rum balls on Christmas Eve at my parents' house!

Summer Home in Minocqua, More Great Memories

Another thing that was just right for me was the family cabin (a summer vacation home) on Sunday Lake in Minocqua, Wisconsin. Minocqua was about a four-hour drive straight north of Madison by car back then, and the cabin is almost exactly 200 miles – door to door – from my parents' house in Madison. Although we weren't poor, there was no way that my father could have afforded this beautiful 300-acre place back then on his UW salary. My grandfather, George, the world famous heart surgeon, bought the place with the plan of eventually breaking it up into pieces and selling off the pieces as he needed money in retirement. George bought raw land, and then he built a 2,000 square foot cabin at the top of a hill overlooking the lake. Then George had a pier constructed about 50 yards to the right side of where the cabin stood (as you looked out over the lake), and all the way down the hill. Finally, George ordered construction of an outdoor white birch staircase that walked down to the hill to the pier. My father, recognizing the beauty of the place, and the convenience of using it as a vacation home for our family (he saved a ton of money on vacations), dug out a sand pit 15 yards away from the marsh-surrounded pier. I remember my brother Dave and me wheeling literally hundreds of loads of sand – in a wheelbarrow – down to the beach (when my father could convince us to help him), while my dad filled up the next wheelbarrow full of sand with a shovel. My father, my brother, and I, over the course of a couple of years, turned that marsh into a white sand beach. We also added a raft and an aluminum canoe to the beach setting. And now we could lounge around on the pier, the raft, or the beach on lazy July days and just sun ourselves, fish, or swim. My brother, my sisters, and I all learned to swim on that little stretch of our own private beach.

The only neighbors in sight from our little beach on Sunday Lake, or even from our cabin on the hill, were the Draegers, and they were a good 200 yards away, straight across the lake. They owned another 600 yards of undeveloped lake front, and between the Draegers and my family, we owned 35% of the lake, all of it undeveloped. This afforded us a ton of privacy! On the 65% of the lake that was developed, there were probably 30 cabins, but all of them were out of our view, blocked by trees, or by various islands or peninsulas. The only time we ever saw anyone else on Sunday Lake was when they were fishing on our side of the lake, or waterskiing across the middle of the lake.

Grandpa George didn't live long enough to break up Minocqua and sell it off piece by piece, but the property did shoot up in value, just as he thought it would. When George died, in 1973, my father, along with his younger brother George Jr, and his sister Julie, split up the property and the assets as best they could. My uncle and aunt took the valuable farmland that George had lived on near Milwaukee, which had its own private lake. And my father took possession of the cabin in Minocqua. And now my parents owned more than 300 acres of land, and some 350 yards of it was prime lakefront property. Sunday Lake is indescribably beautiful, with crystal clear water, white birch trees, islands, beautiful deep-rooted trees, two loons, a few eagles, and an abiding calmness and serenity.

Close Family

The cabin was one huge reason why my family grew close to one another, and we all remain close to this day. With seven of us up there sharing a 2,000-square-foot house for almost a month each summer, we learned to get along with each other, even in close proximity. And owing to the isolation from the rest of the world that we faced up there, we played lots of games together. But as I have mentioned, my brothers and sisters were in my parents' good graces, and I wasn't getting that kind of approval.

Games, Games, Games!

So, naturally, I had to be the best at something. And that something was games, games, and more games. I was the King of Games in my family, and I ruled with an iron fist for about one month each summer while we were at the cabin! We played checkers, hearts, spades, poker, spoons (an intense game that required that you pay close attention to several things at once), multi-player solitaire, Spite and Malice, Scrabble, Monopoly, Risk, and many other games that we would invent. I had the huge built-in edge of being the oldest, and thus a superior understanding of the rules, the tactics, and the overall strategies for these games. I was ruthless – but fair – and I always played to win.

As I grew up, the only thing I was able to hang on to, in the company of my brother and sisters, was my game-playing ability. I worked hard at optimizing strategies for each of the games that we played, and I never missed a trick. I gave every game we played my full and complete concentration, because losing at any game, ever, really shook me up (the birth of the poker brat)! Winning felt good; losing was unbearable.

Birth of the Poker Brat

When I did occasionally lose, then what in my little world did I have to feel good about? My sore loser poker brat mentality was born when I lost games that I had played perfectly or when I lost to a lucky roll of the dice, against one of my siblings. Imagine, I play perfectly for an hour, and you roll double sixes twice in a row to beat me. That's absurd! And when I did lose to an unlucky turn of events, I went off, and told the whole house how lucky my brother or sister was to beat me. Naturally, my brother and sisters did not much enjoy playing games with me! I was unbeatable most times, and unbearable on the rare occasions that I lost!

Part of my ability to win poker tournaments had been nurtured in my all-out effort to be the best at all the games that we played at a young age. I mastered every strategic advantage in dozens of games. And when, eventually, we did make contact with some of the other families on Sunday Lake, the game of choice was poker. These other families assumed that we were rich, because of the land that we owned on the lake, but we were land rich and cash poor. But the other families on Sunday Lake were not cash poor. Thus I began to make some money ($5 or $10 a session) playing poker with our neighbors, and my brother Dave joined the game as well. By the time I was 16 I knew well the concept of winning money at the poker table, and I liked it.

Hello Poker!

Having made money at the cabin playing poker, I brought the game to my Madison neighborhood in the summers, and I pushed for higher stakes, but alas, all my friends would play for was 25 cents max bet. I also hosted small games in our basement on occasional Friday nights. But we didn't play very often in the neighborhood, and never for much money. So it wasn't worth my effort to try establishing a small-stakes game, because there wasn't much money to be made that way.

Reverberations, Dreaming or What?

One memorable night among those Fridays, while I was finishing up hosting a game in my basement, the Eagles song "Take It to the Limit" was blaring on the radio. I recall well that something odd happened to me as I watched my old friend John Huggett mouth the lyrics. It was almost like a religious experience, and as the lyric reached "Take it to the limit one more time," I thought with certainty, "Someway, somehow, I'll be a high roller in Las Vegas someday!"

Cut from a Different Cloth

It seems that I thought differently than my friends as I grew up (there's that slant system!). When we were hanging out at Vilas Park, and we would see a new sports car drive by, like a Corvette, my friends would say, "I want to buy that car someday." Then they would talk about how much the car costs, or how fast it was, or whatever.

I would usually keep mum, or maybe I would say, "That's cool." But I would be thinking, "I don't want that car, I want the souped-up car from the James Bond movie that can go underwater, or fire missiles." Or at a minimum I'd think, "I want a Ferrari, or a Lamborghini." I would always think to myself, "If you're going to dream, then dream big!" I was really a fish out of water as I grew up.

Top-Ten College Plus No Self-Esteem!

It all makes for an interesting portrait: take a low self-esteem guy with a fabricated ego and put him into the college dorms at a top-ten university; how will that person do? (The portrait would be a hell of a lot more interesting to me, and a lot less painful to contemplate, if it hadn't been my life!) As my first rude introduction to college life (and I had it coming), my new dorm "friends" convinced me (duped me) to run for president of the dorm floor during my first month living there. Until right before I was supposed to speak, in front of the whole dorm floor, I hadn't realized that I had been set up. Nice welcome, boys! Then again, I should have seen it coming. My false ego had blinded me from seeing the truth. Why *couldn't* I be president of the dorm floor as an incoming freshman? (Yeah, right!) At least a lot of the women from the other dorms seemed to be interested in me, for the first week or two anyway.

I did manage to have sex for the first time, although it was not memorable enough to mention here in any detail. In fact, it was quite a letdown! It would be another lonely year for me living in the dorms. But because I was under observation by Dean Cipperly in my first semester, I managed to work hard and earn a 3.26 GPA (3.0 is a B, 4.0 is an A). I was pretty pleased with my 3.26, though I knew that I could have worked harder and done better. It was nonetheless the best GPA of my life to that point, and this was the UW, baby. After years of taking a beating, my self-esteem probably broke about even my freshman year of college. I got good grades one semester but not the other. I was still pretty lonely, but at least I was developing some friendships.

During my sophomore year of college, things really fell apart. I went to less than 20% of my classes after I discovered that I could "cram" for tests. I never liked getting up in the mornings, so I just didn't. I now know that I have a sleeping disorder called sleep apnea, which may affect up to 23% of the population. I hate to break it you folks, but if you snore, then there's a high probability that you have sleep apnea. In which case you should go to a sleep center for one night and have it diagnosed. In my case sleep apnea means that I "wake up" (not consciously) over 40 times per hour when I sleep. No wonder I could never get up in time to attend my classes in the mornings. For the first 40 years of my life I could never understand why I needed well more than ten hours of sleep per night, and why it was so hard for me to fall asleep at night. I attributed my inability to get up for classes as simple laziness, or just not caring about school. Looking back now, I understand why I struggled so much in school: ADD plus sleep apnea. The first kept me from getting up for class; the second kept me from learning anything when I did make it to class!

No Effort

At the UW, there was something called "student print lecture notes" that would give you word-for-word what your professor said in class that day. If the notes were available for the class I was taking, then I would never go to that class again, except to take the tests. Eventually, I didn't take any classes that didn't make those notes available. Some people choose classes on the strength of what major they hoped to finish with, and some of us choose classes on whether or not the student print lecture notes are available or not! Once I began to skip classes for which the student print lecture notes were available, I began saying to myself, "Boy, it's a long walk to class, especially when I'm going all the way across campus for just that one class. It probably won't hurt to just skip this class."

Cramming, Of Course

In the classic college tradition, I pulled all nighters and crammed for all of my major tests. Basically, the day before a test I would make sure to buy all of the student print lecture notes. Then I would take the notes and my previously unopened textbook to the library (usually after 10 p.m.) and begin studying for the test the next day. When the library closed, I would go to the basement of my dorm and study for the test the rest of the night, alongside many other students who were also cramming. Nothing was sweeter than comparing test scores with some of my pals on the floor of my dorm who had attended class every day and studied for them every night. More often than not, I would have the better test score! More fodder for my ego.

My cramming successes encouraged bad habits, and sometimes I would have two tests on the same day (bye-bye to sleeping much for two straight days). Then there was finals week, and I would be trying to cram a semester's worth of work into one week! By this point in my life I was beginning to be concerned about my lack of a work ethic. I had never really applied myself to anything, ever. Not yet.

Leaving the Dorms

At the end of my sophomore year I moved out of the dorms, but socially I was still a mess. And because of this, there was another looming problem: I had no one to room with in my junior year. Most of the guys had made friends with each other in the dorms, and thus had already decided who to live with the following year, and this was the conventional way these things were done. But I was a bit backwards socially still, and as a result I was planning on living by myself. Naturally, I felt like I was a social failure because of this decision, but living alone would be OK too, right? I could study more hours, stay focused on my classes and do what I needed to do, and maybe I would make it into business school.

Then one day in August, while I was driving by the Badger Bus Depot on West Washington Avenue, another car ran a stop sign and pulled out in front of me. I slammed on my brakes, the other driver slammed on his brakes, and there I sat with maybe a foot separating the front end of my car from the side of his car. It was so close that I wasn't even sure if I had hit the car in front of me, or not. So I jumped out of my car to take a closer look. I was thinking, "Did we collide or not?"

Hello Room Mates!

It turns out that it was John Mamalakis and Kai Haller, two of my buddies from the dorms. (By the way, John was the one who convinced me to run for president of the dorms two years earlier.) John had just picked up Kai from the bus stop, and they were in town to find housing. So the three of us start talking, and exchanging pleasantries, and the next thing you know we decide that the three of us will live together next year! This story illustrates two things: that I was still struggling socially; and that seemingly random events sometimes conspire to help speed me along my way. What are the chances that I "run into" (less than a foot away from a collision) two of my best dorm buddies at a street corner?

Random Great Things Happen to Me

I really do believe that random great things happen to me a lot and have "great things happen to me every day" written on my bathroom mirror. Does that mean it is so? Let's put it this way; it can't hurt. Eventually the three of us rented an apartment on West Washington Avenue, only a few blocks from where my parents had lived when I was born, and just one block from where I almost crashed my car into Kai and John.

By my junior year in college, I had a clear understanding that in order to do what I wanted to do – go to business school – I would have to have an awesome semester and a little luck. The luck part being the hope that the UW Business School would accept me even though my GPA was not up to snuff. I would show them what I could do in one glorious semester, and then they would accept me, right? Meanwhile, I needed some money, and I took a job cleaning primates' cages (smelly job) every morning from 7 a.m. until 11 a.m., five days a week.

Cleaning Monkey Shit?

Think you have a messy job? At night, the primates, each in their own separate cage with steel mesh walls and a steel bottom, would throw feces and food at each other, and stuff wound up everywhere! I would show up first thing in the morning and hose the stuff out of the mesh of the steel cages, and out of the bottom of the cages. With a flick of the wrist a clear stream of high velocity water came out of my hose. My job was to spray the dried feces and the dried food trapped in the mesh off the steel cages, and off the steel bottom of each individual cage. And the stuff flew everywhere, even back at me! It was a good character-building job, that's for sure. By the time I was done, those steel cages were spotless, at least for an hour or two.

An unexpected bonus afforded to me by that job was that I had to be at work at 7 a.m. every day, somehow. And somehow, I did manage to drag myself in to work every day (pretty impressive, now that I know I have sleep apnea). During that semester I even began grinding my teeth while I slept, but that makes sense to me now – I had never had that problem before, or even after that one semester, because I upgraded my own schedule from then on, making sure to include tons of sleep.

After my work at the Primate Research Center, I had an accounting class that I actually enjoyed attending. For the first time since I entered college, I had a reasonable routine, and a class that I actually liked. I would work every morning from 7 a.m. to 10:55 a.m. and then would rush off to my 11 a.m. class. That summer I purchased a small motorcycle (80 cc) to help me get to those faraway classes across campus. It was my best semester of college, by far. I was working 20 hours a week and still managed to earn a 3.78 GPA. Surely, the business school would accept me now. I assumed that this last semester would show what I was capable of. I had always entertained the idea of going to business school, and now I had discovered that I actually liked accounting. I submitted the appropriate application to the business school, but alas, my overall GPA of 2.9 wasn't going to cut it. My rejection by the UW Business School effectively ended my academic career. Although I continued to take classes at the UW on and off for the next couple of years, I never again found a subject that I was really interested in – it turns out that you weren't even allowed to take further accounting classes if you were not in the business school.

4

Where is that Poker Game?

Early in the second semester of my junior year in college, I was at the Southeast Recreational Facility (SERF) playing some full-court basketball. At the UW, playing full-court hoops is a time-honored tradition! On any given night during the school week, you'll find 12 full-court games of basketball up and running: four full-court games at the SERF, four full-court games at the Camp Randall Sports Center (SHELL), and four full-court games at the Natatorium, all of which have long waits for "next." Students, faculty, and paid members of these three facilities all match up to play some serious full-court hoop.

This night I was having some particularly good games against some relatively weak competition. One of my older teammates and I were really tearing up the other teams. We were passing really well, running at full speed, crashing the boards hard, and pretty much scoring at will. I remember thinking that this random teammate of mine (Dave) was really old! Dave had to be close to 40 years old, but he could still ball. It was about 6:45 p.m. when everyone else decided to quit, he and I struck up a conversation. He said, "I can't decide whether to go home to the wife or play poker tonight." This statement really struck me for two reasons: first because I was super naïve (and innocent) and I couldn't imagine someone not being home with his wife and kids, especially at 7 p.m. at night (after all, my dad was home every night at 5 p.m. for 18 years!); and second, I'd had good memories of playing poker from times when I was a teenager. So I asked him where the game was and if it was open to the public, meaning... me.

Poker Game at Memorial Union?

Dave told me that I had probably walked right by the poker game many times, because it was a fixture at the Memorial Union (famous for being at the center of the 1960s anti-war demonstrations) right in the Rathskeller (the main room)! The reason that I hadn't noticed the game, evidently, was that they used small metallic Austrian coins for chips instead of the cheesy red, white, and blue super thin plastic chips that I was used to seeing as a teenager. Another reason that I didn't notice that they were playing poker was because they were playing a game called Texas Hold 'Em, where everyone was dealt two cards facedown, and five cards were eventually placed face up in the middle of the table. At that point in my life a poker game looked like a Seven Card Stud hand – where everyone started with two down cards and one up card – and the chips were red, white and blue! If I ever did notice this game, then I probably thought that they were playing a German game of some sort. In Wisconsin we play games like Sheepshead, Spades, Euchre, Cribbage, and Hearts, and it's not uncommon to see a group of guys playing one of these games at a bar. In any case, Dave let me know that they were looking for some new blood, and that $20 was enough to sit down with. Upon arriving at the game and letting everyone know that Dave had invited me, I was warmly welcomed to the table by one and all. A fellow named Tuli Haromy – who would become my best friend for years to come – was banking the poker game, as usual.

Tuli Haromy, Early Mentor

Tuli was this black haired, brown eyed, super skinny man who stood at about 6' 1", and had a long beak nose. Tuli always wore a shirt with pockets (he told me on more than one occasion that he liked the utility of shirt pockets – in which he stored pens, note cards, and more), and to complete his nerdy look, Tuli wore thick black rimmed glasses. Tuli was 28 years old, and he was originally from Las Vegas, thus he knew about Texas Hold 'Em and the WSOP. Tuli was an impressive guy! He owned a nice house in Madison, he was a chess master, he played perfect strategy blackjack (he counted), he had advanced degrees in computer programming, and he had a PhD. Tuli was at the UW doing advanced biomechanical research on how to lengthen people's life span. A decade earlier, in 1978, at the tender age of 18 years, Tuli was banking $25 an hour (that's about $200 an hour today) as a programmer for the computer system of the University of Nevada, Las Vegas. Tuli had a satellite dish with a real time connection to the Chicago Board Options Exchange, where he had his own seat, which was worth $20,000 in 1986.

Tuli was truly a super genius and he was a jack of all trades. Tuli believed strongly in two things: he always thought that silver would make a huge run (which it did in the late 1990s); and he felt like we could all live to be 150–200 years old, and he claimed that it was going to happen in the near future. Along with Tuli's genius mind came some huge quirks of personality, and a big-time emotional detachment. Tuli was the only adult that I have ever consistently shouted at in my life. I would tell him that my biggest pet peeve in life was when someone asked to see my losing hand at the end of a pot. You see, as I played poker in Vegas in 1980s, and all throughout the 1990s, it was considered bad etiquette and bad form to ask to see the losing hand. Even though it is within the rules as a player, asking to see the losing hand was more than frowned upon. Tuli would then agree to never ask me to see my hand when I lost a pot. However, about half of the time that we played poker together, Tuli would ask to see my hand a couple of times a night. This would enrage me! Was Tuli trying to get me upset and put me on tilt? I'm not sure, but it did give him an edge when I tilted and I became emotionally unhinged after he would ask. Maybe he did it intentionally. In any case, Tuli and I were best friends, and we spent a ton of time hanging out; playing poker, playing ping pong (I would play him left handed), going out to dinner, golfing (he couldn't break 120), going to movies, etc. Tuli and I were both bachelors, and we both had a ton of time on our hands.

To me, Tuli seemed to be a lot like a computer. He couldn't process emotions at all, and he didn't do well with social boundaries. If you were angry with Tuli, then he didn't seem to understand it, or to be affected by it. Thus I would ramp up my anger by raising my voice. If I had a date with a girl (and there weren't many of those in my early 20s), then Tuli would ask me if he could come to dinner with my date and me. A strange request to say the least! A few years later Tuli had a meeting with a dignitary that was coming into his office, and our mutual friend Morgan Machina told Tuli to change his pants. Machina later told me, "Tuli was wearing white pants with what looked like a brown poop stain on the back. It was a pretty embarrassing sight, so I begged Tuli to change his pants, but Tuli would not change his pants!" Thus I found myself best friends with – and dealing with – a mild mannered autistic super genius who didn't understand emotions and social conventions, and who wouldn't give me much respect. The only thing that he would respect was me shouting at him! At the beginning of our relationship my poker-playing friends couldn't understand why I would occasionally shout at mild mannered Tuli. And I wish I wouldn't have, but believe me they understood it after they spent some time with Tuli and me. For the vast majority of our time together, Tuli and I got along extremely well. The shouting was very rare, and Tuli truly was my best friend for almost a decade, and he was a prominent member of my wedding party.

Tuli was born Patrick, but at the age of four years he told his parents that his name was Tuli, and after a long struggle they agreed to rename him "Tuli." (By the way, "Tuli" was the name of Genghis Khan's younger brother.) Later on, after I moved away from Madison, Tuli designed a commodities trading system for the country of Peru, and he spent years implementing this system. After Tuli left Madison, we completely lost touch with one another. To be sure, Tuli had my telephone number and my parents' telephone number (I didn't always have his), but he never reached out to me, except for the occasional time once every two years where he would come by a poker tournament in Las Vegas (or Vienna) to say hello. I think that this going from "best friend, to never contacting you again" was part of Tuli's strange nature. So it was that one year after it happened in 2006, I found out that Tuli had died in a car accident in Reno.

My First Serious Poker Game

But let's go back to me walking into this poker game at the Memorial Union. I handed Tuli a $20 bill, and some Austrian coins (the chips) were pushed across the table to me. The game of choice was a little-known game in Wisconsin called No Limit Pineapple, which is a just another version of the World Championship game called No Limit Texas Hold 'Em.

In No Limit Texas Hold 'Em, the dealer deals two cards face down to all of the players. Two blinds are posted, the small blind and the big blind. The small blind is to the left of the dealer, or the dealer button, and is usually 50% in size of the big blind. The big blind is always to the left of the small blind, and is usually twice the size of the small blind. Now ensues the first round of four rounds of betting. The action always starts on the person that is left of the dealer. (By the way, you can go online and play Hold 'Em for free, and you will understand the structure of the game – blinds and betting order – within five minutes or less.) After the first round of betting is complete, the dealer turns three community cards face up in the middle of the table. This is the flop. Then the second round of betting proceeds after which a fourth community card is turned face up. Next the third round of betting is completed; followed by the dealer turning up a fifth and final community card. Then the fourth and final round of betting is completed. So we have five community cards in the middle plus the two in your hand. From these seven cards, the best poker hand wins.

One exciting thing about No Limit poker is that you can bet any amount of money on any betting round! No Limit Hold 'Em is the most highly skilled poker game in the world today. Oftentimes, people will win huge pots with just the one big pair they were dealt face down, or even a bluff. Oftentimes, a player going "all-in" (for all of his chips) will suddenly be back in contention. Or gone.

Texas Hold 'Em in Wisconsin?

The chances of anyone in Wisconsin playing No Limit Hold 'Em in those days were pretty slim. Although it's the premiere game in the poker world today, it was virtually unheard of in the state of Wisconsin at the time. The fact that Tuli was from Las Vegas was the sole reason that we were playing a version of it that day.

My first time out, I lost my $20, asked where and when the next game was being held, and went home. My second time out, I lost $40. My third time out, the presence of a couple of wealthy Korean players made for pots much bigger than we usually had. Somehow I managed to win $450 that night. Yippee, I had won $450 in cash in one night! I had never even seen that much money in cash before then. I promptly went out and busted myself paying off my overdue tuition bill. That left me with about $30, which I would use to win a bunch more money at the Rathskellar, or so I thought. Wasn't $30 enough to win another $500? Sure, if you never lose a pot!

My Driver's License is Gone!

The fourth time out to Tuli's game would prove to be my last for a while. I went back to the Memorial Union and promptly lost my last $30. Tuli generously advanced me $110, the hitch being that I had to give him my driver's license until I was able to pay him back. What I didn't know at the time was that I would be without that driver's license for the next five months!

5

Working in the Fields

During the second semester of my junior year in college, having lost all my money – a whopping $30 – in a poker game on campus, at the Memorial Union, I surrendered my Wisconsin driver's license to Tuli Haromy for a $110 loan. With no money, doing what a student must do proved to be difficult. After all, I needed to pay my rent, I needed gas for my motorcycle, and I needed to eat. Naturally, I turned to my father for a loan. It wasn't the first time that I had hit him up for help and, to be fair, I had managed to pay him back every time. But this time around, my father decided to play hardball with me. With no help from dad, my choices were extremely limited, and ugly. I would have to drop out of the UW, and I would have to get a job so that I could eat and pay my bills.

Blain Farms

After dropping all my classes in the spring of 1985, I found a job with Blain Farms, working in their cornfields. I still lived with Kai Haller and John Mamalakis on West Washington Avenue, just a few blocks from the State Capital. As it turned out, a neighbor of mine on West Washington Avenue was also working for Blain Farms. So he and I and a few others carpooled into work every morning at 6:30 a.m. – at least I didn't have to ride my little motorcycle to work on those cold May mornings. It was a 20-minute ride across town to meet the yellow bus. We would drive to the east side of Madison, park the car, and hop onto the yellow work bus at 7 a.m. We were thus on the clock at 7 a.m., and from there we were driven to various Blain Farms fields. For the first month or two, we would "pick rocks" from the field. Picking rocks means that we would physically pick up large and medium-sized rocks, and throw them onto a pickup truck that drove along with us as we walked up and down the fields. It was hard labor, but not too bad. I knew coming in that I was supposed to use my legs, not my back, to pick up the rocks. And it wasn't like we ever saw rocks that were too big. If we did, we would pick them up together. After a month, our duties at Blain Farms shifted, and we helped plant corn.

When I received my third paycheck and paid my rent, I discovered that I had enough money left over to pay Tuli the $110 that I owed him, and thus recover my driver's license. So I called Tuli up and he said, "OK, we have another poker game tonight. Why don't you come over and pay me, and sit in the game and play with us?" I said, "Maybe." That night, I paid Tuli and I observed the poker game for a while, but I decided not to play. I didn't have nearly enough money to feel comfortable playing poker again, at least not yet.

A month later, our duties at Blain Farms switched again, and we were now de-tasseling corn, which means that we were pulling out the tassels on each individual stalk of corn so that the corn wouldn't cross breed. As another month passed and I fell back into the poker game, I began to tell the guys on the bus, "I won $150 last night in a poker game," or "I won $90 last night," or something of that sort. As I began building a poker bankroll, now bordering $800, I began to host poker games at my own West Washington residence. Eventually, I was winning enough money to think about quitting my Blain Farms job.

After working for six dollars an hour in the fields, I had come to know the value of a dollar, and my newly disciplined poker style reflected it. I didn't want to lose any more money, and at that point I began to develop my own tactics for winning at poker. As it turns out, I had been spending my entire life learning the tactics needed to play games perfectly. I had absolutely had to master Scrabble, spoons, Monopoly, poker, and whatever other games contained an element of skill, because it had been too painful for me to lose to my younger brother and my sisters (Chapter 2). Unknowingly, I had begun studying game theory at a young age, and poker was simply another step in my game-theory progression.

Play Tight (Patient) Poker

After playing for a few months, I recognized that Tuli was the best poker player in the game, and I began to talk strategy and tactics with him. He advocated a very patient "tight" style of play, and I agreed with him, but I added my own twists. Generally, Tuli would play more patiently than I would, because I had come to recognize that by adding a few well-timed bluffs, I could throw off my opponents and win a lot more money. Tuli was never much of a bluffer. He was much more like a computer than he was a human being, and he kept his game aloof from its psychological components (the human element). Instead of mixing in bluffs and putting in small money with weak drawing hands in order to win big money when you hit draws, Tuli preferred to play patiently, waiting for great situations to develop, and then he would put as much money into the pot as possible.

Winning with Patience

No imagination was required to win money consistently in those low-level games. There were so many bad players that you could simply wait them out and win money in the majority of sessions. And Tuli was the master of this "wait them out" tactic. To his credit, he was disciplined and unemotional, but he was also predictable and easy to read. I, too, believed in patience, but I added the human element, in order to maximize my wins, confuse my opponents, and outplay them in pots both big and small, but only when the opportunity presented itself. I watched my opponents like a hawk, waiting for signs of strength or weakness that I could take advantage of. If I saw weakness in an opponent, then I would bluff him, oftentimes showing the bluff. But no one likes to get bluffed, and showing my bluffs had a negative emotional effect on my opponents. This then created tons of action in the game, when my opponents became overwhelmed with emotion and made bad decisions (in the poker world, we call this "tilt"). By showing my opponents an occasional bluff, it seemed to induce them into calling big bets when I did have a strong hand.

When I read uber strength in my opponents, then I would fold even my super-strong hand, oftentimes showing it to them. It was at this point that I began to develop the ability to fold these hands, and this has been a hallmark of my game these last 31 years. The more I played the game, the more I came to understand that poker is more about your opponents' hands and less about your own hand. My line of the year at the 2008 WSOP on ESPN was, "Don't play the cards; play the player!" And back in 1985, I had quickly become the best player in the game, as we shall see.

Monroe Street Poker Games

It wasn't long before I dropped my job at Blain Farms and moved out of the West Washington Avenue house when the lease was up, in August. As it turns out, I had worked at Blain Farms for about three months, until right around my 21st birthday, on July 16, 1985. In the middle of August I moved into a house on Monroe Street, which was only two blocks away from my parents' residence. I enrolled once again in a few classes at the UW, but it is fair to say that I had now begun to work full time on my "poker degree." I also hosted a ton of poker games at my Monroe Street house, and in October I found myself staring down the undisputed champion of the local game: Tuli Haromy. We were in my attic on Monroe Street at around 2 a.m., and everyone else had quit the game and cashed in their chips. Tuli didn't even bother taking all of their chips off the table. Instead, he scooped them all up and simply left them all in his stack, almost as if he knew he would bust me. I had been working hard on my poker tactics, but I wasn't sure that I had gained enough skill to take down the game's best player.

The Master, or the Student?

So I reasoned that I would give it a small shot. I saw how much I stood to gain if I busted Tuli (he had left a lot of chips on the table), a whopping $1,200, and my plan was to risk just a portion of the chips that I had sitting in front of me ($150 or so), and then I would quit. I would pay close attention to the play, and if Tuli was clearly bettering me, then I would quit.

So play continued. It was clear to me right away that Tuli was not making the adjustments you need to make when you switch to heads-up play. He wasn't seeing the right strategy, one that seemed obvious to me: play big pots with big hands, small pots with weak hands. Tuli's mistake that day was to over-adjust to one-on-one play, and he was putting way too much money into the pot with hands that were too weak. Thus, I won a bunch of big pots from him when I had super-strong hands and he had medium-strength hands.

So along came the final hand of the night. Tuli was down to $220, and we were playing Pineapple (which is Hold 'Em, except that you start with three cards before the flop, and then fold one of them before the flop). In Pineapple, the starting hands are a lot more powerful than they are in Hold 'Em, and I had K-K. (We had no blinds, just a $1 ante by the dealer.)

I had been baiting Tuli by opening for $10 with starting hands both weak and strong. Naturally, I showed him all of the weak ones. With just a $1 ante, strategically, you could fold a huge number of hands for $10 pre-flop! The game was thus set up for super-tight play, and super-patient tactics. But I was making the game play bigger, as most great players are capable of doing. I opened for $10, Tuli called, and the flop was 9♠-8♠-4♣. On the flop I bet $25, and Tuli called. The turn card was the 6♥, I bet $50, and Tuli moved all-in. With this much money in the pot, my hand was not supposed to be the best hand, and I knew it! But as I studied Tuli, I felt weakness. Finally, I called, Tuli tabled A♦-8♦, and the last card was a 3. I had busted him on this hand, and I was shocked that he was that weak. With a $1 ante in Pineapple, he should have had at least Q-Q for $220!

I should acknowledge that I was much more fresh in these games, having slept all day long, and Tuli had worked all day long. At this point in my life, about all I did was play poker, and I slept on a schedule that kept me fresh for the poker games that I played in. Meanwhile, Tuli was working 10 hours a day doing high-level research. But for whatever reason, the baton was passed that night. I had won all of the chips in front of Tuli, and I noticed that he didn't like paying me all of the money in the bank that night. I'm not sure that he had ever paid another player the whole bank before, and he hesitated as he counted out almost $1,600 in cash. From then on, Tuli looked at me in a different light, and he never again left many chips in front of him when he played me heads up!

Meanwhile, throughout the rest of 1985 and all of 1986 I held poker games at my Monroe Street house. We also had poker games at the Memorial Union, and some of the other players in the game hosted poker games at their houses as well. One of the high-rolling characters that I played with back then was a prominent psychologist I will call Karl S. In daily life, Karl was a talented guy, but in poker he just couldn't get it into his head that he had to play fewer hands if he was to win money in any of the games we played in together. Karl attended about 50% of the games that were held at the Memorial Union, and he had his own game on Wednesday nights. (Everyone else called this one the "big game," but I called it the "doctors' game.") Karl had some skills: he played the hands that he did play really well, but he simply played way too many of them.

Too Many Hands? Can't Win!

In Texas Hold 'Em, you cannot win if you play too many hands, period. The first element that I teach people about the play of Texas Hold 'Em is that patient play is a huge key to winning (I talk about "Phil's Top Ten Hands" in my *New York Times* best-selling book *Play Poker Like the Pros*, in my e-books, my CDs, and my internet poker courses). When a poker game is populated by players who play too many hands, then all you need to do is to play patiently. The poker games that I played in, in the UW community back in the day, were populated by impatient players, and all you needed to do – as Tuli knew all too well – was to play patiently in order to win. Even today, there are tons of poker games, across the globe, where all you need to do in order to win is to play patiently. These "strawberry patch" games always involve players who do not understand the need for patience in poker.

The "Doctors' Game"

In October 1985, Karl invited me to play in the "doctors' game" at his house on Wednesday nights. The game's roster included Karl, himself a prominent psychologist, another well-known psychologist named Ed Donnerstein, two well-known professors, Tuli, Dave (the guy who introduced me to my first game), a famous lawyer, and a few others who rotated in occasionally. It was mostly guys, but there was a female player in the game (whom I had played with just one time) who had written her PhD on poker. She wasn't a good player! I'm sure her math was terrific, but she didn't seem to possess great people reading skills.

In any case, the buy-in was $100, and the rebuys were $50. Here I was, a mere 21 years old, and I was playing poker with a bunch of sophisticated older gentlemen, all of whom were extremely well educated (each of them had at least a PhD!). My father had instilled in me a healthy respect for education, and I had a ton of respect for everyone in that poker game. Indeed, I was amazed to find myself in that company. But as it turned out, I was the best player in the game, by far.

This proved to be a game where I could use all my burgeoning skills. The dealer anted $1, which put Tuli in heaven, because he could play super, super-tight poker and win most of the pots he played in (not many). Meanwhile, I could imitate Tuli and play super-tight and win most of the pots that I played in. Better yet, I could play just pretty tight, and mix it up with the big boys. My style would yield much bigger wins than Tuli's, but seemingly with a lot greater risk. Yes, Tuli won more often than I did, night-in and night-out, but at the end of one year's play, I was the one who was up $30,000 or more in that game, to his $8,000 or so. I discovered that if I gambled with the big boys, then they would gamble with me. At some point, I would stop gambling, and lock it up, but they wouldn't seem to notice my change in tactics. Because the stacks were so deep – by "deep stacks" I mean that we all had tons of chips in front of us relative to the blinds (none) and antes – we had opportunities to make a lot of bluffs, and even semi-bluffs. Oftentimes, there would be over $4,000 in chips in play on the table with only the $1 ante by the dealer, and no blinds. The deeper the stacks, the higher the level of skill required to play it well; and possessing a great reading ability in a game like that is prized. This was the game that separated the men from the boys! I took to this game like a fish takes to water. I began winning so much money that I could pay off all my student loans, and I started piling cash into my bank account as well.

Planning My First Trip to Vegas

So, back in November 1985, I was busy planning my first trip to Las Vegas. I was now 21 years old, and it was time to check out the big leagues. I knew that my buddy Tuli would be in Vegas over the holidays, staying at his parents' house, and I decided to fly to Vegas on December 31st.

6

Vegas, the First Time

By the time I left for Las Vegas on New Year's Eve, 1985, I had almost $12,000 in the bank, and I had paid off all my student loans. I asked myself, how could I make this kind of money by returning to school? It looked like a career in poker for me! I checked into the Dunes Hotel and Casino (the Dunes was on the site where the Bellagio is now) at around 7 p.m., dropped my bags in my room, and then, without unpacking a thing, walked straight into the poker room and noticed there was a seat open right next to... Telly Savalas?

A Celebrity!

Wow, I was shocked; I had never seen a celebrity before, and Telly was a huge TV star and movie star in those days. I knew Telly best as the star of the hit television series *Kojak*. As it turned out, the seat to his left was open, so there I was, my first time in a Vegas poker room, sitting next to Telly Savalas. Telly was dressed in a beautiful black tuxedo – after all, it was 7:30 p.m. on New Year's Eve – and his young wife and infant child (the child was in a stroller) kept coming down to tug on his sleeves. Apparently, there was a big party upstairs that they were all attending, and Telly's wife kept trying to drag him away from the table. I could see that Telly was happy playing poker and didn't want to go anywhere! In any case, he leaned over to me and said, "Kid, we're the suckers here!" I didn't answer, just smiled, but I thought I was definitely not a sucker. After all, I had made all of my money playing poker. But I suppose that Telly was right (I just didn't know it!): this was Vegas, this was the big leagues, and the game we were playing was one I had never played before. We were playing $20–40 limit Stud 8/b (Seven Card Stud 8-or-Better).

Sleep, Who Needs It?

I had checked into my room at the Dunes on December 31, and I left the hotel on January 2nd, but I could just as easily have left my bags at the bell stand those first two days. I played poker for roughly 40 hours straight, and it was only when I remembered (foggily) that Tuli Haromy and his mother were supposed to come by the hotel to pick me up at 2 p.m. that very day that I finally went to bed at 11 a.m. I slept like a stone for three hours, and awoke only when my door opened. Apparently, I had slept through four phone calls to my room, and I hadn't even budged when hotel security pounded on my door. Finally, Tuli and his mother had to have the hotel security guard open my door! I was unconscious, and one wonders what Tuli and his mom thought, when they were admitted to my room, and I looked up at them all bleary-eyed, and half-conscious! In Madison, I had never had to quit a poker game. I would just play until I had busted everyone else, or they had all quit. I was the one who had no job, who had no classes and no responsibilities; I was the one who slept right up to the time the poker game began. I never had to quit in Madison, but in Vegas the poker games ran 24/7. I would have to learn to quit, or I would kill myself from exhaustion.

Tuli's Parents' House

On the spot, I moved out of the Dunes and into Tuli's parents' house. I had brought $5,000 with me, mostly in travelers' checks, and had already burned through about $1,800 of it. After a day of rest, Tuli took me to the poker room at the Stardust Hotel and Casino (right down the street from the Dunes), where they had limit Texas Hold 'Em. Even though I had never played Limit Hold 'Em, Hold 'Em was a game that I understood, and loved to play. Right away I held my own playing $10–20 Limit Hold 'Em, but I discovered a few dangerous games called blackjack, craps, and baccarat. These and video poker machines, and baccarat are considered "casino games." And casino games are the reason Vegas is thriving!

Random Walk Downward

Take a look at all of the wonderful hotels and casinos that exist today in Vegas. These magnificent properties were built mostly from tourists' losses in the casino games. When you study these games closely, you will see that each has a "random walk downward" element. Blackjack is a bit different. Perfect blackjack strategy may net you a "close to breakeven" random walk, and if you can count cards as well (without being thrown out of the casino), then you can expect to make some money (random walk upward). In any case, these casino games are fun to play, and extremely addictive. After I discovered (and came to love) craps and baccarat, then it was just a matter of time before I lost all my money. That first trip to Las Vegas I lost my $5,000 bankroll, and flew back home to Madison with my tail between my legs. I had held my own at Limit Hold 'Em, but I had gotten crushed at Stud 8/b, as well as the casino games.

7

Vegas Busts Me, Again and Again!

For all of 1986 a familiar pattern developed around my card play. I would win big in Madison, and then would lose big in Las Vegas. After returning home from my first unsuccessful foray to Vegas in January 1986, I attacked the games at home with a new vigor. First, I had learned a lot while playing poker in Vegas. Even though I lost all of the money that I had taken with me, I learned some valuable lessons. It didn't take a genius to figure out that the Las Vegas poker rooms were filled with hometown champions. Everyone seemed to have the same familiar story: they won big at home and then tried to take their game to the next level. So I was cutting my teeth against some tough competition. Second, the stakes in the "doctors' game" at home now seemed paltry to me.

Vegas Trips, Losing Trips

So again, I crushed the poker games in Madison for about $7,000, and two months later I headed out to Las Vegas for the second time. This time I stayed at the Stardust Hotel and Casino and played Limit Hold 'Em, but I also played craps and baccarat. Again, I brought $5,000 with me, and broke even playing Limit Hold 'Em, but I lost big playing craps and baccarat. After about 12 days at the Stardust I went broke, and flew home for the second time with my tail between my legs. Two trips, two $5,000 losses, and two times that I went home completely broke. I began to understand what would happen to me if I kept messing with the casino games, but I wasn't ready to give them up quite yet.

Big Al Emerson

A month later, I was ready to head to Las Vegas for the third time. In the meantime, I had crushed the games in Madison again, and this time around in Las Vegas, at the Stardust, I played more poker, and less casino games, for the first few days anyway. And on this third trip I was introduced to another Wisconsin-ite named "Big Al" Emerson. Big Al was a professional poker player based in La Crosse, Wisconsin, which is about 90 miles west of Madison, located right on the Mississippi River. Big Al was this 6' 7", 320-pound man with light-brown hair, brown eyes, and a pleasant personality. He was warmly received in poker games all over the Midwest, although he was often the big winner in these games. Big Al and I hit it off right away, and when we were back home he introduced me to some of the biggest poker players, and some of the biggest poker games, in the state of Wisconsin. In fact, Big Al knew tons of poker players all over the Midwest.

Even though Big Al and I lived 90 miles apart, over the next few years we trav-eled the Midwest together quite a bit. At that point in my life, I didn't know any poker players outside of my small UW crowd. As it turned out, there were poker games in Madison, La Crosse, Minneapolis, and Fargo, North Dakota, to name but a few. In Big Al's hometown of La Crosse, there was a regular $5–$10 limit poker game four days a week at Freddy Wakine's Fayze's bar and restaurant. This $5-$10 limit game was way too small to capture Big Al's full attention, unless he was broke. If he had over $2,000 to his name, and was home in La Crosse with the wife and children, he would usually skip Fayze's game. But if he had less than $2,000 to his name, he would "pump up" in the game there.

Big Al's Ups and Downs

Big Al had had some serious ups and downs along the way, and just listening to his latest "state of Big Al" stories was, and still is, gripping! His stories went something like this:

> On Monday I started the day with $2,000 in cash, but then lost it all playing $20-$40 limit. You know all the crazy limit games that we play up there in our poker game in Minneapolis. I hit the couch, and six hours later they woke me up to start another poker game, and Jerry loaned me $500, which I ran up to $4,000 in a Pot Limit Hold 'Em game (which is my best game anyway), and these guys in Minneapolis never play it. Then I put all of my money in before the flop, the whole $4,000, with pocket kings, and Mike had A-K. An $8,000 pot, and it comes down 7-6-2-4-A! I blow this $8,000 pot to an ace on the river! But Mike owed me $500, and I ran that

up to $7,500. Then on Wednesday there was no poker game, so I bet $4,000 on the Milwaukee Brewers, and can you believe it? They were up one run in the ninth, and they blew the lead with two outs in the top of the inning, and now they lose by two runs. So now I ran into the bookie and had to pay the $4,400 off, and now I had $2,600 to my name.

All of those twists and turns, and we still hadn't made it to Thursday yet!

"Broke and Borrow" System

Big Al was living on an old system, but one that still exists in poker today. A poker player would go broke, borrow money from another player, and then work hard to climb out of the hole he had put himself into. Not much changed whether you had $20,000 in cash to your name or were $5,000 in debt. You still traveled around to the biggest poker games you could find, and you still played in them, whether you were on borrowed money or your own money. Actually, one thing did change. When someone like Big Al was pumped way up (say with $50,000 in cash to his name), then he would play worse poker that day than he would when he was actually broke and hungry for a win. There is a good reason why they say "broke and hungry!" The same thing happens to a lot of professional poker players and, occasionally, to me.

Hanging out with Big Al, I learned some valuable lessons. Since I knew that I wanted to be a professional poker player, and Big Al was a pro, I paid close attention to his lifestyle, and his habits. First of all, he bet on sports compulsively at times, and because of this predilection he never seemed to have money for too long. If he had a lot of money, he would bet a lot of it on sports. If he was pumped up and betting sports, he would bet every game on the sheet! He might know something about some of the games, but he would usually know relatively nothing at all about most of the games. Since the bookie collected 10% juice on each of his losing bets, if Big Al bet 30 games at $1,000 a pop and won 15 and lost 15, then he was out $1,500 in juice. I equate it to this: if you bet $1,000 a game on 30 games every day, then it is like flipping 30 coins, and paying 10% juice every time you flip tails. So the first thing that I learned from Big Al was to avoid sports betting. The second thing I learned was this: I didn't like the whole "broke and borrow" money system. Basically, I was never involved in this system as I climbed my way into the poker world. The whole thing just seemed way too stressful to me! I wanted to be able to pay my bills, at all times, and it seemed to me that if I managed my money well, then I would always be able to pay my bills, on time.

Avoiding this "broke and borrow" system worked well for me for several reasons. First, I felt the hunger to win before I went broke, not afterward. So I more or less raised my "desperation bar" higher than Al's "broke and borrow" system allows. I've learned firsthand that desperation and inspiration cause people to achieve great things. And most times when I've been desperate, I've played great poker. Second, because I was usually the best player in the game, I would be the one who was doing the lending, and almost never the one who was doing the borrowing. Because I managed to avoid this system, I have a "debt sheet" (a list of people who owe me money) from the 1980s (which I threw away), a debt sheet from the 1990s (fewer names, greater amounts!), and a debt sheet from the 2000s (not too many names). Third, I was always able to pay my bills, because I never really ran out of assets, other than once in January 1987. I did run out of money occasionally, but I always had equity in my house, stocks, and a SEPP fund (a retirement fund), and my cars have always been paid for in full.

Still, with Big Al, I had found a professional poker player I could hang out with, learn from, and observe. From Day 1, I felt like my Hold 'Em skills were vastly superior to his, seeing as he had the common Hold 'Em disease called "playing too many hands." But in the other tricky poker games that I was introduced to by Big Al, the high-stakes poker games (like Stud Hi/Lo and Monty) that they played in Minneapolis and Fargo, Al was clearly a better player than I was for the next several years.

Over the remainder of 1986 I made six more trips to Las Vegas, and each time I came home broke. Meanwhile, I continued to crush the games in Madison, and in July 1986 I introduced Pot Limit Omaha to the "doctors' game." In Hold 'Em and Pineapple, my edge in the "doctors' game" was huge, but in Pot Limit Omaha my edge was off the charts! I began to win more than $1,200 a night in that game, routinely (my biggest win ever in the "doctors' game" was $2,600). It was about this time that Karl and the UW gentlemen began asking themselves, "Why are we inviting Phil to this game? He wins a fortune each week, and he rarely loses." By October of that year I found myself banned from my first poker game, because I was too good! And without that $1,000 a week coming in from the "doctors' game," I no longer had the ammunition to keep losing $5,000 a trip in Vegas.

Going Broke, Yuck!

In Las Vegas in January 1987, I went completely broke for the first time. I had won well over $100,000 by then playing poker, but I had lost most of it playing casino games in Vegas. The good news was that every time I saw a craps table, I began to feel sick to my stomach (a trend that continues to this day). Finally, the lure of the casino games had left me forever!

8

Home Poker Games in Madison and Beyond

In writing the last chapter I left off the moment when I went broke in January 1987. But in telling my story, a little overlap is in order. In late 1985, my best friend Tuli Haromy and I were invited to play in a poker tournament at the Park Grill on Park Street in Madison. It was there that we found the tip of the iceberg, that being the thriving poker scene in Madison. It was there that I made some new poker friends, Dewey Weum and Wayne "Tilly" Tyler (more on Tilly below). Dewey, about 6' 1" with light-brown hair, was the best No Limit Hold 'Em player in the state of Wisconsin. Dewey was a hardened veteran poker player who had been through many campaigns and wars in Las Vegas, and was the biggest winner in the poker games that were held in the state.

Dewey Wins!

Dewey had a great style of poker for Pot Limit Hold 'Em, playing super-tight, and playing aggressively. He was also tricky. He could play his strong hands fast, as when he had K-Q and the flop was K-Q-6, and he somehow would get all of his money into the pot right on the flop. Or Dewey could play his strong hands weak and trap his opponents, as when he had A-2 and the flop came down J-2-2, and he didn't raise it up until the last card fell (J-2-2-4-9). He had played in the WSOP, and he had played successfully for years in the Pot Limit Hold 'Em – and No Limit Hold 'Em – side games in Vegas. Years later, Dewey would win some huge poker tournaments in Las Vegas. As good as Dewey was at poker, he was sort of a one-trick pony. By that I mean that he played Pot Limit Hold 'Em and No Limit Hold 'Em almost exclusively (Pot Limit and No Limit are almost the same game in the side games), and any other games that we played in over the years – like Seven Card Stud, Stud 8/b, and Limit Hold 'Em – he just skipped. Dewey may not have played all the other forms of poker, but he was smart enough to stay in his own lane and win all the money!

Ken's Bar Game – Playing with Cash!

The iceberg expanded when Tuli and I dug deeper and found another regular poker game. It was a $10-$20 limit game, and it was held on Friday nights at Ken's Bar, which was located one block away from the state of Wisconsin's Capitol building. This game had a unique feature: we used cash only to bet, to call, and to raise it up – no chips! I'm not sure that I've played in another poker game, before or since, where we used cash only, and not chips. And this cash-only feature led to the eventual demise of the Ken's Bar game. But for one year I played with the boys with stacks of five-dollar bills, $10 bills, and $20 bills, with $100 bills sprinkled in. This game was exciting! We played in a public place, with stacks of cash in front of us, and you could win or lose $1,500 a night in the game. We also played some interesting games like the super-old-school Five Card Draw, and Seven Card Stud, and some Texas Hold 'Em. In the one-year period when I played in the Ken's Bar game, I probably won a small amount, maybe $100 per Friday night. The Ken's Bar game thrived until the day after Thanksgiving in 1986 (November 21, 1986), when the bartender got into an argument with her boyfriend, and her boyfriend decided that he would try to get her into trouble at work. So he called the police to inform them that there was some high-stakes gambling going on at the bar. So two policemen come waltzing into the bar – one in plain clothes, the other in uniform – just as my old friend Bruce DeWitt was dragging in a big pot. Bruce, about 5' 10" with what seemed like orange hair, had tons of freckles everywhere. Just an instant before, I had asked Bruce to give me change for three $100 bills, and he was counting out the change for me when the policemen walked up to the table. The rest of us immediately moved our stacks of cash into our laps, our pockets, and anywhere else out of plain view, but Bruce was in the middle of his count, saying, "90, 100, 110, 120."

With a loud voice I said, "Bruce!"

Bruce, distracted and irritable, replied, "Wait a minute! 130, 140..."

Speaking even more loudly, I said, "Bruce!"

Then Bruce looked up, and if it is possible, he turned even redder than the red he already is! Suddenly, whoosh, the money in front of Bruce disappeared into his lap. One of the plainclothes policemen, looking very much amused, told us, "Look, we don't care if you play poker here, but we do care if you use cash. It just looks bad. If you use chips, then everything is cool."

Personally, I think that the guys were a bit too paranoid when they quit the game right afterwards, thinking that the police might come back if we continued to play.

The Demise of the Ken's Bar Poker Game

None of these guys wanted their name in the newspapers. Dewey was a businessman who was married to a school teacher; Bruce was a postman for the US Postal Service, and two of the other guys in the game were postmen as well, Tuli was a highly respected researcher, and then there Wayne "Tilly" Tyler. Tilly probably didn't mind too much, as he was a poker player who ran and organized poker games throughout the state of Wisconsin. In any case, when we showed up the following Friday night to play the Ken's Bar game, we were told that Ken (whom I never actually met) didn't want us playing there anymore, because he didn't want to risk losing his liquor license. So ended the super-juicy Ken's Bar game that had been running since 1984.

Wayne "Tilly" Tyler

As I mentioned in the preceding paragraph, Tilly ran poker games, and Tilly was the most connected of anyone that I knew, when it came to knowing where the poker games were held, and who was playing in them. Wayne "Tilly" Tyler is about 6' 3" with black hair, brown eyes, and a putting stroke that is pretty pure (but the rest of his golf game sucks!). Tilly's father owned and ran a junkyard, and Tilly had been briefly in the junkyard business himself. Over the years, Tilly moved away from the junkyard and toward poker. He eventually started playing in, and organized and ran, poker games in Madison, Fort Atkinson, Jefferson, and places in between. Tilly was, and still is, a fixture on the Madison poker scene, and he and I have had a long history of trying to beat each other at poker, golf, Dirty Clubs, darts, pool, bowling, and many other games that offered venues where we could compete against each other.

Tilly's poker skills were not ready for prime time the way that Dewey's were, but he held his own in Las Vegas, and he made money in the local games that he played in, and ran. Tilly occasionally traveled with me, and roomed with me (in 1986 and 1987) on trips to Las Vegas, Reno, and such other destinations as Minneapolis and North Dakota, which I will talk about in the next few chapters. Everyone loves Tilly! He has a fine personality, but as the man who ran the poker games, he also knew how to tell you like it was. Tilly wears his emotions on his sleeve, and you always know where you stand with him.

Fort Atkinson Poker Game

One of the poker games that Tilly ran was a $5–10 limit game that he spread at the Polish Palace in Fort Atkinson (55 minutes east of Madison). I really enjoyed this game, as it featured some loose – and rich – players, and on a good day I could win $300. It was there that I began playing poker with Tommy Hun, and Hun seemed to beat the crap out of me in poker for years to come.

Tommy Hun "Holds Over" Me!

In poker, when Player A seems to beat Player B out of an extraordinary number of pots, we say that Player A is "holding over" Player B. Tommy Hun held over me for years! Tommy was overall a losing player who played way too many hands, but we all loved the man.

Tommy was about 6′ 1″ tall, with wispy light-brown hair, and brown eyes, and he was thin as a rail. Tommy had been in the US Army during the Korean War, and had been injured around the mouth area. Tommy had a southern accent, and a pleasant way about him, whether he won or lost. When Tommy was losing big on any given night, his chips flew around the table as he tilted! But when he became desperate, he also became a dangerous opponent, more than capable of winning a big pot when his bad hand outdrew your good hand. This would lead to some bad beats for the rest of us, or to an even bigger loss for Tommy, and more often than not, I was the victim of his bad beats! On the other side of the coin, when Tommy was a big winner in the game, he played a more tightly controlled game as he protected his win. One thing is for sure: Tommy seemed to have an inexhaustible supply of money, and he played like it!

The Nora Bar Game

Fort Atkinson was almost an hour-long drive for the Madison contingent (the vast majority of the players were from Madison), and by January 1987 Tilly decided to move the game to a small bar just a few miles outside of Madison on Highway 15 called Nora's. When one poker game goes down, usually others spring up to take its place, especially when you had an ever-growing poker community, like we did in Madison back then. With the Ken's Bar game gone, the players in it were looking for action. And with this new and closer location, Nora's attracted a big crowd. Madison poker was growing, and as the games became intertwined, more and more players began to know where all of the poker games were being held. I remember that we would often have *two* tables, with over 20 players in attendance, playing at Nora's at one time. The new game at Nora's originally began as a $5-$10 limit game, but that lasted only a few months. The big guys like Dewey Weum wanted in, and Dewey played pretty much exclusively Pot Limit Hold 'Em. So the game switched to a Pot Limit Hold 'Em game, and I played there twice a week. Tilly would run a $1-$2 blind Pot Limit game in the afternoons, and a $2-$3 Pot Limit Hold 'Em game that began at 6 p.m. The game at Nora's always ended at 1 a.m. (bar time), but when the right people were in town, we would go to the Wolf's Den (see below) to extend the game. I rarely played in the afternoon game, because there wasn't enough money on the table to sustain my interest. By that point in my life I understood that I couldn't play my best game when the stakes were relatively modest.

The Wolf's Den Poker Game

Nora's Bar served as one of the two big homes of the poker community. And especially it served as a home for the higher-stakes games. The other home was the Wolf's Den (the actual name on the building was the Sportsman's Club) in Waunakee, which was about 25 minutes from my Monroe Street rental house. A colorful character named Wayne Wolf owned the Wolf's Den; and the Sportsman's Club was actually a private club whose members included a few fishermen and a few hunters from the Madison area. These sportsmen paid dues, and received discounts on hunting and fishing trips that Wayne Wolf himself served on as a professional guide. These trips were usually to Northern Wisconsin or Eastern Michigan, but I never knew any members of the club, and from what I saw, Wayne used the club primarily to host poker games. Wayne was a nice guy, mild mannered, but you knew that you didn't want to piss him off! He was a burly guy who stood at just 5' 7" tall, with black hair and black eyes, and he really was an expert in hunting, fishing, and survival tactics. Wayne raked the game (he lifted money out of some of the pots), and in return he provided food and drinks, and a place to play. Although Wayne raked the game pretty heavily at times, no one minded much, because he usually lost the rake right back to the players in the game.

The Wolf's Den game, even though it was only $2-$4 limit (sometimes $3-$6 limit), was an important source of income for me back in the day. And it was a fun game to play in because we played tons of poker games other than Texas Hold 'Em, like Stud 8/b (Seven Card Stud 8-or-Better), the game in play when I made my first final table at the WSOP (Chapter 12), Omaha High-Low Split, Seven Card Low, and other High-Low Split games that gave me the base of knowledge that I used for decades afterwards. The regular players in the Wolf's Den game were waitresses, shop owners, businesswomen, businessmen, accountants, and a wide array of players who came from a more normal, everyday walk of life. Oftentimes, when the games at Nora's and the Wolf's Den overlapped, I would skip the bigger game at Nora's to take a guaranteed $200 or $300 victory at the Wolf's Den. I have fond memories of playing in the Wolf's Den game, with its relaxed atmosphere and fun mix of poker games, and I played there tons of hours.

The Player's Bar Game

There was one other game that I played in back in 1987 (and they still play there in 2017). It was held at Player's Bar on the near east side of Madison on Saturdays, and back then it was $2-$4 limit. The game started at noon, and ended at bar time (12:30 a.m.). And it was by far the most uncomfortable poker game that I have ever played in! Back then, six to eight of us were crammed in like sardines around a tiny raised circular bar table that was made for just four people maximum, while we sat on ludicrously uncomfortable bar stools. Meanwhile, while we played our poker game, we had to get out of the way of the people right next to us, who were playing pool. (Player A would say, "I'm all-in for $43." And right then a player who had a shot at the pool table next to us would ask our Player A, "Can you move a little to the right, please?") Meanwhile, the jukebox was blaring out tunes so loud that you could barely hear yourself think, and the later it got, the louder the jukebox was cranked up! I love "Guns and Roses," but how often can you hear "Paradise City," "Sweet Child of Mine," and "Welcome to the Jungle" in one day? Still, this low-limit $2-$4 game at Player's Bar sustained me big time for a few years. Back in 1987 I was no longer strutting around with $20,000 in my bank account. By then I had gone broke, and these small-stakes games at the Wolf's Den and Player's Bar are the reason that I could pay my bills and build my bankroll. It was pretty normal for me to win $400 every Saturday at Player's Bar, and I rarely lost money there. On occasion I would win over $1,000.

Phil's Cocaine Overdose?

I'll never forget what happened to me on the way to a Player's Bar game back in 1987 or so. Back then I would pretty much win all of the money that the guys had at the time, and then I would leave. One fall on a Saturday night, I decided to buy some cocaine from one of the players at the table, who offered it to me in order to keep himself in chips at the table. Because it was a "free roll" (a zero-risk proposition) for me, the drug dealer would put the money back on the table and lose it, and it would keep the game going. Eventually, because I was the best player at the table (and because I kept the game going), I would win at least as much money as I spent to buy the coke. Having tried cocaine only twice in my life and both times while I was drinking, I was curious to try cocaine without drinking any alcohol. So I put my purchase away and thought, "OK, snort this next Saturday night before you come to the poker game here at Player's Bar." I felt like the Player's Bar game was so easy that I could win no matter what state I was in, drunk, tired, or high. So the following Saturday night at around 7 p.m. I left my car at my Monroe Street apartment, called a Yellow Cab, and snorted a few lines of coke. On the way to the bar, while sitting in the back seat of a Yellow Cab, my heart started to flutter uncontrollably, and began beating super-fast! "Oh my god," I thought, "this could be it! Please don't let me die like this!" And the recent Len Bias tragedy jumped to the front of my mind.

Len was a superstar college basketball player at the University of Maryland whom the Boston Celtics had drafted second in the 1986 National Basketball Association (NBA) draft. Larry Bird himself had said that he, personally, was going into mini-camp early in 1986, just because he was so excited about playing with Len. Then two days after the draft, it was reported that Len Bias had died of a cocaine overdose. This sad story was flashing through my mind as I sat in that cab with my heart fluttering out of control: it felt like it was beating so fast that it could have been the heart of a hummingbird. I tried to slow my mind and my body, in order to slow my heart beat. No response. After a few minutes of this madness, in the calmest manner possible, and with the clearest possible thought process, I said to the powers that be, and to myself, "God or the universe, please help me make it through this alive, and I'll never do cocaine again!" I did make it through that night alive and intact, and believe me when I tell you that I never did cocaine again!

9

Serious Progress and a New Resolve!

At the end of Chapter 1, you will recall, I was hungrily gobbling down huge amounts of peanuts on a flight back to Madison after burning the only "get out of jail free card" that my mother would give me. But on the positive side of the ledger, I had seen something in Las Vegas on that trip. It seemed to me that the best poker players in the world weren't playing Texas Hold 'Em the way they ought to play it. The day before I ran out of money and was forced to beg my parents for a way out of Las Vegas, I had watched someone named Stu "The Kid" Ungar (a poker legend) blow away the competition in a No Limit Hold 'Em poker tournament at the Riviera Hotel and Casino. From what I saw that day, Stu had thoroughly outplayed his opponents on his way to winning the tournament and the $67,000 first prize. I watched the final table as Stu raised it up before the flop almost every single hand, and his opponents folded meekly, hand after hand, letting Stu pick up the blinds and antes at will, and thus accumulate a ton of chips risk-free. I saw clearly the way he dominated play three handed. It seemed as if the two other players were playing for second place, while Stuey was playing to win.

Why Can't They See?

How could his opponents not see this? How could they play so poorly? I knew that if I were one of Stu's opponents, he would not have been rolling over me that easily. I would have re-raised him, with or without a strong hand, but I would not let him win the tournament uncontested. So, I knew a lot more about No Limit Hold 'Em tactics than two of the final three players still alive at the end of that tournament did.

I was broke on that trip because, for some reason, I had been incapable of playing my best poker, and because I foolishly played the casino games like baccarat and craps. I wasn't broke because the players in Vegas knew Texas Hold 'Em tactics better than I did. No, from what I saw playing in the Stardust Hotel poker room, it was just a matter of time before I would learn to play my best poker consistently. In my mind, a plan began to take form: I would go back to Madison, lick my wounds, and figure out what went wrong, but I would be back... with a vengeance!

My "Monk's Robe" Vision

When I returned home to Madison, I began mulling over a vision: I saw myself in a brown monk's robe with a hood over my head, sitting stone still at the poker table. No one could see my face, and I ignored all of those who tried to interact with me. I sat still as a chair, I gave nothing away. As I envisioned myself as this monk, I also imagined being unstoppable at the poker table. Even as the chips on the table flowed to me, I stayed quiet and still.

I guess what it all meant was that I needed to have the discipline of a monk if I was to succeed in poker. I needed to exercise patience relentlessly, and to allow no negative emotion to affect my mood, or put me on tilt (tilt, a poker term: to lose control of your emotions and thus your poker game). At that point in my life, I would still go on tilt too easily. One bad beat, even if I had been winning big, and I would lose control and go on tilt. More often than not, tilting costs you tons of money, but occasionally you will get lucky in a succeeding pot or two and recoup both your composure and your recent losses, the losses that put you on tilt in the first place.

Or did the monk vision mean that I needed time to train myself to be great, much as a Jedi Knight of the *Star Wars* movies might have done? I already knew that poker was a lot about discipline and patience, but discipline and patience were two of my greatest weaknesses. I would have to learn to overcome them if I was to become a great poker player.

Winning Feeling

In January 1988 I was still making most of my money playing in the poker games around the Madison area. But by then I had booked a winning trip or two to Las Vegas. I recall distinctly the first of these trips. After ten losing trips in a row, where I basically lost all the money I had brought with me, I was finally ahead around $6,000, and it freaked me out! I called my mother and told her, "I don't feel very good." After we discussed my situation for a while, and I couldn't seem to find a reason why I should feel so poorly, my mom finally asked, "Do you feel poorly because you're winning money?" For a fleeting moment her theory struck me as absurd. Then I realized that there was truth in her theory. It seemed that

I was feeling poorly *because* I was winning money! Then Mom said to me, "You have gotten used to losing, and losing is hard to deal with. But remember that winning can be even harder to deal with." She was right. Thanks Mom! From that point on, I was determined to make sure that I left Vegas on that trip a winner, if for no other reason than that I wanted to get used to winning. Winning is hard, and no one can prepare you for that reality, because most of us do not experience that concept. I left that trip a winner, and I was determined to make a habit out of winning money in Vegas!

As I played more and more poker in Las Vegas – and fewer and fewer casino games – I became more aware that there were poker tournaments being held at various casinos in Vegas and in places like Los Angeles. Surrounding these poker tournaments, I learned, was a ton of juicy side-game action (good poker games were going 24/7 at these tournament venues). It seemed as if chronically losing poker players flew in four or five times a year to take their shot at the big poker tournaments, and then play in the side games that surrounded those events. The bookies, the hometown champions, the big sports bettors, and the bad gamblers seemed to flock to the big-league poker tournaments. In more ways than one, these tournaments had become a dream come true for the top professional poker players!

Poker Tournaments

In January 1988 I found myself in Las Vegas, at a poker tournament being held at the Tropicana Hotel and Casino. As that event wound down, another big-league poker tournament was just getting under way at Caesars Palace. It was Amarillo Slim's "Super Bowl of Poker," and it was to begin on February 1st. I still had a room at the Trop, but I was playing poker at Caesars. It was 11 a.m., I hadn't slept much, and I hadn't had anything to eat in about 24 hours. I hadn't even noticed how hungry I was because I had been playing Pot Limit Hold 'Em at Caesars for the last 24 hours straight (Big Al was at the table with me), and poker is pretty all consuming. By then, I had decided to switch hotels from the Tropicana to Caesars, but since Caesars was sold out, I was going to share a room with my buddy Big Al. So I left my seat at the poker game and headed over to the Tropicana to pack my bags before noon and move them into my new room at Caesars. I was aware that my stomach was acting up, but I needed to get to the Tropicana before they charged me for my room for the night. So I put my head down, made my way over there, grabbed my bags, and checked out. Again, my stomach was bothering me, but I kept thinking that I would get back to Caesars and eat.

I Collapse at Caesars Palace!

When I arrived there, I went to the poker room and waited a few minutes for Big Al to get up from the table and go upstairs to the room with me. Finally, as he and I arrived at the elevators, I suddenly collapsed and fell to the floor! A security guard by the elevator called the paramedics. But within a minute I pulled myself up from the floor and got into the elevator to head up to the room. When I got out of the elevator, I collapsed again. What the heck was going on here? Big Al hopped onto the elevator and went down to alert the security guard that I had collapsed again. The paramedics arrived promptly, and I was carried out of Caesars on a stretcher.

Paramedics Involved

I seemed to be conscious all the way to the hospital, and when I arrived there, they couldn't find anything wrong with me (in truth, it didn't seem like they had tried very hard). But what were they going to test a healthy 23-year-old for? As the doctors asked me questions, they could see that I was allergic to nothing, I had no history of sickness whatsoever, and I had enjoyed perfect health. Believe it or not, the doctors finally gave me some Saltine crackers and released me. I was sick for a few days afterwards with something like exhaustion: I couldn't seem to eat much, and I was pretty weak physically. Basically, I spent a few days in bed sleeping and recovering. Later on, it was speculated that I was hypoglycemic (I need to have food at least every 10 to 15 hours).

Exercise – Running

In any case, nothing like that had ever happened to me before, and I was concerned and freaked out. Being scared like that gave me the momentum I needed to begin exercising every day. As I recovered, I started running up the strip every day, and as the Caesars tournament drew to an end, I found a nice $10-$20 Limit Hold 'Em game at the Stardust Hotel and Casino. I hadn't done well at Caesars, but really, up to this point in my poker career there had been too many lows to go with few highs. I was still too emotional at the tables, always battling with myself over the fear of going on tilt. And it just seemed as if my bankroll would never begin a steady upward climb! There were always so many downs. But at least the recent trend was positive.

Racking Up Huge Wins in Limit Hold 'Em

During my three-week stay at the Stardust, the house was running a contest whereby they would give away, each week, a total of $3,000 a week to the five biggest winners of the week in the $10-$20 Limit Hold 'Em game. First place was $1,000, second was $800, third was $600, fourth was $400, and fifth was $200. The week began at noon on Monday, and the top-ten leaders' numbers were posted on the wall throughout the week. The casino tracked our wins and losses closely. The players would buy into a particular $10-$20 game, the dealer then would verify the amount that we bought in for, and then sign our card. When we cashed out to the dealer, they would count us down and sign us out. It turned out that I had won the $1,000 first place prize in the promotion two out of three weeks, and finished in second place the third week.

The Best Unknown Player in the World

During that three-week-long financial boon, I had an encounter at the Stardust with the "best unknown poker player in the world," Don Williams (sadly Don died in April 2013). Don came into the Stardust one day with his southern accent and said to me, "Son, I hear you're quite a poker player. How's about you and I play some heads-up Limit Hold 'Em?" I had heard of Don Williams, and Don Williams had heard about all that money that I had sitting in my box. I passed at first, asking myself why I would ever play against a great player like Don. But as we hung out for a few hours, I thought, "Why not play him? If I lose, then I'll quit early, like maybe I'll risk $1,000, but if I win, who knows how much I'll win." Don and I started playing $10-$20 Limit Hold 'Em, and Don was complaining the whole time that the stakes were too meager for him. I was glad he saw things that way, because I realized that he might not play his best at that limit! But, as I felt more and more comfortable and started winning big, I agreed to switch it to $20-$40 Limit Hold 'Em.

After a few hours, I was not only holding my own, but came to realize that I had a better natural understanding of Limit Hold 'Em than Don did. I just needed to avoid getting unlucky, and I would be grinding out a decent win. I was up around $800 or so when a bunch of other players joined the game. This was about the biggest limit poker game I had ever played in, and by the time the smoke had cleared, I was winning about $4,500.

Don and I played a lot of tournament poker together over the next few years, and he was tough as nails. In 1993, I would play Don heads up in Limit Hold 'Em again, but this time for a WSOP bracelet, after we had busted the other 100 players in the tournament. I won that bracelet, with my wife and parents in attendance, for my record-tying third WSOP bracelet for that year!

By the way, Ted Forrest had just become the first player ever to win three WSOP bracelets in one year, just a week before I did it. The 1993 WSOP featured four men winning a total of ten bracelets: Ted had won his three, I won three, John Bonetti won two, and Costa Rican Humberto Brennes won two.

But I digress. Back to the story: near the end of my three-week-long stay at the Stardust, I heard about a tournament called the Cajun Cup, which was to be held in a few months (in April 1988) in Lafayette, Louisiana.

10

I Can See the Light!

In March 1988, an incident that fell my way became a defining moment, a turning point, so to speak, for the ensuing years of my life. On this random Tuesday – a cold, bleak day devoid of sun – the poker game began, at 11 a.m. with seven players. Nonetheless, at noon, I found myself wanting to leave. I felt restless, and I simply didn't want to be playing poker that morning. Maybe the dimensions of the game were a little too meager for me, or perhaps I was just burned out. In any case, I craved the outdoors! Perhaps I had spent too much time playing poker indoors, over the last few weeks.

In any case, I convinced two of my poker pals, Gary Miller and Larry Warmke, to leave the game with me. We took Larry's car, smoked some pot, and we drove to a bar down the road. When we arrived, we had a drink and began playing pool, each against the others for $10 a game, and then for $20 a game. Still, I was a bit frustrated with the action. First off, because I was the worst pool player in the group, I couldn't get a fair game. Second, we were playing for stakes so modest I thought, "Why bother? What a waste of time. What am I doing here?"

I See the Light!

When I was preparing to leave, I noticed a side door, and walked over to open it. As I opened the door, the sunlight outside came flooding over me! As my bleary eyes adjusted to the white light that seemed in abundance everywhere around me, I gazed out over the beautiful snowy landscape, and over the busy street that was about 15 yards in front of me. The snow on the side of the road in front of me was still about a foot deep, lying in half-melted icy piles. Because it had been overcast all day, I was surprised to find that the sun was out at all, much less out in full force.

Out of nowhere, it seemed, I woke from my odd life and was shocked to realize where I was, and what I was doing. Did the vast amount of light symbolize, to me, that I was falling slowly back into darkness? Why was I here? What was I doing with my life? Jarringly, I realized that I was in a bar having a drink, after I had smoked pot: and it was noon, no less! Perhaps you have heard that song by Talking Heads, "Once in a Lifetime?" My interpretation of the meaning of the song is that it is about waking up years later and finding that you are living a life you don't want, asking yourself how you got there and realizing that the answer was just by letting things happen…" I felt as if I was waking up, and just now seeing that my new poker life had become a tedious nightmare. I made some excuses to Gary and Larry, called a taxi, and got out of there, fast.

Putting Pen to Paper

The moment that I arrived at my nice new University Avenue apartment, which I had moved into a few months before, I sat down at my desk, pulled out some pen and paper, and pondered what, exactly, I was going to do with my life. OK, I loved poker, and was good at it, but if I was going to continue playing, then I might as well work toward becoming a great player, maybe the best poker player in the world. Why not? Even though I didn't smoke pot more than once a month, and then in moderation, it was nonetheless a habit that needed to go, and I decided that I would never turn to it again (I did smoke it three or four times in the next 30 years). I then resolved that I would be looking at poker as a scientist would look at math and physics; I would redouble my efforts to examine Texas Hold 'Em, the great variable of all, and learn everything about the game I could. I would dedicate myself to learning how to improve my poker tactics, to learn how to play consistently at a world-class level, and to learn (modestly enough) what it would take to become the best poker player in the world. I would then do what I needed to do to reach that level. And I would continue to do it the right way, unwaveringly, with honor, and ethics.

The "Winning Pyramid"

Now it was time I put my pen to paper. First I came up with the concept of the "winning pyramid." This "pyramid" entailed the building blocks needed to achieve world-class success in poker. On the bottom row of the pyramid, I put the biggest "leaks" (a leak is a trap that drains cash from your bankroll), which many of the poker players nonetheless seemed to tolerate. The bottom row is thus "casino games," "sports betting," "drugs," and "alcohol in excess." On the next level up I listed "exercise," "eating healthfully," "proper rest," as in not playing poker when you're tired. On the third level up of my "winning pyramid" I inserted: "emotional control," as in having the ability to avoid pressing in the moment (no more tilt!), and "discipline," playing the game the right way at all times, over all of my of future poker sessions. At the top of the "winning pyramid" I put "money management," because the only thing that can potentially trump talent at the poker table is good money management. You can have all of the talent in the world, but if you allow yourself to run out of money when a juicy game appears, then you'll be on the sidelines (probably watching less talented players pursue that amazing game). I figured that in order to become great at poker, I would have to learn to master each one of these blocks of the "winning pyramid" the right way. I listed them in order of importance, the bottom being the least important, and easiest to rid yourself of, and the top being the most important, and most challenging to master. It was a key day in my life because for the first time I clearly understood where I wanted to go, who I wanted to be, and how I could get there, using my "winning pyramid."

The "Poker Pyramid"

After I formulated my "winning pyramid," still drawn by inspiration, I began formulating and conceiving my new life plan, and I came to the realization that the entire poker world could be looked at as a "poker pyramid." The poker games at the bottom of the "poker pyramid" represent the low-limit games that the nonprofessional poker players might play in their homes. The poker games on the second level of our "poker pyramid" represent the medium-limit games that the "hometown champions" comfortably reside in. The poker games on the third level of the "poker pyramid" represent the high-limit games that persist here and there in the Vegas, LA, New York, Paris, Moscow, and Atlantic City. And finally, the poker games that occupy the top rung of the "poker pyramid" are the WSOP tournaments, the World Poker Tour (WPT) tournaments, the mega-high stakes games that can be found today primarily in Bobby's Room at the Bellagio Hotel and Casino, and the Ivey Room at the Aria Hotel and Casino in Vegas, the private games in LA and Manhattan, and these days a few mega-high stakes games that persist on the internet. The various games in the "poker pyramid" model, which I fashioned, even roughly match the numbers in a normal pyramid, with greater numbers of squares (or players) on the bottom rung, fewer numbers of squares on the second rung, still fewer on the third rung, and finally only one square on the top rung. Throughout the world, then, there are tens of thousands of low-limit poker games (bottom rung), thousands of medium-limit poker games (second rung from the bottom), hundreds of high-limit poker games (third rung from the bottom), and just dozens of mega-high stakes games (top rung).

Money Flows to the Top of the "Poker Pyramid"

The most important thing that I noticed about the "poker pyramid" is that the money flows upwards! Naturally, the winners in the low-limit poker games bring their winnings (money) to the medium-limit poker games to test their mettle. Some of these low-limit guys hold their own, or even move up to the wealthier limits with even more money, but most of them leave their money in the medium-limit poker games – and now, the money has moved up a level. Naturally, in due course, the big winners in the medium-limit poker games bring their winnings to the high-limit poker games, to do battle. But most of these medium-limit guys are forced to leave their money in the high-limit games (not good enough to win at this level), and then return to the medium-limit games, where they can comfortably beat the slackers. It is easy to see that most of the money in the poker world eventually ends up at the top level of the pyramid! Only a few dozen players ever reside on that top level for long. Pondering the upward flow of money in the "poker pyramid," I realized that I would have to climb all the way to the top of the mountain if I was to accumulate that kind of money, not to mention the kind of success I was after.

Life Goals

When I was done mulling all this over, and done putting the "winning pyramid" and the "poker pyramid" concepts to paper, I decided that the next step to take was to pull out pen and pencil and write up a list of life goals. I couldn't decide whether I should write up a short-term list first, or a long-term list, but finally I realized that it didn't matter, that I should just plough ahead, drawing upon this great stock of energy and clarity that I had assembled, and continue to write. I thought then, and I feel more strongly now, that my goals would be even easier to reach once they were crystal clear. Here, then, is the list that I wrote up, in March 1988:

Life Goals
1. Win the "big one" (the main event) at the WSOP.
2. Meet and marry a wonderful woman, one who can abide me.
3. Write a *New York Times* best-selling book.
4. Buy a beautiful house.
5. Buy a beautiful car.
6. Win tons of big poker tournaments.

When my wife, Kathy, found the list in 1990 she exclaimed, "That's amazing. You've already accomplished a bunch of your goals." In any case, these days I keep a list of my "goals" on my bathroom mirror. Side by side with that list is another list of my "blessings," and at the top of the blessings list I have a quote from President John Adams, "Rejoice everyday and be thankful." In the morning, while I'm brushing my teeth or combing my hair, I can see clearly what I want to accomplish with my life (my goals). By gazing inches to the right, I can also check out my list of blessings (I have "perfect health," "great wife and kids," "14 WSOP wins," "a *New York Times* best-selling book," "great friends," and "a beautiful house" listed as a few of my blessings). When I leave the washroom, I'm more aware of what I'm trying to accomplish, and I'm also happy and thankful for what I already have.

I believe that writing a list of "goals" is an essential ingredient in moving on to serious levels of success. Otherwise, how will you know exactly what you want to accomplish with your life?

Prologue: The Greatest Poker Player of All Time!

In 1993, after winning three WSOP bracelets (Chapter 23), I upgraded my life goals. My new stated goal was simple: I would become the greatest poker player of all time! I had five WSOP bracelets, and I decided that I would find a way to win 24 WSOP bracelets. I'm not sure how I settled on 24, but I figured that that ought to be enough to be the all-time WSOP bracelet leader, forever!

11

My First Trophy!

At the close of Chapter 8 I was still at the Stardust Casino, having won $21,000 in 21 days playing $10-$20 limit Hold 'Em, when I heard rumblings about a poker tournament called the "Cajun Cup." The tournament was to be held in Lafayette, Louisiana, March 17-28. Big Al and I decided to check out the action. Although I wasn't really a poker tournament player yet, I did well at the Cajun Cup; I was pleased to make three final tables in the preliminary events. And, the night before the Cajun Cup main event, all the players gathered into the tournament area to have a Calcutta.

What Would I Sell For in the Calcutta?

A Calcutta is basically an auction pool where you bid on players (and ultimately buy those players), and all the money in the pool is then split up and awarded according to order of finish. For example, 40% of the prize pool in the Calcutta would go to the person who bought the winning player, 20% of the pool would go to the person who bought the second-place finisher, and 10% of the pool would go to the person who bought the third-place finisher. Basically, a Calcutta gives you a chance to buy the players you fancy will win the tournament, and Calcuttas are tons of fun!

I watched as the reigning World Champion of Poker Johnny Chan went for $2,100, World Champion Jack Keller went for $1,800, and T. J. Cloutier (no slouch either) went for $1,700. Seems about right, that the three best poker players of that era went first, second, and third in the bidding.

When my name came up, I was nervous! I thought, "I know I'm an unknown player, but please, oh please, I don't want go too low and get embarrassed." By then I had watched a couple of players go for a mere $50, and it was awkward. I also thought, "On the other hand, if I do go too low, then I'll just buy myself for cheap and get great value." I was both surprised and pleased that a couple of "groups" (players combined their money in this Calcutta to spread the risk) started bidding me up. I mean, who was I? I had never won a tournament before in my life. I watched the bids roll in, "$300, $500, $700, $800, $900, $1,000, $1,100, $1,200." Somehow, for no apparent reason, I was bid up to sixth place in the standings in the Calcutta, out of over one hundred players on the board. It was nice to get that much respect, and certainly I had craved respect throughout my life, but even I thought that I was overvalued. The winning team then asked if I wanted to buy a piece of their bid, and I passed (I guess I had no ego issues that day!).

The Cajun Cup Rules!

As I turns out, I didn't do any good in the final event, but I fell in love with the Cajun Cup. All of the poker players loved it down there. The action was first rate, and the food was even better. I was introduced to crawfish: in Louisiana, they boil crawfish with corn and potatoes and serve heaping plates of it. The Cajun Cup had to be the poker tour's favorite stop back in 1988 and 1989, as evidenced by the fact that over 800 players had descended on the Lafayette Hilton in 1988.

Reno

Right after the Cajun Cup ended, there was an event in April in Reno, at the Hilton Hotel and Casino, called the Pot of Gold poker tournament. Two of my poker-playing friends, Wayne "Tilly" Tyler and Gary Miller, headed out to Reno with me. Tilly and I had had a golfing rivalry at the time, and we headed out to a course one day in Reno, where the scenery was awesome. There were mountains on three sides of us. Tilly claims that I'm the luckiest golfer that he has ever played with! He used to tell me, "Phil, you had better just aim for the trees, because if you hit them then your ball will end up in the middle of the fairway!" To give you an idea of how competitive Tilly is, after he beat me at golf that day, he bought the rental clubs he was using (though he already had two sets of golf clubs at home). I asked Tilly, "Are you crazy?" He replied, "You're the one who paid for them!" That shut me up.

Easter Sunday Trophy

Anyway, I was really getting into this poker tournament thing, and I made a final table at the Pot of Gold tournament. I seemed to go deep in every tournament that I entered. Specifically, I was doing well in the Hold 'Em events, and on Easter

Sunday (I was raised a Catholic), April 3, 1988, I won my first poker tournament. It was a $300 buy-in No Limit Hold 'Em tournament at the Pot of Gold, and I won $12,000 and this trophy for first place. I called my parents to tell them about my victory. (They weren't all that excited, but at least they were still talking to me.)

Perry Green and Reno Hilton Main Event

In the Pot of Gold main event – the big buy-in No Limit Hold 'Em finale – I reached the final table, where I ran into a gentleman named Perry Green. Perry was a tough poker player from Alaska who had been playing in the biggest poker tournaments in the world for decades (he still plays today, in 2017). Perry isn't a pro, but he had finished second to Stu Ungar in the 1982 WSOP main event (the poker world's World Championship event).

Although Perry wasn't a pro, he certainly was a wily old veteran! I recall well having the chip lead at the final table, but then losing my patience. When I didn't win a single pot for almost two hours, I began to panic and tried to make something happen. By then, I had already tried to make something happen more than once, but to no avail. In other words, I had already lost a lot of chips by repeatedly pressing the action with weak hands. Finally, I called a big raise with A♥-2♠ and flopped a monster when the flop came down A-5-2. At this point, I was more than happy to put all of my remaining chips into the pot. But alas, Perry had pocket fives, and I was eliminated in fourth place (for $5,500)!

It was an unlucky flop that would have busted anyone, to be sure, but why had I decided to call a raise with A-2 before the flop? No, I should have maintained my patience, and let my natural abilities give me a chance to pull out the win. Still, looking back, I had won my first poker tournament, I had reached two other final tables, and I had given myself a chance to win the main event! All in all, it was a terrific trip for me.

12

The 1988 World Series of Poker

On May 5, 1988, one month after the Pot of Gold poker tournament ended, the 1988 WSOP began, officially. With my first trophy – and a bunch of final tables from the Cajun Cup and Pot of Gold tournaments – under my belt came a sky-high confidence level! So for the first time, I headed out to Binion's Hotel and Casino in Las Vegas, to play in the WSOP. In May 1987 I didn't even know the WSOP existed! But by now I understood that the WSOP was the single most important poker tournament on the planet. The WSOP is where the poker world crowned the World Champion of Poker in a huge $10,000 buy-in poker tournament that paid at least $500,000 for first place! Poker's biggest prize by far. And one of my stated "life goals" (Chapter 10) was to win the WSOP's main event and be crowned a World Champion of Poker forever! (The honor persists essentially forever.)

Twelve WSOP Tournaments in 1988

The 1988 WSOP was actually a series of 12 poker tournaments (one was the Women's World Championship), with buy-ins ranging from $1,000 to the $10,000 buy-in to the main event. It was time to use my "winning pyramid" principles to navigate me successfully through the 12 tournaments that made up the 1988 WSOP. Or so I thought. You see, at the beginning of the 1988 WSOP I had about $20,000 in cash to my name, and I brought $12,000 of that cash with me to Las Vegas. On the strength of my "winning pyramid" principles, I had brought too high a percentage of my net worth to the WSOP (60%, or $12,000 out of $20,000), but I reasoned that this was the big leagues, and I needed some ammunition. The fact that I was hitting the big leagues was not a sufficient excuse to violate my "winning pyramid" principles! A proper amount to risk, given my money-management principles, and given that it was the WSOP, should have been $6,000.

Bad Money Management!

I arrived at the 1988 WSOP a few days early, so as to play in the legendarily juicy side games. These were always populated by once-a-year players, book-ies, big-time gamblers, and millionaires. I arrived May 2nd, and by the night of May 4th I had lost $10,000 of the $12,000 that I had brought with me. I was beating myself up pretty good and I thought, "Wow, what a colossally stupid move! What were you thinking? You brought enough money to play in the first six WSOP events, and now you're broke before the first event begins?" My early failure caused me to feel some serious pain. What had happened to my new-found discipline, which was based on the principles of my "winning pyramid"?

Rash Move!

At that point I made another rash maneuver. I took $1,500 of the $2,000 that I had left with me in Las Vegas, and I entered the first event of the 1988 WSOP, a $1,500 buy-in Limit Hold 'Em event, along with 399 other players. About then I was feeling terrific about my Limit Hold 'Em skills because only a few months earlier I had won $21,000 in 21 days at the Stardust Hotel in the $10-$20 Limit Hold 'Em games (herein Chapter 9). Also, I knew that I had to wait a few days for another WSOP Hold 'Em tournament to get under way, and so I decided to take a big chance. I made it to Day 2 with about 60 other players, but they were only paying 40 players.

Val Carpenter and I "Save"

While I was walking into the WSOP tournament room to play Day 2, I ran across a tough player named Val Carpenter. Val was a good-looking young man with blond hair who wore stylish wire-rimmed metal glasses. Val, from Alabama, had a pleasant demeanor; everyone loved Val. Val was a disabled player. When I say Val was a "disabled player" I mean that he was permanently in a wheel chair, but make no mistake about it; Val's poker game wasn't disabled! In any case, Val asked me to make a 5% "save" with him (where we would swap a 5% piece of each other in the tournament, so that if one of us won $100,000, then the oth-er would receive $5,000). So I agreed, and Val and I made that 5% save before the tournament began.

At the beginning of level 12 – with the limits now at 400–800 – I had around

5,000 in chips when I was dealt pocket kings. The only problem was that my opponent was dealt pocket aces! No one could have avoided going broke with my hand, with the number of chips that I had left. And I began to lament my bad luck. They had dealt a "cooler" (a hand that you are likely to lose everything with) to me, when we were close to making the money, ouch! Now I headed back to my room at the Horseshoe all depressed, and I was still whining about the cooler to anyone who would listen. To make matters worse, I didn't have enough money left to play in any more WSOP events, and I was beating myself up at having managed my money so poorly. For that matter, though, how could I not play in the WSOP main event? After all, the 1988 WSOP main event was my chance to make history, and it would pay at least $600,000 for first place.

Wasn't it a "life goal" of mine to win the main event and be called World Champion of Poker for the rest of my life? What was I thinking when I lost almost all the cash that I had brought with me? Why hadn't I used the money-management principles from my "winning pyramid"?

Super Satellite?

With only $500 in my Las Vegas bankroll, I was really in a funk when I walked back to my hotel room at the Horseshoe. Thoughts of my own stupidity, thoughts of flying home, and thoughts that were dark and depressed passed through my mind. When I arrived back at my room and told my roommate ("The great J.P." Havenor) my bad-beat story, he gave me no empathy at all. Rather, he said, "Are you going over to the Hilton to play in that super satellite at 7?" I asked, "What is a super satellite?" Then J.P. explained that it was a $100 buy-in tournament with unlimited rebuys, and that the winner would receive a seat in the $10,000 buy-in WSOP main event.

I didn't have much money at that point, but I did have $500, which was more than enough to play in a super satellite. So I boogied over to the Las Vegas Hilton and played in my first-ever super satellite. I bought in for $100, along with over 300 other players, and it seemed to me that everyone I knew was in the room.

How could I not have known about this super satellite? Since I didn't have much money left in my pocket that day I avoided re-buying and adding on, so that I was in for a total of $100. Lasting deep into a super satellite for "one bullet" (one buy-in total) is pretty rare! I'll bet that the average player that day was in for over $300. As it turned out, first place here was an entry fee into the $10,000 buy-in WSOP main event (plus $6,000 cash).

As time passed, I continued to play tough poker, and somehow I had gained the chip lead when we hit the final table. At around 3 a.m. I won the super satellite, and the crushing depression that I had felt only nine hours earlier seemed to be from light years ago. Now I was in the main event, and had $6,400 in cash in my pocket!

Things Get Even Better!

I was on top of the world, but it was about to get even better. I headed back downtown to the Horseshoe and immediately ran into Val. He was crossing the street in his wheelchair, moving away from the Horseshoe and toward the Golden Nugget. I was excited, and as I began to tell Val of my good fortune, he excitedly interrupted me and said, "Where were you? You just missed the whole final table! I just won the Limit Hold 'Em tournament for $223,800! I thought for sure that you would be there sweating me; I owe you over $11,000, and I've been looking for you to pay you!" What a guy!

Wow, things sure had changed very quickly for me! Now, while I was feeling a huge momentum swing in my favor, I hopped into a $100-$200 Limit Hold 'Em game at the Horseshoe, and won almost $9,000. This was the biggest limit that I had ever played, and that $9,000 win was my biggest side-game win in a limit game, ever. But I felt comfortable playing Limit Hold 'Em, and this $100-$200 was a juicier game than the $10-$20 game at the Stardust!

So, after losing with pocket kings to pocket aces, to fall just short of cashing at the WSOP at 1 p.m., and feeling incredibly depressed, and having a $500 Las Vegas bankroll earlier in the day, I was now playing in the "big one" ($10,000 buy-in to the WSOP main event), and I had nearly $27,000 in cash!

As I often find when a big cloud appears to be taking out some of my sunshine, there is usually a silver lining, and losing with pocket kings earlier in the day now seemed to be a blessing in disguise.

My First WSOP Final Table

A few days later, on May 10th, still in Vegas, I made my first WSOP final table in the $1,500 buy-in Stud 8/b (Seven Card Stud 8-or-Better) tournament. There were 206 players there that day, so I was feeling pretty good about my accomplishment. And Stud 8/b was a game that I had played often in the Wolf's Den game (Chapter 8) in Madison, Wisconsin. I felt like my training down in the trenches was starting to pay off, and I felt really comfortable playing Stud 8/b. I also noticed that a lot of the other players in the tournament didn't feel comfortable – frankly, many of these players didn't know what they were doing. With three tables remaining in play and about 24 players left vying for the bracelet and the cash, Joe Petro (who was sitting next to me) leaned over and asked me if I wanted to save 15% (that seemed a lot to save, but I said yes). Joe was a Cajun guy through and through, with a slow speech pattern and a heavy Louisiana accent, but Joe was sharp as a tack. And one of the nicest guys on tour. I knew Joe from the Cajun Cup days, and I respected his play. So a save made sense to me, especially after I collected so much cash a few days before from Val! So I shook Joe's hand and agreed to the 15% save. First place in this WSOP Stud 8/b was $123,600, and tenth place was only $3,090, so why not increase my chances of getting paid some decent money?

With five players left, and the limits at $5,000-$10,000, I started play with (8-7) 6, and I called a $5,000 bet against Lance Hilt's up card, an ace. I then caught an eight, and Lance caught a four. Lance bet $5,000, and I called. Now I hit a five [(8-7) 6-8-5] and Lance hit a ten. We both checked, and then I hit a nine [(8-7) 6-8-7-9] and Lance hit a jack [(X, X)) A-4-10-J]. Lance checked, I bet $10,000, and Lance called. On the last card (dealt face down), Lance checked, and I peered down at a portion of the card (I sweated it) and I noticed that it had four spots on its outside. (I knew that it was either a ten to complete a straight, or a nine) and I bet $10,000. Lance asked how many chips I had left, and when I informed him that I had $8,300 left, Lance called the $10,000 and raised it up my last $8,300! Oh shit. Now I felt a ten would lock up 50% of the pot for me, but a nine wouldn't help (I had two pair, eights up, already anyway), although I would probably receive 50% of the pot. I sweated the card slowly, praying for a ten, but alas it was a nine. I called my last $8,300 anyway, as Lance may well have made a low hand, and this was High-Low Split – meaning that 50% of the pot goes to the best low hand, and 50% of the pot goes to the best high hand. Then Lance declared, "Aces up," (two pair) and he scooped the pot beating my "nines up." I was deeply disappointed as I thought, "If that last card had been a ten, then I would have scooped the pot with a straight, and then I would have had the chip lead! Instead, I'm out in fifth place; what a huge swing, considering that there was exactly a 50% chance that that card had been a ten, sigh."

Still, I collected $15,450 for fifth place, and I had a shot at collecting a lot more, as Joe was still in there. Completely trusting Joe, I left the building at something like 2 a.m., and the next day Joe found me to tell me that he had finished in second place for $68,000, and proceeded to pay me $10,300 or so (15% of $68,000).

Limit Hold 'Em $100-$200

Over the next week I managed to win some more money playing in the juicy $100-$200 Limit Hold 'Em side games, and I played in a few more WSOP tournaments. On May 16th, at noon, I sat down to play in my first WSOP main event. On Day 1, I managed to hold my own in the "big one." I did play one big hand of note against the backgammon prodigy Jason Lester. I had J♠-10♠, and the board came down 9♠-8♥-5♠. I had flopped a huge drawing hand; I had an open-ended straight draw, two over-cards and a flush draw. On the flop, Jason and I put a bunch of money into the middle of the pot. The turn card was the 6♦, and Jason moved all-in. I was sick calling a big bet with jack high, but I was getting the right price to call his bet. Thus, I called, and flipped my hand face up. Now Jason smiled, and as the last card was the 4♣ (9♠-8♥-5♠-6♦-4♣), I was starting to turn green. I knew that I had blown most of my chips, and I was just beginning to get aggravated at myself for losing so much money with a drawing hand (and jack high!). But then Jason flipped up J-10 as well. Miraculously, it was a split pot! Things were going well: I made it to Day 2 of the 1988 WSOP, and I had close to $60,000 in cash in my box!

Day 2 of the WSOP Main Event

During Day 2 of the "big one" I ran my chips up to about 90,000, which was near the chip lead, when I was introduced to a new player who just sat down. His name was Johnny Chan, and he was the reigning World Champion of Poker, but I barely knew who he was. I certainly knew his name, but I certainly didn't know what he looked like. I had been going along nicely all day when a huge pot came up between Johnny and me. I opened up the pot for a raise, with a pair of red pocket eights (8♥-8♦) in first position, and Johnny called in the big blind. The flop was K♠-Q♠-2♠, Johnny checked, and I bet. Johnny called. The turn card was the ace of spades, which put four spades on board (K♠-Q♠-2♠-A♠). Now Johnny made a bet, and I had an easy fold because I had nothing, but I sensed weakness. I didn't think Johnny had a flush, but if he did have a flush, then I sensed that it was a weak one.

Again, at this point in the hand, I had nothing. But acting on my read, I mus-cled up and tried to bluff the reigning World Champion of Poker out of this pot. Thus I went ahead and raised it up a good sum of chips. Undeterred, Johnny called my raise. Even after Johnny called my first bullet (bluff), I still didn't think he was strong. As it turned out, I was right, as Johnny had A-K in his hand, which amount-ed to top two pair: aces and kings. But that was really weak considering that there were four spades on the board, man! I had made a good move, but Johnny must have sensed weakness in me just like I had sensed weakness in him, because he called me. After the last up card hit the board – it was the 2♦ – Johnny checked, and I fired another big bullet (I made another big bluff). For the second time in this hand, Johnny made a great call. Johnny could only beat a bluff with his A-K! Again, even though I correctly sensed weakness in Johnny, he correctly sensed even more weakness in me! As it turned out, I bluffed off about 35,000 in chips to Johnny, and I nearly doubled him up in the process.

T.J. Cloutier's Advice

A month later poker legend T.J. Cloutier came up to me and said,

> I was at the table and saw the hand that you played against John-
> ny Chan. If you're going to try to bluff the best players in the world,
> then you should really learn to just stare at a spot on the table when
> you bluff. You gave away too much information to Johnny when you
> opened your mouth, and when you looked around. To me, you looked
> a like a scared deer caught in the headlights of an oncoming car. I like
> to practice my bluffs as I look at myself in the mirror.

T.J. was right. Bluffing great players requires that you give away nothing, and it was a skill that I needed to work on. I knew that I would need to learn how to bluff the great poker players if I wanted to become the best poker player in the world.

I Cash in My First WSOP; Johnny Chan Busts Me!

Late on Day 2, we made the money in the main event. In the 1988 WSOP, 36 players were paid, although 27th through 36th place would receive only $7,500, which was a $2,500 loss! With 33 players remaining and the blinds at $1,000-$2,000, Steve Kopp (a tough young professional player from Chicago) raised it up, making it $6,000 to go in early position, and Johnny Chan called in late position. From the big blind, I decided to move all-in with my pocket tens. So I called the $6,000 bet, and I raised it up my last $27,000 ($33,000 total). A minute later, Steve Kopp threw his hand away, and Johnny called me with pocket jacks. I was a 4½-to-1 underdog to win this pot with my 10-10 vs. Johnny's J-J. Still, I had a really good flop when it came down 9-8-7. Now I needed a jack or a six to complete a straight. Alas, Johnny's hand held up, and I finished in 33rd place and collected $7,500.

This encounter with Johnny Chan would be the first of many duels between us over the next 25 years (including a classic duel the very next year, in the 1989 WSOP main event!).

Johnny Chan Wins 1988 WSOP

Johnny went on to win his second consecutive World Championship of Poker (the 1987 WSOP and the 1988 WSOP) and $700,000 for first place in a classic showdown between Johnny and Erik Seidel! This Chan–Seidel showdown even has a scene in the movie *Rounders*, where, in the final hand of the 1988 WSOP Johnny has J-9 and Erik has Q-7 and the flop comes down Q-10-8. In this famous hand, Johnny flops a straight, and Erik flops top pair, but Johnny craftily checks twice to try to lure Erik into making a big bet. On the last card Erik moves all-in, and Johnny calls and wins the 1988 WSOP.

Big Al Goes Off!

Immediately after I had been eliminated, I felt sick to my stomach as I questioned my tactics. Like why had I bluffed off my money with 8♥-8♦? And why had I moved in with 10-10? I was beginning to torture myself way too much as I questioned my play, wondered what I could have done better, and lamented the fact that I was now out of the most important event of the year.

And to make matters worse, I had had a lot of chips, and I didn't really need to be on the sidelines. I felt as if I had unnecessarily busted myself out. I could have easily made Day 3 with at least 70,000 in chips, right? Yes sir, there was no doubt about it, I had lost my patience. My old buddy Big Al picked this exact moment to come over and get in my face, "How could you bluff off all of your chips to Johnny Chan?!? You probably won't get many chances to win the World Championship throughout your whole life! What were you thinking?"

Big Al's timing was off. I was steaming out of my mind! Sure, I was torturing myself a bit, but I surely wasn't going to let anyone else torture me! I immediately and loudly responded, "Al, trust me when I tell you that I will have a chance to win the WSOP every single year for the next 50 years! I'm not done here at the WSOP, I'm just beginning! So back the hell off!"

Along with the greatest disappointment that I have ever felt in my life (I always feel the most disappointed from a poker point of view every year when I bust out of the main event), there was lots of good news: I was headed home with almost $50,000 in cash in my possession and some good results under my belt; and I now knew that I could play poker with the big boys! I knew that my style was topnotch, and I felt like my time was coming...

13

The 1988 Bicycle Club: My First Major!

After the 1988 WSOP concluded, I headed home with bolstered confidence, and my bankroll at an all-time high. I continued to do well throughout the summer in the poker games in Madison, and by July had a record $70,000 to my name. My money management still left something to be desired, though, because I spent $25,000 of my $70,000 bankroll on a new car! (One down on my list of "goals.") By then I had been looking to buy a new car for a long time, and I had thought a great deal about the kind of car I wanted to buy.

Old Gray Cadillac

I liked the idea of purchasing a "conservative" car, one that would balance the not so conservative choice of career that I had made. I reasoned that if I bought a nice sports car, then everything about my life would be "fast!" I thought that if everything about me was going to scream "fast," then I would indeed be living too fast and I wouldn't be able to hold on to money. In retrospect, this sounds a bit adolescent, but I can see why I decided to go in the conservative car direction. With the financial swings that I was taking, I felt I needed some stability, and a Cadillac seemed a stable, conservative choice.

So I went out to Aaron's Cadillac dealership and bought an absolutely gorgeous 1988 gray four-door Cadillac de Ville Sedan – four doors was part of that conservative mode I was looking for. I had never been to a car dealership before, because my parents had never bought a new car before in their lives (not yet anyway). Once I was there I found the car that I wanted right away, and asked the incredulous salesman to put it "on hold" for me for one day. And much to his amazement I came back the next day with a "cashier's check" for the full amount of the purchase.

Diamond Jim Brady

Two big tournaments were coming up in August 1988. One was the Diamond Jim Brady tournament at the Bicycle Club Casino in LA. The other was a smaller tournament down in South Carolina, which was a first-time event. Even though the big money was in LA, I chose South Carolina. I knew that the great players would all be in LA, and that the easier lineups – and cash games – would be in South Carolina. I thought that this South Carolina poker tournament might be another Cajun Cup, so to speak. And as I said earlier (Chapter 11), all of the poker players loved the Cajun Cup! So tons of us flocked down to South Carolina, but unfortunately (though fortunately for me as it would turn out!), at the last minute the Governor of South Carolina decided that we couldn't have a poker tournament there that year. So I flew from South Carolina back home to Madison, and then a week later I headed to LA to play in a couple of the bigger buy-in Hold 'Em tournaments at the Bicycle Club.

Before I left for LA, and after careful consideration, I decided to improve my skills in one of the blocks on my "winning pyramid"; it was time to take the next step in money management. My new plan was to manage the amount of money that I won or lost on any given trip. With $35,000 in cash to my name, I knew that if I risked only $10,000 on my trip to LA, then I would be keeping myself comfortably flush. By this point in my life I was sick of the big swings that go hand in hand with the life of a professional poker player. Thinking back just a few months to the swingy 1988 WSOP trip, where I had $500 one minute, $26,000 the next, I was depressed and dark one minute, and elated the next; I concluded that this Jekyll and Hyde lifestyle was for the birds!

Good Money Management, Please!

I already saw that these swings could yield some serious depression, and even then I understood that this big-swing lifestyle could lead to alcohol and drug abuse. Rather, I would be disciplined and strong, and keep myself in cash! No matter what, I would stick to my plan. And if I could stick to that plan, my life would be a lot smoother. Thus, I brought exactly $10,000 with me to LA. My plan was to play in two big No Limit Hold 'Em tournaments at the Bicycle Club, one of them the $1,000 with rebuys event, the other being the $5,000 buy-in Championship event, which was considered a "major" (the Professional Golfers' Association tour has four majors, and back then this was one of the poker world's majors). I figured that $8,000 would cover the entry fees for the tournaments, and this left me with a little less than $2,000 to risk in the side games, before going home.

Upon arriving in LA, I messed around with the side games and went over budget; basically, I lost a lot more than I was supposed to lose. I left myself with only $2,700 in cash going into the $1,000 buy-in with rebuys (at $1,000 a pop) No Limit Hold 'Em tournament. Still, even though I had made a bad money-management decision, when I risked too much money in the side games, I would honor my "winning pyramid" $10,000 maximum risk concept for the trip.

With $2,700 left in my LA bankroll I would simply have to live with the fact that I didn't give myself a chance to play in the main event. But, I did enter the $1,000 buy-in preliminary event with $1,000 rebuys and 104 other players. After I lost my first $1,000 buy-in, I bought in one more time (there were 132 rebuys that day, among the players), and I made a last longer side bet with "Captain" Tommy Franklin for $400.

Phil Uses Every Dollar of His LA Budget

So I had $2,400 of my last $2,700 now at risk. I was moving all-in for my maximum $10,000 exposure for the trip! I knew that I could fly home for $150 without having a reservation on an airline (airfare was cheap that summer).

Trying to be realistic about my situation, I was expecting to lose my chips, hop into a taxi, and fly home at any moment – though I was hoping for the best. I was all-in with pocket twos vs. the "Captain's" A-J (I was even money to go broke and fly home), but I survived. And eventually I thrived; by 11 p.m. we were in the money! Somehow, someway, I made it to Day 2 of the event, with eight other players, including Erik Seidel (the second-place finisher in the 1988 WSOP main event to Johnny Chan; see Chapter 12), Ralph Morton (at the time a top-ten tournament poker player), Mike Sexton (a poker legend and eventual voice of the WPT), Dewey Tomko (admitted to the Poker Hall of Fame in 2010), Curt Knight, Glen Cozen, Wally Wong, and Fred White.

Day 2, Diamond Jim Brady

On Day 2, the nine of us came back to finish the poker tournament. The five players remaining (Morton, Sexton, Cozen, Seidel, and me) talked about making a deal. Officially, first place paid $100,800, second place $44,800, third place $26,880, fourth place $15,680, and fifth place $11,200. Throughout poker history in the 1980s and the 1990s, making deals when you hit the final three or four players in a poker tournament was standard practice. It was unusual when a deal wasn't made. After all, first place was usually 40% of the prize pool, second place was 20%, third place 10%, fourth place around 8%, and fifth place about 6% of the prize pool. In our case, the difference between first-place prize money ($100,800) and fifth-place prize money ($11,200) was almost $90,000! A deal eliminates some of the financial swings that routinely exist in poker tournaments. One unlucky hand could cost you tens of thousands of dollars. The proposal on the table was that the five of us would get paid out, "according to the value of our chips." We would all get $11,200 at minimum (fifth place money), and then get paid by a simple formula whereby you multiply your chip stack by the value of each chip.

The Old-School Math Behind a Deal

For you aspiring poker players, here is how the math works. You add up the total amount of prize money that remains (100,800 + 44,800 + 26,880 + 15,680 + 11,200 = 199,360), then you take out the guaranteed minimum cashes (11,200 × 5 = $56,000), then you subtract the minimum cashes from the total prize pool (199,360 – 56,000 = 143,360), so that the total that you're all playing for in this case was $143,360. That day we had 237,000 in chips on the table. So then you divide the $143,360 unclaimed money by 237,000 in total chips (143,360 / 237,000 = .60489) to come up with how much each chip is worth: $0.60489. Then you multiply your chip stack by that amount, and add $11,200 to that number to see what your "fair value" is. So if I had 40,000 in chips, I would be entitled to receive $24,195 (40,000 × .60489) plus $11,200, or $35,395. That figure, $35,395, is more than third-place money, even though there were five of us remaining, and a lot more than you would receive if you were the next one to be eliminated ($11,200). You can see why deals were so commonplace! But before the five-way deal was sealed, Seidel insisted that he receive a little extra money. Erik simply wanted an extra $4,000 or so, but I refused. Everyone else at that final table was willing to give Erik extra money, but I said, "No way!" So no deal was made, and I knew that playing for all of the money was risky, but it does put more pressure on everyone at the table!

Seidel vs. Hellmuth for the Title

Eventually, it came down to Erik and me, but by then I had the chip lead. So we ended up splitting most of the money, according to the value of the chips. With $145,600 left to be claimed, we agreed that I would get $70,000, Erik would get $66,000, and we would play for the last $9,560. For more than two hours we played our hearts out, and Erik finally prevailed. Unbelievably, I had Erik all-in eight different times! I wanted that title so badly, and the fact that I didn't win it made me analyze the way I had closed the tournament. Thus I kept running all of the heads-up hands that we had played over and over in my mind. Had I closed properly? Had I taken a few too many chances? I reached the conclusion that I could have been a little bit more patient. In one hand, because Erik was super short on chips, I had called his all-in bet with 4-2 offsuit. Although I had called him with 4-2 for a small amount of chips (roughly four big blinds worth), I should have folded. After I called, Erik showed 7-7, and the cards came down A-A-Q-Q-6. He won that pot with seven high! I remember thinking that with anything decent I would have won this hand. Playing Erik heads up for a big title taught me a lot, and I knew that the next time I was heads up I would do a better job closing the deal, but who knew how long "next time" would be?

What a Swing!

On the plus side, I went from leaving town broke and in a taxi (the day before), to having $70,000 in cash! At noon the next day the $5,000 buy-in Championship event at the Diamond Jim Brady would begin. After having such a huge win, I knew that I wouldn't be able to sleep. I knew that I would run the heads-up hands vs. Erik over and over in my head all night, and I concluded that I needed to be sharp for the following day's tournament; thus at 11 p.m. that night I went out for a three-mile run in the Bell Garden area, to clear my head. My "winning pyramid" was clearly influencing my actions more than ever, seeing that I now used "exercise," along with good "money management" on that trip. Cardiovascular exercise helps clear my head from the day's play, and helps me turn my gaze toward winning the tournament the next day. I wouldn't recommend that anyone run in Bell Garden, California, at 11 p.m. at night, but back then I didn't know what a dangerous area I was jogging in!

The Bicycle Club Main Event

The next day, I entered the $5,000 buy-in main event along with 75 other players. Erik Seidel was the first one out of the Championship event, and I said to myself, "I'm glad that I finished second because I'm still hungry for a title." Of course, it was a lie! I wasn't happy that I had finished in second place as badly as I wanted that title, but I needed a positive way to put away the disappointment of yesterday and focus on winning today. Even though I was exhausted from the previous two days of playing poker, somehow I reached down deep and made it down to the final ten players in the Championship event, although we were playing down to nine-handed before Day 1 ended.

It was then that I caught an enormous break! With ten players left, a player raised it up under the gun (in first position), and two other players called. I was sitting in the big blind with K-J. After a little time was spent considering my options, I moved all-in! But sadly, I was called instantly by the-under-the-gun player, uh oh! A super-fast call meant that I was in deep trouble. Indeed, the player under the gun held pocket aces! I was over a 6-to-1 underdog to win this pot for my tournament life. I was in bad shape; tenth place was calling my name, and loudly. I watched as the flop came down... Q-10-9. Wow, no problem, I had flopped a straight! I went on to make the final nine, and to come back at noon the next day to play Day 2. Again, I was exhausted after three long days of tournament poker. Again, I turned to exercise to clear my head, and I made one more late-night run through the city of Bell Gardens. I knew that winning this poker "major" the next day wouldn't be an easy task, seeing as the best three poker tournament players in the world were sitting at that final table with me!

Diamond Jim Brady Main Event Final Table

On Day 2 of the main event I played at the final table along with: Johnny Chan (the number-one poker tournament player in the world, as well as the two-time defending World Champion of Poker), Jack Keller (the second-best poker tournament player in the world, who was also the 1984 World Champion of Poker), T.J. Cloutier (the third-best poker tournament player in the world), Rod Peate (another tough player who was the runner-up to Chan at the WSOP main event in 1987), Glen Abney, Gary Lundgren, Hugo Mieth, and Jeff Rothstein.

Wow, what a lineup! And even the tenth-place finisher the night before is legendary and was the youngest member ever admitted to the Poker Hall of Fame: the late great David "Chip" Reese. Early on, Chan was all-in with A-Q vs. Peate's A-K, and Chan hit a queen to win the pot, prompting Peate to say, "Not again!" A few minutes later, Peate was the first player out, followed by Chan, when Johnny and I played a huge pot. Chan raised it up with K♠-J♠, and I re-raised it a sizeable amount with A♦-Q♦ from the small blind. In fact, I raised it up enough to move Chan all-in, if he called. Chan studied for a full minute, and then called me. I flipped my hand face up, but Chan didn't show me his hand. Instead, he had some fun with me. The flop was 10♣-7♣-4♣, and Chan shouted, "Club!" As it turns out, Chan didn't really need a club, but I didn't know that. Then the deuce of diamonds hit, followed by the six of clubs; I grimaced, because I thought that I had lost the pot, but then Chan showed me his K♠-J♠ (thank goodness!), and he was out, in eighth place.

After Hugo Mieth busted in seventh place, T.J. Cloutier and I played a big pot. T.J. raised it up with K-10 offsuit, and I called with 7-7. The flop was Q-10-5, T.J. checked, I bet out a small amount, and T.J. called. The turn was a seven, and T.J. moved all-in! I actually said, "You flopped three tens, didn't you?" But within 20 seconds I knew that I had to call his bet, and I busted T.J. out in sixth place. Jeff

Rothstein finished in fifth place, and then I played a big pot against Gary Lundgren with my A-K high to his A-J high. Gary was all-in before the flop, and neither one of us made a pair, so I busted him out of the tournament in fourth place.

Now the last three standing – Jack Keller, Glen Abney, and I – started negotiations on a potential deal; as it stood, the third-place finisher would get $38,000, the second-place finisher $64,000, and the first-place finisher $145,000.

I noticed that I had around 60% of the chips in play, that Keller had 30% of the chips and Abney about 10% of the chips. As I ran the numbers in my head, I thought, "All of us are going to receive $38,000 minimum, so we are playing for $133,000 ($145,000 + $64,000 + $38,000 – ($38,000 × 3) = $133,000).

Without running any numbers, I thought that I should be getting around $110,000, but Keller is a great player, so maybe I'd ask for $105,000. Keller, however, didn't see it that way and said, "Son, anything can happen from here on out. If I double through you, then I'm the chip leader. You can have $50,000 plus the $38,000, or $88,000 total." Knowing that I could always go back and accept that deal, I made a counter offer and said, "Now Jack, you know that I have a massive chip lead. Let me lock into $97,000."

Please understand that we were talking about a ton of money moving to me at that point in my life. There was far more money at stake in this three-handed scenario than I had ever played for, by far! I was acutely aware that the difference between $145,000 and $38,000 is $107,000. Thus, I really wanted to lock in a deal, especially for an amount that was well above second-place money. But I wasn't willing to get screwed too badly, either.

I knew that Keller was right, and that anything could happen, but then I also knew that I had a ton of control over the outcome. Eventually, Keller responded, saying, "No deal." And he walked over and sat back down at the final table. No counter offers. No more discussions. No more talking at all. I took it all in, and I thought, "OK, I really want to make a deal. But if I show weakness, then I won't get the right deal. And Keller doesn't want to talk, so be it." I reasoned that if I could simply hold on to my chip position, then I could make a deal later. I was also aware that if Keller or Abney went broke, then I would be locked into at least $64,000, and the deal negotiations would begin anew. At that point, my whole focus was on protecting my chips, and playing great poker. But the pressure was on!

Let's Play for All of It

Over the next 45 minutes, Keller put the heat on us. He was doing a lot of raising and re-raising, and he began chipping away at my lead. Then, suddenly, I won one big pot, and I had my chip lead right back to where it was when we started, 45

Poker Brat

minutes earlier. When you use the tactic of playing fast and raising and re-raising a lot of pots, then you will pick up some chips, because the other players will continually fold their hands, until you step over the line one time too many times. Keller stepped over the line, and I nailed him; and his 45 minutes of dominance were gone in one second. Within ten minutes, Keller was all-in, with his K-Q to my A-Q. My ace-high stood up when five low cards hit the board, and Keller was out in third place. One more time at this final table I would win a huge pot with ace-high, without making a pair!

Heads Up for my First "Poker Major"

Now I was staring down only one opponent: Glen Abney. I was now locked into at least second-place money of $64,000, and I held over 90% of the chips in play. There was no need to talk about making a deal. Hopefully, I would bust Abney and win the whole $145,000. Still, I knew that it wasn't over yet: my thoughts flashed back to two days earlier, when I had 80% of the chips vs. Erik Seidel. I had had Erik all-in eight times but couldn't finish him off! I remembered the hard lesson that I had learned about playing heads-up No Limit Hold 'Em for a title.

Lesson Applied

I smiled as I recalled a thought I had had about 46 hours earlier:

> *I have learned a great lesson here today, about how to play heads up at the next level, and the next time that I am heads up I will do a better job closing the deal. I won't be reckless, I will wait until I have the best hand, even if my opponent is short on chips. But it's a shame that I may have to wait a long time before I can apply this new lesson, because who knows how long "next time" will be?"*

Turned out that "next time" was now, a mere two days later! Against Glen I would wait until I was nearly certain that I had the best starting hand before I moved him all-in. And, I would fold a lot of weaker hands, even if he did have a short stack.

Here is a radical concept: why *shouldn't* I have the best hand when my opponent had the short stack? About 20 hands into our match I had A-J, and I called Glen's all-in move with his A-9. If I could hold him off, then I would win the money, the title, and the glory! When the board came down Q-8-7-4-10, my hand held up and I was the champion! One more time at that major final table, I busted an opponent with merely ace-high!

I Win!

It was all so surreal to me. Add it all up: four days, two final tables, a second-place finish, a first-place finish, $220,000 in cash, and a major title. Had it really happened, or was this a dream? Wasn't I supposed to be in South Carolina? Wasn't I "even money" to be broke (2-2 vs. A-J) and back in Madison three days earlier? Just like that, I went from leaving the Bicycle Club broke, in a taxi cab to the airport, to having $220,000 in cash and leaving in an official Bicycle Club stretch limousine for the world famous Spago Restaurant!

Back in 1988, well before Wolfgang Puck was a big name in the food industry, his Spago Restaurant was already a huge hit in LA. Right after I collected my trophy and converted most of my cash into the form of a check, I asked around about where I should eat and celebrate my victory. I was told without resort that I should hit Spago on Sunset Blvd. in Hollywood. As an unsophisticated kid from Wisconsin, I remember watching in shock and awe as Johnny Carson's righthand man Ed McMahon walked up to the bar at Spago. Seeing an "A list" star like Ed McMahon was a really big deal to a young Wisconsin boy like me, who had never been exposed to even any "C list" stars. Even the palm trees were a big deal to me back then. I recall that the first time I was in LA, I asked the taxi to pull over, so that I could see the palm trees up close. Over those last few days I had been on the ride of my life, but people seem to peak like that right before they fall.

14

Why Do I Act Like a Jerk Sometimes?

I've often pondered the reasons for my becoming the "poker brat." I know that it is closely related to the low self-esteem I developed while growing up (Chapters 2 and 3). Why is it so hard for me to lose a decent-sized pot? Why do I act out after losing that pot? Here I am, playing with some of my best friends, and I'm lecturing them (!) about why they shouldn't have done this, or done that, when they beat me in some pot. Basically, I'm alienating my friends! Thank goodness my best friends these days just laugh at me and my antics (Chapter 48), and just enjoy the show! I'm happy that they seem to see right through my poker brat behavior.

When my blood starts to boil, after losing a meaningful pot, it doesn't make sense, on so many levels, and yet there it is. Consciously, I know that I shouldn't let one bad pot, one bad hour, or one bad day affect me so deeply emotionally. Consciously, I know that I shouldn't berate other players for their winning play, or complain about how unlucky I was to lose a pot.

Consciously, I know that I should stay in the moment. Consciously, I know that when I'm beginning to feel like a loser I should focus on the fact that I have accomplished so much over the years, and that the players at the table are conscious in recognizing that I'm a great poker player. But for some reason, consciously knowing all the above has no effect on my actual behavior!

Losing a pot, especially one where I had outplayed my opponents, harkens back to the days when I felt that I had to beat my brother and sisters at every game, or else what did I have going for me? My brother and sisters had better grades and better athletics, and they played instruments and I didn't. Basically, my brother and sisters had everything that my parents valued. At least let me beat them at the kitchen table when we played games!

The positive part of the fragile self-esteem that I built for myself, the first 20 years of my life, was solely based on the fact that I was just fine at games, and that I could beat my parents, brother, and sisters at those games. Beyond that, I didn't have much to hang my hat on. So when I lost a game back then (or I lose a pot in poker now), I feel pretty worthless and I search for the reasons why I lost, eventually going off on someone else for being lucky, or for playing poorly.

In 1998, when I watched Martina Hingis lose the French Open final to Steffi Graf, I was struck as I watched Martina's behavior, and embarrassed for her, because it brought to mind my own conduct in the poker arena. Over the course of the last few games, Hingis served the ball to Graf underhanded and skipped the post-game ceremony and interviews. Before witnessing Hingis's epic meltdown I thought that she was a classy champion, so watching her act in this bratty way made me feel sick (in Hingis's defense, she was still a teenager then). At that moment, while watching Hingis, I realized the impact that I had on other people who witnessed my tantrums. I wasn't disrespecting the game the Hingis did in her meltdown, but still, it was hard to realize that I could act like that too.

Good Person

I know that I am a great person. I am honorable, honest, and respectful toward everyone (away from the table!). I know I am really good to my wife, kids, parents, brother, sisters, and extended family. I am solid, loyal, and supportive to my friends. I respect my relationships with people, and I constantly strive to improve myself, but what comes over me at the poker table I may not ever fully understand.

I can compare my behavior to the following situation: imagine a kid standing in the batter's box taking a nice cut at the ball and hitting the ball harder than he has ever hit it before. The ball flies off into the sky, where the outfielder barely catches it in "snow-cone" style (where the ball is sticking out of the glove as it is caught), and the outfielder is moving at flat out speed on the dead run. Now the kid trots back to the dugout, and starts the following tirade:

> I cannot believe it; first off it was the longest ball that I have ever hit in my life, so I deserve that home run. Second, the outfielder barely caught it in snow-cone style! Third, why was he playing so deep in the first place? I have never hit a ball that far in my life. That guy should never have been playing that deep! Fourth, how can that outfielder run that fast? I mean there was only a slight chance that he would catch that ball, running full speed backwards like that! I was so unlucky; I deserved to have a home run!

Is the kid right about everything he said? Yes, the outfielder should not have been playing that deep, it was a lucky catch even for a speedster to make, it was a fluky snow-cone catch, and he did hit the ball farther than he has ever hit one before.

That kid is me losing a poker pot! This guy played poorly before the flop, I was unlucky that the turn card hit, and how could he call the all-in bet, etc?

For the last 30 years I have been trying to rid myself of the poker brat behavior that I am so famous for, because I'm 100% sure that getting that emotional hurts my play at the tables. In 2006 I actually controlled myself near perfectly for the whole WSOP, and the results were spectacular: I had a first, a second, a third, a fifth, and a 13th! And finished second in WSOP Player of the Year. Somehow for that one month, whenever something negative happened I was able to say, "Oh well, that's poker."

Phil's New Technique for Calming Down: Three Questions

When I lost a big pot, I used a new technique that I invented; first I would count down my chips, then I would figure out what the blinds were, and then would ask myself how to play optimal poker. Three questions. Somehow, this thought process took my mind off what had just happened to me, and put it squarely back in the moment. With my emotions in check in 2006, I remained calm at the table, instead of going off with a load of negative emotions, and all along tainting my own thought process. Thus, my entire focus was on playing the game the right way.

Hooded Monk!

I hope to get back to that non-emotional way of playing poker, where I act more like my earlier vision of a hooded monk at the table, completely in the moment and focused on winning, and I hope to stay that way for the next 30 years!

15

Big Ego Trip Leads to Cascading Fall

After my stunning triumph at the Bike (the Bicycle Club), *Poker Player* (the poker industry's leading magazine, really like a bi-weekly newspaper) had me on the cover page, touting me as one of the "brat packers" of the game. The three players who were being touted as the "brat packers" were 28-year-old Johnny Chan, 28-year-old Erik Seidel, and a 24-year-old Phil Hellmuth Jr. I guess they picked a pretty good group, seeing as how Seidel has nine WSOP wins (fourth all time), Chan has ten WSOP titles (second all time), and I have 14 WSOP titles (first all time through May 2017).

The Poker Majors

In golf, there are four "majors" per year; in poker, winning the Championship event at the Bike was like winning a major. All of a sudden, I was a name known in poker circles everywhere. All of a sudden, I had $250,000 in cash and a new Cadillac. I made a triumphant return home (Madison, Wisconsin) and the various poker games that I had cut my teeth on there, and wallowed in the attention that these successes had brought me.

But things were changing quickly for me. First of all, the games in Madison seemed way too modest for me to play in now. It was pretty hard for me to concentrate on winning or losing a $40 pot, when just the week before I had won $215,000 in LA. Along with this new lack of concentration and focus in the "little games" came a prolonged losing streak. I'd always been a gracious winner, but an obnoxious loser.

Slowly Losing Money, Painful!

Between the time when I came home from the Bike, in early September until March 1989, I gradually lost most of the money I had accumulated. In those days, nothing felt worse to me than losing almost all of my bankroll. My confidence and my ego were at an all-time high after winning the Bicycle Club main event: I thought I was a great poker player, and I had stacks of cash. Thus this prolonged losing streak, and the slow disappearance of my bankroll, didn't make sense to my fragile but pumped up ego. The long losing streak smashed up my ego. To me, the process of losing steadily, over a long period of time, seemed like torture! And caused me to have more than a few sleepless nights and a fair level of depression.

My Brother Dave and I Take a Poker Cruise

In late September that year my brother Dave accompanied me on board the S.S. *Rotterdam* for my first poker cruise. (See the picture in the photo section.) To this day I love having my younger brother and sisters around me, as often as I can. Back then, they were able to travel around freely, because they had no serious responsibilities (they were all still in school), and I would always pay their way in these gatherings.

My Younger Brother Dave

Dave is only 14 months younger than I am – two grades behind me in school – and different from me on so many levels. Whereas I was one of the youngest kids in my grade (born July 16, 1964), David was one of the oldest kids in his grade (born October 24, 1965). Whereas my GPA (2.8) hindered me, Dave's GPA (3.4) was good enough to advance him to business school at the University of Minnesota, and Law School at William Mitchell College of Law.

Whereas I struggled with social issues of every kind, including friends and girlfriends, Dave sailed along smoothly, with many friends and lots of interest from girls. Whereas I was super skinny and not exactly good looking – I looked a bit gawky back then – Dave was well built and good looking. Whereas I wasn't cool and was way too sensitive, Dave was cool and detached. Dave became president of his fraternity (Phi Kappa Psi), primarily, he jokes, because he could match you drink for drink late into the night, but still get up early in the morning for classes. Even on the poker cruise, Dave had a smoking hot girl after him for the whole ten days. But Dave did nothing with the girl, because he, like me, respected his relationships, and he had a long-term girlfriend at home in Minneapolis. These days, Dave has an amazing law firm (Hellmuth and Johnson) in

Minneapolis, staffed with over 60 attorneys.

But back to 1988 and the S.S. *Rotterdam*, where we spent ten days touring the Caribbean, with stops all the way from the Bahamas to Curacao. There was poker onboard, in the form of high-stakes side games, and small-stakes poker tournaments. The $200-$400 limit games that I played in, while onboard, were the biggest poker games I had ever played in. And as the losses in the side games mounted, I was deeply depressed when I hit $35,000 loser for the trip. In retrospect, I understand that $35,000 isn't all that much to lose at $200-$400 limit, but back then, not being accustomed to those numbers, I was devastated – that was the most money that I had ever lost on a trip. Never mind the fact that I had just won $220,000 at the Bike a few weeks before, this loss bummed me out.

Losing Sucks, But It Can Lead to Great Things

I guess that I was too much of a perfectionist, but being bummed out did serve a purpose. It caused me to pay closer attention to how I was incorporating my style of play. Why was I losing? What was I doing wrong? How could I improve my side-game results in the $200-$400 game? Ultimately, my depression caused me to improve my $200-$400 limit poker game.

On the other side of the coin, when I could get the side-game losses out of my mind, my brother and I had a great time. After all, I was the newly minted Bicycle Club champion; and my brother and I were definitely celebrating that trip. "We" (I paid for it!) had a bar bill of over $1,000 by the end of the trip, as I inaugurated my tradition of buying drinks – rum punch and Dom Perignon on that cruise – and dinners for the rest of the poker world. I still love to pay the bill when I'm with my poker player friends. I figure that I'm one of the guys who make the most money in poker, so why not be the one who buys for the players at the clubs or restaurants?

On one stop in St Thomas, Dave and I took a helicopter tour of the island, flying over Charminol, the most beautiful beach in the world. On the same day we rented out jet skis and wave runners for the entire afternoon! Still, for as much fun as we had, my depressing side-game results were never too far from my mind. At that point in my life, I was too intense about poker, and I hadn't learned to separate a loss from feeling down. If I lost, then I felt down for a while, period. These days I can lose, and then hang out with my friends, smile, and enjoy life. But back on the *Rotterdam*, I would be off having fun with my brother, and I would ruminate for a while over my poker losses. And then I would go back to having fun.

Hello Malta!

The very next day, after returning to Madison from the poker cruise, I headed by plane to Malta, a small island nation in the Mediterranean, right south of Italy. A bunch of players from the USA decided to attend a poker tournament being held there at the Dragonarra Palace Hotel and Casino. Poker legends Seymour Leibowitz, T.J. Cloutier, Hans "Tuna" Lund, world champions Brad Daugherty (1991), Jack Keller (1984), and Mansour Matloubi (1990) were in attendance.

Phil Locked in his Hotel Room?

Because I had fallen off the money-management wagon on the poker cruise – I was supposed to risk no more than $20,000 on the cruise, but in fact I had lost $35,000 – I had brought only $20,000 to Malta with me. I was back to using all of the concepts from the "winning pyramid," and my plan was simple: if I lost the $20,000, then I was done playing poker for the trip. After three days, I was already about $12,000 loser for the trip, and I figured that I needed to save the last $8,000 for the last two big poker tournaments on the schedule. Thus I'm embarrassed to acknowledge that I spent the next three days in my room!

I'm also proud to tell you that I was sticking to my money-management principles and had strayed away from further losses. How easy would it have been for me to ask Jack Keller or Tuna Lund to lend me $20,000? But I stuck to my plan, and figured that I couldn't lose any more money while sitting in my room.

Get Out and See Malta

After I spent a few days alone there, Tuna, Brad, and I rented a car and drove all over Malta to check out the island. Brad and Tuna were shocked at the way everyone, including me, was driving around Malta. For one thing, the streets are as narrow as any I've ever seen. For another, they drive on the "wrong" side of the street there. After about an hour of driving, I realized that these people were used to what us Americans would term "close calls." In other words, the Maltese people would drive very fast, even though there was literally just 18 inches between them and the car driving in the other direction.

I got used to this after about an hour, so the next thing you knew I was driving at the same speed as the Maltese were, much to Tuna's and Brad's dismay. I relished the reaction that I got from them, and freaking them out was hugely satisfying! They would see a curb 18 inches away and a car approaching us in the other lane at 30 miles an hour, missing us by another 18 inches, and they kept flipping out. To me, driving in Malta was all about tactics, like playing a new poker game, or a new video game, and I prided myself on mastering these games. I felt really safe after becoming accustomed to that crazy style of driving. After a bit, we moved out of the fast-paced urban environs and visited the cliffs that the Allies had stormed, to retake Malta from the Germans in World War II.

We also visited the set of *Popeye the Sailor Man*, and I don't think I'm exaggerating when I say that the water there was the bluest that I've ever seen. During our extended travels around Malta, I repeatedly told Tuna and Brad that I was going to win the 1989 WSOP "big one." They both thought I was crazy! But the mind is a funny thing. Tuna and Brad eventually listened to me for nine months while I told them that I was going to win it, and then I went out and won it. How did seeing me pull off the win affect Tuna and Brad? Well, no one knows, but I suspect that they dug down deep and raised their own expectations, telling themselves, "If this young punk kid Phil thought he could win the 1989 WSOP, and pulled it off, then why can't we win it?"

Lo and behold, the very next year, in the 1990 WSOP "big one," Tuna made it down to heads up vs. Mansour Matloubi. Tuna had Mansour all-in on a flop of 9-5-2 while Tuna was holding A-9, to Mansour's 10-10. Amazingly, the turn was an ace, and Tuna was more than a 20-to-1 favorite (Tuna had 42 cards to win, to Mansour's two cards to win!) to achieve his lifelong dream and win the 1990 WSOP. But alas for Tuna, the last card was one of the last two tens left in the deck! And Tuna went on to finish in second place. The very next year, Brad Dougherty won the 1991 WSOP "big one."

You are what you think;
You become what you think;
What you think becomes reality.

You might as well think big, folks!

Blown Out to Sea!

One memorable day early in our trip, I asked Brad to watch me as I went for a swim in the cold Mediterranean. What was I doing swimming in that cold water? It was simple: I wanted to be able to tell people that I went for swims in the Caribbean and the Mediterranean in the same week! So Brad watched in horror as I jumped into the water and was sucked 150 yards straight out into the ocean. Fortunately, I had been on a swim team for about five years when I was younger, and I was able to work my way slowly back to shore. Now I know what they mean when they say "Beware of strong ocean currents!" One more time I freaked out my friend Brad, but this time I was pretty shaken up myself.

Phil Becomes "Number 2"

One day, while I was still hanging out in my room in Malta, T.J. Cloutier invited me to dinner. As he mercilessly needled me about locking myself in my room for three days, I decided to tell him the way things were in the poker world at that time. I told him that I was the best No Limit Hold 'Em player in the world, except for one other. And the only reason that I gave Johnny Chan the nod over me was because he was, after all, the two-time reigning World Champion. I also told T.J. that I would win the 1989 WSOP. T.J. got a laugh out that, and he looked at me with bewilderment in his eyes. Here was this wet-behind-the-ears 24-year-old kid telling the grizzled veteran (who already owned dozens of No Limit Hold 'Em Championship titles) that he was the second-best No Limit Hold 'Em player in the world! I guess I deserved what happened next: T.J. gave me a nickname, and for the rest of the trip everyone called me "number 2." Fortunately, I have discovered that a nickname sticks only when the person whose nickname it is, likes the nickname. Needless to say, I didn't like it! Even so, they managed to call me "number 2" for a couple more months after that. By the way, "number 2" proceeded to lose the whole $20,000 that he had allotted for the Malta trip. But, there was one big victory for me that trip: I had stubbornly stuck to my money-management principles.

The Losing Continues

But the losing continued for the next month back, in Madison, and as a result I became quite insufferable to play with. I had never had so much money as I'd had in August, and thus had never been able to lose so much money straight away. My ego couldn't handle the losing, so again I got cocky at the table and continued to lecture down my opponents, or whine insufferably, when I got even a little bit unlucky (that's me, the poker brat!).

Many hours of the day I was consumed with poker. I thought constantly about Hold 'Em. How could I improve? How could I become less emotional at the table? At random times during the day, I tortured myself over past mistakes that I'd made along the way, in particular the mistakes that had cost me poker tournaments. If only I hadn't got reckless here or there, I would have won another title. If only I hadn't got unlucky here or there, I would have won another title. On and on I went, constantly reviewing my sorry poker history in my mind. But this somewhat painful process eventually paid dividends. How could I play a hand better in a certain situation? Why had I lost $55,000 in the last two months? What was I doing wrong? How could I stop the bleeding?

Dad Wants to Go to the WSOP!?!

One day in September I asked my father where in the world he wanted to visit, on my dime, just he and I, while I hinted strongly that an Australian trip would be terrific. He suggested that he wanted to come to the 1989 WSOP. I had to smile, because he was finally showing me support, but I knew that his physical presence could throw me off. So I strongly discouraged him from coming to the 1989 WSOP. By November 1st, my father was insisting on going to the WSOP "big one" to watch me play. He kept saying to me, "You are going to win the thing, right?" To which I kept answering, "Yep." Then I told him, "You won't have much fun. I'll be ignoring you for most of it. I really think Australia would be great. I'll come back again in December and ask you where you want to go."

High-Stakes Golf

In early November, I went to play in my poker friend Yosh Nakano's golf tournament in Lake Tahoe. Yosh is a short Japanese gentleman with the heart of a lion. He is known for his ability to play poker for 40 hours or more straight, with no sleep, and his Limit Hold 'Em cash game skills were nothing short of world class. In the old days, Yosh would almost never quit a game while he was losing, and he has been known to play over 100 hours straight.

Back then, he also had a reputation for being a big-time gambler. He would play golf with you for big money in the light of the day, play liar's poker or backgammon with you for big money at dinnertime, and then play poker with you for big money all night long. Then without sleeping, he would do it all over again! (Yosh and I gambled against each other all over the USA at poker, golf, backgammon, Liar's Poker, and much more!)

High-Stakes Golf: Hustled?

Yosh's golf tournament was being held at the famous Edgewood Country Club, and I broke about even during Yosh's two-day scramble. The next day, a well-known gambler named Tab challenged me to a golf match. When we made the match, I overestimated how well I played golf (I didn't want to be viewed as a hustler) and he underestimated his golf abilities, and, well, he just plain hustled me. It was the first time that I had ever played a big golf match one-on-one, and I had lost the match in the clubhouse even before I picked up a club. I continue to wonder now how I could have been a professional poker player all this time and yet still be so naïve elsewhere. Out on the course at Edgewood Golf and Country Club, Tab and I played straight up, with no one receiving shots. Here's the way it was: Tab claimed to shoot 88 (but he really shot 84) and I claimed to shoot 88 (but I really shot 94); so he absolutely crushed me! After Tab beat me every hole we gambled on, I doubled up on 18th hole, a famous par five hole at Edgewood, and I shot a 7, which was good for the way I was playing, but Tab beat me anyway by making a par 5. I lost $5,000 for the day, and I was furious at Tab for hustling me. Nonetheless, I had to pay in full.

Since I didn't know the players or their golf games, I quickly decided to make a two-man team match to ensure that the match was fair. The next day, my new partner Mike Sexton, (recently the voice of the WPT), and I were going to scramble (best ball) against Yosh Nakano and Richard Dunberg. Mike and Richard would hit the ball twice each and Yosh and I would hit the ball once each. So Mike would hit twice and I would hit once, and then we would play the best ball. Then we would drop three balls and do it again. Obviously, this promotes very low scoring. Especially when you have one of the greatest putters in poker history, Mike Sexton, on your team putting the ball twice! When the smoke cleared I was up $6,000, and we happily made a match for the next day. This time we would let them add their buddy Dale to their team.

So Dale, Yosh, and Richard would hit once each for their team. And Mike would hit twice, and me once for our team. Little did I know that Dale was a much better golfer than advertised. Dale was a ringer! I bet a lot of money ($4,500 Nassau, two down automatic presses – which means that you could win or lose 5-bets maximum) on the match. Yosh and Richard, by the way, continued to play like dogs. Over and over Dale would hit last for their team, after Yosh and Richard hit two bad shots, and over and over, Dale hit "Gin" (perfectly).

Like on one par-four hole where Mike and I had a ball about 15 feet from the pin, putting for birdie. This was a key hole late in the match (the 16th hole), so that everyone was feeling a lot of pressure on them when they hit their shots. Yosh, stone-cold chunked his shot and Richard pulled his shot badly. Mike and I were feeling really good about the comeback we were mounting, and in particular, we felt good about our position on this hole, with only Dale left to hit for their team. Dale stepped up under all the pressure, and hit his ball "stiff" (about three feet away from the hole). I remember thinking "Not again, what the heck is going on?" I ended up losing $18,000 (4-bets) for the day, which was one of the biggest losses of my life. To make matters worse, I lost the money on the golf course, not at the poker tables, where I could at least justify it to myself. This really ate me up, how could I lose so much money on the golf course? I immediately hopped on the next plane back to Madison, to lick my wounds, while feeling like a terrible money manager, and a complete loser. After this trip – I had lost about $25,000 – I managed to go through about $80,000 straight.

A Dark Time for Me

In December 1988, I headed out to Las Vegas to play in the last "major" tournament of the year, at the Horseshoe Hotel and Casino. The Hall of Fame poker tournament there was a huge and important event, and it was also where the poker world admitted one person just once per year to the Poker Hall of Fame (now they admit two players per year, and I was accepted by the Hall in 2007).

I was coming off of the worst run of my life going into the Hall of Fame "big one" (Championship event), and the money-management wheels had fallen completely off of my poker cart. I had brought about $20,000 with me for the trip, and I ended up losing that amount playing $400-$800 limit poker, before I even went to bed on the first night. The next day I borrowed $15,000, and wired home for $40,000. I promptly lost the $15,000 in a Deuce-to-Seven No Limit side game. And the next day, when the $40,000 arrived, I paid back the $15,000, and I was left with $25,000. I was already over budget and pressing badly, and the "winning pyramid" concepts that I had labored over, and that I believed in, were completely hidden from me on that trip. Patience, no; discipline, no; exercise, no; and my money management was atrocious! Thus I sat down in another Deuce-to-Seven No Limit game and lost the last $25,000 that I had with me in town.

Now things seemed really dire to me, but I decided to make a stand! I would risk it all, if I had to, but I would turn this losing streak around. Talk about bad money management, it doesn't get much worse than risking your whole bankroll in a matter of days. I was completely out of control, and had no idea what I was thinking. Somehow, some way, for some reason, I ended up wiring home for $80,000 more, leaving myself with $30,000 left in my bankroll at home. And I proceeded to lose $70,000 of it, playing higher and higher limits, and that really put me over the edge into a state of shock, a real state of depression, and a state of panic. What had happened to the $250,000 bankroll that I had once had? How was I going to recover that?

Now in the midst of my panic, it was a very dark time for me at the Horseshoe. Even though I was never suicidal, I would joke to my mom and dad on the phone about how perhaps I should go jump off the roof of the Horseshoe. Obviously, my parents didn't take well to my dark humor. And I placed way too high a percentage of my self-esteem on how much money I had.

I believe that it is really hard for someone who has had no money to speak of over the course of his life to suddenly acquire a bunch of money. I believe that it takes some time to become "used to having money." And while people evidently get used to having money, I have noticed that they tend to head toward the financial state that they were in before they had money. In other words, people –

when they're unaccustomed to having money – tend to go broke after a sudden surge in cash.

Just take a look at the people who win the lottery. Often, winning the lottery tends to ruin lives, and studies show that – on average – these lottery winners end up broke within a couple of years; $50 million to zero, pretty scary! Or take a close look at the young sports stars who get hold of riches. Most times these young athletic stars just don't know how to handle their new-found wealth. I have seen case after case of athletes going broke by the time they are 40 years old and out of the game. Studies show that the average millionaire tends to fluctuate between being broke and having a million dollars close to ten times before they finally hold on to the money. This all makes sense to me, after having lived through it. After all, accumulating money is one talent, and managing money and holding on to it is another. In any case, it seemed like I was speeding down the highway toward going broke.

Hall of Fame Main Event

In the $5,000 buy-in Hall of Fame Championship event (the year's fourth major), I had literally one-third of the chips in play with 17 players left in the event. Now I had a great chance to reverse course on all of the damage that I had done in one fell swoop, because first place was over $194,000. I could veer right off of that "Broke Highway" in short order! All I had to do was win this one poker tournament.

Late in the tournament, T.J. Cloutier (the third-best tournament player in the world), and the two-time defending World Champion Johnny Chan (the best tournament player in the world) sat at my table.

All I had to do was to avoid any big confrontations, play patiently, and I would cruise into the final nine and Day 2 with the chip lead. In this Crown Jewel event, the structure gave you plenty of time to work your chips, relative to what ensued in the other tournaments of the day.

First, I busted T.J., when I raised it up under the gun with J-J, and T.J. moved all-in for a huge re-raise with A-7, and I called him. Now I had almost 50% of the chips in play! A little while later, I raised it up under the gun (as the first player to act) with 9-9, and Johnny Chan made a big re-raise from the small blind with Q-Q. I studied a long time, and decided to move all-in. I reasoned that everything had been going my way, and that I probably had Chan beat. If Chan did have A-K, then it would be a coin flip. If Chan had a bluffing type of hand, then I would win the pot right then and right there. If Chan had an under pair, then I would be a big favorite to bust him. I have used this line before, but I'll use it again here: I was giddy with the chip lead.

In any case, I ended up doubling up Chan, and for many months afterward I was tortured by the thought of how badly I had played this hand. I had reached the conclusion that I simply didn't have to move all-in with my pocket nines. If Chan was a short stack, then I would have had to play my 9-9, but Chan had enough chips in front of him to strongly suggest that I would do well to fold my hand. I should have made a very good lay-down and avoided doubling up the two-time defending World Champion. Had I just called Chan's re-raise before the flop, an ace did hit on that flop, which would have allowed me to fold my 9-9, and thus lose a minimal amount in this hand. But after I lost the hand against Chan, I seemed to fall apart emotionally and I blew a ton of chips. I kept thinking about how I should have folded against Chan, and my negative emotions had a big effect on me as I tilted off handfuls of chips at a time. Hand after hand, it seemed as if I was giving away piles of chips to my opponents.

When it came down to the final ten players, I had to last just one more spot in order to make it to the final table. I should have been patient, but foolishly I tilted and moved all-in for my last 60,000 before the flop, with my A♦-10♦. My opponent had almost exactly the same number of chips that I had, so that it was he or I who was going to the final table that night. Unfortunately for me, my opponent had J-J, and he was a 2½-to-1 favorite to win the pot. Fortunately for me, I hit an ace and won the pot! I had badly overplayed the A♦-10♦, and I saw Chan shaking his head, like, "How could Phil get it all-in *there*, and how could he be so lucky as to hit the ace?" Making the final table should have been a cakewalk for me; it should have been smooth and easy for me to take that massive chip lead and convert it to a final table appearance. But I knew the reality: I had tilted off tons of chips, and at the end of the day I was lucky to make the final nine.

Hall of Fame Main Event Final Table

Joining me at the final table that day were to be Chan, Pete Knowles, Paul Rowe, Wendeen Eolis, Brad Dougherty, George Rodis, and Jesse Alto. It took me a long time to fall asleep that night (that's typical for the night before the final table of a major), and right when I was about to fall asleep, my brother Dave – with whom I was sharing a room – came bursting into the room and screamed with excitement, "Yo, bro!" That did it; I was up again and feeling both the excitement of the moment, and the pressure of the occasion. Unfortunately, I had a lot of trouble falling asleep after that, and I'm afraid that I played like a sleep-deprived man the next day, while finishing in seventh place and cashing for $15,000.

Johnny Chan won it and Jesse Alto finished second that year. Looking back now, I realize that I had a great year in the four majors in 1988: I made the money in my first World Championship (finishing 33rd), I won the Bicycle Club big one, and finished seventh at the Hall of Fame big one. This didn't stop me from looking back at the Hall of Fame big one for many years to come, and blaming myself for not "closing the deal." That tournament haunted me for years, at random times, like for example when I was taking a shower, or when I was lying in bed, or right before I fell asleep.

Chan Crushes!

By the way, how about Johnny Chan's run in those majors? He won the WSOP main event in 1987 and 1988, then finished second in 1989. He won the Hall of Fame main event in 1988 and 1989. And he made it to the final table in the 1988 Bike main event (Chapter 13). A man of both wisdom and courage.

Although I had cashed for $15,000 or so by making the final table, by now I had lost over $200,000 straight, and I was really feeling down and depressed. We could debate all night long whether or not it was inevitable that I ended up broke, but we cannot debate how lousy I felt on the way down. Still, I think I handled it better than most would. During the darkest times that I have ever faced in my life, my mind would always wander out of the darkness of the present, and look toward the brightness of the future. If I was struggling in the present, that was OK. I was simply laying the foundation for success in the future. I felt that if I kept my wits about me when things were bad, then I would be back on top at some point in the future. This outlook of mine helped me avoid the standard trap that so many young poker players fall into these days, on the way down: I avoided alcohol and drug abuse.

Back in Madison for Christmas in 1988, I again prodded my dad to come to Australia with me, on my dime. He replied, "Australia would be fun, but I want to go to the WSOP." Having seen the car my father was driving at the time (it was an old rust bucket), I had formulated a plan for this response from him. So I answered, "Dad, that's fine with me. If I win it I'll buy you a new car." So my father, who had never watched me play poker, and didn't even know how to play Texas Hold 'Em, would be coming out to the 1989 WSOP. This was the granddaddy of them all, the main event, and I was sure that my father's presence would be great for me!

Big Comeback at the Super Stars of Poker Tournament

In January (1989), I headed back to Lake Tahoe to play in the Super Stars of Poker tournament at Caesars Palace. I managed to win the Omaha 8-or-Better tournament – after staying up all night – and to finish second in the Seven Card Stud 8-or-Better tournament for about $20,000 total.

It was there that I first ran into a very obnoxious poker player named Sam Grizzle. Sam was quite a character! He was a motor mouth running, insult flying, always attacking, huge personality. Sam would insult everyone at the table, and if you defended anyone, then he would start on you. Sam was so good at tilting the other players that I was forced to develop a couple of tactics for dealing with him. First, I decided that I would never let him put me on tilt through personal attacks, like he is wont to do, by just enjoying the show. I would simply enjoy his sharp wit, and terrific sense of humor, even if it was directed at me. Once you view his attacks (or anyone's) in that light, and laugh at yourself at the table (this is key!), then they lose their potency.

One time, when I was in the room at the Hall of Fame main event, Sam told the legendary Stu Ungar that they ought to take down all of the photos of the World Champions of Poker (they were sitting below all of the photos of the world champions), and just put up one big photo of Sam. This struck Stu the wrong way, and he and Sam got into it, disrupting the whole tournament. I saw so much humor in all this, that I couldn't stop laughing!

In any case, Sam had to be dealt with, daily, at Lake Tahoe, and my second line of strategy went like this: if Sam started on one of us at the table, then we would all gang attack him, verbally. And most of all, we would stick together. So I approached the other regular players in the game, who were all fed up with being insulted by Sam, and suggested that we neuter his attacks thus. And it worked! Apparently, Sam wasn't used to seeing everyone sticking together, and he quickly saw that he couldn't win the spats anymore. He was forced to give up his attack tactics, on that trip anyway.

During my trip to the Super Stars, there were a couple of incidents of note. First, there was a small confrontation between Johnny Chan and me in the Championship event, over a pot of no consequence. Player A raised it up, and Chan called with A♥-J♥. Then Player B called, and I re-raised it with 4-4. Player A folded, Chan called, and Player B folded. The flop was 10♦-8♠-3♥, and Chan checked. I wasn't sure what Chan had called with, holding such a big re-raise, but I feared that he had a strong hand, perhaps a bigger pocket pair than my fours, so I checked. It wasn't the best check, but not too bad, because I was planning on betting on fourth street, assuming that Chan would check one more time. Fourth street was the 9♥, for 10♦-8♠-3♥-9♥, and Chan checked his open-ended straight draw and flush draw to me. I bet out 50% of the pot size, and now Chan raised it up a big amount. I folded quickly, and then Chan showed me his hand. I believe he was thinking that he had the best hand with his ace-high, and with a straight and a flush draw to boot. I knew that Chan was not needling me, or showing me up, but I got upset anyway and I told him, "Johnny, you will never beat me again in a big poker tournament, ever!" Everyone at the table laughed at this because Chan had been winning tons of the big major tournaments over the last several years. Everyone laughed at this, except Chan. These words would have a somewhat more salient meaning on May 18th of that year (1989).

The second interesting thing to happen in Tahoe at the Super Stars was in a $200-$400 Limit Hold 'Em game that went down with Yosh, Clone, Sam Grizzle, and me being the only four players involved. Sam had just won the Irish Eccentric $2,500 buy-in No Limit Hold 'Em event (for about $100,000), in the Championship event held at the Super Stars of Poker. After his big win, Sam hopped right into the biggest game in the house, and had Yosh, Clone, and me squirming in our chairs with his phenomenal luck and his motor mouth running at full blast. When at one point Sam left the table, I looked over to count his stacks and stacks of black $100 chips, with $500 chips in stacks as well, and he had nearly $80,000 in chips in front of him (he had bought in for $20,000). He was "barbecuing" us all.

We all prayed that Sam wasn't going to quit the game, because often when someone leaves the table it is because they have decided to quit the game. Or, after they leave, they then decide that quitting the game is a prudent move. In this case, quitting would have prudent for Sam! He had finished off two days of intense poker while winning the Irish Eccentric main event, hopped straight into the game with us, and now it was 5 a.m. Sam should have booked the win! I was about $14,000 loser, but I didn't feel all that bad, because I was losing the least of the three losers. Twenty minutes later, here came Sam, and here *went* Sam, for the whole $80,000 that was in front of him. Then he went back to his box (safety deposit box) and got the rest of his money, which was about $30,000, and that didn't last long either. After Sam left, I quit, because we had been playing all night and I was $32,000 winner.

Yosh told me that Sam had lost all of his money that night. I felt a little bit bad for Sam, but it is hard to feel too sorry for someone who is that obnoxious at the tables. I was also feeling pretty good about my largest side game win ever! I remember taking racks and racks of the black $100 chips and stacks of $100 bills to the cage, at 10 a.m.

16

Choppy Waters Lead to a World Championship

In its February 1989 issue, *Esquire* magazine did a major piece on poker. Although the article dealt mostly with poker's current events, focusing on Johnny Chan, there was a quote in there that really stoked my WSOP fire. It was inspiring, to say the least, to see Chan himself, the defending two-time WSOP Champion (World Champion), saying, "Phil Hellmuth will win the World Series of Poker main event as soon as he learns to tuck it in a bit." It was clear now: I knew that the best player in the world knew who I was, and respected my play. I had already received major props from the two other big tournament champions of that era, Jack Keller and T.J. Cloutier. By then I had played with Keller and Cloutier extensively, in a bunch of high-profile tournaments, and I had acquitted myself quite well.

With a renewed sense of confidence, I headed out to Las Vegas to play in Amarillo Slim's Superbowl of Poker tournament, where I broke about even. In Slim's Championship event, our first major of the year, I played with poker legend David "Chip" Reese for the second time (the first was when Chip finished tenth at the Bicycle Club's main event). It was said by the top poker players that Chip was the best all-round poker player in the world. Chip was still considered the best all-round poker player in the world until his untimely death in 2007, but in the side games, not in Hold 'Em. Everyone in the poker world knew of Chip's stature, but his successes never seemed to extend to tournaments, for whatever reason. One reason perhaps was that he didn't play in as many tournaments as many of us. Chip did win one of the biggest and most prestigious tournaments in the poker world, when he won the $50,000 buy-in Players Championship at the 2006 WSOP. In any case, there we were at the same table, and I had a ton of chips.

I was getting a bit giddy with the chip lead, and I began to be a bit reckless. With the blinds at $100-$200, and with a $25 ante, I raised it up to $700 to go with 8♦-3♦, trying to win the blinds and antes, and Chip called. The flop was 9♦-8♠-5♦, at which point Chip checked. I bet $2,000, Chip moved all-in for about $14,000, and I called with my pair of eights and a flush draw. I felt a bit sick getting involved for so many chips with a drawing hand – not to mention holding 8♦-3♦ – but that's what can happen when you play those types of garbage hands. In those days we didn't show our hands when we were all-in, so when the J♦ came on the turn, I thought I had probably won the pot. But Chip rolled over the K♦-2♦ – which completed a higher flush – to claim the huge pot. It turned out that I had been a 3-to-2 favorite when the money went in on the flop, but still, I was left wondering why I had let myself get involved with 8♦-3♦ for so many chips, when I'd had such a comfortable chip lead, of around $36,000, before the hand began.

After I lost that pot, I was berating myself quite a bit (internally), and I was beating myself up for losing my focus and discipline. My winning plan involved playing a patient game of Hold 'Em, and it certainly didn't involve ever playing the 8♦-3♦. I believe that it was because I was so emotional after I lost with 8♦-3♦ that I cost myself a chance to make it to the end of Day 1! My negative emotion had definitely caused me to "go on tilt," and thus to blow the rest of my chips, in short order.

Beating Myself Up

After I was eliminated I promptly hopped on a jet and flew home. But I wasn't through with that hand yet. For weeks, I'd wake up in the middle of the night in a cold sweat, regretting the way I had played that hand.

This trend of being upset when I played poorly has continued even to this day, and sometimes I need to pull myself back and say, "Forget about it, you'll get an ulcer if you worry too much about the hands that you played in the past." The act of punishing myself over the bad plays that I had made helped me improve my game, because I wanted to play perfectly and not face my own wrath! When I made mistakes playing poker, if it rocked my world too much emotionally, and for too long, then I would pay extra close attention in the moment, and learn to make fewer and fewer mistakes. At some point though, I had to shift my focus to the fine things that I had accomplished in the game in order to stay happy (and respectful of the blessings on the bathroom mirror).

Cajun Cup II

In March 1989 my old friend Gary Miller and I hopped into my new car (my Cadillac) and headed south to the Cajun Cup poker tournament in Lafayette, Louisiana. On the way down south, Gary and I stopped in Bloomington, Indiana, to visit my sister Kerry. While in Bloomington, Gary and I caught the last home game of the season for Bobby Knight's Indiana Hoosier basketball team. After the final home game each year, the sold out crowd hung around because Bobby always gave a long inspirational speech to his team, thanking his seniors, and praising his basketball team for their work and their effort over the previous season. It was a pleasure to be there. Knight is a master at giving these types of speeches!

My Little Sister KK (Kerry) Hellmuth

In any case, my sister Kerry was really coming into her own. In March 1989 I was 24 years old, David 23, Ann 22, Kerry 19, and Molly 17. Kerry was a sophomore in college at Indiana University (IU), and blessed with the looks of models. She's 5' 10" tall, with black hair, green eyes, and a slender athletic build. She had a nearly straight A average in both high school and IU, and eventually she was invited to join the Phi Beta Kappa Honor Society. Kerry also has a great winning personality: she is modest, but bubbly and as sharp as a tack. And she had a long-term boyfriend (Bob Soderstrom) that the whole family loved. Bob eventually became the Homecoming King at IU, and married Kerry a few years later. As her older brother, ever since Kerry was a baby I felt the need to protect her from all kinds of harm.

My family was tight knit, and part of my brother Dave's job and my job, was to look after our younger sisters: Ann, Kerry, and Molly. We still joke about a classic line that Dave and I used on our little sisters as they grew up, "When a boy comes to the door to pick you up for a date, we'll greet him with a baseball bat in our hand so that he knows not to mess with you!" At IU Kerry was into riding bicycles, and she entered the inaugural women's Little 500 race in 1988. The Little 500 race for the men was made famous by the movie *Breaking Away*, which was nominated for the Best Picture Award at the 1979 Academy Awards. Kerry won the race! Then in 1990 she won the women's Little 500 race again, and she eventually rode bicycles professionally in Europe and in the USA for several years. She raced in the Tour de France, and the Giro de Italia and every other big women's race from Europe to California to New Zealand. But before Kerry embarked on her bicycle-riding career across the world, she finished Law School at the UW.

I remember one day when Kerry called me in tears saying:

> *I just spent three days talking a power bar company into giving me a free box of power bars for my new team. I have a law degree, and I spent three days of my time trying to get a box of bars worth $50!*

Sometimes chasing your dreams is a tough deal financially! Kerry and I always had a special bond. Perhaps it was the fact that we were the two dark-haired kids in the family (Dave, Ann, and Molly had blond hair), or the fact that we looked alike – Kerry and I share many facial features but somehow they came out looking great on her, and only OK on me! One thing that made me feel great, and that made me play harder, was that I wasn't just playing for my own benefit. The fact that I helped my brothers and sisters pay for their college and law school tuition gave me extra incentive to win my own battles. When I was trying to win poker tournaments, and money in the side games, I would imagine that I was a huge oak tree with a ton of people standing below me. That visualization (or image that I carried in my head) helped remind me that I wasn't playing poker just for myself, and my own needs, but that I was also playing poker for my family. For example, I remember that I gave Kerry $5,000 in cash at Red Rock Canyon (outside of Las Vegas) for her last year of law school. Reflecting on memories like this help rev up my sense of entitlement. Why shouldn't I win big? I'm not going to blow the money on drugs, alcohol, strip clubs, or casino games, I'm going to help my brothers and sisters go to school! In giving to my family, I was also giving to myself!

After a couple of days in Bloomington, Gary and I drove on to Lafayette, Louisiana. In Chapter 11 I mentioned how much the poker players loved the Cajun Cup poker tournament, what with the boiled crawfish, and the great southern ambience and all. The tournament action and the side-game action were equally fantastic. I'll never forget the older Cajun gentleman who would shout, day and night, "Lock the doors, don't let nobody out!" In 1988 that was the line of the year in the poker world, and it seems the players couldn't hear him say that enough. We would all just break out laughing whenever he shouted it out. He was implying that the action was off the charts (the action there was always off the charts!), and that given enough time he would bust everyone in the room.

No Limit Ace-to-Five Lowball Draw

I seemed to be holding my own on that trip when I decided to enter a poker tournament I had never played in, or even heard of before. It was the No Limit A-5 Lowball Draw Tournament at the Cajun Cup. One thing I had going for me was that reading and bluffing your opponents make up a big part of what No Limit A-5 Lowball Draw is all about. Since there are only two rounds of betting, before and after the draw, picking off bluffs is a big key to success. And I have always felt that one of my biggest strengths was reading people. Another thing that I had going for me in No Limit Ace-to-Five Draw was that it presented No Limit, and I had shined at No Limit Hold 'Em.

Somehow, I muddled through the tournament, gaining confidence – and insights into the game – with every passing hand. It got down to Joe Machivernia and me, heads up. Joe had had a small chip lead when he asked me to make a deal and split the tournament's cash prize. After a quick negotiation, it was agreed that I would get the first-place title and trophy, and we would split the money evenly.

Two Trophies in Two Days

With my first Cajun Cup title under my belt, and about $20,000 in my pocket, I attacked the No Limit Hold 'Em tournament at noon the next day with vigor and new-found enthusiasm. By 3 a.m., this event came down to Larry Satterwhite and me, heads up. But this time I had so many chips that there was no talk of deals. I won $55,000 for first place! Bang, two titles in a row (and another $75,000 in cash for the bankroll).

Two tournaments in a row is quite a feat, and it had only been done a handful of times, but how about three in a row? No one had ever done that before! The third day, the event was Seven Card Stud, which was my worst game. Although I was severely sleep-deprived (you try winning two poker tournaments in a row on back-to-back days!), I began to take the chip lead in this event as well. My old acquaintance "Chicago Scotty," sitting next to me, was telling me all day long how badly I was playing Seven Card Stud, as I was slowly busting him. I was happy to be rid of Scotty, but he would have the last laugh that day. I had a big chip lead relatively early in the stud tournament, but then the tournament director Eldon Elias got on the microphone to tell us that the Governor of Louisiana had ordered him to shut down the tournament. Eldon (the director) went on to say that we could finish the poker tournament, and that we could then continue to play poker until midnight with no legal issues.

Shut It Down, Now!

At this point I saw my old friend Dewey Weum run across the room to his safety deposit box. A lot of us noticed Dewey's run, and the next thing we knew, there was a huge rush for the safety deposit boxes. Roughly an hour later Eldon announced that they were treating our stud tournament as if it had never started. Everyone would get a refund from the day's buy-in, and the tournament was now officially over. But "Chicago Scotty" got in one last needle ("Phil, see this 300?") as he left the room with his $300 buy-in back in his pocket, even though he had (technically) already lost it in the tournament. I never got to find out whether I could have won three in a row that trip, but at least I have the distinction of winning the last two Cajun Cup tournaments ever held, back to back!

A Pile of Cash in the Trunk

Right after that event, at about 4:30 p.m., I took my $75,000 in cash to a local bank, but for some reason they wouldn't accept it. I recall that I was both young and paranoid, and I actually hired a security guard to ride with me to the bank! After I moved 60 miles east to a hotel in New Orleans I tried again to take the cash to a bank, but I began to suspect there was a banking regulation of some sort against accepting over $8,000 in cash. I never did fully understand why I had to carry that $75,000 in the trunk of my car throughout my stay in Lafayette and New Orleans, and then all the way back to Madison. But I can tell you this much: because a lot of people knew that I had that cash, I was pretty nervous about it – especially while I was making my way across hard-times Louisiana.

With an extra week of free time, now that the remainder of the Cajun Cup poker tournament was canceled, and Gary Miller had headed home with Big Al, I asked my sister Molly if she wanted to meet me in New Orleans to hang out for a week during her spring break. At the time, it was easy for my brother and sisters to come with me on my trips because they were young and they didn't have to be concerned about money, jobs, or family. Besides, I would happily pay for their trips, because I dearly love hanging out with my family.

My Little Sister Molly Hellmuth

So Molly joined me in New Orleans, and we had a grand old time! We ate well, we hung out on Bourbon Street every night, we listened to jazz, and we watched a lot of movies. Molly was 16 years old at the time, a junior at Madison West High School. Molly is a beautiful girl: 5' 9" tall with blond hair and blue eyes. She has an engaging personality, and we have always had fun hanging out together. In 2005, Molly was voted one of the "Top Forty Most Powerful Scientists in the World under the age of 40." And these days she is one of the leading climatologists in the world! Specifically, Molly is a water engineer, and if there is a big global climate conference, then you can expect to see two people at it: Al Gore and Molly. Molly is also a world-class skier, and she has three children.

Molly and I thought we were pretty cool when we walked into the Hard Rock Café, New Orleans, with my new car phone (they weren't called cell phones yet)! Back in 1989 you didn't carry a car phone in your pocket. You didn't carry a car phone anywhere really, because the cutting-edge car phone (I had it) was 14 inches long, 14 inches wide, and 5 inches thick, and it was bulky, heavy, and you carried it in its own case! Back then it was rare that you could carry a car phone outside of your car. When I carried the thing into the Hard Rock Café, and set it down on the table, I think that no one in the place even knew what it was. Then

I pulled out the receiver (which was attached by a black wire) and I dialed up my parents' house, and I talked to my mom. ("Hi Mom, yes Molly and I are in the Hard Rock Café sitting at a table calling you from my car phone.") But before we walked in to the Hard Rock, I thought that I would feel like James Bond, with this rare, cutting-edge toy in my possession. I was the cat's meow: calling people on a car phone in a booth at the Hard Rock Café in New Orleans! No one was particularly impressed by my little "show," and I felt as if the waitress there was taking my ego the wrong way. My ego was huge at that point. I had just won two tournaments back to back only a few days before. But to the waitress I wasn't James Bond. I was quite the opposite: I was the spoiled rich kid with an unbearable ego. Despite my problems, Molly and I had a great week in New Orleans, and we told many jokes that week about the pile of money that was just sitting in the trunk.

C'mon Phil, just say, "Thank You, Officer!"

So Molly and I pointed my Cadillac and its car phone toward Madison and off we went. We foolishly decided to drive the whole 14 hours in one day, and we paid the price for that decision. In southern Illinois, I was speeding when a policeman pulled me over. When I rolled my window down the policeman asked me, "Do you know why I pulled you over?" I asked, "Was I speeding?" The policeman said, "Yes you were, you were going 70 miles per hour in a 55 mile per hour zone, but I'm going to let you go. Have a nice day." Now I said, "No, I don't think I was going 70." (What was I thinking? Why didn't I simply say, "Thank you very much," or "Have a nice day?") A policeman lets you off the hook for speeding, and you argue what, exactly? I believe that the weird response I made had something to do with my ego. In any case, now the cop shakes his head and looks at me like I'm an idiot and he says, "I'm going to give you a ticket. Give me your license and registration please." Now I tried to be polite and gracious, but it was too late. After I received the ticket, I read it quickly and I noticed that there was a court date. I said, "Can't I just pay the ticket and be done with it? Do I have to go to a court date?" The policeman said, "You can write a check right now." I said, "I don't have a check. Sir, I'm not trying to bribe you or anything, but is there a way that I can pay cash?" He said, "Yes, you can put cash in the ticket and mail it in." I said, "Can I put cash in there, seal it up, and just give it to you to take in for me?"

I could tell that the policeman was getting tired of me by then, but he said, "OK. The total is $137." It was at that moment that I realized that I didn't have enough cash on my person, and that I would have to go into the trunk (where there was $75,000 in cash) to get a $100 bill out! Thinking quickly I told the policeman, "I don't have enough money on me, but I have a $100 bill in my suitcase in the trunk for emergencies." My sister Molly and I exchanged nervous glances. So I grabbed a $100 bill from the trunk, paid the ticket, and got the heck out of there. The rest of the trip went really quickly, as Molly and I laughed about that incident all the way back to Madison!

Cheated on a Caribbean Poker Cruise

I wasn't back in Madison long before I headed out on another poker cruise in late April (without my siblings), this time right before the 1989 WSOP. By now, I was getting known as a big-time poker player, but I wasn't very "street smart," and couldn't seem to put two and two together on this cruise. World Champion of Poker Jack Keller (now deceased) was on the cruise this time around, and when I asked him why he wasn't playing in the big side games he said, "Phil, Player A (now also passed away) and Player B are both known cheaters. You'd better stay out of that game." But I knew Jack to be very paranoid, so I didn't listen to him. My mistake. There were no cameras, and no one watched the games closely, and when Yosh Nakano asked the poker cruise director about the fact that there were well-known cheaters on board, the director said, "Poker players will be poker players." Nice, thanks.

Meanwhile, I had proof of just how naïve I was in short order. I had been hanging out with a bunch of poker players that whole trip, and I had made friends with the wife of one of the known cheats. I was the only single guy who hadn't brought a girl along among our merry little group. So a lot of the women in the group were trying to set me up with women on the cruise. I had been getting massacred in the side games on the trip, but at that point I still didn't believe that there was any cheating at all, in the known poker universe. If there was cheating going on, then how could a young clean-cut man from Wisconsin come out on tour and win all this money playing in poker tournaments? To me, cheating was nonexistent in poker.

Anyway, the wife of Player A, who knew I was winning big, became close enough to me to say, "Please do not go back into that big poker game." I said, "Why not? Unless you can tell me that I'm being cheated, then I can handle these guys in the long run." She hesitated, then said, "I can't tell you that, but please don't go back in that game." Young, naïve, egotistical, and apparently unable to read between the lines, I kept on playing. I reasoned that this woman was concerned that her husband was a better player than I, and she was telling me not to play because she thought he would crush me. But, as they say in the National Football League (NFL), "upon further review." A week later I realized that she had been trying to tell me that her own husband was cheating me! It was amazing that she would tell me that, especially when it involved her own husband, but it was comforting to know that she liked me well enough to try to warn me off. (I have to find something positive to think about from that cruise!)

In any case, I lost $57,000, and I believe it was one of the only times in my entire career when I was cheated. One particular hand from that cruise still sticks in my mind; something just wasn't right. I woke up in the middle of the night still intently disturbed about that hand. I had K-J, and the bad guy (Player A) had what turned out to be A-J. Something just didn't seem right with his hole cards, the way the betting went, whatever. Maybe my unconscious mind saw the bad guy slip an ace into his hand, or discard three cards instead of two, or something of the sort. The final board was J-8-8-2-6, and that hand stuck with me.

By the way, this guy (Player A) could have made a fortune by playing the game straight up! Everyone knew how much talent he had. I heard later that he was serving time in a Washington prison for cheating in a casino. The fellow who told me this was happy to report that the bad guy was in prison, because he knew what had happened to me on the cruise. But I couldn't get happy about someone else's suffering. It was probably supposed to make me happy, but what good did his going to prison do me? (A few years back, the bad man passed away.)

The problem with being on a poker cruise is that everyone settles up later. At the end of the cruise I owed $57,000, and I had only about $75,000 to my name, after paying my taxes for 1988. Losing $57,000 out of your last $75,000 in cash, talk about bad money management! The "winning pyramid" building blocks had come a long ways, but I was far from mastering them. Still, the application of the "winning pyramid" building blocks had taken place: I had completely given up all the casino games, I had completely given up smoking pot, I was never a big drinker anyway. I exercised regularly, I ate a decent diet, my discipline and focus were now at a world-class level, and my money management, for the most part, was terrific.

But this trip I had made a horrible money-management move and lost way too much: $57,000 of my remaining $75,000 cash. At that point I did something which no experienced gambler would do: I wired the full amount out to the person that I owed. So even though I knew by then that I had been cheated, and even though it wasn't smart to pay the full amount immediately, I did. (Usually if he had a debt of $75,000 a professional player would give himself a chance to recover, by, say, paying $40,000 of the money immediately, leaving himself with $35,000 to build on.) In other words, I left myself financially crippled (with $18,000) heading into the 1989 WSOP, but (and do not underestimate this) I felt great about myself, and about the fact that I owed no one in the world one dime. Paying my debts in full in a timely manner, giving money to my brothers and sisters for college and law school, keeping my ethics and honor intact, these things all made me feel a larger sense of entitlement. Trust me, you need an outsized sense of entitlement if you want to win millions of dollars and make poker history!

No Sex for a Reason

Somewhere over the past year, I had made up my mind that part of my having a shot at winning the 1989 WSOP would be abstinence. I felt, if I could avoid sex, then I would win the main event. If I did have sex, then that would hurt, or cripple my chances of winning. God knows how or why I thought this way, and I'm not saying that it makes sense. I'm just saying that I believed it, and thus I respected it. I'm not particularly religious, and at the time I didn't have a girlfriend, so when I had a great opportunity on the cruise to sleep with a beautiful woman, it pained me to turn it down. I recall passing on that great opportunity, and the strength it took! Still, I figured that I was going to win the WSOP first, and then open up my life a good bit. But first things first. I felt I had to avoid sex for another month or two, until the WSOP was over.

It had been almost four years since I had had sex, and I wasn't feeling very normal. In fact, I felt pretty abnormal! A 24-year-old guy who hasn't had sex in four years doesn't sound particularly cutting edge, or cool, or natural, or even quite normal. For me, abstinence was partly about the fact that I broke some-one's heart when I was 20 years old, and I didn't want to mislead someone else, and break her heart too. I remember well the searing pain that I had caused my last girlfriend. Hookers were always available too, but that idea wasn't particu-larly appealing to me. I suppose I was waiting around for the right woman, and I thought I could always tell on the first date if they were right or not. Back then it was hard to find a good woman on the poker circuit. Still, enough was enough, and I vowed to open up my life, and my sex life, after the 1989 WSOP ended.

Other than remaining true to my vision of celibacy, the other thing that hap-pened on the cruise was that I kept telling all who would listen that I was going to win the 1989 WSOP. If they told me I wouldn't, that I couldn't, or that I was plain crazy (plenty of people did tell me that), I would just ignore them. I had a clear vision, and I refused to accept anyone else's assessment, or anyone else telling me what the odds were. I also told people that the only guy that I would even consider making a deal with, if I were heads up, would be Johnny Chan. I was so confident that I bet Tommy Fisher and a couple of others, at even money, that I would win one of the 13 WSOP tournaments in 1989, even though I had never won one before.

The rumor of my "stupid bet" preceded me to Las Vegas. And when I arrived at the Horseshoe for the 1989 WSOP, I was accosted by dozens of players, all trying to bet me that I wouldn't win a WSOP tournament at even money. As I dealt with this barrage of scorn, and people trying to goad me into making serious bets, I realized that I had made a bad bet (or at least one seen in the eyes of the world as a bad bet). Did this change my thinking at all? Nope, I was sticking to my vision, but I will say this much: I should have taken better odds! Although I hated all the derisive laughter, I would have the last laugh this time.

After the cruise ended, but before the WSOP began, I played poker for two weeks in Madison, and I kept telling my incredulous poker friends that I was going to win the "big one." I told any and all of them that if they were out in Las Vegas at the Horseshoe Hotel and Casino to witness it, then I would fly them all home on a private jet. Right before I left town for Las Vegas, I changed the message on my answering machine to, "I am not home right now. Please leave a message for the 1989 World Champion of Poker, after the beep."

17

The 1989 World Series of Poker

From the outset of the 1989 WSOP, I was asking people to "stake me" for the last five events, as a sort of package deal (they would receive 60% of my action for putting the money up). I knew it would cost about $20,000 to enter the last five events, and I just didn't have enough money to play in them all. (After paying the $57,000 loss from the cruise, I was left with only about $13,000, and I had left $3,000 at home.) Plenty of people said no, and others said that they would have to wait and see, since the closing events of the WSOP were still ten days away.

As the days flew by, my financial standing wasn't improving much. I was still short! And no one had stepped up to back me. I had had discussions with many people – who later reminded me that they had almost agreed to stake me – but nothing had panned out yet. On the morning of Friday May 12th, I had $6,500 left in my Vegas bankroll. A quick look at the 1989 WSOP schedule told me that there were four events left: today's $2,500 buy-in (with unlimited $2,500 re-buys) Pot Limit Omaha, Saturday's $2,000 No Limit Hold 'Em, Sunday's $2,000 Limit Hold 'Em, and the $10,000 World Championship (the one where, should you win, you are called a World Champion the rest of your life; the one I dreamed about winning, the one I had a lifetime goal of winning – indeed, the one that I told everyone I was going to win).

Violating Money Management Principles for Main Event

Because the WSOP had huge numbers of players, and thus huge payouts, this was the only time that I felt justified in violating my money-management principles. I couldn't help thinking, "Go for it now, and if you fail, then you'll have plenty of time to rebuild your bankroll with your new skills." So I decided to play the last three tournaments before the big one with my own money. I would need to cash well enough in one of these last three events, if I was to place myself into the main event. Or win a satellite, as I had done in the 1988 WSOP. Or find someone out there who would step up to stake me!

Dad Watches Me at WSOP Final Table

At 10:30 p.m. that night, Dad's plane landed in Vegas. Because I was still in the Pot Limit Omaha tournament, I dispatched my brother Dave (who had arrived earlier, Friday) to the airport to pick him up. At 11:15 p.m. or so, I made the final table – where first place was $184,000. Fifteen minutes later, my father arrived at the final table, having never watched me play poker before. I'm pretty sure that the major reason I was at this final table was that I knew that my father would be arriving in town that night, and I wanted to impress him. Even to this day, I perform better in poker tournaments when my parents are around, or when I know they will be arriving that day to watch me. I even planned for it! For more than a few years now I have been scheduling my parents to fly in late on Day 2 of the Big One. I reason that I will still be in knowing they were coming in to watch me play!

In any case, I sought out Jack McClelland – the now legendary tournament director – to give my dad preferential seating right next to the final table. Whereupon my father proceeded to sit down and tell everyone at the final table a joke! I whispered, "Uh Dad, you're not supposed to talk to the players. We're playing for a lot of money and a WSOP bracelet." But his joke didn't bother me, and I didn't blame him for it. I was deeply grateful to have him there! It just so happened that the first time he ever saw me play serious poker was at a WSOP final table.

Amazingly, two of the three top tournament players in the world were at that final table with me, just as had been the case in the 1988 Bicycle Club Championship event, which I had won nine months earlier: hello again to Jack Keller and T.J. Cloutier.

Pot Limit Omaha can be a very treacherous game, and Cloutier and I went out on the same hand. Technically, he finished sixth and I finished fifth, since I had started the hand with more chips then he had. Fifth was worth $25,300, and my worries were over, so far as getting staked for the main event was concerned. After busting out, I immediately bought into the main event and felt as if a lot of pressure had been lifted. I was in!

The hand that I lost with at the Pot Limit Omaha final table had taken an interesting twist. Remember that Omaha is a game where you start with four cards in your hand, face down. T.J. was already all-in before the flop, for a small amount of money. I had 7-6-5-4 in my hand while I sat in the big blind, and the flop was A♣-6♥-5♣. My opponent, Kevin Redican, laid out a big-sized bet. And I called, with my two pair and an open-ended straight draw. The turn card was the 10♥, and this time Kevin made a huge-sized bet, enough to put me almost all-in too. After studying for a while, and feeling that I smelled some weakness, I moved all-in. Kevin called my small raise, and showed his hand: A♥-Q♣-9♥-3♣, with two flush draws and a pair of aces. To win the pot he would need an ace (for three aces), a nine, or a queen (for two pair), or a heart or a club (a flush) that wasn't a six or a five. As it turned out, I was almost even money to win this huge pot, but alas for me, the river was the jack of clubs, and Kevin made his flush.

I'm In the 1989 WSOP Main Event

At least I had cashed for enough to play the next three Hold 'Em tournaments in comfort, including the main event. And I now had 100% of myself in the main event! I had told my dad that he could not watch me play during the main event, because I felt it would distract me. This he already knew, because I had put that condition on it before he came out to Vegas. In Saturday's WSOP tournament, I didn't last particularly long. And I decided taking Sunday off to rest up for the big one would be a good move.

On Sunday, then, my father, my brother, and I went golfing at the Dunes Golf Course. (A few years later, Steve Wynn famously blew up the Dunes Hotel and Casino on national television, and now the Bellagio Hotel stands where the Dunes used to stand.) I recall that I was, as usual, frustrated with my golf game! And that day we staged the family golf championship, and my brother won it, as is his custom.

Day 1 at the 1989 WSOP Main Event

Monday, at 11 a.m., my father showed up at my hotel room at the Golden Nugget Hotel and Casino, with breakfast in hand (fresh fruit, orange juice, and cornflakes), and I was irked with him because he forgot to bring a banana for me to slice up onto the top of my cornflakes! At noon, we walked over to the Horseshoe, which is where and when the 1989 WSOP main event began. I was wearing a sharp new Ralph Lauren blue-and-white oxford button-down polo shirt, and some khaki pants. I also had a dark midnight blue Ralph Lauren jacket on hand, should the temperature change suddenly in the casino. The event began by recognizing Johnny Chan, who was the two-time defending champion. (It was Chan who had busted me out the year before.)

Day 1 was relatively uneventful, and I accumulated an above-average stack without much difficulty. The only notable moment was when I seemed to be the only player in the room with a Walkman on. Back then I had a new yellow Sports Walkman made by Sony that was supposed to be waterproof, had thin yellow head phones, a Bobby Brown tape cranked up ("Dance!... Ya know it!"), and a Van Halen tape standing by. The yellow Walkman stood out, too, in photos. With 178 entrants, we lost 78 of them on Day 1, and thus were down to the final 100 after one day's play. We each started with 10,000 in chips, and I ended the day with 24,575 in chips, which put me in 24th place out of the 100 remaining players.

Notable Chip Counts After Day 1

These were some of the notable chip counts after Day 1: two-time defending WSOP Champion Johnny Chan $31,500 (ninth place), Poker Hall of Famer Lyle Berman $30,425 (tenth place), actor and semi-pro poker player Gabe Kaplan $27,600 (19th place), poker legend Erik Seidel $21,475 (34th place), two-time WSOP Champion and poker icon Doyle "Texas Dolly" Brunson $21,175 (36th place), Hall of Famer Chip Reese $20,350 (38th place), the "Grand Old Man of Poker" and three-time WSOP Champion Johnny Moss $18,625 (43rd place), WSOP Champion Walter "Puggy" Pearson $17,150 (51st place); and future WSOP champions Hamid Dastmalchi $36,400 (third place), Noel Furlong $26,800 (22nd place), and Jim Bechtel $24,000 (27th place).

Day 2 at the 1989 WSOP Main Event

At 11 a.m. my father came to my room with food in hand, and this time he remembered not only to bring a banana for me, he had even had it sliced onto the cornflakes already. I said, "Well done, Dad! Thank you so much for the support. It's great to have you out here with me." I just loved having my father there for me, and it gave me a lot of extra power! By the way, I wore the same clothes that I had worn on Day 1; even the same socks and underwear.

Bono vs. Hellmuth

Day 2 was where the fireworks began for me! After an hour or two, they broke my table down, and I was moved to a new one – table 22, seat 2. I discovered that the late great John "Bono" Bonetti was sitting two players to my left. Bono and I later became great friends, for 20 years, but I had to forgive him for what happened next. As the day progressed, it became apparent that Bono was the most aggressive player at the table, and I was the second most aggressive player. One hand, I had A-K, and I played against Bono for a huge pot before the flop.

But I had a bad feeling on the flop of J♣-10♣-6♠ and bailed out when I made a huge bet, and Bono moved all-in. All day long it seemed, Bono and I had been jabbering back and forth, and after he beat me for this monstrous pot he said (quite loudly), "Never send a boy to do a man's job!" This provoked laughter from both the table and the ever-growing numbers of spectators who were watching play from the rail. That comment stung, and I turned pretty red. It hurt to lose a big pot, and then on top of that to receive a big needle!

So the Bonetti–Hellmuth war was heating up, when all of a sudden I found myself calling off a big stack of my chips with the 9♥-3♥ (a flush draw), on a board of A♥-K♥-J♠. Bono, who was all-in, flipped over his hand. He had the Q♥-4♥ (a higher flush draw along with a straight draw), and with a harmless 7♠-6♦ finish, he raked in the nearly 60,000 pot with queen high.

I was feeling like a real idiot, and thinking, "This is how you're going to go out in the World Championships, with 9♥-3♥? Get your head out of your ass, and play the game right!" It didn't help that right after I had that thought, Bono once again shouted, "Never send a boy to do a man's job!" This time there was an ever louder response – tons of laughter – from all of the gathered spectators, and oh boy, did Bono get under my skin with that swipe. Now I started really tilting, and I was either going to bust out quickly or get over Bono and my mistakes quickly. It was my first serious emotional test of the 1989 WSOP, and I was really struggling to keep myself under control. I kept thinking, "I've worked too hard to get here, and I have too many chips left to be losing control now. Patience, Phil, you know the game. Patience."

My once big chip lead had all but evaporated, but I was still in there with 24,000 or so when the following hand came up: with the blinds at 200-400, Ali Farsai made it 1,400 to go, and Ralph Morton called. I called on the button with 8♣-6♣ – a hand that I wouldn't ordinarily play. The flop was 7♦-5♠-3♣, and they both checked to me. I bet out 4,000 with my open-ended straight draw, Ali folded, and Ralph called. The turn card was the 8♦, Ralph checked, I bet out 7,000 with my pair of eights and an open-ended straight draw, and Ralph moved me all-in for my last 12,000 or so. I wanted to fold, and badly. But I didn't see how I could. After all, I did have top pair and a straight draw, and half of my chips were already in the pot. I was pretty sure that I was beat, but I called. I flipped my hand face up, and Ralph waited until the last card was dealt, before he showed me his hand. The last card was the 5♣, and Ralph flipped up K♦-7♦. I had life! Ralph had a pair of sevens, but I had a pair of eights. Ralph had flopped sevens for top pair, and had turned a diamond flush draw, so that he needed a king (three of those), a seven (two of those), or a diamond (nine of those), to win the pot. Ralph had 14 cards in the deck that he could win with, to my 30 cards. Now that I had safely dodged that draw, I was back in the hunt! I was lucky to win this hand, because I was tilting more than a little bit, and winning this hand seemed to settle me down and get my head back into the game.

Late on Day 2, Noel Furlong (who would become 1999 World Champion) was moved to my table. And right away we had some big action. After a few players limped in, George "Diamond Jim Brady" Hardie raised it up on the button to 3,000 to go, Furlong called in the small blind, and I called in the big blind with K♥-Q♣. The flop was Q♥-2♦-7♥. Noel checked, and I bet out 15,000 into the pot. I had bet while still trying to figure out if I had the best hand or not. Everyone else then folded to Noel, who called. The next card was the 6♥ (completing a flush draw), and Noel checked. I bet out 18,000 this time, and Noel moved all-in for another 40,000 or so.

It was decision time for me. I had top pair with a good kicker, and I had the K♥, which gave me a flush draw. (I also had 80,000 in front of me, so that if I was wrong I would still be alive.) But I didn't have enough information about Noel, and I studied him for a long time. I thought, "I'm in bad shape if Noel has a flush or trips, but I did bet on fourth street because I thought Noel was weak."

"Click" Goes the Camera!

If I folded, then I still had an above-average stack, and I had a great chance to persist to the end of the day. If I called, and I was right, and I won the pot, then I would have the chip lead! But if I called and I was wrong, then I would be a bit low on chips and at risk of being eliminated. I chose the conservative play and folded my hand face up. Now Noel flipped up his hand, the 9♥-9♣. He had bluffed me out! Noel could still have won the pot if he had hit a nine (two cards to my 42 cards), but I had folded when I was over a 20-to-1 favorite! Right then, a *Las Vegas Sun* photographer snapped a picture of Noel and me, and they put it on the front page the very next day, captioned, "Hellmuth gets bluffed by the Irishman Furlong."

No matter, at the end of the day I was still alive and kicking, with 92,800 in chips. We ended play at midnight, when we were down to the final 27 players. I had survived the Bonetti–Hellmuth wars (as had Bono with 173,800), and Noel's big bluff (Noel had 98,600). I was feeling pretty good when my father and I walked out of the Horseshoe late that night and ran into Humberto and Alex Brennes. Humberto said that he was sorry that I had let Bono take me out of the tournament with all of his needling chatter. I said, "I'm not out yet, baby! In fact, I'm up over 92,000 in chips again." Humberto replied, "Don't let Bonetti get to you! *Tranquillo*, Phil, *tranquillo*." And Humberto took his right hand and pointed to

his temple as repeated, "*Tranquillo*." He and his brother reminded me that I needed to stay calm and focused. To this day, Humberto and I still greet each other
with a point to the head, and a nice loud "*Tranquillo!*" I still remember, with great
fondness, that the Brennes were rooting hard for me in 1989!

Here are some of the notable players left after Day 2 ended: Ralph Morton
177,600 (chip leader), John Bonetti 173,800 (second place), Jay Heimowitz
136,800 (third place), Johnny Chan 99,000 (sixth place), Noel Furlong 98,600
(seventh place), Phil Hellmuth 92,800 (eighth place), Lyle Berman 61,700 (11th
place), and David "Chip" Reese 40,800 (16th place).

Day 3 at the 1989 WSOP Main Event

On Wednesday at 11 a.m. my father woke me with the usual food tray in hand.
Again, I wore the same Ralph Lauren blue-and-white button-down oxford shirt,
I brought the same midnight blue polo jacket and, sadly, I wore the same pair of
socks for the third day in a row! Since I couldn't sanitarily wear the same underwear (I didn't want to smell bad!) I went without wearing any underwear at all.
I figured that if something worked, then why change it? I like superstition, at
least when it's positive for me. I believe that some things *are* lucky for me, but I
try hard to believe that there isn't anything out there that is unlucky for me. As I
mentioned in Chapter 2, I grew up with this sign on my bathroom mirror:

> *You are what you think;*
> *You become what you think;*
> *What you think becomes reality.*

If this is true, and I believe it to be true, then why shouldn't I choose to believe in good luck? Why not believe that something, whatever it is, makes you
lucky? If "What you think becomes reality" is true, then why not believe in good
luck? Perhaps good luck will become your reality. Is there a downside? Conversely, why should I believe that something makes me unlucky? Is there an
upside? Consequently, I believe that some clothing is lucky for me. Thus, if I'm
at a tournament – like the 2012 WSOP – that lasts over a month, and I win a
tournament, then expect to see me wearing precisely the same clothing many
more times before the tournament ends.

Day 3 wasn't nearly as turbulent as Day 2. We were scheduled to play down
to the final six players, from the 27 remaining, and fortunately for me I had never been all-in. When we hit the final table (nine players), I watched one player
simply fall apart in front of my eyes, much the way I have seen a PGA tour player

fall apart on the back nine of the Masters. It was weird, watching that meltdown, but now, a little older and a little wiser, I understand the reasons for it. Perhaps this gentleman was so close to his dream, and so close to making some big money, he couldn't handle it anymore. Perhaps he had been bad to his family, and felt like he didn't deserve to win. Maybe he didn't think he was good enough to be called World Champion the rest of his life. Maybe he just couldn't handle winning the $755,000 first place prize. Maybe he was an alcoholic or drug addict, and felt he didn't deserve success. Maybe he couldn't handle the pressure. Or maybe he was tired of the fight, and he found it easier simply to give up and get out of the pressure-cooked WSOP final table. Who knows the exact reasons why people self-destruct?

But I have seen PGA tour golfers melt under the pressure, or self-destruct, many times on the back nine of one of the four major golf tournaments. When we reached seven-handed play, we had to lose only one more player to advance to Day 4. I recall raising it up with J-J, and Fernando Fisdel moved all-in with 2-2. I called his raise of 25,000 more with my J-J. When we flipped our hands up I was thinking, "No deuce," but when the flop came down J-7-3, giving me trip jacks, I stopped worrying. My hand held up and we ended play for the day. The final six players counted down their chips, and here's what it looked like: seat 1, veteran Don Zewin with 188,000 in chips; seat 2, high-stakes gambler Noel Furlong, 302,000; seat 3, Johnny Chan with 350,000; seat 4, veteran Steve Lott with 413,000; seat 5, uber successful businessman Lyle Berman with 185,000; and seat 6, Phil Hellmuth Jr. with 344,000.

This lineup made for a pretty tough final six, with two-time defending World Champion and Poker Hall of Famer Johnny Chan, future 1999 World Champion Noel Furlong, WPT Founder and Poker Hall of Famer Lyle Berman, super successful high-limit poker pro Don Zewin (who finished second to me in the 2012 WSOP in Seven Card Low), multi-final-table finisher at past World Championships Steve Lott, and me.

Early Day, Long Dinner!

We ended play well before 9 p.m. on Day 3. Each night I would have dinner with my dad and my old friend Tuli Haromy (Chapter 2), who happened to be in Vegas to visit his parents. After Day 1 ended, Tuli decided to extend his stay as long as he needed to, in order to watch me play. I was mostly quiet during these dinners, as I was consciously trying to save my energy for the next day. After Day 3 ended, we headed to dinner at the steak house at the top of the Horseshoe, and Tuli asked me, "What happens if you pick up kings, and someone else picks up aces?"

Under the pressure of a few intense WSOP days in a row I flipped out, saying loudly, "Do not even suggest something like that. What's wrong with you?! It will not happen like that tomorrow!" Tuli then answered, "Well, what if it does?" Now I really flipped out, and shouted, "Have you lost your freaking mind! It will not happen like that tomorrow, period!"

I felt that I had a great chance of winning it all the next day, and this seemed like way too much negativity, and it was coming from my own camp! How much of what we say and what we do influences future events? We are what we think, we become what we think; what we think becomes reality. I was seriously thinking about asking Tuli (my best friend) to leave the dinner table, since I simply didn't have time to hang out with someone that negative. But I realized that I didn't need any serious conflict like that going on in my life right then. Thankfully, my dad jumped in there saying, "Tuli, what's wrong with you? Leave it alone, please just leave it alone." Now that Tuli went down this path I was thinking about trying to "will it not to happen" in order to make sure that I didn't have K-K vs. someone else's A-A, but I quickly decided that I really didn't want to think about that possibility, period. To think about it would give it energy. Besides, who knows if "willing" something like that could work? Although it does seem that great players, like Tiger Woods and Michael Jordan, can will the ball into the hole when they really need it to go in.

On every level, I knew that I wanted to stay positive, and I thought:

> *Tomorrow is my big chance to make history. I have already seen myself win it in my own mind, and now I have to convert my vision into reality. But it will take everything I have left in the tank. No one is going to give me the win, and if I play poorly, then I will bust out. To win it, I will have to play perfect poker on Day 4, start to finish.*

Day 4 at the 1989 WSOP

On Thursday May 18, 1989, at 11 a.m. my father knocked at the door of my hotel room at the Golden Nugget. As he had done every day during the four-day-long main event, my father was faithfully serving me as a food bearer (fresh fruit, cornflakes with sliced bananas, and no coffee), and as a human alarm clock. By then, sleeping for me was a huge issue. You try sleeping at night after you have made it down to the WSOP main event final table! With my dad – the guy I trusted the most in the world – getting me up every morning was one less thing that I needed to worry about. When I walked into the tournament room, with my father still completely out of my line of sight, I saw that there were stands set up on all four sides of the final table, and the stands were full of people hoping to see poker history being made. Chan and I were both trying to make history, and we were both trying to break some records. Chan was going for his third WSOP Championship win in a row, and I was trying to become the youngest winner in the history of the WSOP. ESPN was there with cameras rolling. But, in 1989, ESPN wasn't the huge worldwide network that it is now. Still, it was great to know that someone was watching. In 1989 the only event that was on television, without hole card cameras, was the last day of the WSOP main event.

PH Showmanship!

After play had ended the night before, on Day 3, I had an idea: I was going to make a show out of pulling out, and putting on a pair of sunglasses when play began (showmanship for Johnny Chan!). Thus I went to the store and bought a pair of sunglasses, and as soon as Chan sat down at the final table and pulled out his sunglasses, I reached into my pocket, fumbled around a bit for effect, and pulled out my own pair of sunglasses. I just wanted to get Chan's attention, and the game was on! I had never played poker with sunglasses on before (boy, did that one go the other direction over the next 20 years!), and I wasn't sure how long I would wear them on that fateful day. As it turned out, over the first 40 minutes of play at the final table I didn't win many pots, and I pulled those sunglasses off. (I never wore them again.) Meanwhile, Furlong was playing a super-aggressive game, and he was beginning to pile up the chips.

In one big hand, 90 minutes into the action on the final table, with the blinds at 3,000-6,000 and the ante at 1,000 a man, I raised it up to 21,000 to go, with 10-10, and Furlong made it 80,000 to go (a 59,000 re-raise). But I hated to call Furlong's 59,000 raise! I hated that idea because I didn't want to play a big pot early on and risk being eliminated. First place paid $755,000, second place paid $302,000, third place $151,000, fourth place $83,050, fifth place $67,950, and sixth place $52,850. If I wanted to make the big money, then I had to last at least until we were three handed. I wanted to last as long as possible, but I couldn't let Furlong run me over either. I called, and the flop was J-J-10; I had flopped a full house! I checked, Furlong bet 80,000, and I moved all-in. Way too conservative! I should have just called, but I kept thinking that Noel would hit some miracle, like running queen, queen, to beat me. So Furlong took a small hit from me on this hand, but he took some big hits from Chan over the next hour.

First, Furlong played a huge pot against Chan when Furlong held pocket nines, and Chan had pocket jacks. There was a raise and then a re-raise before the flop, and the flop came down J♠-5♥-3♣. Furlong checked, and Chan, who now had the best possible hand, also checked. Chan was trapping Furlong. The turn card was the eight of spades (J♠-5♥-3♣-8♠), Furlong checked, and Chan bet. Now Furlong raised it up, and Chan just called. The river was the A♠, and Furlong moved all-in! Chan called off all of his remaining chips in an instant, although the flush had hit. Chan doubled up, putting a huge dent in Furlong's stack. Chan had managed to pull off a perfectly executed trap against Furlong, reaping the rewards with that beautiful double up.

The next big hand between Chan and Furlong came along when the blinds were set at 3,000-6,000 with 1,000 a man ante. Chan limped in under the gun (in first position) with Q-Q, Lott limped in for 6,000, Zewin folded in the small blind, and Furlong raised it up 30,000 with 4-4 out of the big blind. Chan studied for a few seconds, counting out some stacks of chips, and then said, "I raise." Chan raised it up 100,000 more, Lott folded, and Furlong called. The flop was K-10-3, Furlong moved all-in for his last 138,000 or so, and Chan called him in an instant. Furlong was all-in, and in bad shape; he needed a four to survive. When the next two cards came down 7♣-K♠, Furlong was eliminated in sixth place.

About an hour later, with the blinds still at 3,000-6,000, and 1,000 a man ante, I folded under the gun, Zewin limped in for 6,000, and Chan, too, limped in for 6,000, on the button. Lott called 3,000 more in the small blind, and Lyle Berman looked down at A♦-K♣ and raised it up 30,000 more, to go. Because there was 29,000 in the pot, Berman's raise was a big one. Zewin folded, and Chan called 30,000 with his 7-7. The flop came down K-7-6. That was a very unlucky flop for Berman and, conversely, a very lucky flop for Chan.

Berman bet out 60,000 and Chan put enough chips into the pot to cover him. Berman then called all-in for 170,000 in total (60,000 + 110,000). Even though Berman had a monster top pair and top kicker, he would need two perfect cards to win the pot. The pot had basically concluded, but then a king came up on the next card (K-7-6-K), and Berman hit the table hard with his hand. Berman had hit one of the perfect cards that he needed to give him a chance to win the pot. But he was still in bad shape! Berman needed to hit an ace, a king, or a six, to win the pot. Berman had seven wins – three aces, one king, and three sixes – compared to Chan's 37 winning cards. The river was a jack, and Berman was gone, in fifth place. And then there were four!

The Old 6-4 Suited!

A little while later, with the blinds still at 3,000-6,000 with a 1,000 a man ante, I was in the small blind, and everyone else had folded. I called 3,000 more with the 6♠-4♠. From the big blind, Zewin raised it up 20,000 more, and I called.

I'm not sure why I called his raise: 20,000 with 6♠-4♠? I guess I thought that Zewin had A-5 or something weak, and that I could outplay him after the flop. I do know that I thought he was relatively weak, because I didn't think he would raise it up that much with a medium pair, or a big pair.

In any case, I caught an amazing flop when it came down K♠-9♠-3♠! I had flopped a flush, but if Zewin had a higher flush, then I was going to be eliminated. I checked, Zewin bet out 80,000, I moved all-in for my last 330,000, and Zewin called. I thought that he had trips, like three threes or three nines. Since Zewin didn't show me his hand, and because my tournament life was on the line, I watched the next two cards come off of the deck with great angst; and naturally I was thinking, "Please do not pair the board, and please do not turn a spade." If he had trips, and the board paired, then I was out. If he had a higher flush, then I was out. But if I had the best hand, I still needed it to hold up. The next two cards came off 8♦-4♣, for a final board of K♠-9♠-3♠-8♦-4♣, and Zewin flipped up his hand. He had the A♠-3♦, so that he had flopped a pair of threes and an ace-high flush draw. As it turns out, I would have been eliminated if a spade had come off the deck. Still, I had put my money into the pot as roughly a 3-to-1 favorite, and thankfully my flush held up for the 700,000 chip pot.

Fifteen minutes later, with the blinds still at 3,000-6,000 and 1,000 a man ante, Chan opened the pot under the gun (first position) for 21,000, holding 9-9, Lott folded, and I peered down at 10-10 in the small blind. It was decision time for me! Re-raise, and risk a pile of chips, or just call? After studying for nearly one minute, I decided just to call. Now Don Zewin, from the big blind, announced that he was going to raise it up. Zewin decided to make it 100,000 more to go, with his A-J. Now Chan announced that he was going to raise it up, and he made it 200,000 more to go, more than enough to put Zewin all-in. I muttered to myself as I studied the situation with my pair of tens. But when faced with all of those raises and re-raises my decision to fold was fairly easy to make.

As it turned out, Chan's 9-9 was about a 6-to-5 favorite to win the pot over Zewin's A-J, but the cards came down J-5-3-Q-A, and Zewin doubled up to over 400,000 in chips. It didn't take a genius to figure out the ramifications of what had just happened. If I had re-raised with my 10-10, then it's 100% that Zewin would have folded, and I would have had a chance to double up through Chan. I was stewing about my missed opportunity, but not too much, because I knew that I wasn't going to play a big pot with a medium pair, just like the rest of the poker world; this was one big difference between me and the rest of the poker world in 1989. Still, when you watch the video of the hand, after Chan calls and they show their hands, I reach into the muck and shout, "Damn, I had pocket tens!"

My Lucky Ace!

Ninety minutes later, with the blinds now at 5,000-10,000, and a 2,000 a man ante, I opened in first position (under the gun) for 35,000 with my A♣-10♣, Zewin called in second position on the button with 10-10, Chan folded from the small blind, and Steve Lott moved all-in from the big blind for another 83,000. I was thinking, "Steve doesn't seem that strong to me, and if I call, then Zewin will probably fold, or maybe he will just call, and we will check it down and look at five cards." When someone is all-in and there are multiple callers, then checking it down to try to bust the all-in player is a pretty standard tournament strategy. Thus, I decided to call, figuring that I could look at five cards. But after I called I was shocked to hear Zewin say, "I'm all-in!" I asked for a chip count, and was told that it was 163,000 more for me to call.

The math at that moment broke down like this: there was 527,000 in the pot (35,000 × 3 + 5,000 Chan's small blind + 8,000 for four antes + 83,000 Lott's all-in + 83,000 my call + 83,000 Zewin's call + 163,000 Zewin's raise = 527,000), and it cost me 163,000 to call. Thus I was getting laid well over 3-to-1 on my call, and I had a chance to bust two players. If I won the pot and busted the two players, then I was guaranteed $302,000 for second place.

From a math point of view, I had to call. But I don't always play the math: 163,000 was a lot of chips to keep in my stack that I could use later to bust someone when I was a big favorite to win the pot.

More important than the math was the read. And I kept wondering what kind of hand Zewin could have just to call my 35,000 bet, but then move all-in over the top with an 83,000 re-raise. I pretty much eliminated A-A, K-K, Q-Q, A-K, A-Q, or A-J from the possible hands that Zewin held. Did he have a medium pair like pocket eights, or pocket nines? It seemed likely to me, and if so, then I was in good shape (only about a 12-to-10 underdog) with my A♣-10♣. Or did he have J-J or 10-10? I didn't think Zewin held J-J. But I was in bad shape with my A♠-10♠ if he did have J-J, or 10-10. I had the chips I needed to make the call stacked up and ready to slide into the pot. Finally, I slid those chips into the pot and called, thinking Zewin had a medium pair. Lott showed 2-2, I showed my A♣-10♣, and Zewin showed 10-10.

Damn, it was 10-10! Bad for me. I was over a 2½-to-1 underdog to win the pot. But I caught the luckiest and most important flop of my life, when it came down A-7-7.

Now I had to hold off a ten or a deuce. I was so nervous now that I couldn't bear even to watch anymore! So I walked over to the edge of the rail, and looked the other way (with a straight face). Jack McCelland was announcing and I heard him say, "The turn card is the queen of hearts." I was thinking, "One more card to go! No ten! No deuce!" McClelland then announced, "And the river is the eight of diamonds, Phil Hellmuth is going to win the pot and eliminate Don Zewin and Steve Lott." Zewin officially finished in third place, because he had started the hand with more chips than Steve Lott had. Chan and I then took a small break as ESPN interviewed Zewin and Lott.

Chan vs. Hellmuth for the World Championship of Poker

And there I was, staring down the two-time reigning World Champion of Poker, Johnny Chan. Chan had a red and blue Fila warm-up suit on (as was the custom and style of the late 1980s), with red on the top half of his chest, and blue on the bottom half of his chest extending down to his waist. The suave Fila warm-up suit had a one-inch-wide white stripe across his chest and back, separating the red and blue. Although I was only one player away from winning it all, that one player was certainly the toughest of them all! I had to get by the best poker player on the planet to realize my lifetime goal of winning the WSOP.

But I didn't lack confidence. I felt as if I was every bit as good as Chan at No Limit Hold 'Em, but with what he had accomplished in the poker world, I wasn't about to underestimate him. If I was as good as, or better than, Johnny Chan at No Limit Hold 'Em, I would have to put up some serious skins on the wall before any else would believe it. When play started back up I whispered to Johnny, "I'm going to play perfect poker. You're going to have to play perfect poker, *and get lucky*, to beat me."

And so the heads up, *mano y mano*, one-on-one match to make history began. With me trying to become the youngest World Champion of Poker in history, and Chan trying to win an unprecedented three consecutive World Championships of Poker. I had 1.2 million in chips vs. Chan's 600,000 when heads-up play began.

We both started out slowly, feeling each other out. I was trying to play small pots until I had a super-strong hand, but Chan didn't mind putting in a lot of chips if he thought he had the best hand. I think Chan may have bluffed me in a pot or two, or maybe I made a good lay-down or two. Back then we didn't record the hole cards, so I'm not sure.

Chan Steps Up his Aggression

About 30 minutes into our match, Chan stepped up his aggression. I could see that he was doing it, but I continued to fold some hands. I decided that my best counter-tactic to his aggression was to move all-in when I was strong, or when I thought that I had the best hand. So I was looking to raise it up, have Chan re-raise it, and then move all-in. Notably, with the blinds still at 5,000-10,000, and 2,000 a man ante, I opened on the button for 40,000 with A♦-7♦. Chan announced, "I raise," and then he made it 130,000 more to go. This was a huge over-the-pot-size raise! Who raises 130,000 into an 84,000 pot? I decided that now was not the time to make my stand, and I folded.

Two Black Nines!

But exactly four hands later, 32 minutes into our heads-up match, I made my move. I was looking down at two black nines, and I could see the writing on the wall. I was going to raise it up, Chan was going to re-raise, and I was going to move all-in. Again, not wanting to change anything from four hands prior, where I folded the A♦-7♦, I opened for 40,000. Chan announced that he was going to raise it up, and I didn't want to move a muscle or give any small indication of what I was going to do next (move all-in). Chan again made it 130,000 more to go. Immediately, I announced, "I'm all-in." Jack McClelland announced that I was all-in, and there was a lot of "oohing" and "aahing" in the room. The fact that Chan didn't call me immediately told me that I had the better hand. But how much the best of it did I have? Did I want to be called or not?

Chan studied for nearly four minutes, and my emotions zigzagged wildly as I calmly (on the exterior anyway) waited for him to decide what to do. I was still as stone, because I didn't want to move my eyes, move my head, move my hands, or utter a single word. The great T. J. Cloutier's advice from the 1988 WSOP (Chapter 12) had seeped in. T. J. told me, "Give away as little information as possible to the great players, just stare at a spot in the middle of the table." No doubt, I was a more mature, and better player than I was only one year before. There was no upside to showing any emotion or movements to a great player like Chan—he would be able to pick whether I was strong or weak if I gave him anything, anything at all. I told myself that I didn't care whether he called or folded. The ball was in his court, and whatever happened, would happen.

My mind wandered; What did Chan have? Was I rooting for him to call, or to fold? I knew that I didn't want to flip a coin for 1.2 million in chips, even though I had another roughly 600,000 left in my stack. In other words, I didn't want Chan to call me if he had two over-cards like K-J, or K-10, Q-J, or A-10, where I was a small favorite to win the pot. I knew that he didn't have a pair higher than mine, or A-K, or A-Q. He would have called instantly with those hands.

I thought about showing strength or weakness to induce a call or a fold. But I ruled that out. After all, I might induce what for me was a wrong move! I had done that before. In the biggest moment of my life, I decided to let it play out and witness it as calmly as possible. Finally, four minutes after I announced that I was all-in, Johnny Chan shrugged his shoulders and said, "I call."

Chan flipped up the A♠-7♠, and I didn't have a great feeling. I was surprised that he was that weak, and yes, I knew that I was now a 2½-to-1 favorite to win the pot, but I had watched Chan get lucky when he really needed it, more than once. As in the last hand of the 1988 Hall of Fame main event in this very room, six months earlier, where I finished sixth, but I knew that Chan had put it all-in with A-10 vs. Jesse Alto's A-J. The flop was ten high! With such a disparity between $755,000 for first place and $300,000 for second place, I wanted to make sure that I at least locked into a big payday. So before the cards were dealt I asked Chan to step outside and talk with me about a deal. We left the room, and I said, "I know that I'm a 2½-to-1 favorite to win this pot. Here is my offer: if I win the title I pay you $100,000, so that you'll make $400,000 minimum, but if you win the title, you give me $200,000, so that I'll make $500,000 minimum." Chan said, "No deal, let's go back and finish this thing." His confidence scared me even more; how could Chan not take that deal? He would be getting way the best of it! The fair save was more like $275,000 to $100,000. How could he say no to $200,000 to $100,000? I said, "Hold up, how about $150,000 to $100,000?" An amazing deal for Chan, he actually studied for a while before he said, "OK, you have a deal."

Deal or No Deal?

Then we walked back into the room, and now Jack Binion, who was standing there, said, "What's going on? I rushed down here as soon as I heard that they stopped the tournament. There's a lot of press here, and I don't want anyone making deals or casting aspersions on the WSOP." Chan knew Jack, and answered, "Nothing, we were just making a save." Binion said, "OK." I said to Chan, "Are we on?" Chan didn't seem to care either way, but he said, "Yes, $150,000 to $100,000."

The flop came down K-10-10. Now Chan needed a king or an ace. The turn card was a queen, and now, with one card to come, Chan needed an ace, a king, a queen, or a jack to win the pot. There were three aces left, three kings left, three queens left, and four jacks left. Chan had 13 wins, and I had 31 wins. I was still roughly a 2½-to-1 favorite, just like I was before the flop, but now it was all on one card. My lifetime goal, my dream of becoming a World Champion of Poker, was hanging on one single card.

Lifetime Goal Achieved!

Amazingly, the last card was the 6♠, and my arms shot up into the air! When I watch the video on YouTube, I see myself raising my arms up in triumphant jubilation, but within seconds I begin to scan the room. Where is my father? And suddenly Dad appears, running up between the stands. There is $1 million in cash on the table and the security guard stops Dad, but I wave him through, and the embrace that I have with my father at that moment was one of the sweetest embraces of my life! Dad tells me how proud he is of me. He tells me how much he loves me. My father is there when I achieve my lifetime goal. To me that's absolutely priceless. Believe it or not, I'm almost in tears right now as I write this. All of the fighting over poker, all of the conflict, disappears in an instant, and never to return.

A few minutes later, as I'm doing interviews for ESPN, and a dozen other assembled media, I look over at my dad, who is earnestly answering questions about me for a reporter. I smile. I know in that moment what it is to be truly happy.

18

The Reigning World Champion Wins More

After I finished up all the interviews, and with a smile plastered on my face, I invited a group of friends to go out for a victory dinner at the Bacchanal restaurant at Caesars Palace Hotel and Casino. At dinner I managed to spend around $1,700, which was by far my biggest dinner bill ever. By the way, we spent a lot of that money on champagne! After my victory dinner ended at the Bacchanal, and I put my father on the red eye flight home, I made my way back to the Horseshoe, where I ran into T.J. Cloutier who said, "I guess you're not 'number 2' anymore, now you're number 1." T.J. managed to bring an even bigger smile to my face than the one that was already plastered on it! In light of the "number 2" nickname that I earned in Malta, it was a really cool thing to say.

By now it was after midnight, and I was still considering whether or not I should rent a private jet for the flight home. On the "do not rent a jet" side I had these points: my dad had already flown home; it was expensive; and my father didn't think I should do it. On the "rent a jet" side of the coin was the fact that in the weeks leading up to the beginning of the WSOP I had told my Madison poker friends, "If you're there when I win it, then I will fly you home with me on a private jet." Even though five of my poker friends were around, only two of them had actually been watching me play at the final table. Still, all five had come out to the epic victory dinner with me afterwards, to celebrate. After another hour of deliberation, I finally decided that I had no choice; I simply had to rent the jet. I kept thinking, "I said I would rent the jet, and I'm a man of my word, thus I must do it!" Plus I figured that I had marked the occasion of achieving a lifetime goal with something special. So I had Susan Albrecht, from the Horseshoe, call around and check out prices, and I ended up renting an eight-seat Lear jet for $6,500.

On a night like this one, you can pretty much forget about sleeping, although I was brutally exhausted from four days of the most intense poker there is. Somehow I pulled off three, or maybe four hours of sleep. On the way to the airport on Friday I grabbed the two major newspapers in town, the *Las Vegas Sun* and the *Las Vegas Review Journal*. The *Las Vegas Review Journal* had a huge picture of me on the front page, top flap, with my arms raised up in victory; and another, smaller picture of Johnny Chan and me standing side by side and smiling while we held over $1 million in cash in our hands. Underneath the big picture, and above the smaller picture the legend said, "'Golden Boy' Plays His Cards Right." I was thrilled with the pictures, with the words "Golden Boy" in the legend, with the size of the pictures and the article (60% of the cover), and with the placement on the cover (and I'm smiling now, 28 years later, as I look at this old newspaper). The *Las Vegas Sun* also had a nice picture on the cover of Johnny and me, but the legend beneath said, "College Dropout Youngest Champ." Why did they have to say "College Dropout"? (The goofy legend reminds me of the newspapers in England.)

Private Jet Home

Gary Miller, Tommy Keisler, Tuli Haromy, and Bill "Porky" Dearth joined me on the jet ride home, and we played low-stakes hearts for the three-and-a-half-hour ride home. I remember looking out the window of the jet, high enough that I could see the curvature of the earth. When I asked the pilot about it, he told me that we were flying at 42,000 feet, 6,000 feet higher than the commercial jets flew. Flying that high made for a spectacular view!

When we landed in Madison, I was greeted at the airport by my mother and my sisters Ann and Molly. The three of them had made a big sign, about ten feet long and two feet high, that said, "Congratulations to the New World Champion of Poker." It was all still so surreal to me, but one thing was certain: I was absolutely thrilled, finally, to have my family 100% behind my poker career.

It was now Friday night, and I took my parents and my sisters out to the best restaurant in town for a big dinner and some Dom Perignon, and we celebrated my victory. On Saturday the *Wisconsin State Journal* had a nice little picture on the cover of someone holding two nines, and five cards behind the nines (K-K-10-Q-6). The legend was "A Big Deal!"

As it turns out, Wayne Tyler was having a $300 buy-in poker tournament on Sunday in Madison at Nora's, and because of all of the excitement in the poker community over my win, we had over 50 players show up to play in it. When I walked in, a few minutes late, as the newly minted World Champion of Poker everyone in the room gave me a standing ovation, and that really made my day. It is one thing to be recognized by the whole poker world, but another to be recognized by the poker players that you came up with. Having just won the WSOP I felt like I had a huge amount of positive momentum, so I bet Dewey Weum $500 at 5-to-1 odds that I would win this tournament as well. When I made it the final table with the chip lead, Dewey paid me $1,250 to settle the bet. I went on to win it, and about $4,000 for first place. This win wasn't about the money. This win was about showing my local group of poker player friends that I was indeed a great player.

Hello London!

A few weeks later, on Friday June 2, 1989, I flew over to London, England, to play in the All England Grand Prix (AEGP) poker tournament that was being held at the Barracuda Club. There were only eight events in the AEGP, and the final event was a £2,500 (£ = British pounds) buy-in – about a $3,800 buy-in No Limit Hold 'Em tournament, but there was also a number of interesting tournaments involving obscure poker games leading up to the main event. They played No Limit Five Card Draw, No Limit Five Card Stud, and No Limit Seven Card Stud Low, and to my knowledge these games were rarely spread anywhere else in the world.

On Wednesday, in the fifth tournament, I finished in second place in the Pot Limit Omaha for £6,000 ($9,291) with around 35 entrants. On Thursday I finished in second place in the No Limit Five Card Stud event for £5,000 ($7,742) with about 30 entrants. I was pleased with this result, because I had only played No Limit Five Card Stud once or twice in my life. On Friday, despite never having played No Limit Five Card Draw before, I finished in third place in the tournament (out of 37 players) for £3,975 ($6,155). Even though I had almost zero experience at these two games, both the Five Card Stud and the Five Card Draw games were No Limit. And in No Limit, no matter what the type of poker game, ideally you want to put the big chips in when you're a big favorite (written "favourite" in London). The players in London were a bit reckless, and often played huge pots when they had a small edge. I was patient, and I waited until I had a big edge, and that served me well. And, the players over there panicked and moved all-in with weak hands when they were short-stacked, and I waited, which allowed me to move up to third place with no chips.

As the reigning World Champion of Poker I was getting a ton of respect in London, and some great press coverage. On Sunday June 11, there was a full-page article about me on page nine of the *Mail on Sunday*. The top flap on page nine blared, "No Kidding the Kid." Apparently being in the *Mail on Sunday* was unprecedented for a poker player, and that kind of coverage was a big deal for the fledgling poker world in the UK. The guys over there were feeling pretty good about that article, and I was too. In fact, I still have a copy!

Yeah Right, Mansour Matloubi will win the 1990 WSOP!

Now let's take a closer look at my second-place finish in the No Limit Five Card Stud tournament. The legendary Seymour Leibowitz won it, and Mansour Matloubi finished in third place. First, let's talk about Mansour. I had a nice run in the AEGP in three tournaments in a row; including a second-place finish, then another second-place finish, and then a third-place finish (£15,000 total). But Mansour's run, in the last three tournaments in a row, was even better when he took a third-place finish (£3,125), then a first-place finish (£13,250), and then a second-place finish in the main event (£16,000). Mansour won more money (£32,375), he had one of his higher finishes in the main event, and he won a title. I'll never forget what I was told by a gentleman one day, while we were playing poker together in a high-limit Five Card Stud side game. He said, "Mansour is the best player in the world, and he will win the WSOP next year." No one over there had minimized what I had accomplished, but I felt minimized by that comment, and frankly I felt incredulous, regarding his prediction. Did this guy think that anyone could waltz in and win the WSOP? C'mon man! I knew that every winner in the 1980s was a great poker player, and I hadn't seen, or even heard of Mansour. Besides, Mansour didn't even play Hold 'Em! But sure enough, Mansour was a great poker player, and he did win the 1990 WSOP. By the way, my boy Hans "Tuna" Lund finished in second place (more on that in Chapter 22) when Mansour won it in 1990.

As to Seymour Leibowitz, he was a legend on the poker circuit. Seymour was a hardnosed player who never, ever, gave away a chip at the poker tables. He was about 5' 10", bald, about 100 pounds overweight, and must have been in his 70s back then. Seymour had a habit of wearing green combat jackets at the table, which suited his game perfectly, because he was a warrior! I believe that Seymour loved the game of poker because he loved to compete. In any case, on this trip to London, Seymour won two of the eight poker tournaments, and he challenged me to play him a heads-up No Limit Hold 'Em match for $10,000. I said, "How about for $5,000?" Seymour agreed. We sat down, and I discovered that I had a big edge when I played him heads up, as Seymour overvalued some hands, and thus lost too much money to me when I had him beat.

As the match marched on, Seymour won a big pot when he overplayed his A-8 vs. my 9-9. Seymour put way too much money in before the flop with his A-8. He was trying to push all-in before the flop, but I chose to wait until after the flop. The flop came down A-Q-2, Seymour moved all-in, I folded, and I flipped my 9-9 face up.

For some reason, Seymour showed me his hand. Perhaps he thought that he could tilt me? It certainly did put me on tilt! I was tilted seeing how badly he had misplayed this hand! I went on a little mini tirade about how badly he played his hand. It sounded something like this:

> *How could you put in the third raise with A-8 offsuit? You know how tight I'm playing! When you raised it up, and I re-raised, then you should have known I had A-8 crushed! You should have folded, not re-raised it! In fact, you had an easy fold. Seymour, if you want to put in your money 2½-to-1 underdog, just let me know, and we'll go to a different table!*

Back in those days in the card rooms in London, you weren't allowed to show any emotion, or even talk about any hands that had been played, or that were happening. So although I felt like using the exclamation points above, and although I pushed it to the limit that I could get away with, I was struggling to keep myself under control.

Twenty minutes later, I had most of my chips back in front of me, and I moved them all-in before the flop with K-K. The cards came down A-8-3-3-7, and Seymour flipped up his hand: 8-8. I said, "You win." Seymour said, "You want to play again?" I said, "Seymour, I'm better than you are in this game, and I'll play you as many times as you want when we get back to the USA, but I'm done playing with you over here, you're too lucky." Then I showed him my pocket kings, and I said, "See, I was a 4½-to-1 favorite this hand for 80% of the chips." Seymour laughed heartily and said, "I don't blame you." When the smoke cleared, I ended up winning about $30,000 in London.

From London to Fargo

My next stop was Fargo, North Dakota, for a small poker tournament with my old buddy Big Al. So I flew to Minneapolis, Minnesota, to meet Big Al and drive with him to Fargo. Knowing that my brother Dave lived in Minneapolis, and that I would hang out with him for a day before we went to Fargo, I picked up a bottle of Louis XIII for him in the London airport. Back then, you could pick up a bottle of Louis at Heathrow for only $350. Over the years in Fargo I had won the first three poker tournaments that I had played in, and this was the fourth. I didn't win this one, but I won around $5,000 in the side games, and I was able to hang out and golf with my brother for another couple of days before I drove back to Madison.

19

Hello to the Love of my Life!

By now I was nearing the end of my lease in the Allen House apartment building (just off of the UW Campus). The building was filled with graduate students, and in my two years of living there I had the following observation: not only did I rarely see anyone else on my floor (the second floor), but I didn't even know what my next-door neighbors looked like! It was one of those buildings, it seems, where everyone had a purpose, and a goal, and where everyone was always in a hurry. There was simply no sense of community because who had the time?

On Monday June 19, 1989, I went out for dinner and drinks with my brother Dave in Minneapolis (end of preceding chapter), and then slept until noon and drove for four hours, back to Madison. I parked my Cadillac in the Allen House garage, and walked up two flights of stairs to the second floor. As I opened the door to the second floor, I looked up and, bam, this beautiful woman turned the corner at the end of the hallway and walked right at me as I continued walking right at her. I noticed that she was tall (5' 10"), thin, and athletic, with medium-length brown hair. I thought, "Whoa, who is this?" Then I said, "Hello," and she replied, "Hello." And that was that. I walked on, turned right at the end of the hallway and walked past the laundry room to my room, which was just down the hall from the laundry room. Less than a minute after I passed her I remembered that this mystery woman was carrying an empty laundry basket. As I arrived at my door, I reminded myself that I still hadn't followed my post-WSOP plan of getting aggressive about meeting new women. (Then I thought, "I haven't had sex in over four years!") My deductive reasoning then kicked in, as I thought, "An empty laundry basket can mean only one thing: she will walk back to the laundry room sometime soon." I wracked my brains to try to remember how long the washer cycle was, and how long the dryer cycle was. I hadn't done my own laundry for a few years by then, but I remembered that it was roughly 45 minutes for the wash cycle, and about 20 for the dry cycle. So she could be back in as soon as 20 minutes!

Locked Out!

I quickly opened my apartment door and walked straight to my bathroom, where I brushed my teeth, shaved, wetted down my hair and brushed it to perfection, washed my armpits and put on fresh deodorant, then changed my clothes and jumped back out into the hallway. As my door slammed shut I suddenly remembered that I had left my room key in the pants I had just changed out of, still in my room. I was locked out!

I ran downstairs to the front desk, but recalled that they didn't keep spare keys there. The woman manning the front desk suggested that I call a locksmith, but I wasn't allowed to use her phone, sigh. At that point I realized that I would have to either call a locksmith, or call my sister Ann (the Special Olympics star), who had a key because I paid her to do my laundry every week. So I ran back upstairs and ducked my head into the laundry room, because I certainly didn't want to miss that girl now, not with all of the extra effort that I was putting into this deal.

For my next move I knocked on my neighbor's door, and he barely cracked the door open – with the lock chain still in place – and said, rather icily, "Can I help you?" I said, "Hi, I'm your next-door neighbor and I locked myself out. Can I please use your telephone?" Then I called my sister Ann (who doesn't have a driver's license), and asked her to give the key to my other sister Molly, who could drive it over to me as soon as possible. It was agreed. While awkwardly standing in the hallway waiting for the mystery girl to make an appearance, I realized that Molly didn't have the credit-card-sized "key card" that would have allowed her to swipe in through security at the front door on the first floor. Now I had to run downstairs every few minutes to make sure that I could let Molly in, but I didn't want to miss this mystery girl either, so I ran back and forth. At this point I was beginning to work up a sweat!

Great Story if You Marry Her

Finally, Molly arrived, with two friends in tow, and they wanted a beer. As the older brother, I didn't mind letting Molly and her friends have exactly one beer, but no more. As the older brother, I wanted to encourage light social drinking, and to discourage Molly from drinking too much – because (in part) it goes against my "winning pyramid." As we sipped on a beer in my apartment, I told Molly and her friends the somewhat embarrassing story of how I had quickly cleaned myself up in my bathroom in anticipation of seeing the mystery girl, and then how I promptly locked myself out. Everyone was laughing heartily when Molly said, "Wouldn't it be something if you married this girl? Whenever anyone asked you how you met, you would have a hilarious story to tell them!" Uh... for real, Molly! By now over an hour had passed since I had seen the mystery girl, and every five minutes or so I managed to walk over and check out the laundry room. Almost ten trips back and forth from my apartment to the laundry room, and there was still no sign of her.

Finally, I walked out into the hallway, and there she was. Now it was time to get aggressive. We chatted awkwardly for a few minutes, and I learned that the mystery girl's name was Kathy (no last names). When a lull hit in our conversation and we said our goodbyes, I added, "Wait a minute; I don't think that I'll see you around here again. Do you want to go to dinner tonight?" Kathy thought for ten long tortuous seconds, and then she said, "No." OK, that was a bad sign, but I needed to stay aggressive. I then asked, "Would you want to catch dinner tomorrow night?" After another ten long tortuous seconds, wherein Kathy appeared to be thinking, she said, "No." Another no, and another one-word answer spelled real trouble in my pursuit of Kathy. I thought, "Stay aggressive, Phil." So I ventured out there one more time and I asked, "Do you want to catch dinner Thursday night?" This time she studied for about 15 seconds, and then finally said, "No, I'm busy." I thought, "OK Phil, being aggressive is fine, but that's it! You've been shot down."

But before I could say anything else, Kathy said, "But I can have dinner on Friday night." I said, "How about seven o'clock?" Kathy said, "That would be fine." How many people with the intent of accepting an offer to go out on a date say no to dinner three nights in row like that? A UW graduate school student does, that's who!

Now, with the date set, Kathy and I continued to talk for a while before she asked, "What do you do for a living?" "Uh, oh," I thought. But I answered, "Now don't judge this, or take it the wrong way, OK?" She said, "OK." I said, "I'm a professional poker player." Kathy was good at bluffing, because her facial expression didn't change one bit when I told her this, but later she told me that she almost canceled our first date because of my profession. She had to be thinking, "This guy does drugs, drinks heavily, is a compulsive gambler, and sleeps until noon." Well, I do sleep until noon!

On Friday night I picked up Kathy in her room, and we walked downstairs and hopped into my Cadillac. We then drove to one of my favorite restaurants, called the Whitehorse Inn. On our way over there, Kathy opened the glove compartment at my request to grab some breath mints, and she saw my gold-plated Cadillac tire changer, which evidently looked a lot like a marijuana pipe. Since I had previously mentioned to her that I wasn't a drug guy, she confronted me about it immediately, and I said, "Look at it a little closer, it's a tire changer!"

Once we hit the restaurant, things started to go more smoothly. At one point, after a couple of glasses of wine, Kathy was telling me the four reasons that she liked something or another. She talked about one point for 90 seconds, and then abruptly said, "And the second reason is..." I thought to myself, "Wow, this girl is really smart." And that was a huge turn-on for me. As the night grew late, I realized that I was really impressed with this Kathy girl, and that this could potentially lead to something big. Kathy was brilliant, sexy, engaging, fun, and driven. Even though I was way into her, when I dropped her off that night I didn't even try to kiss her. I didn't go for the kiss for two reasons: first, I had taken to Kathy so well that I was going to play this one really slow and easy; and second, by then I knew that she had her grad school final exams next week, and thus she wouldn't be around at all for the next week. On top of that, I was leaving town for Las Vegas next Friday. So I knew that I wouldn't see her for a few weeks. Still, there was something special about Kathy, and I knew it from the moment that I met her! She had style, grace, and tons of class, but did she like me?

Back to Vegas

The following Friday I was off to Las Vegas to play in the $10,000 buy-in final event of Bob Stupak's America's Cup Poker Tournament, which was being held at Stupak's Vegas World Casino (Vegas World used to sit on the strip in the same location as the modern-day Stratosphere). Back in the Vegas World days, Stupak would play heads-up poker with anyone, for any amount. As it turned out, Stupak would say no to challenges from the world's best poker players like Chip Reese and Doyle Brunson, unless they happened to want to play his favorite game, No Limit 2-7 Lowball – a game at which Bob was considered to be one of the best in the world. By the way, Stupak was an excellent poker player for decades, and a huge character in Las Vegas until he passed away in 2009. In 1987 he ran for Mayor of Las Vegas, but when he lost, he held a press conference the next day in which he showed up so drunk that he fell over during his speech! I had a lot of respect for Bob, and I played poker with him for decades in Las Vegas.

It was my first trip back to Vegas since I had won the WSOP main event, and things had changed for me drastically. Now everyone in the poker world knew my name, and I showed up with some serious cache and swagger as the reigning World Champion of Poker, and I now had a big target on my back! The number of entries for the America's Cup main event was a very disappointing 14. Thus first place paid $80,000, second place $40,000, and third $20,000. Although the main event was originally scheduled to last three days, we decided to play it in two days. I remember one hand where I dodged a small bullet at the final table vs. T.J. Cloutier. T.J. had raised it up pre-flop with A♦-Q♦, and I called with J♠-10♠. The flop came down J♦-9♦-6♥, and we put all of our chips into the middle of the pot. T.J. was almost a 3-to-2 favorite, but I came out on top when the last two cards came off an eight of spades and a four of clubs. I still remember T.J. mumbling to himself about how he never likes to put his money in on a draw, but we both knew that he was the favorite to win the pot.

In the end, it came down to Poker Hall of Famer Roger Moore and me, and I had a huge chip lead. Roger battled me toe-to-toe for six hours, and I finally got him to commit his chips with 8♣-7♣ on a K♣-10♣-2♦ flop. I had K-Q, the turn card was the deuce of hearts, and thus I had the trophy and the cash in my hands; I just had to dodge a club on the last card. I remember being pretty upset when the last card was Roger's club! I shouldn't have been so tilted; so Roger hit his flush draw, so what? But I was tired from battling Roger for hours, and I was upset that I lost the title on the last card. Even though I still had a nice chip lead, I guess that I was running out of steam, because I pretty much blew it from there. A second-place finish, when I had that kind of a chip lead? Rough, but it hurt more than it should have! I flew home the next day.

Hello Kathy!

One night, about a week later, when I was just chilling in my apartment, Kathy knocked on my door. She said, "I was walking by on my way to the Jacuzzi, and I saw your light on and thought maybe you were home." Kathy had a tight-fitting black Speedo swimming suit on (she looked great in that swimsuit) and she invited me down to the pool with her. I leapt at the chance to chill with Kathy in the Jacuzzi. By then I had been living in the building for almost two years, and yet I had never made it down to the basement for a swim, or to hit the Jacuzzi. While we were hanging out in the Jacuzzi I set up another date with Kathy for the next day. After two more happy dates with her, and still zero attempts at a kiss, she was off on a driving trip to Vancouver with her friends for a few weeks, and before she made it back to Madison on August 4th, I was off to the Bicycle Club for a month for a poker tournament.

I really liked this Kathy girl, but at one date per month, and zero kisses over our first three months of hanging out, this romance was moving at a snail's pace.

The Baller Condo

One of the goals on my lifetime goal sheet, which I had written only a year or two earlier (Chapter 10), was to buy a nice house. So I started looking around

Madison and the surrounding area with a realtor. In the summer of 1989 I was sitting on over $700,000 in cash, but $225,000 of that was set aside to be used to pay income taxes for 1989. As I read through a real estate magazine, one description of a property really piqued my interest, "Penthouse condominium on Lake Mendota with dock slip, underground parking, teak floors, huge balcony, huge master suite with walk-in closet, and every room faces Lake Mendota." When the realtor brought me to see the place, I instantly fell in love. Condo number 701 at The Cove was spectacular! As I toured it I was envisioning turning it into my dream bachelor pad. I decided to buy this dreamy pad, and I put in an offer of $180,000. My offer was accepted (another goal from my lifetime goal sheet accomplished!), and I didn't even bother taking out a loan, I just wrote a check for the entire amount at the closing! I paid for this penthouse with cash, because it seemed like a great place to park cash, and I reasoned that once I paid taxes for 1989, I would at least have a beautiful home for the rest of my life.

I then asked my mom and her good friend Patty Koval to help me furnish the place. They helped me pick out some wonderful furniture that befitted my castle (to me, it was a castle) and a beautiful $4,000 oriental rug that was supposed to be worth $15,000 (my mom gets value, baby!).

Meanwhile, I continued to live in my apartment while I waited for the condo to become habitable. And after a month of waiting, in early September, I decided that enough was enough! I needed to go out right then and there and buy a bed, so that I could move in that day. How could I continue to live in a small apartment when my dream three-bedroom condo was sitting empty? I found the best mattress in Madison for $2,000, and I paid extra to have it delivered that day. That night, I was sleeping in my dream condo. My friends needled me about spending $2,000 on a mattress, but I had the right response to their needling, "C'mon man, I sleep over 10 hours a night, so I spend like 40 percent of my life on that thing!"

I Will Win Best All-Around Player Award

The Bicycle Club was using a quote of mine in their advertising for their month-long (32 events) Diamond Jim Brady Poker Tournament. The quote was, "I am going to win the Best All-Around Player Award at the Diamond Jim Brady this year, and no one can stop me! [signed Phil Hellmuth]." The Bike was giving away $100,000 in prizes to the top-ten points earners in their best all-around player contest at their Diamond Jim Brady Poker Tournament in 1989.

In the very first event (Ace-to-Five Lowball), Johnny Chan finished third, picked up a ton of points, and the race was on! The only problem was that I was never really in the race. Day after day I played in the poker tournaments, and nothing happened; I had no cashes, no final tables, and I wasn't even close to cashing. I was giving it my all, but I was pretty much a one-trick pony back then. I was world class in No Limit Hold 'Em tournaments, but in the other poker tournaments (like Seven Card Stud, Lowball, Omaha, etc...), including Limit Hold 'Em, I was worse than average, never mind world class. Still, I went for it hard for the first 15 days, but then I thought, "Oh well, there is always the side games, and the main event – one of the majors in the poker world – and I am the defending champion!" So I hopped into the side games with vigor and won a pile of money, and then somehow I made it to the final table of the main event. I was down after I fanned in those Diamond Jim Brady events day after day, but now I was at the final table of another poker major! My confidence quickly grew as I realized that I was defending champion, and I was the reigning World Champion of Poker. I would win this thing, and I would show the world how great I was. With first place at $240,000, second place $120,000, and third place $80,000, it came down to Chip Reese (I talk about the late great Chip Reese in Chapter 16), Bob Veltry, and me.

This was the first poker major since the WSOP main event, and the Bicycle Club had stands set up all around the final table, which were filled with people. I took a huge chip lead, and I was well on my way to winning another major when a hand came along that bothers me to this day. I raised it up with A-7 on the button, Chip called from the small blind, and Bob called from the big blind. The flop was 6-5-4, Chip checked, Bob made a big bet, and I studied for a minute. I had options: I could fold, I could call, or I could raise it up. Back then the standard play was to raise it up. A raise would give me a good chance to win the pot, by forcing my opponents to fold their hands, and even if I were called by someone holding say, the 9♣-6♣, then I would be the favorite to win the pot. Against 9-6, I needed a three (4 threes) or an eight (4 eights) for a straight, an ace (3 of them) or a seven (3 of them) for a pair. Still, I even considered folding, but I finally decided that calling was the right play. I called, Chip folded, and the turn was an ace. Now Bob bet out big, and I decided that I had to move all-in. I moved all-in, Bob called me, and I showed my hand. Bob looked at my hand, then he shook his head in disgust and said, "Wow, you really have me in bad shape." Immediately, I realized that he had to have 7-6, 7-5, or 7-4 in his hand; or possibly 8-6, or 8-5. He had to be drawing slim, man! I knew that I didn't want the board to pair, or a seven to come up. Bob picked up his cards, holding them high so that the audience in the stands behind him could see them. Then the dealer dealt a deuce. Suddenly, the audience behind Bob started rising out of their seats, and I was like, "Uh oh, but how did I lose this pot, deuce looked pretty safe to me?" Bob flipped up his hand, an A-3, to claim the pot with a straight.

There was a pile of money in this pot. I would have busted Bob and taken a 6-to-1 chip lead heads up vs. Chip, but at least I still had the chip lead. I tried to stay in the moment, and settled down without too many poker brat antics. Eventually I was back in the flow of the game, and we played for another two hours. Bob was super-aggressive, and I had been letting him steal pots left and right, just waiting for the right time to play back at him.

Finally, I decided to make a stand. Bob popped it up on the button, and I re-raised with 6-5 offsuit, expecting to win the pot right then and there. Bob called, the flop was K-8-7, and now I checked (I had had a great flop for 6-5, an open-ended straight draw). Bob bet, and I put in a big raise. Bob called, and the turn card was a queen. Now I made another big bet, and Bob called. The river was a ten, and I moved all-in. Bob said, "I call," and showed me his hole cards: pocket queens.

I give Bob a lot of credit here for his call on fourth street. It must have been tempting to raise it on fourth street, and protect his hand when he had three queens, but in just calling he allowed me to hang myself with a big bluff on the river!

Make no mistake about my play in this hand: there was no shortage of guts and heart in there! I fired four barrels worth of bluffs, bluffing pre-flop, on the flop, on the turn, and on the river. But along with tons of guts and heart sometimes comes a massive loss, and I had pretty much cost myself the tournament with this crazy, gutsy bluff. So, there it was, a third-place finish and an $80,000 cash prize. Was I unlucky to have lost that big pot to Bob to a river deuce? Yes, I was, but so what. I still needed to close better. That was my tournament to win, and, I should have grinded it out and won it. I should have trapped the super-aggressive Bob when I had the Q-Q, not bluff him when I had six-high. Still, I didn't completely blow it like I had at Vegas World; in this case, I just misfired on a big bluff.

Midnight Blue Porsche

Before I left LA, a friend of mine told me that he had a Porsche for sale. It was midnight blue, with a racing clutch, it was in perfect condition, and it was fast, fast, fast! Another cool effect was that at night the car looked black. By now, I was winning $120,000 for the trip between the side games and the tournaments, and I decided to buy the car for $35,000. I really loved that car, and *man* was it fun to drive! I also learned a few lessons while I owned it. If I was driving 90 miles per hour in my conservative gray Cadillac, then the police would let me go. But, if I was going 75 miles per hour in the Porsche, then I would get a ticket every time. I lost my license for a while because of that car! By the way, I asked a couple of police officers why they ticketed cars like my Porsche more often, and I was told that it was because they were sick of pulling bodies out of fast cars that had crashed!

When I returned to Madison, Kathy was back in graduate school, and I was still living in my apartment for another week or two. Now it was time to get this relationship thing rolling! I took Kathy out on our fifth date, and still I didn't try to kiss her. But the very next night, on our sixth date, I took her to my new condo (still no bed), and then took her to the dock, right at twilight, and I asked her if I could kiss her, and she said yes. By now, I was ready to speed up any, and all, physical contact! But now it was Kathy who slowed things down. We started dating three times a week, or more, when I could get her to go out, but she was in grad school and she took it very seriously.

Energy Match? Magical...

Do opposites really attract? Kathy and I often talk about what happened one night at her apartment in September 1989. It may sound a little strange, but the energy when we touched was absolutely incredible! It was like we were opposite magnets in close proximity; we were drawn to each other, and it felt absolutely amazing when we touched or hugged. This weird energy thing really threw us for a loop. What did it mean? I have no reasonable explanation for it to this day, but I do feel that we're perfect for each other, and that the two of us were opposites in a lot of ways.

Is there an explanation in physics? Like opposites attract? I don't think so, but we certainly were opposites. Kathy is born January 17, and I'm born exactly six months away, July 16.

Kathy had never received a grade less than an A, I had rarely received a grade as good as an A. Kathy gets up early every day, I try to sleep in, every day. Kathy has a huge sense of responsibility, whereas I couldn't even get myself to pay my bills on time. Kathy always shows up on time, I never show up on time (back then, especially). Kathy likes to be on a schedule, I like to be spontaneous. Kathy isn't sure things will always go well in her life, and I feel that things will always be just fine in my life. I feel that I will always have tons of money and security. Kathy hates to write, I love to write. Kathy is patient and measured, and I am impatient and impulsive. Kathy is more or less an only child; there are five kids in my family. Kathy is quiet, I'm loud. Kathy has advanced emotional intelligence (EQ) and empathy, and I've had a hard time giving anyone empathy. Kathy has no ego, and I have a huge ego. Kathy is financially conservative, whereas I take some chances with my money (not as much in 2017!). Kathy went to Las Vegas with other grad school students to protest nuclear bomb tests, I went to Las Vegas to play poker and stay in big suites. Kathy hates the spotlight, I love the spotlight. So is it possible that our puzzling "energy attraction" had anything to do with opposites attracting? I'm a romantic, and I prefer to think that our energy attraction was about the two of us being in love, meeting our match!

Kathy and I also had a lot in common. We were both driven, we both value family highly and are family oriented, we both wanted children, we were both liberal (back then), we are both loyal, we are both highly principled, we are both smart, we are both logical, we are both independent, and neither of us holds a grudge (we are both forgiving). One more: we are both dragons on the Chinese calendar, and the Chinese say that dragons get along really well.

Around this time I brought Kathy home to meet my parents, which was a significant event for me, because she was the first girl that I ever took home with that in mind. It was apparent to all of us that she would fit into our family like a glove fits on a hand. When Kathy entered my folks' house and sat down on the couch, she soon met my mother, and they hit it off immediately, discussing art and politics. My mother is an artist, and most of Kathy's friends were artists. Kathy tells me now, "When I walked into your parents' house that day, I immediately felt like this was the kind of home that I had envisioned for my future." It's an older house, located right on Lake Mendota, and it's filled with woodwork, antique furniture, and artwork, and to me it was the quintessential professor's abode. As we chatted with my mom, the two got along instantly, and they could easily discuss art, meditation, and our interests in other cultures.

Then my father invited Kathy outside to see the backyard, and while they strolled around he casually probed into her academic background, asking, "So hon, you're in grad school at the UW, very good. Where did you go to undergraduate... University of Chicago! Well you're all right then, I'm a Chicago man myself."

My wife says:

> When I mentioned UC, he put his long arm around my shoulder and gave me a hug. That was all your father needed to know about me. I was welcome in as far as he was concerned! Of course, then, you left town for Las Vegas, and I attended your grandmother's birthday party at your parents' house, without you. I must say that I was shocked when they made your 75-year-old grandmother finish eating her birthday cake underneath the table, because she talked after eating a bite! [In my family, if you talk after you eat a bite of your own birthday cake, then you go under the table to finish your piece of cake, no exceptions!]

After our magnetic night, Kathy was back in town pretty much every day to attend grad school, I continued my pursuit of her by asking her out every night for the next month. Although Kathy was busy with grad school, we managed to make it out to dinner at least three times a week. The more we dated, the harder I fell for Kathy! By now, I was feeling pretty good about my life. In October 1989 I was the reigning World Champion of Poker, I had a beautiful penthouse condominium along Lake Mendota, I had a Cadillac, and midnight blue Porsche, and a top of the mark girlfriend. The goal sheet that I had written only two years earlier was now nearly empty! The only goal remaining was to write a *New York Times* best-selling book. In 1993, I decided that I wanted to be the greatest poker player of all time, and I placed that goal on the top of my list. My 14 WSOP wins is a good start, but I need 24 WSOP wins, and I need to win a few WPT titles.

As my relationship with Kathy turned hot, I invited her to come to Las Vegas with me for a long weekend, and we flew to Vegas on Thursday November 17, 1989. Kathy was there for just the weekend, but I was staying on in Las Vegas for the grand opening of Steve Wynn's spectacular Mirage Hotel and Casino, on Wednesday November 22, 1989. Back then, it was widely reported in the press that Wynn needed to make $1 million a day at the Mirage in order to pay off his construction loans in the next eight years, but the Mirage did so well that Wynn paid off his loans in 18 months! Right after the Mirage opened, I was scheduled to fly to LA to get on a poker player cruise (my second of the year) that had planned stops along the west coast of Mexico at Puerto Vallarta and Mazatlan.

Upon our arrival in Las Vegas I rented a nice spa suite at the Golden Nugget Hotel and Casino (I was back at the Golden Nugget again) and over the weekend Kathy and I caught some shows and hit a few of the nicest restaurants in Las Vegas, before the trip ended badly for our relationship.

I Drop the Ball with Kathy

On Sunday night I found myself involved in a high-stakes poker game across the street from the Golden Nugget, in the poker room at the Horseshoe Hotel and Casino (where I had won the WSOP main event a few months back). A few of us were playing Pot Limit Omaha with $10-$25 blinds. And 1986 World Champion of Poker Berry Johnston (both of our pictures were on the wall as world champions) was also in the game, and I was pretty buried as time flew by. (One common flaw that almost every poker player shares is this one: we have trouble quitting when we are losing!)

Now I knew that Kathy would be leaving the next day at 10:45 a.m., and I made a mental note to myself to make sure that I made it over to the suite by 8 a.m. to have breakfast, and then I would escort her to the airport. But at 8 a.m. I was losing $5,000... and then I was back to breaking even in the game... and then I was losing $6,000, and then it was 8:30 a.m. I decided that that was OK, that it was 8:30 a.m.; I would miss breakfast but still escort Kathy to the airport. I told myself that ten more minutes were fine, and then suddenly it was 9 a.m., and I was losing $8,000. Just a few more minutes of play, I thought, and then suddenly it was 9:30 a.m. and I reasoned that Kathy must have left for the airport by now (cell phones and pagers hadn't become hot yet). So I completely blew off my wonderful girlfriend Kathy, and I felt horrible about it!

I ending up losing $14,000 in the poker game when Berry busted me on the K-6-5 flop, and I shoved too much money in with my A-A-Q-7. Berry had 8-5-5-4 in his hand (he had three fives), and I remember the hand well, because a few of the poker players in the room were taking a piece of Berry in the game, and they were screaming for a seven to come off the deck so that Berry would make a straight, and then I couldn't even hit my ace to make trips and beat his trip fives and win the pot. The last card was a seven and this provoked a cascade of celebration in the room! Even though I still had a lot more money with me, I wisely quit the game at around 2 p.m. As I left the poker room, utterly exhausted, I wondered, "What have I done?"

The next night I checked into a nice suite at the Mirage for the grand opening. My suite was facing the volcano in front of the hotel that went off every 30 minutes or so. Back in 1989, it was quite a sight to behold. One reason I was there was that Steve Wynn always had a poker room in his casinos, and it was important that the poker players support his efforts. As reigning World Champion of Poker, I was supposed to be downstairs for a ceremony that would open the poker room for business. But here I was, in my room, and didn't know where I was supposed to go, or when I was supposed to be there, so I waited for them to call me. But no call ever came! No problem, I was happy in my suite, and I was happy that poker had a home in the world's swankiest casino. By the way, I'm sure that I was handed an invitation to the poker room opening, but I lost the darn thing. After two days at the incomparable Mirage, where I mostly slept, I headed off to LA to catch my poker cruise.

I was now the champ, and this time around I was going to win big on the poker cruise. There would be no losing, and for certain I wouldn't lose $57,000 (out of my last $75,000!), like I did on the poker cruise in April. But just like last time, I started losing money right away on the cruise. I'm not sure if I was cheated, but I don't think so. This time around I wasn't playing with known cheaters. Instead, I was playing with a more honest group of guys, like poker legend Chip Reese, who was considered the absolute best poker player – in the side games – in the world. So it wasn't surprising that I lost money to him! Also onboard, playing high-stakes poker with me, were Yosh Nakano, Ralph Rudd, David Shue, and a few other seasoned cash game veterans. These guys were all tough players! Along with the high-stakes poker, a high-stakes backgammon game developed on this cruise. As it turned out, my roommate, Tommy Keisler – an old poker friend from Madison – had some serious backgammon skills. Eventually, I decided to take a shot at staking Tommy in the high-stakes backgammon games. I thought, "Why not, I might lose like $10,000 at $100 a point, but if Tommy wins, then perhaps he will win hundreds of thousands of dollars." As it turned out, Tommy was about equal with Chip at backgammon, but much better at backgammon than Yosh was.

As my poker losses mounted – I think I lost every single day – my backgammon wins rolled in! At first, the game was $100 a point, and then Chip dropped out, to spend more time with his family. Yosh owed us $18,000, and then Tommy told me that he was out of Yosh's league at backgammon, and we upped the stakes to $200 a point. By the end of the cruise they were playing for $300 a point, and Yosh owed us $47,000. Yosh was frustrated, and threw the board on multiple occasions. Apparently, Tommy had lucky roll after lucky roll, right at the end of the games, when he really needed them; and this augmented his skill advantage. But Yosh could see only the "lucky roll" side of the equation, and not the tactical advantage that Tommy had on him. At the end of the cruise I owed the boys $50,000 for my poker losses on this cruise, although Yosh agreed to pay $27,000 of those for me off of the $47,000 that he owed me.

During the cruise I called Kathy two or three times, but every time I called her, her machine answered.

20

December 2, 1989, Magical! Marriage Already?

The poker cruise pulled into the harbor in Los Angeles on the morning of December 2, 1989. While Tommy (who had made me $47,000 playing backgammon on the cruise) was driving me from the harbor over to Los Angeles International Airport to catch my flight, I spotted a pay phone, and I asked him to pull over. I simply had to call Kathy! I really missed her, and I had talked about her way too much on the cruise ship while Tommy patiently listened to me. So, I picked up the pay phone and called Kathy's apartment, and she picked up. I told her that I was mortified about how things had ended so badly for us in Vegas (Chapter 19), and that I would love to take her to dinner that night. Her preference: she would pick me up from the airport and cook dinner for us at my place.

Magical Night!!

When we hit my penthouse, the whole night seemed magical. While we ate Kathy's home-cooked gnocchi dinner, I told her that I wanted to take things more seriously. I told her that I wanted to commit to her, fully, and she responded likewise, that she wanted to commit to me on similar grounds. We were both happy, and after the way we had parted in Vegas, we were both relieved. After dinner, we made it into the bedroom. Old gypsy lore says that when you get someone pregnant, the "earth spins." I can tell you now, first hand, that it felt like that to me! It really was as if I was spinning around outside of my body, or something weird and hard to explain. Whatever it was, it was wonderful! It was a stunning experience, and we have talked about that night for decades since. Kathy and I had a happy week after that, but I headed back to Las Vegas for the Hall of Fame poker tournament at Horseshoe Hotel and Casino, on December 12th.

While I was playing high-stakes poker in Las Vegas, Kathy was back in Madison studying for exams, except that something weird was happening to her. Suddenly, for no apparent reason, she couldn't drink coffee anymore! Kathy wondered how that could happen, especially when she was pulling all nighters studying for her rigorous medical school exams.

Meanwhile, I was getting crushed at the poker tables again! I risked way too much money on the first day in town, and lost every dollar that I had brought to Las Vegas with me: $26,000. And things got worse from there. On my second day in town I borrowed $20,000 from Hall of Fame poker player Puggy Pearson, and I lost that in short order playing No Limit Deuce-to-Seven Lowball. Then I threw my "winning pyramid" principles into the garbage when I decided, "OK, now it's time to make a stand against this losing streak. I will wire every remaining dollar that I have left in my poker account into town, and I will find a way to win, period." I reasoned that I performed better when my back was against the wall, which was true, but risking 100% of my bankroll in one trip was clearly a horrendous notion. It's a good thing that I set aside the money to pay my taxes in a separate account, because I wired in everything else (about $90,000).

By the end of the trip I had lost it all! I was back to feeling down and depressed, and my ego was in such a state of shock that I'm sure that I wasn't much fun to be around.

Wasn't I the reigning World Champion of Poker? Wasn't I a poker superstar? How could this happen to me? It happened because my ego was bursting at the seams! I had the amazing Kathy, I had a main event title, I had a beautiful penthouse condominium with a spectacular view, I had a midnight blue Porsche with a racing clutch, a beautiful gray old-school Cadillac, and I had trophies in my trophy case. I also had an ego the size of Wisconsin. How else could it go? In two short years, I went from rags to riches, from struggling college drop-out to reigning World Champion, from a lifetime of low esteem to mega-success. It could have been worse, my ego could have led me to dark places, like alcohol abuse or drugs, but instead it led me to poor money management, and I always preach that money management is more important than poker talent.

On the plus side, I owned my condo, and my cars outright, and I had my taxes from 1989 covered. Basically, I had $250,000 in assets free and clear. All in all, it was a great year for me, but there was no excuse for losing that kind of money that quickly. The idiom "easy come, easy go" comes to mind.

When I arrived back home in Madison on December 22nd I called Kathy at her mother's house in Pewaukee, Wisconsin (near Milwaukee), and she told me that she couldn't drink coffee anymore, and that she was eating foods that she rarely ate before. Kathy now ate fruit like three times a day, she hated mayonnaise, and she liked steak! We both understood what the wonderful earth-spinning love making on December 2 probably meant, but Kathy hadn't taken a pregnancy test yet. I encouraged her to take a test as soon as possible, and get back to me. On December 24, Kathy called me to tell me that she was pregnant. My brother Dave and I had talked extensively about the possibilities of Kathy being pregnant over the last two days, and I was ready to act. I told Kathy that I was hopping into my car and driving to her mother's house right away (Pewaukee is about 70 miles from Madison).

I arrived at her mother's house and asked Kathy to marry me. But she didn't look as if she wanted to marry me! Maybe Kathy was thinking that I was egotistical (but loyal), cocky (but honest), self-centered (but loving), unstable (but well principled), and that I bordered on narcissism (you try winning the main event with low self-esteem!). Kathy later told me that she thought of me as her "knight in shining armor" when I rushed over to her mother's house so quickly.

There was no doubt that Kathy thought I was eventually going to be a diamond, but also no doubt that she saw a lot of coal in me. She undoubtedly knew that I still needed to be pressed from coal into a diamond.

I believe that Kathy and I would have been married eventually, but this kid in the making, forced our hand. We made to move our wedding date up! After a few days of pondering and planning, Kathy decided to accept my proposal.

Meanwhile, my brother Dave was planning a surprise engagement party at my place, on New Year's Eve. He would ask his long-time girlfriend to marry him, at 8 p.m., and Kathy and I would celebrate with them until late. Then, with Dave's blessing, it would be a double engagement party!

Phil's $12,000 in "Show Money" Stolen by Friends?

We had one hell of a party at my condo on New Year's Eve! We were celebrating a new year, a new decade, and two engagements. I made sure that we had a lot of cold Dom Perignon in the place, but Kathy couldn't drink any of it. And, because I was leaving for Lake Tahoe with Kathy for a poker tournament on January 3, I had secured $12,000 in cash, and it was stashed in my condo somewhere. Because I had lost so much money in mid-December in Vegas, I had to free up about $25,000 from my underfunded pre-paid taxes account. After all, I could subtract poker losses from poker winnings in 1989, so less winnings meant I had to pay less taxes.

I remember seeing that $12,000 and thinking, "I should really put that money away. But then that would seem to show that I don't trust people, and I don't want to think that way tonight." Weird thought, but then my ego was acting up quite a bit. And the money was in my walk-in closet in my private bedroom. Even though I knew everyone at the party, somehow the money disappeared! Best not to tempt people, even your friends! There just weren't that many people there capable of pocketing the money, but what was I going to do? Ask everyone who was still there when I discovered the theft to turn out their pockets?

It occurred to me that in my youth, eight years ago, I had stolen a gold necklace worth exactly $1,200 (Chapter 2). That old 10-to-1 rule that I postulated as a gambler seemed to have come back to bite me! My 10-to-1 rule: if you win money playing games of chance (craps, blackjack, slot machines, roulette) when you first play those games, then you will lose back at least ten times what you have won initially. Considering how low I was on cash at the time, that $12,000 theft really put a damper on my evening. Worse, my poker friends teased me for months about how my "show money" was stolen! "Yeah, right!"

21

Our Wedding and Honeymoon Cross Paths

As 1990 began, Kathy and I began discussing possible dates, and places (a church?), wherein to stage our upcoming wedding. Because Kathy would clearly be pregnant, and showing, when we staged our wedding, we joked about the concept of a "shotgun wedding": a wedding where the pregnant woman walks up the aisle, while her father holds a shotgun on the groom to make sure he doesn't leave! Jokes aside, we both thought it a good idea to get married before we gave birth, as some religious folks may have held it against us if we gave birth before we were married. My grandmother, Agnes Slattery, was devoutly Catholic, and everyone in the family was so afraid to tell her that Kathy was pregnant.

When I finally told grandma Slattery that Kathy was pregnant, with all of my siblings present, we all held our collective breath! We were all expecting her to sermonize, regarding Catholic doctrine about how you were *not* supposed to have sex before you were married. But grandma, god bless her soul, snapped back saying, "I'm happy that you didn't use birth control!" We were all pleasantly shocked, and greatly amused. Grandma had ignored one Catholic principle, and invoked another one (no birth control). I didn't want to ruin the memorable moment by mentioning that we had used not one, but two forms of birth control!

Kathy and I are both more or less spiritual, but neither of us is religiously denominational (I was raised Catholic), so she suggested a Unitarian church. The church was the very church that her parents had been married in, in Madison, and I agreed. Kathy chose Saturday March 31, 1990, as the big day, and she wanted the two of us to write our own nuptials. For my part, I wanted the ceremony to be reasonably short, and I wanted it to end the wedding with a jolt. I wanted to end it with a rock song. (I disliked long, drawn-out, ceremonies!) I selected my favorite song, "Free Fallin'," by Tom Petty and The Heartbreakers, and Kathy agreed... Until a month later when she listened closely to the "bad boy" lyrics!

Whoops! So we chose Bobby Brown's "Every Little Step," and this song succeeded.

Since we were having a big ceremony, and most of the guests were my friends and family, I asked Kathy's mother Margaret if I could pay for the wedding. Traditionally, the wife's family pays for the wedding, and the groom's family pays for the rehearsal dinner. I insisted on paying for both.

The Wedding

As my brother and I arrived at the Unitarian Church on March 31, 1990, the first thing I noticed was that my Porsche was covered with a few "just married" signs, some streamers, and some cans (nice). We were hoping for sunshine, but instead it rained steadily most of the day. I'm told that rain on your wedding day means that you will be prosperous, so bring on tons of rain! Twenty minutes into the ceremony, at the appropriate time, "Every Little Step" came booming onto the sound system at the church, to end the ceremony. Apparently, my friend Gary Miller had accidently had the sound cranked up way too high, and it jolted energy into the assembled crowd. I loved it! Twenty minutes in, boom, loud music, and we were off to our wedding reception filled with energy. (I had knocked off another goal from Chapter 10's lifetime goal sheet: meet and marry a wonderful woman!)

When I drove us over to the reception in the Porsche, my fast, semi-reckless driving (safe driving to me) managed to upset Kathy. I reasoned that it was the only time in my life when I could drive crazy (because of the "just married" signs) and not get pulled over! Not my smartest move, but things picked up quickly from there with lots of speeches, and merriment, until well past midnight.

The Honeymoon and the Cat

The next day Kathy and I were off to Hawaii for two weeks for our honeymoon. Upon landing in Maui at dusk, I went off script and rented a small propeller plane to fly us across the island to Hana, and thus avoid the dangerous road along the cliffs. We had been hearing horror stories about this treacherous 90-minute drive, but I asked the pilot to come back twice more. First, to give us a private plane tour of the island; second, to fly us back at the end of our trip (no need for us to be on that dangerous road, ever!).

We checked in at the Hotel Hana Maui Resort and Spa, and began walking down to our private cottage in the dark, when we ran into an attention-seeking, but sweet, Calico cat. There was something about this cat... we seemed to bond with the cat immediately. As I picked the cat up, I quickly realized that the cat was very pregnant! At this moment, Kathy pointed out that keeping the cat was not a good idea, because a pregnant woman shouldn't be in contact with cat feces (it can lead to birth defects). I understood, we simply couldn't keep the cat. But this cat was not going to be rejected easily, and she proceeded to follow us all the way (for 150 yards) to our honeymoon cottage. I had never seen, or heard of, a cat following (unknown) people for hundreds of yards! I had also known cats to be fiercely independent. I wanted to keep the cat inside our room, but Kathy put her foot down. Instead, we ordered milk for the cat from room service, and put the milk on the doorstep.

That first night of our honeymoon in the cottage was intense, and I'm not talking about the intimacies (we were both tired from traveling all day). The most intense thunderstorm of my life was raging outside our little cottage. The walls of the cottage were made of little more than linen cloth that retracted up in the day time.

The lightning cracked, the rain deluged down, and the 40-mile-an-hour wind blew hard off the ocean and rocked our little linen-walled cottage. The linen was battened down tight, but even then it flapped wildly in the stormy wind.

In the morning, Kathy woke up with a start, and a shout. There was something in our bed next to her! Upon examination, it was the pregnant cat. I decided to take a long look around the room, and I couldn't, for the life of me, figure out how this cat had managed to gain entrance into our cottage. Kathy reiterated that we couldn't keep the cat, and so we ordered a bowl of cream and put it outside the door with the cat. (But there was something about that cat...)

Kathy is a Doctor, But Not a Gynecologist, Right?!?

Five days later, I went for a horseback ride with the plan of meeting Kathy on the beach for a luau (a traditional Hawaiian feast accompanied by entertainment) that the hotel was putting on. Kathy was two hours late, and a little shaken when she finally showed up. Apparently, the cat had showed up on our bed, in our cottage, and tried to give birth! Kathy could see that the cat was struggling mightily, and she called a veterinarian. The vet told Kathy that the cat would die if it couldn't finish the birthing process. The vet further instructed Kathy that she would have to reach into the cat and pull the first of the litter out, if she wanted to ensure that the cat would live. So Kathy pulled the first of the litter out, and then three other kittens quickly popped out!

According to Kathy, the cat and the kittens were resting comfortably, back in our room, and the hotel staff had already changed the bloody covers and sheets. What could we do? This cat had clearly chosen us. So, we boarded the cat and kittens with a local veterinarian, and flew them home with us, to live in our condo with us! I named the mother cat Kakeeyu (Ka-kee-you), and Kathy named its male black offspring, the one we eventually kept along with the mother, Molokai. I would be the one to change the litter box... A few months later, we found nice homes for the other three kittens in Madison.

22

It's a Boy!

From my poker point of view, the 14 events of the May 1990 WSOP didn't yield much for me, so I was looking forward to the Bike (Bicycle Club) and its month-long schedule of poker tournaments in August. But for my boy Hans "Tuna" Lund, who had been my traveling companion from Malta (Chapter 15), the 1990 WSOP main event represented his chance to achieve a lifetime dream. Just 13 months before, Tuna thought that I was crazy to predict that I would win the 1989 WSOP, but then he witnessed me do exactly that. Did Tuna have extra belief in himself after that? I'm sure he did. And, so, Tuna made it down to heads-up to play vs. Mansour Matloubi, and hence to be crowned World Champion of Poker.

In a classic poker hand, Tuna had A-9, and Mansour 10-10, and on a flop of 9-4-2, they both put all of their money into the pot. Mansour was a huge favorite, but if Tuna won this pot, he would be 1990 World Champion of Poker, and retain the title of World Champion forever. Stunningly, the turn card was the ace of spades, and the packed room screamed approval for the beloved Tuna Lund. All-in, with one card to come, and with Mansour drawing to a ten, or it was over. There were two tens left in the deck for Mansour, leaving 42 cards from which Tuna would win the 1990 World Championship, but alas for Tuna, the ten hit and Mansour went on to win. Tuna, a poker legend, never did win the World Championship before he passed, but he left his mark on the poker world, emphatically.

Family First, Even If…

Poker is my life, but I've always been a family man, and the birth of our first child trumped everything else. Kathy would give birth, and I would be there; no matter what. As I pondered what that might mean for me, I realized that there was now some chance that I would miss the Bike's main event, which got under way August 30, 1990. This poker major was one of the most important of the year, and I had won it in 1988 (Chapter 13), and then finished third in 1989 (Chapter 19). I had had great history there, and I didn't want to miss this one. But I wasn't worried, for Kathy was due August 19, 1990, and the Bike main event was scheduled for August 30th.

As August 19th came and went, I started to consider the possibilities. One option, which I loved, was to fly to LA on the 29th, play in the Bike's main event on the 30th, and fly home whenever I was eliminated, or won it (on the 31st). Or I could hop on a private jet when Kathy went into labor. Since I had flown on my first private jet after I won the WSOP World Championships (Chapter 17), I knew that that was an option. So I told Kathy about my burgeoning plan, stressing that the private jet could have me back within eight hours of her going into labor.

But she was not impressed with my plan! August 29th came and went, and I resigned myself to the fact that I would miss the Bike's main event. I was bummed out at having to miss it, but I had proved to everyone else, and more importantly to myself, that family truly was first for me. Meanwhile, the legendary T.J. Cloutier (Chapter 16) won the Bike's main event in 1990, and oh, by the way, T.J. won it again in 1991, and once more in 1992! What a legend.

Finally, on September 7, 1990, after being over two-and-a-half weeks late, and after an arduous 24-hour-long labor, Kathy and I welcomed a healthy son into the world. We decided to name our son Phillip Jerome Hellmuth III. It was a great day for Kathy and me, and I was happy. As a couple of weeks flew by, I believe, I was in shock, and I retreated from my young family. Over the next ten months, I found myself traveling a lot, and when I was home, I seemed to be busy playing Nintendo's Super Mario Bros. all night long, golfing, playing basketball, and playing a lot of hours in the local poker games.

Looking back now, it made sense. By that I mean that the changes were huge, and the pace of change was fast, fast, fast. In a couple of short years, I went from struggling young poker player to World Champion of Poker, from living in an average apartment to living in a beautiful penthouse condominium, from having no girlfriend for four years, to being married with child, from driving an old Buick to driving both a new Cadillac and a sporty Porsche. And I didn't abandon Kathy and Phillip, not even close, but I certainly wasn't around as much as I would have been had we had a child when I was, say, 30 years old.

When Phillip turned 10 months old, I was fully present once again. Day after day I would wrap Phillip up tightly, put him in his car seat, and then tell him exactly what we were going to do for the next three or four hours. I was never sure he understood me, but I thought he did, and I wanted him to know what his next few hours looked like. I suspected, in any case, that this routine was good for him. It would go like this, "Phillip, first we are going to grab some food at Panini House, then we are going to the bank to grab some money, then we are going to the post office, and then I'll drop you off back home with the nanny." And with the trappings of success, I thoroughly enjoyed buying Phillip the best fine clothing, and giving him the nice things that I didn't have when I was a kid.

The 1991 WSOP, Nothing to Report

The May 1991 WSOP came and went, and in those 17 open tournaments (up from 14 in 1990), it didn't seem that I had done anything special. Brad Daugherty won the 1991 WSOP main event and became a World Champion of Poker. And Tuna Lund had staked him! So, Tuna made a bunch of money, and was there to witness his best friend become a World Champion of Poker. I'm sure it was bittersweet for Tuna, but mostly sweet! I sensed that I had been a small influence on the outcome, for Brad had been traveling with me and Tuna Lund in Malta (Chapter 15) when I proclaimed that I would win the 1989 WSOP. They both had laughed at me for a week, but then I won it in 1989, Tuna finished second in 1990, and Brad won it in 1991 (positivity!).

My First Hall of Fame Poker Classic Watch

In October 1991, I was back in Las Vegas at the Horseshoe Hotel and Casino to play in the Hall of Fame Poker Classic, and I crushed it! I made four final tables in one week, and I won my first Hall of Fame Watch! I finished in the top four in all four Hall of Fame tournaments: on October 26th, I finished in third place in the $1,500 Limit Ace-to-Five Lowball Draw; on October 27th, I finished fourth in the $2,500 No Limit Deuce-to-Seven Lowball; on October 30th I won the $1,500 buy-in Pot Limit Hold 'Em tourney for $80,400, when I beat a field of 134 players; and on November 4th I finished fourth in the $2,500 Pot Limit Omaha. The Hall of Fame watches were only a little bit behind the WSOP bracelets in stature, and I had one in the bag!

A More Nuanced Meaning of Family, Support, and Love?

In March 1992 I learned a real lesson. I had been playing Pot Limit Hold 'Em in Madison, Wisconsin, and I was up $3,500 at 2 a.m., when the game broke down to just three of us. It was a good, natural, normal time to quit; take a win, and go home. But part of me said, "You just lost a $2,600 pot that you were a big favorite to win. You've been playing great poker, and you're not up as much money as you deserve to be. These guys have chips, and you might as well stay and play awhile." My old friend Big Al Emerson had $4,200, and Matt Cooney had $3,800. I stayed, and by 2 p.m., 12 hours later, I was losing a Madison record $17,400, and couldn't take it anymore. So, I quit. The lowlight of that night was when I tried to bluff Big Al out of a pot when he held four nines!

Even though I had a $150,000 cash bankroll, I kept needling myself about setting the new record loss for a poker game in Madison. I knew what the records were, and no one had ever lost over $10,000 before. If I was going to set the Madison record for biggest loss, then I was going to punish myself for it, so that it wouldn't happen again. I hate losing anyway, and I was in a bad mood and beating myself up, and I refused to let myself off the hook, and thus I felt an ever-growing level of pain and frustration. I told myself that it might take six months for me to win that much back in the local Madison poker games. I wasn't feeling self-destructive, but I was close; the thought that I should crash my car, not violently, but slowly, into a wall, flashed through my mind. I didn't want to hurt myself, but still, that dark vision flashed through my mind, and even though it quickly vanished, it was shocking! I was in a foul mood on the 25-minute drive home.

When I opened the door to my condo, my negativity was near its peak, and Phillip came running up to me and shouted, "Daddy!" Instantly, I fell to my knees to hug him. The second I held Phillip in my arms, the negative energy began to dissipate. As I held Phillip tightly, all I thought was, "I'm so blessed to have this perfectly healthy son!" After ten seconds of hugging, all of that brutal, negative energy had dissipated, and I felt only thankfulness, and positivity. It was as if I was waking up suddenly, and clearly seeing all the blessings: love, family, a World Championship of Poker, a beautiful penthouse, smooth cars, and a lot more. I was shocked, and pleasantly surprised, at the quick transition. One hug from my 18-month-old son, the power of family, had instantly trumped one of the worst moods of my life.

Not surprisingly, I didn't have $17,000 in cash with me the night that I lost, but I agreed to meet Big Al any time he wanted, so that I could pay him the balance of cash that I owed him. Al lived in La Crosse, Wisconsin, but seeing as how he had won $25,000 that night, and I owed him $15,000, he was happy to stick around for a couple days to collect the cash from me. I decided to take a few weeks off from poker to recover from that loss. It felt like a wise move, but Big Al suggested that we play again in two days. Since I had to drive across town to meet Al to pay him off anyway, I decided to play. I thought it would be smart to risk only $2,500. If I lost, then I would quit.

Somehow, someway, I won $14,000! Sometimes, when I'm focused on pro-tecting my bankroll, and I'm once again worried that I might lose a lot of money, my hyperfocus emerges. Hyperfocused or not, my win did involve my outdraw-ing Big Al for a monster pot when I held 9-7, and he had Q♦-10♦ (top pair and a flush draw!), on a Q♠-9♦-4♦ board. We put $1,800 each in on the flop, and I hit a nine! Lucky.

That $17,000 loss had caused all that negative emotion and grief, com-pounded by the fact that I beat myself up, and then, I won most of my money back two days later. Seems like there are good lessons here? First, I shouldn't beat myself up, and cause myself to feel so much negativity over one bad day. And the second lesson, I heard loud and clear: my wife and son's love trumps a bad day at the poker tables!

23

Crushing the 1992 and 1993 WSOP

After a terrific performance at the Hall of Fame Poker Classic seven months earlier, I had some confidence heading into the 1992 WSOP in late April. And the 1992 WSOP (now 19 open tournaments) turned out to be a terrific one for me. I made five final tables, and won my second WSOP bracelet.

My 1992 WSOP run started on April 26th, when I made the final table of the $1,500 buy-in No Limit Hold 'Em tournament with the chip lead. But alas, I finished ninth (254 players) when I overplayed pocket sevens before the flop. I was lucky enough to flop a seven against my opponent's pocket aces (7-5-3), but the last card was an ace. I busted out a few minutes later; and I was irked with myself for losing way too many chips (50 big blinds) with pocket sevens. What a rookie mistake!

Seidel vs. Hellmuth: Again!

Five days later, on May 1st, I finished fourth in the $5,000 buy-in No Limit Deuce-to-Seven Lowball Draw. Then, on May 3rd, the $2,500 Limit Hold 'Em Championship (168 players) came down to me, and a familiar opponent: Erik Seidel! Erik had beat me in our last heads-up match (Chapter 13), in the Bicycle Club preliminary event in 1988, but I went on to win the main event two days later. And the next week, in September 1988, *Poker Player* magazine called Johnny Chan, Erik Seidel, and me, the "brat packers" of poker. In that preliminary event at the Bike, I felt as if Erik had been lucky to beat me. After all, I had had him all-in nine times! But I also knew that I could have closed better.

This time it was for a WSOP bracelet, and I was going to finish with a flourish; there was no way I was going to lose! But after a couple of hours battling just the two of us, I lost... Give Erik Seidel the credit; he is a great player, and to date he has eight WSOP bracelets.

My WSOP run continued three days later, on May 6th, when I finished eighth (134 players) in the $2,500 Pot Limit Hold 'Em tournament, and played at the final table with my old friend Tuna Lund.

I Win My Second WSOP Bracelet

Six days earlier, after finishing second to Erik Seidel in the preliminary WSOP $2,500 Limit Hold 'Em tournament, I felt like my Limit Hold 'Em tournament game was sharp. So I was looking forward to playing the $5,000 buy-in WSOP Limit Hold 'Em Championship event on May 9th. At noon, on May 9th, Huck Seed called my room at the Horseshoe and asked if I was playing. I was super sleepy and said, "No, I'm really tired, and I'm going to take the day off." Huck said, "Are you crazy? You're hot right now, get down here and play!" I knew Huck was right, so I bought in, along with 83 other players.

Mom Watches Me Win a WSOP Bracelet

I always do well when my parents are in town to watch me play. So I always have them come in during the WSOP, especially around the time when there are tournaments I think I can win. I think it has something to do with the fact that I want to impress my parents. I believe that wanting to impress our parents is deep seated in nearly all of us. In any case, my parents flew in May 7th, and my wife Kathy, another one that I want to impress, was in town as well.

After knocking on the WSOP bracelet door four times (four final tables) in the last ten days, I finally busted through that door with a victory in my fifth 1992 WSOP Final Table! WSOP bracelet number 2 (and $168,000 first prize) was in the bag! And it was sweet that my mom was there to witness it!

After reading an article about how Magic Johnson gave away all his trophies to family and friends, I decided to take a page out of his book and give all my bracelets away to family and friends. I gave WSOP bracelet number two to my wife, and I decided that I would give my mom and dad bracelets numbers three and four.

A Second Child?

Over the next few months, Kathy and I had serious discussions about having more children. We both wanted more kids, but when? I was smart enough to tell her, "I want more children, but I will not pressure you, and I will leave the timing up to you." In October 1992, she decided that it was a good time for her to get pregnant. And within a few weeks, Kathy was pregnant!

Meanwhile, I fanned in the 15 tournaments that comprised the 1992 Hall of Fame Poker Classic (October 27 – November 12) and as the 1993 WSOP rolled around, no one, not even me, could imagine how well I would do.

Am I Dreaming?
Three Bracelets, and a Second in the 1993 WSOP?

It started April 26, 1993, when I won the $1,500 No Limit Hold 'Em tournament with 284 players. First place was $161,400. I had a calmness over me. I was on a roll. My reads were perfect. My timing was perfect. My luck was strong too. When you "know" your opponents are weak, or strong, then No Limit Hold 'Em is a relatively easy game. You still need the stomach to make the tough calls, and the heart to make the big bluffs.

Four days later, on April 30, I made it down to heads up in the $5,000 No Limit Deuce-to-Seven Lowball Draw. My opponent was (and still is) the best Lowball player in the world: Billy Baxter. Nonetheless, I had Billy all-in and drawing when I had a "pat ten." I would win the WSOP bracelet unless Billy completed his draw. Billy needed a ten or under, one that didn't pair him. Basically, he had 17 cards to win the hand, but I had 25 cards to win the bracelet. But sadly, he caught his card, won that key pot, and went on to win that bracelet. Alas, I'm still chasing my first Deuce-to-Seven bracelet, but at least I picked up $72,500 for second place.

Can Anyone Win Two Bracelets in One Day?
Uh, Yeah... My Parents Were There!

Exactly one week later, on May 7, 1993, I won my fourth WSOP bracelet (second from the 1993 WSOP) in the $2,500 No Limit Hold 'Em tournament, with a field of 173 players. I clearly remember that a "tell" from one of the other players at the final table contributed mightily to my win. My reads were already "sharp as a tack," but this particular "tell" won the tournament for me. First, I lost a massive pot on a "coin flip" at the final table, with my Q-Q to their A-K, and this left me no room for error. Second, I noticed that the player on my left would move his chips halfway into the pot whenever he was going to fold! OK, I saw what I saw, and I was ready to bet my entire tournament on it. One flop came down A-9-8, and I had 7-5. I checked, he bet, everyone else folded, and I began to study (I had an easy fold). After a minute, he moved his chips halfway into the pot and, boom, that was my signal, so I instantly moved all-in. He folded. From then on, I would take a moment after he bet, and every time he slid his chips forward, boom, I would move all-in. Finally, he raised it up in first position, and I called in the big blind with A♠-8♠. The flop was A♥-J♠-2♠; I flopped top pair and the nut-flush draw. I checked, he bet, but he didn't slide his chips halfway into the pot. Well, he may have had me beat, but I was going ahead with this hand. I raised him, he moved all-in, and I called. Surprisingly, he had A♣-6♦, so I was a huge favorite to win the pot, although there was a 15% chance that we would split the pot. My hand held up, and I went on to win the bracelet and $173,000. Again, it was sweet to have Mom and Dad there watching me win! Kathy was seven months pregnant, and I encouraged her to go to bed at 1 a.m., and she did.

After I won the No Limit Hold 'Em tournament, I knew I couldn't sleep, so I went for a run until 5:30 a.m.. It reminded me of when I finished second to Erik Seidel at the Bicycle Club in 1988 (Chapter 13), went for a run through the dangerous neighborhoods in LA, and then came back and won the Bike's main event over the next two days. It was near the end of the WSOP, I had been playing intensely the day before from noon until 4:30 a.m., I was high from my big win and couldn't sleep, and I was using a run to hit the reset button.

The very next day, or should I say, that same day (the No Limit Hold 'Em tournament ended at 4:30 a.m.), I entered the $5,000 Limit Hold 'Em tournament at noon, along with 68 other players. Actually, I wasn't there at noon, and thus I missed a great WSOP moment in my life. When WSOP tourneys begin, they announce last year's winner (the defending champ), and yesterday's winner. Well, I was both the defending champion in the WSOP $5,000 Limit Hold 'Em (from 1992 WSOP), and I was yesterday's champion in No Limit Hold 'Em, and that's kinda cool!

I walked into the tournament area at 2 p.m., two hours late, and exhausted. My goal was to make it to the dinner break, so that I could nap and come back fresh. I barely made the dinner break, but after my nap I came back and quickly took the chip lead.

When we hit the final table, I recall, I busted Jack Keller with a funky hand. I called a raise with 5-3 offsuit in the small blind to try to take out "Miami John" Cernuto, who had only three small bets left, and was on the button. John raised to 2-bets, I called, and then Keller re-raised from the big blind to 3-bets, and John moved all-in for 3½-bets. Having called 2-bets, it was easy to call 3½-bets, so I called, and Keller re-raised again to 4½ bets, sigh. My sigh turned to enthusiasm as the flop came down 7-3-3. Keller put in so many bets that I wondered if he had flopped sevens full! When the smoke cleared, Keller had busted himself (he could have saved some bets) with J-J in third place, Miami John busted in the same hand for fourth place, officially. Don Williams (Chapter 9), known as the "best unknown poker player in the world," smiled and, surprisingly, said, "Thank you." Don was super short on chips, and happy to move up two spots from fourth place money ($24,150) to at least second place money ($79,350). After about four hands, I picked up pocket aces (A-A), and won my fifth WSOP bracelet (the third one from 1993 WSOP), and $138,000, in style (with pocket aces!). It happened so quickly that I won that bracelet at 10:45 p.m., my second bracelet of the day!

Did I mention that having my parents around, watching me play, works out pretty well for me? One or both parents were there for four of my five WSOP wins, although they were in Vegas for only 20% of the tournaments that I entered.

No matter how prepared we are for success in life, and I wasn't, achieving great things can have a weird effect sometimes. Having won the last two WSOP tournaments going into the main event, having won three WSOP bracelets in two weeks, and then taking the chip lead on Day 1 and Day 2 of the 1993 WSOP main event, sort of, kind of, blew my mind. It was too much to believe. It was too much to handle. In the 1993 main event I basically fell apart and blew my chips. I'm sure it was partly due to exhaustion, but something else was going on with me as well. I'm not sure that I could have handled four WSOP bracelets in one year, especially if you include the main event bracelet to my haul. Later, I was mad at myself for blowing the main event, but how mad could I be considering I had just won three WSOP bracelets and over $500,000 in cash!

Sadly, the 1993 WSOP was over for me after I blew myself up in the main event, but I had a beautiful son, an amazing wife who was pregnant, five WSOP bracelets, a pile of cash, a beautiful condo, and more. Life was good! But I wasn't through with the fight, and I wasn't through with my own struggles...

24

One More Son!

On July 11, 1993, at 2 p.m., we rushed Kathy to the hospital to give birth. Four hours later, it was over, and we were blessed with another healthy son: Nicholas Hellmuth. When Kathy gave birth to Phillip, she had been in labor over 24 hours, but with Nick, it took a mere four hours. The boys came into the world at different speeds, and in many ways they are opposites. From the time Phillip came home, he needed constant attention (we hired a nanny for at least four hours a day), and we couldn't set him down on his back for even 30 seconds without him crying. We could set Nick down for an hour, and we would hear nary a peep. Phillip woke up during the night multiple times, needing to be nursed. Nick slept through the night. Phillip had green eyes, Nick had brown eyes. Phillip preferred fruit and steak, Nick preferred fish and chicken.

1993 was a great year for me: we had brought another healthy son into the world, and I won three WSOP bracelets! With such great momentum, it's a shame that there wasn't a 1993 Hall of Fame Poker Classic.

Meanwhile, Kathy and I had long discussions about where she would do her residency, and this involved some randomness. Kathy would rank residency programs in order of preference, and residency programs would rank applicants in order of preference, but where she ended up was a coin flip, and it was a binding coin flip! Knowing that Vegas was not a great choice for Kathy residency-wise, and because she said she wouldn't even consider Vegas, I lobbied for LA. But her first choice, and I was fine with it, was Stanford University. Still, being accepted at Stanford seemed like a long shot.

Her second choice was UCLA Harbor, and I thought, "Hello LA, here we come." One liability (we thought) in the application process was that her husband was a professional poker player. But Kathy spun that to: my husband is a World Champion of Poker. It might have been that that "liability" was the grain of sand that tipped the scales in our favor at Stanford! We will never know, but the chairman of the department at Stanford seemed awfully interested in the concept of World Champion of Poker. Stanford, here we come!

The 1994 WSOP rolled around in late April, this time with 20 open events. And on April 25th, the $1,500 WSOP No Limit Hold 'Em tournament kicked off with 328 players. When we reached the final three players, I had a massive chip lead, as I stared down professional poker players George Rodis and Howard Lederer. I was a super-aggressive player, and George found an interesting tactic to use in combating my aggression. George would call on the button, I would raise it up out of the small blind, Howard would fold, George would move all-in, and I would fold. This pattern repeated itself more than a few times, until I finally realized that George was going to continue this unusual tactic. So, as a good counter-tactic, I stopped raising out of the small blind or the big blind.

Fast forward an hour; I was dealt A-A in the small blind, and I could see the writing on the wall. And just as it was in the script in my head, George limped in, I raised a lot (to make sure Howard would fold, and to protect my hand), and George then moved all-in. I snap-called him! George flipped up a K-10, and I was a huge favorite to bust him. I had 300,000 in chips, George had 100,000, and Howard had 100,000. But, alas, the flop was J-10-10, so sick! The last two cards rolled off J-8, and instead of my having 400,000 to Howard's 100,000 in a heads-up situation, George had 200,000, I had 200,000, and Howard had 100,000. I was stunned! I had George set up perfectly, and nonetheless lost.

I took Howard out when he raised my big blind, I defended with 9-7, the flop came K-7-7, I checked, and Howard moved in with A-5. Then George and I played heads up for hours. (I remember that he was super lucky.) On the final hand, I put in 105,000 with 9-9 vs. George's K♦-8♦ (I was 68% to win), and the flop came down Q♦-J♦-10♦, sigh. After that loss, for some silly reason I decided that I would focus on the side games, and not the tournaments, for the rest of the 1994 WSOP play. (What was I thinking?!?) I had just won $93,900 for second place! I had picked up three WSOP bracelets the year before, as well as $546,000, and now I was going to focus on the side games?

To be fair to my 29-year-old self, the one I'm tongue lashing now, many other poker players would have a tough decision when it came to playing cash games vs. tournaments at the WSOP. The late great Chip Reese once told me that he averaged $300,000 in winnings per year in the WSOP cash games, and many of the greatest players (Chip, Doyle Brunson, Johnny Chan, Billy Baxter, Stu Ungar) focused primarily on the cash games. Maybe it was my own ego. But I wanted to be one of the greatest poker players in the world, like so many I was confronting, and it seemed like following that side-game script made sense to me. So, I played a limited tournament schedule the rest of the 1994 WSOP, and focused on cash games. I won $19,000 in cash games the rest of the 1994 WSOP, and when the 1994 Hall of Fame Poker Classic rolled around in December, I lost money by focusing on the cash games. Although I was clearly world class in tournaments, and I had won more than anyone else had over the last six years (1988–1994), excepting Johnny Chan, I was not a world-class cash game player, at least not yet.

In July 1994, Kathy and I moved our young family to Northern California. And we brought Kathy's niece, Claire Sanborn, to be with us, to be a nanny for Phillip and Nick. Claire was only 18 years old, and just out of high school, and she had not been trained as a nanny, but she loved our boys, she was responsible, and that was good enough for us. What a great move! Claire lived with us for two years, and she was wonderful in every way. Claire put up with Kathy and me (my ego was up and down, but I was always too self-absorbed), and she was perfect for the boys. Claire sang songs to Phillip and Nick, she read them stories, she dropped them off at school, and when I was on the road, she picked them up from school and helped us out night and day.

In September 1994, Kathy entered her residency at Stanford. I knew that it would be at minimum tough, but it was brutal! She would be up and at the hospital at 7 a.m., and oftentimes home at 7 p.m. And when she came home, she was exhausted. Then there were whole months when she would be "on call," which meant either that she would have to have her pager next to our bed, or she would have to stay at the hospital (napping here and there) for 36-hour blocks. The self-centered Phil of 1994 still needed a huge jolt of energy from Kathy, and she just didn't have that much energy to give.

I was still struggling with the low self-esteem problem that I had accumulated growing up, and now I was trying to balance it with the great successes that I had achieved in the poker world. The result was that I was still self-centered to the line of narcissism. I learned that I couldn't talk to Kathy on the phone for an hour straight, looking for empathy, and expect her to stay focused on me the whole time. Kathy made me grow up and get away from my attention-seeking behavior. Kathy was still waiting for the "diamond in the rough" that she had married to see him become more of a diamond!

When It Rains, It Pours

The 1995 WSOP was a bust for me. Yes, I focused on the cash games, but I didn't have a single cash in a WSOP tournament. By now, I had developed a strong theory that explained my poker successes, simply, that when it rains, it pours. It seemed that when I began making deep runs, that would continue for weeks. In the 1991 Hall of Fame Poker Classic, I finished third, fourth, first, and fourth in one week. At the 1992 WSOP, I finished fourth, fourth, second, and first in one week. In the 1993 WSOP, I won three bracelets and added one second-place finish. And at the 1995 Hall of Fame Poker Classic, it was about to pour!

The 1995 Hall of Fame Poker Classic

On December 16, 1995, at the Horseshoe Hotel and Casino, I won the Hall of Fame Poker Classic $1,500 buy-in Limit Hold 'Em tournament (195 entries) and $117,000. It was my second Hall of Fame Poker Classic watch, to go along with my five WSOP bracelets. Four days later, the $5,000 buy-in main event started, and I had gained momentum. In fact, the WSOP main event was the only tournament that I wanted more than the Hall of Fame Poker Classic main event. In 1988 (Chapter 15), I had been close to winning the Hall of Fame Poker Classic when with a huge chip lead I fell apart, which opened the door for Johnny Chan to take down the 1988 Hall of Fame Poker Classic main event.

I made the final table of the main event, and my super-busy wife agreed to fly in to watch. Kathy was scheduled to land at 5:30 p.m. But somehow, we hit the final three players at 4:30 p.m., well ahead of schedule. And I knew my two opponents well: Humberto Brenes and Howard Lederer. I had history with both, and I knew that they would give me a real battle for the prized trophy. After Humberto busted, Howard and I began heads-up play. I noticed that Howard's parents were present, and I thought that was great. It meant they were giving him support as a professional poker player. It was nice to have more families supporting our profession, and the journey that that entailed.

At 5:15, the flop came down 6♦-5♠-2♠, and I had the 6♠-4♠. Wow, what a flop; top pair, a straight draw, and a flush draw, I had flopped a straight flush draw. When Howard made a huge bet, I sensed strength from him, and just called, and moving in, I thought, might scare him off! I didn't want a seven, an eight, or a nine to come off, in case he had a straight draw. I didn't want a five, or a deuce, in case he had a pair of fives or a pair of deuces. The turn card was an eight. Howard bet huge again, and I just called. The river paired the deuce, and he bet huge again. After talking out loud, and studying, I folded. Howard then flipped up 9-5 offsuit! He bet a pair of fives on the flop, then picked up a straight draw on the turn. So he bet again. On the river, he turned his hand into a bluff. I berated myself! All I had to do was move all-in on the flop, with my huge hand, and I would win the title, or at least win the pot. On the turn, if I move all-in, then Howard calls and I win the title. Or finally, if I call the river bet, then I win the title.

I still had a nice chip lead, but moving all-in on the flop is the way the rest of the world would have played that hand.

Kathy came strolling in at 5:45, and 20 minutes later I had the title, and the $236,000 first place prize! As a perfectionist, it still bothered me that I had folded the 6♠-4♠, but I joked that I folded it because I wanted Kathy there to see my victory.

Taking stock of where I stood, I now owned five WSOP bracelets, including the one that us pros want the most, the main event; and three Hall of Fame watches, including the main event, arguably the second most prestigious title in poker. Plus, I had won the Bicycle Club main event, arguably the third most important title on the planet. Not a bad little resume, and I hoped that I was just getting started!

After I took the Hall of Fame main event, hitting it for $353,000, Kathy and I began talking about buying a house in Northern California.

1975 – me, David, Ann, Kerry and Molly

Class of 1982, Madison West High School

The family 2006! Me and David, Ann, mom and dad, Kerry and Molly

1988 Bicycle Club Main Event final table. T. J. Cloutier on left

With World Champion Brad Daugherty, and Tuna Lund on cliffs of Malta, 1988

My brother Dave and me, 1988 "poker cruise"

Main Event, changing tables

Old friend Tuli Haromy and his mother in Austria, 1989

Jack Binion looking down: me winning 1989 Main Event!

First trophy, Reno, Easter Sunday 1988

Just won 2001 "Poker EM," Baden, Austria. With sisters Kerry and Molly, Kerry's husband Bob Soderstrom (Mike Sexton in background with glasses)

With games-lover grandma Slattery; left is my brother Dave

With oldest son Philip at sus restaurant, California 1996

With Mom and Dad - bracelet number 10, 2006, when I tied Johnny Chan and Doyle for all time bracelet lead

My favorite picture, deep in 2001 WSOP Main and I'm smiling!

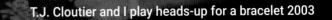

T.J. Cloutier and I play heads-up for a bracelet 2003

President Bush and Condoleezza Rice with billionaire philanthropist Bill Austin on left

Bronze sculpture by Lucky Eight Olympic artist Jon Ha

NBA legend Tim Duncan, Eva Longoria, Leeann Tweeden at "Eva's Heroes" Charity Poker Tournament, 2008

With Joe Lacob and Warrio NBA Championship trophy

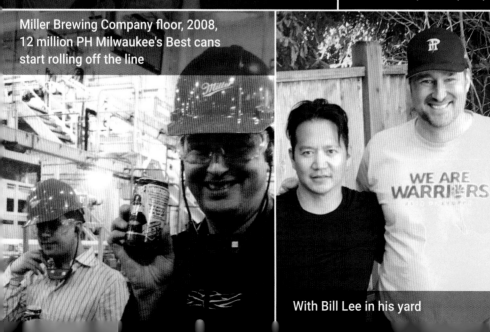

Miller Brewing Company floor, 2008, 12 million PH Milwaukee's Best cans start rolling off the line

With Bill Lee in his yard

With Bill Lee and Liv Boeree filming on *Poker Night in America*

With my best friend
Chamath Palihapitiya in his office

Chamath Palihapitiya, NBA all star David Lee,
Vivek Ranadivé and me on floor 2016 Warriors

3 Philips — with Dad and son, 2015

Doc Sands, Steph Curry
and me pre-game, 2014

2015 and 2016 NBA MVP Steph Curry's pocket
aces hold up at Warrior Foundation Charity Tour

With the amazing Carl Westcott, 2016

With Floyd Mayweather at his
training camp for Pacquiao fight

2016 Olympic basketball practice: Heisman trophy winner Des Howard,
NBA Champions Draymond Green and Kenny Smith

ike Tirico, ESPN announcer,
at Mich Basketball game

Nice shot at the 2015 WSOP!

Newly-crowned
2015 NBA Champions
Golden State Warriors
id Lee and Draymond Green

With Kara Scott and Daniel Negreanu
on ESPN set of WSOP Main Event 2015

h guru Tony Robbins on floor
Game 5, NBA Finals, 2015

With Kirk Lacob, coach Jim Harbaugh and Warriors
GM Bob Myers in VIP area Mich Basketball game

With President Clinton in San Francisco, 2014

With Philippe Ramos and world fa
soccer star Neymar at 2015 WSO[

With President Clinton, I'm MCing his Clinton
Foundation Charity Poker Tournament in SF, 2015

With President Clinton, at the Clin
Foundation Charity Tournament 2
discussing White House chip set!

WPT President Adam Pliska (behind Tiger Woods)
at TigerJam Charity Poker Tournament 2015

With Tiger Woods and at TigerJan
Charity Poker Tournament 2016

Warriors eliminate Houston Rockets, 2015 Western Conference Finals

Showing bracelet #14 to Floyd Mayweather at Game 5, 2015 NBA finals

2015 NBA Finals: LeBron James, Klay Thompson, Bill Lee and me (Floyd Mayweather on left)

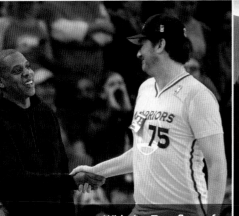
With Jay Z on floor of Golden State Warriors game

2015 NBA Finals: with Barry Bonds, Tony Robbins and Bill Lee

With Tony Romo at Nick and Sam's, Dallas, 2016

With Tiger Woods at TigerJa
Charity Poker Tournament 20

Selfie with businessman Sky Dayton,
businessman and Warriors owner Joe Lacob
and Nicole Curran on floor

November Nine
commentary for ESPN, 2016

Steph Curry is all-in and reveals: pocket Aces! I'm setting up on
microphone at 2016 Warrior Foundati n Cha it Poker T urnament

With NASCAR legend Jeff Gordon
at a trade show

The amazing Facebook COO
Sheryl Sandberg with her
NY Times best seller *Lean In*

With mega-star Damian Lewis
on the set of *Billions*

Aria Hotel High Limit Bar, 2016,
with Charles Barkley, blackjack all night!

With Heisman Trophy winner Des Howard, coach Jim Harbaugh
and Allan Mishra (who cured tennis elbow)

Crashed this NASCAR while filming and was ESPN "Top 10" highlight!

NASCAR driver at the 2007 WSOP

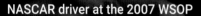

General Patton entrance, 2008 WSOP

General Patton inspects his troops

General Patton at the Main Event featured table

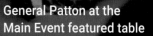

2009 WSOP
esar accompanied by 100 Roman women

Caesar at the Main Event featured table

London Caesar entrance going 5 mph,
double decker buses whizzing by!

Caesar in London, 2009 WSOPE

MMA fighter in the Hallway
of the Rio, 2010 WSOP Main

25

Bono Buys Our California House, and Televised Poker Begins!

Right before the 1996 WSOP began, my good friend John Bonetti lost his backer. I had staked Bono on and off for a couple of years, and he had always made me money. Now, the day before the WSOP began, Bono needed me to stake him. But I had vowed never to stake someone while I was playing in the biggest tournaments in the world. It was simply too distracting! For example, I would have 30,000 in chips in a WSOP tournament, and meanwhile, a couple tables over, two guys I was staking had 40,000, and 50,000, in chips. I couldn't ignore them, as I always felt like my horses needed positivity and emotional management. So, I would wander over to my horses' table, and check in, and if they were off, then I would talk to them and straighten them out.

I felt like the practice of staking others had a high cost for me, notably my own tournament success. In spending so much energy managing other players, as well as their emotions, I had a lot less energy for my own game. Horse management was time-consuming, for I had to coach them up, keep track of their numbers, make sure they were happy and emotionally stable, and make sure that they were staked at an appropriate level in a particular tournament (they needed cash to play, whether I was in town, or not).

I haven't talked about it in this book, but I staked a bunch of players over the years (T.J. Cloutier, John Bonetti, Dave Crunkleton, to name a few) to mixed results. But, the one horse who made me the most was John Bonetti. And now John was begging me for help!

I've been involved with many "50% with make-up" staking deals, and it works like this: you put up 100% of the money for someone else to play in particular tournaments, as well as their airfare and hotel, and they pay you back off the top with any cashes that they make, plus 50% of the profits. So, if a player lost $20,000 on one trip, and another $33,000 the next trip, and then hit for

$100,000, the backer would get his $53,000 back off the top, then 50% of the $47,000 profit. Tournaments are so hit and miss, that sometimes you had to stake someone for a year or two before they hit for enough money to get out of the hole.

After paying taxes for my big year in 1995, and then some small losses before the 1996 WSOP, I wasn't in great shape cash-wise. I had set aside $61,000 ($74,500 was the maximum spend, including rebuys) for me to play, stress free, the whole 1996 WSOP (23 open tournaments). If I tried to stake both Bono and me, then it could get bumpy, and thus stressful. But Bono needed me.

Fine, I decided to stake him, but sparingly. And the way Bono and I rolled up titles, we would surely hit something big along the way, and then the stress would be gone, right? Uh, wrong! Man, so much stress at the 1996 WSOP! Weeks passed while my bankroll shrunk, day after day. Going into the second to last event, the $5,000 Limit Hold 'Em Championship, neither Bono nor I held any cashes of significance. Somehow, by both Bono and I skipping a bunch of WSOP tournaments, I had managed my money well enough to stake us both into this penultimate event, with enough left over for me to play the $10,000 WSOP main event. But not enough cash for Bono to play the main event. With only one event to go, one of us would have to cash, if I was to stake Bono in the main event.

I busted early in the $5,000 buy-in Limit Hold 'Em tournament, but it was Bono who made it happen! Bono (and this may well have been his worst game) not only cashed, but made it to the final table. And then, with me watching nervously from the rail, Bono made the final three. Deals were common back then, but these guys never even stopped to talk. Bono finished second for $135,700, and since his make-up number (from the past) was higher than that, the whole $135,700 was mine, sweet! But more important, we had life! The pressure was off. So Bono and I sat down comfortably, Monday May 13th, to play the WSOP main, and I had 50% of him. I busted late on Day 2, but Bono flirted with the chip lead.

On Day 3, with me sweating him from the rail, Bono began an epic meltdown. He blew through tons of chips (290,000 down to 40,000) while he was on massive tilt, then put his last 40,000 in with 10♠-9♠ vs. his opponent's A♣-8♣. Bono somehow flopped a straight (Q-J-8), and then, thankfully, the players went on a long dinner break.

In the six years that I had staked Bono, I had never shouted at him before, but at dinner break at the Horseshoe Buffet, in front of his lovely wife Jean, I lit into him!

What the hell are you doing?!? You blew off 250,000 in chips for no god damn good reason, what the hell is wrong with you?!? You're tilting off the WSOP main event! How many more chances do you think you'll have to win it?!? It's $1 million for first, and you're going to regret this for years! Show some patience, get it under control!

Bono took it all in, and he didn't say a word. He knew that I was right, and at the end of our meal, Bono said, "I'm tired, I'm going up to my room for a nap."

About 30 minutes later, when Bono walked back into the tournament area, I could smell the aftershave, and his intense stare said, "Back off!" Bono looked like he was seething! I instinctively knew that I shouldn't say a word. I could see it in his eyes: Bono wasn't taking any prisoners!

Based on his reckless pre-dinner performance, the table was expecting Bono to raise every pot and continue playing like a madman. They were expecting him to bluff, bluff, and bluff. And frankly, they were all scared of him. "Aggressive Bono" was not someone you ever wanted at your tournament table. With his piercing eyes, and his huge bets, with or without having a good hand, he could scare the crap out of you. Yeah, you might pick him off once in a while, but the rest of the time he would put the fear of god in you!

So, Bono sits down and folds, and folds, and folds, and folds some more; he folded 13 hands in a row. Finally, he raised, and I have never seen a table fold their hands so quickly! Bono raised, and within seconds every other hand hit the muck; it was shocking to witness! No one wanted a piece of him. They couldn't wait to get out of his way.

For at least an hour, Bono didn't say a word to me. Meanwhile, he was in the process of building a healthy chip stack. And by the end of Day 3, Bono was a top three chip stack. I was excited! Bono had made it to Day 4, the final table of the main event, and first place was a cool $1,000,000!

My best friend at the time, Huck Seed, also made it, along with the legendary Men "the Master" Nguyen. I sat in the audience, which was large, with my parents, and Jean Bonetti.

Kathy was in the middle of residency and perpetually tired, and flying down on the spur of the moment, on a random Thursday, only to be back working on Friday, didn't sound particularly fun, or appealing, to her. So she stayed home.

One More Toast, to a Lucky Eight!

When they were five-handed, Bono called with 8-8 in early position, everyone else folded, and Huck Seed, with 7-3, checked, in the big blind. The flop came down 7-3-2, Huck checked, Bono bet, Huck raised, Bono re-raised, Huck moved all-in, and Bono called, for his remaining chips. Huck had us (I mean "us") all-in, and in bad shape. Surely it couldn't end for us here? The turn card was a five, and now Bono needed a deuce (three of those), a five (three of those), or an eight (two of those). Huck had the rest of the deck, or 36 cards, to win the pot with, and to bust us. I can't say that I was expecting it, but, miraculously, the river was an eight, and we went absolutely crazy in the stands! I'll let you know how much that eight was worth to us, in a minute, but for now I'll say that fifth place would have been $128,700.

When they made it down to three handed, Huck Seed, Bono, and the big chip leader, amateur poker player Dr. Bruce Van Horn, Bruce said, "Hey, let's split the money, three ways." Wow, what an amazing offer for Huck and Bono, who nonetheless weren't sure they wanted to make a deal. Until they saw the numbers! They would get $600,000 apiece, and play for $126,000 for first place. So, first place would get $726,000, and second and third place would get $600,000. Because Dr. Bruce had a big chip lead, he was offering Huck and Bono a great deal. Huck and Bono both thought that they could get Bruce's chips, but they couldn't pass up that deal. No sane person could. So, they reluctantly agreed to a deal.

Eventually, Bono finished third, and we went out to Piero's Restaurant, a classic, where mobsters used to eat, and movie stars still eat to this day. While we ordered stone crab claws, live Maine lobster, steak, and Dom Perignon, we repeatedly toasted the lucky eight that Bono had hit on the river, the one that made us an extra $500,000!

Yes, there had been some pain, some sacrifice, stretching $61,000 out to stake us both, but what a beautiful reward at the end. Bono cashed for $735,700 in the last two 1996 WSOP tournaments. His make-up number had been $240,000, so I collected that off the top. We split $495,700, meaning that I left the staking table with nearly $500,000 in cash.

Northern California House Hunting

A few months earlier, in early 1996, Kathy and I had started looking at houses in Palo Alto. We were in shock! Or should I say we were in "sticker shock." In 1989, I had bought a top-of-the-line penthouse condominium for $180,000 in Madison, Wisconsin. Now we were in Northern California, and we knew it was expensive, but $800,000 was the minimum price that we could find for a house that we liked.

For a few months, we had put off house hunting, while our financial position slightly worsened, but when I came home May 17th, with a check for $500,000 in my pocket, we knew it was time to buy. We revisited a four-bedroom place that we had loved a few months ago, the first time we saw it. And now, on the second time around, we knew that this was the place for us! This house had great energy! It was 3,700 square feet, had a swimming pool, two orange trees, a lemon tree, and over one-third of an acre, and it was on a tree-lined street. It was listed at $980,000. We knew that we were stretching, because we would have a hefty tax bill, but further research showed that we could get in for 10% down, and that the mortgage payments would be around $9,000 a month.

So, we put in an offer for $918,000, and I bluffed when the agent called us back to see how high we might go. First, I thought that it was illegal for an agent to call me back and probe me like that. Second, I thought that we will pay more, but I'll tell this agent that we liked another house a lot, and thus we would not make another bid. It worked, we bought the house for $918,000. Who says you can't play a good hand of poker, and win a big pot, in the real estate world? Now we had a beautiful place, and our boys absolutely loved the swimming pool. We were not top-of-top anymore, but at least we were above average in an amazing neighborhood.

Trump's Taj Mahal Televised Main Event

About then, another major poker tournament popped up in the poker world, when Donald Trump (yes, US President Donald Trump) announced the 1996 US Poker Championship at the Trump Taj Mahal in Atlantic City. The final event, the $7,500 buy-in Championship tournament, would be televised, with actor–pro poker player Gabe Kaplan commentating. The tournament was three days long, and first place was $500,000, guaranteed.

When I hit the final table, one of my opponents tried an interesting tactic on me. It appeared as if he was playing against me, and me only, and not trying to win the tournament. Every time I raised, and he was in the blinds, he moved all-in, and I kept folding. This went on for a couple of hours, until I had pocket nines, and called him. He had 5♦-4♦, and the flop was A-K-3. Fortunately, he missed his deuce, and I took the chip lead to the final six the next day.

Yes, $500,000 for First Place, But...

I was cruising along, with a massive chip lead, when we hit three handed. I was against European legend Surinder Sunar and seasoned poker veteran Kenny "Sky-hawk" Flaton. The thing is, first place was $500,000, and third place was merely $63,000! Yes, they met the $500,000 guarantee, but there wasn't much left over (second was $122,500)! I thought, "Man, I better hold on to this chip lead, and bust them both and win it all, or, at minimum, make a deal of some sort." Finishing third, without some sort of deal, would be a disaster! And if I could hold on to the chips, I had a good shot at winning it all.

We had Skyhawk down to 17,000 in chips, and in the small 5,000 blind (the big blind was 10,000). I had A-3 on the button and opened for 30,000. Skyhawk called, and Surinder studied and studied. I was shocked that he studied! He was in the big blind, and for 20,000 he had a chance to take out Skyhawk. Good tournament strategy dictates that he make that call. I wanted to say something out loud like, "What are you thinking?" Or, "How can you not call?" But, I realized that doing so would violate rules and etiquette. Other guys might say that when they're not supposed to, but I would never say that. My move was to shut up, and let Surinder figure it out.

Surinder folded his 10-9, and I said, "What were you thinking? How could you fold?" Skyhawk had 10-8, and the board ran out K-10-4-9-8. Instead of going broke to Surinder's 10-9, Skyhawk more than doubled up and went on to play a 400,000 pot with me an hour later, when he moved in with 2-2, vs. my A-Q. Skyhawk won that one, and now I was forced to make a deal! Because I had had a massive chip lead, I had a great shot at winning the whole $500,000 first-place prize. But now, after losing three or four big pots, I was forced to talk, and to look at a potential deal. First place was $500,000, second $122,500, and third was $63,000. I took $240,000 in the deal (the most, and then we played for $50,000 for first and divided up the rest), and went on to finish in third place. Skyhawk came all the way back from 17,000 in chips to officially win first place.

Afterwards, I blamed myself. I should have just called on the button with A-3, or opened for 20,000 and forced Surinder to stay in. This play still bothers me today, in 2017! However, I certainly looked good, as I watch it right now on YouTube (as I write this), in my patterned white Gianni Versace shirt!

26

Toughest Table Ever? Risking it all in 1997

Coming into the 1997 WSOP, I realized that it had been four years since I won my last bracelet. I had five WSOP bracelets by then, and I had a plan for becoming, as I have said, the best poker player of all time. If I wanted that lofty title, then I would have to do it primarily in poker tournaments. It is hard to make that lofty claim, just by playing in cash games. Some cash game players are better at borrowing money, or asking to get staked, selling a piece of themselves in high-stakes cash games, making money from assorted other sources, playing in easier cash games, or managing their money, than others. In cash games, it is hard to tell who the best players are. For example, did a player stay comfortably in the high-limit cash games, despite losing $2 million straight, because they had other sources of income?

On May 6, 1997, I picked up my sixth WSOP bracelet in the $3,000 buy-in Pot Limit Hold 'Em, with 170 other players. And with that terrific momentum, the following week, I made a deep run in the 1997 WSOP main event. We started with 312 players, and with three tables left, we confronted one table that proved to be remarkable. The press loved that table, and claimed that it was the "toughest table in the history of poker." It included four World Champions of Poker: the late great Stu Ungar, Bobby Baldwin, Doyle Brunson, and Berry Johnston.

With those legends at the table, it nonetheless seemed as if Stu Ungar and I dominated, as we battled each other like crazy people! Raising, re-raising, moving all-in, and the dance continued for hours. Stu did nail me in one big pot when he had Q-J in the big blind, I limped in with A-10, and the flop came down J-9-2. I tried to bluff him out on the flop, and then again on the turn (a jack). Then, when I bet the river for value, I hit an ace (J-9-2-J-A). Stu went on to win his third WSOP main event, and I went on to help commentate on his victory for ESPN. (They played outside, on Fremont Street, and it was a little windy!) It was painful to commentate, feeling as I did; I felt that I should have been there, but well done Stu, what a legend!

There was a hand (one that I commentated on from the windy television booth on Fremont Street), where the board was A♠-9♥-6♠-8♣, and Ron Stanley bet out 25,000 with his 9♦-7♦ (there were no hole card cameras, but Ron showed his hand when he folded), and Stu raised it up to 60,000 to go. The river was the K♦, Ron checked, and Stu bet 220,000. Ron folded, and Stu, then, within an instant of Ron's fold (this hand is on YouTube), flipped up his bluff; the Q♣-10♣. A well-timed bluff! Stu went on to win his third World Championship of Poker (his third WSOP main event).

A Whisker Away from Losing All My Cash, but for the Grace of God...

In August, the 1997 Hall of Fame Poker Classic rolled around, and simultaneously, we sold our place in Madison, Wisconsin. We had moved from Madison in 1994, but it had taken three years to sell our place. When we finally sold it, for $220,000, the real estate agent asked Kathy where she wanted the check sent. She was busy, and had complete trust in me, so she told them to send the check to the Horseshoe Hotel and Casino. I was surprised she had it sent to me, at a casino, but it was no stunning moment; I would just grab the check, and then mail it to her, right? Well... no!

I was playing way too high that trip, and risking way too much money, when things went south, way south. One bad decision led to another bad decision, and I found myself up all night, playing $1,500-$3,000 Limit Hold 'Em, and asking Bobby Baldwin if he could cash my check for $185,000.

Bobby, a poker legend, a Las Vegas legend, and a World Champion of Poker, had risen to number 2 in Steve Wynn's organization, it seemed, overnight! According to majority owner Guy Laliberté, Bobby championed Cirque Du Soleil with Steve Wynn. There would be no $9 billion Cirque, and all its massively entertaining shows, without Bobby fighting to keep it on track at Bellagio Hotel and Casino! Later, Bobby came up with the idea, and then built, City Center. Bobby married Miss Nevada, was Casino Executive of the Year, and plays, and wins, in the biggest No Limit Hold 'Em poker games on the planet! Bobby runs all of City Center now, and at the same time he still crushes the high-stakes No Limit Hold 'Em games held at Aria Casino and Hotel!

Back to August 1997, where Bobby asked me, "This check looks a little dog-eared, is it good?" I said yes, and then, without a word, Bobby passed me $180,000 in chips. Just like that. And now, I had 95% of my cash (not my net worth) sitting on the table, in a game where it was all at risk. Up all night, buried in the game, and suddenly realizing my predicament, something deep inside me awoke. I can't explain it. Maybe it was a surge of energy? Maybe it was adrenaline kicking in? I suspect that it was a deep desperation that demanded that I wake up, right then and there. In any case, I felt as if I had no room to fail. My back had never been more against the wall, and then there was the pressure of Kathy, Phillip, and Nick, and all of them depending on me!

By the time Bobby handed me the chips, I already owed Johnny Chan $40,000, and Hamid Dastmalchi $30,000, which left me with $110,000 in chips. Despite the deep awakening within, and the ability to ratchet up my game to its highest level, my chips dropped down to $18,000 or so. I was a whisper away from going down, and who knows what that might have meant?

Playing four-handed, Bobby called, Chan raised it up, and I looked down at A♠-8♠ in the small blind. It was an easy call, but I so wanted to fold my hand and protect this last $18,000! But I made the right move, and called. Hamid and Bobby called, and the flop came down Q♠-10♠-2♠. I had flopped the best possible hand! So, I bet out $1,500, Hamid called, Bobby raised it up ($3,000), and Chan called. I should have re-raised to $4,500, but instead I opted to call, and Hamid called. In my defense, I thought everyone was drawing dead, and I reasoned that slow playing made sense. The turn was the 8♦, I checked, and to my surprise, everyone checked (I had lost a lot of value!). The river was the 10♣. I bet out $3,000, Hamid called, and Bobby and Johnny folded. I flipped my hand up, and claimed the pot, but Hamid flashed the 6♠-4♠! He had flopped a flush and was also slow playing it, sigh. I had won the absolute minimum. Had I put in all the raises and re-raises, then I would have won a lot more, but as it was, I now had $39,000 in front of me, and a little breathing room.

After that close call, I began to hit some hands. Within three hours, I bought the check back, and quit with $80,000 in front of me. I was roughly even for the trip, and before I went to bed, even though I had been up all night, I mailed that check off to Kathy: whew, crisis averted!

Having almost buried myself, I vowed that I would never do it again. I had a family depending on me, and who can live on the edge like that? I would manage myself better. (I would go back to the drawing board. I would design a plan that would help me avoid future disasters.)

A New Financial Plan

Over the next few months, I came up with a new financial plan. I knew, from my close call, that risking all my cash in one night, or all my net worth, was easily doable in the poker world. But I could never let that happen. My wife, my kids, and I had a nice life, in a beautiful house, and I needed to protect that, at all costs. I would rather give up some great opportunities than put my family in financial jeopardy. I had to be stronger, and I had to be smarter. Thus, I decided that getting staked was a great idea. But, at what point should I get staked?

Initially, I decided that I would get staked when my net worth hit $700,000, but I was ready to move the bar still higher, as my net worth grew. So, if I had $650,000 in SEPP funds, stock market investments, my house appreciation, and $150,000 in cash (a net worth of $800,000), and I lost $100,000 ($700,000 net worth), then I would get staked. And I began talks with various parties, like Ted Forrest, Huck Seed, and Chip Reese, about getting staked if or when I needed it. Ted was ready to go, if I ever needed him.

The Status Quo "Borrowing and Lending" Money Management System for Top Pros

My friends in the poker world lived by a different financial system. The "borrowing and lending" system was established, and frequently used by the top pros. They would go broke, borrow money from one or more professional poker players, and eventually make their comeback and pay off their debts. On the surface, this system has it merits for professional poker players. First, us pros have natural and normal swings, and this system could help when things went bad. Second, the "borrowing and lending" system allowed you to take a chance and play in a "juicy game" when you were short on money, and not fear the consequences of going broke. Thus, you wouldn't miss good opportunities.

But I Hate the Status Quo "Borrowing and Lending" System!

I decided that the reigning "borrowing and lending" system was a bad one. First, if you engage in this system, then you accept the fact that you can be cash broke at times, and are willing to go into debt. And, where does that end? As both a borrower and a lender, it's in your best interests to keep the money moving. As a borrower, you need to keep borrowing (more and more) until you turn things around. You have no choice! As a loaner of money, you need to keep loaning, to make sure that your friends are still in action, and will have a chance to pay you back. I figured that if I was going to be a long-term big winner, then the system would not balance well for me in the end, because I would have to loan out a lot more money than I would ever have to borrow.

Staring down future decades, and knowing that I had a long list of people who owed me money from my poker-playing days in Madison, Wisconsin, I felt like the "borrowing and lending" system would end with me loaning out millions of dollars to professional poker players who wouldn't make it (I would never get paid back), and on the other side of the ledger, I would end up owing no one. So, short term, when I needed cash, it was easy to borrow money from my friends with no pay-back date, but then, as a standup guy, I would have to offer such loans to them when they were in need.

Second, you can lose friends by loaning them money! Personally, I have had bad experiences lending money to family (not my parents or my brothers and sisters), and friends. Sadly, it affects relationships. It is hard to say no, but whenever I have been asked, I reflect on the fact that it would be bad for my relationship with that person and for my own financial health in the long run.

Great Start in 1998, Bad Ending

A new, hugely popular, poker tournament emerged unexpectedly in January 1998: the Carnivale of Poker, which began life at the Rio Hotel and Casino. It seems to me that the reason the Carnivale became so big, so quickly, was location and timing. It was held in Vegas, in January. In any case, poker players flocked out to play! And, I was absolutely stunned to learn that 480 players had signed up on January 3rd to play in the $500 Limit Hold 'Em tournament. (Poker legend T.J. Cloutier took that one down.)

Chan vs. Hellmuth II, Not Exciting

On January 17, 1998, my wife's birthday, I hit the final table of the $1,500 buy-in Limit Hold 'Em tournament, along with my boy John Bonetti, and the legendary Johnny Chan. I seemed to have decent chips the whole time, but Johnny was all-in several times. I don't ever root against people, but I wasn't rooting for Chan when he was all-in, because I knew that he would be a tough, tough, opponent. But somehow, someway, it came down to Johnny and me for all the marbles (again). Only this time, first place was only $78,000, and second place was $39,000. But before we played a single hand, we counted down the chips, and ran the math for a potential deal. This wasn't a history-making tournament, like a WSOP bracelet tournament, or a Hall of Fame Poker Classic watch tournament, or a poker major. Thus, we were loose. It was 2:30 a.m., and we both had respect for the other's poker skills. So, without playing another hand, we made a deal, and split the money, based on our chip counts (I was paid $60,250, $3,500 more than Johnny). One good reason to chop it up was that we could go right to sleep, and then play the next day's tournament.

World Champions Collide:
Huck Seed vs. Phil Hellmuth vs. Johnny Chan

Four days later, on January 21, 2000, the Carnivale of Poker main event began, with 153 players. Whenever I hit a final table (or win a tournament), within a week or two of a main event, it seems as if I'm in form. So, I was looking forward to the main event. And, the Carnivale of Poker main event had risen, overnight, to "poker major" status. And the final table reflected it. That final table included three of the hottest players in the world, World Champions Huck Seed, Johnny Chan, and me. But Chan went out in ninth place.

With seven players left, I made a stand, with 7-7 on a J-J-9 flop. My super-aggressive opponent moved me all-in on the flop, but I felt like something was wrong. I was sure that I had him beat. I really felt as if he had A-K, and I was sick of being pushed around by his aggressive tactics. So, I called his all-in, for a mountain of my chips, and my opponent did indeed have A-K. My hand held up (I was 65% to win the pot) when a four, and then a three, came off. This pot gave me the chip lead, and it was apparent to everyone else at that final table, after watching me call it all off with 7-7 on a J-J-9 board, that they should not try to bluff me! Even Huck, my best friend at the time, marveled at my call. It is easy to play No Limit Hold 'Em when everyone else at the table is afraid of you.

Huck vs. Phil

When we made it down to two players, Huck Seed vs. me, we took a break to see what a deal looked like. First place was $306,000, and second place was $153,000. It was Huck vs. Phil, my best friend vs. me, two of the best players on the planet squaring off, head to head! We had a big audience, and my wife Kathy, who loves Huck, was there to watch the spectacle. I had the chip lead, so Huck was reluctant to make a deal measured by the value of the chip counts, and thus receive less cash. Eventually, though, we wound up making a deal: I took $213,000, Huck took $203,000, and we played for $43,000, and the now prestigious title.

A couple hours into our heads-up match, after a 15-minute break, we came back to the table and I picked up 8-8 to Huck's K-K. I had Huck all-in, and I could win it all, but Huck was a 4½-to-1 favorite to win that pot. Huck's hand held up, and he went on to win the title. This second-place finish hurt, but it was to Huck, we did split up most of the money, and I had the Green Bay Packers Super Bowl on my mind! My exciting week wasn't over yet. It was Thursday evening, and I knew where my next stop was.

Dad and I Hit Super Bowl XXXII: Packers vs. Broncos

I had planned to watch my Green Bay Packers in the 1997 Super Bowl, which was held in New Orleans, but as time slipped by, my plan failed to come to fruition. I couldn't find anyone else who had the money, the freedom, and the love of the Packers, to go with me to New Orleans. But this time around, I had a plan. If the Packers made it to the Super Bowl in 1998, then I was going, and I would bring my dad with me!

About a week earlier, after splitting the tournament with Johnny Chan, I called my dad to confirm that we were going to San Diego to watch the Packers win the Super Bowl, on my dime. He was worried about getting tickets, but I said, "Trust me, I'll find tickets. Buy a plane ticket, make hotel reservations, and I'll reimburse you."

On Friday January 23rd, I hopped a flight from Las Vegas to San Diego, and met up with Dad. On the flight to San Diego, I felt a stunning amount of gratitude. I kept thinking, "Man, don't pinch yourself, or you might wake up. How lucky am I? I have six WSOP bracelets, I just won $250,000, and I'm bringing my dad to watch the Pack in the Super Bowl." And we were going to win it, too, because the Packers were 11-point favorites! Brett Favre, a gunslinger himself, and the most-fun quarterback to watch, ever, was going to lead the Packers to a second consecutive Super Bowl victory.

On Saturday, Dad and I hit the pavement to scout out tickets, and we found good ones, 20 rows up, on the 40 yard line, for $5,400: $2,700 a pop. As I was buying the tickets, Dad said, "That's an awful lot of money, why don't you save the $5,400, and we'll go watch it on television." I said, "Thanks for the concern, Dad, but we didn't come down here to watch the game on television! And, I have just won over $250,000 this week. Let's enjoy it."

After the Packers scored a quick seven points, I actually felt sorry for the Denver Broncos fans sitting next to us. They seemed like such a nice couple. Poor Denver, they never seem to win the Super Bowl, and now we were going to blow them out. Boy, did I get that wrong! Late in the game, John Elway did some crazy, headfirst dive, risking life and limb, and was hit in mid-air. From there, he flipped around like a helicopter, and I thought, wow, he'll risk his own life to win. The Broncos players noticed it as well, and I'm sure that that signature play from Super Bowl XXXII gave them extra energy. Eventually, the Packers lost the game. But at least Dad and I were there!

The 1998 WSOP, Money Management Plan Solidified

By the time the 1998 WSOP rolled around, I figured that I had a net worth of $1.2 million. Our house had really appreciated, we had a SEPP fund, cars, and stocks. The plan was that if things went south, then the minute that I hit $1 million in net worth, I would get staked. My friends in the poker world thought that this was the most conservative plan in history! A $1 million net worth, and you're going to get staked, what?

I reasoned that if I'm going to take swings, then let them be ones where someone else faded the down drafts for me. I had a family and a way of life to protect. My worst-case scenario did *not* involve me losing my house because I couldn't pay the mortgage! To my friends, my worst-case scenario is that I would miss some upside when I won some big tournaments. But I could live with that, if it left my wife and kids protected.

Hedge Fund Found a Loophole, Yum Yum!

The 1998 WSOP was a bust for me: I had a 16th and a 14th-place finish. The cash games went well though, and I invested $92,000 into a hedge fund run by some poker players. Their premise was that they would make big trades on information, before it hit the streets. So, they would listen in on earnings calls, before they were widely released (it was a great legal loophole), and then buy, or sell, ahead of the public report. Their hedge fund was averaging 137% per year! By January 2000, 16 months later, our balance was $260,000. But then the big crash hit, in February, and shortly thereafter the loophole closed. I still had $180,000 in that account, which was a huge win, but man, I needed that loophole to stay open for another decade!

28

Millionaire Gets Staked in 1999?

In 1999, I made eight final tables in the poker world (only one at the 1999 WSOP), but nothing worth mentioning. By then, I was playing $400-$800 limit, mixed games, mostly in LA and Vegas. We played primarily five games in the mix: HORSE (Hold 'Em limit, Omaha 8/b, Razz – Seven Stud Low, Seven Card Stud, and 8-or-Better – Seven Card Stud). The mix would always be HOE, or HOSE, or some combination of HORSE. As good as I was in Hold 'Em tournaments (I had the best results on the planet for the preceding 12 years), I wasn't a world-class player in HORSE, yet. And, when I played $400-$800, I was oftentimes matched up against the best players in the world.

If I was off my game, then I could lose $40,000 in one session, or more. I believe that most professional poker players struggle for a few years in their 30s, and I was no exception. Most of these struggling pro players end up going broke, and it takes a while for them to come all the way back. I have witnessed this "struggle in their 30s" phenomenon with at least ten of the top players in the world. I don't why it happens. I simply can't explain it.

For me, I had drawn a line in the sand. I wasn't going to go broke! I had to protect my family. I had to protect my beautiful way of life. My plan was that I was going to get staked if I fell to $1 million in net worth (Chapter 27). By October 1999, I hit that line. And Ted Forrest knew a good thing when he saw it. Ted would stake me, on make-up deal (where he put up cash for me to play, then took his money back off the top when I started winning, plus 50% of the winnings).

Hubby, Are You Crazy? Celebrating This?!?

I remember the day that I decided to get staked. Kathy and I were spending the night at the Four Seasons Hotel in San Francisco (45 minutes from our house) in

September 1999, and that night I toasted the fact that I was getting staked by Ted. Kathy was confused, and thought that I was toasting the fact that we were running low on cash! She said, "That's nothing to celebrate, are you crazy?" I said:

> *Honey, I'm not celebrating the fact that I lost $7,500 last week and fell down to $1 million in net worth. I'm toasting the fact that I'm smart enough to get staked, even though we are worth $1 million on paper! I'm toasting the fact that it is a smart thing to do, and no one else has ever done it before. I'm toasting the fact that we will never go broke. Raise a glass to great money management!"*

Things started well for Ted Forrest, and me. But before I go into that, I want to say that I owe Ted for his kindness, and his help. When I had bills due, late in the month, Ted would transfer $9,000 into our bank accounts. For nine months, starting in September 2000, Ted had to transfer cash to our accounts so that we could pay our bills. Now, it is true, Ted knew that I had at least $350,000 in my SEPP fund, and in my stock funds. And Ted and I had a deal that I would eventually sell my funds, if I had to. But Ted had my back, and he was rewarded, eventually.

Meanwhile, my wife was going crazy! Poor Kathy. No cash in the accounts on the 26th, with $9,000 in bills due, and I never broke a sweat. How do you explain to your wife that you're never worried about money, that worrying is a waste of time? How do you explain to your beloved that you *know* you will always have plenty of money, for the next 50 years, even though there was no cash at that moment? Did I sound crazy? Do I sound crazy?

As I was saying, things started well for Ted and me, when he gave me $20,000 to go to Atlantic City to play cash games in November 1999. Ted said, "I'll give you $80,000 in cash to go play cash games." I said, "Just give me $20,000, maybe I can run that up. If I need more, then you can send it." That trip, I won $90,000, and we split it 50/50. Good, that gave me a few months of breathing room.

January 2000, Carnivale of Poker III

The popular Carnivale of Poker began life in January 2000, but this time, they switched the location from the Rio Hotel and Casino to Harrah's Hotel and Casino, right on the strip (Las Vegas Boulevard). Most of us greatly preferred the Rio to Harrah's, but the numbers were off the hook again, and this tournament continued to gain serious momentum.

After two final tables in 1998 (a first and a second) and two final tables in 1999, I made three more final tables in 2000; I was building quite a nice little record at the Carnivale of Poker! I was also proving to be good, and consistent, at Limit Hold 'Em tournaments, while I made my third consecutive final table (1998, 1999, and 2000) in the $1,500 Limit Hold 'Em tournament on January 22nd: I finished in sixth place.

On January 27th, with a record field (194 players), the Carnivale of Poker main event began. After two final tables in the last ten days, I was in form. And I took that good form, grabbed the chip lead, and made it to the final table, again. When we hit three-handed play, I had a big chip lead, and the prize pool looked like this: first place was $386,900, second was $201,400, and third was $100,700. This seemed to be a familiar position for me; I had the chip lead in a No Limit Hold 'Em poker major, with three players left. And the usual 40% of the entire prize pool went to first place, 20% to second, and 10% to third was in effect, again. That's 70% of the cash to the top three places. Thank goodness I made it to the top three a lot!

This final three was peculiar. Take note that Angelo Besnainou, from France, was spreading sugar on the table! Yes, actual sugar was being dropped onto the table, and it made the cards a bit sticky. I complained, but what could I do? When confronted about it, by me, or by a floor man, Angelo pretended that he didn't speak much English, and didn't know what we were talking about. I suppose the sugar appeared on the table by itself? In any case, Angelo obviously thought that the sugar made him lucky, and maybe he was right!

We battled three handed for hours. I could have made a deal that would lock up second place cash ($200,000), we could have taken $200,000 apiece and played for $100,000 and the title, but because I was getting staked by Ted, I was willing to gamble more. I knew that Farzad "Freddy" Bonyadi, the third player in our sugary three-way drama, was an excellent poker player, but I thought that I had a good edge on him in No Limit Hold 'Em tournaments. With 70% of the money in the top three spots, and some luck when we hit three handed, most of the time I made a financial "save." But this time I passed.

I had a theory that these guys would crack, playing for so much money, especially Angelo. And Angelo was over-playing his hands, as he kept moving all-in for big numbers, and Freddy and I kept folding. Eventually, one of us was going to pick Angelo off! Finally, he moved all-in from the small blind, with K♠-10♠, and I picked up A♠-Q♠ in the big blind, and quickly called him. I was about 64% to win this pot with my A♠-Q♠. The flop was K-Q-5, which hurt, but I reserved judgment until the turn card, which was... an ace! What a great card! But, it wasn't over yet. Angelo would need a jack (four of those), or a king (two of those) to win the pot. I had 38 wins to his 6 wins. I was counting on the win now; I would have a massive chip lead, lock into at least $201,400, and take down this poker major. After finishing second to Huck Seed in this Carnivale main event two years prior, winning would be extra sweet! But alas, a jack came off, Angelo made a straight (K-10 on a K-Q-5-A-J board), and I lost the pot. And an hour later, I went on to finish in third place.

This one hurt even more, because I didn't make a save, and I had always made a save! I walked away with third-place money, when all I had to do was agree to lock into $200,000, or perhaps $250,000 (I had a big chip lead). Maybe Angelo had cracked under the pressure, maybe he didn't, but either way, he won the tournament. Well, at least I made more cash for Ted and me.

Jack Binion, World Poker Open 2000, and the 2000 WSOP

Benny Binion started the WSOP, way back in 1970, and now his son Jack, who had been a good steward of the WSOP until he sold the Horseshoe Casino in 1997, started the Jack Binion World Poker Open in Tunica, Mississippi, on March 28, 2000, at the Horseshoe Hotel and Casino Tunica. The players came out in decent numbers, and I picked up my first World Poker Open bracelet in the $1,000 Limit Hold 'Em tournament, along with a third-place finish in the $1,500 Pot Limit Omaha.

The following month, the 2000 WSOP didn't turn out to be great, especially by my standards. I finished sixth in the $2,000 Pot Limit Hold 'Em, and fourth in the $2,500 Pot Limit Omaha. A bad beat cost me in the Hold 'Em.

In the Pot Limit Hold 'Em tournament, I defended with 4-2 offsuit in the big blind, and it came 8-5-4. I checked, my opponent, the late Dave "Blondie" Col-clough bet, I raised, and he called. The turn was a deuce, and I counted down my chips as I thought, "I think Blondie has an over-pair, like K-K, or J-J, and I have him beat with two pair. I have 60,000 in chips, so I'll bet 20,000, then 40,000 on the river to get maximum value." So, I bet 20,000, and Blondie studied forever, before he called. I would bet 40,000, unless an eight, or a five, hit the board. (If Blondie had an over-pair, then an eight, or a five, would beat me.) The river was a nine, which looked perfect to me, and I moved all-in. Blondie, however, had 9-9, and made trips on the river! The only way he gets my 40,000 in chips, is if a nine were to hit on the river, sigh.

I didn't have a great WSOP in 2000, but I would make my mark in two big, international competitions in Europe.

29

Hello Europe, Hello Hole Card Cameras

On Sunday morning, October 1, 2000, I landed in Vienna, Austria, for the Poker EM Seven Card Stud Championships. The Poker EM was held 20 minutes south of Vienna, in Baden, Austria, at the magnificent Casinos Austria. The Poker EM is a beautiful poker tournament, with all its pageantry and flair! The 72 finalists are introduced to the whole casino, one at a time, and the flags of their different countries are held aloft proudly during those introductions. The final table is surrounded by hundreds of people, and broadcast live on the internet. The money is brought out on a silver platter, in plastic packages; and the green and red euro bills are quite colorful.

At the Poker EM, there are three qualifying events, in which 24 people advance to the main event. There is a maximum of 456 players in each qualifying event, and these events are always sold out! So, 24 out of 456 advance to final day. And, with three qualifying events, a total of 72 players advance to the final day. The buy-in was $300 to enter, $300 to rebuy, and $300 to add on.

I didn't fancy myself a great Seven Card Stud tournament player, but I had attended the tournament the year before (1999) with my wife Kathy, my backer Ted Forrest, and an up and coming poker pro named Layne Flack, and I finished in ninth place. Ted made the final table, the final eight in Seven Card Stud, but finished in fourth place. The tradition, the pageantry, the flair, the grand old casino, and the fact that I almost won it the year before, brought me back to play the Poker EM in 2000.

Surrounded by Family, I Told Them, "I'm on a Boat!"

Since my sister Molly (Chapter 16) lived in Vienna, I flew over four days early to hang out with her. But Molly had to work during the week, so I spent two days studying Gustav Klimt paintings at the Belvedere Museum. In particular, I marveled at his famous painting "The Kiss." I love Klimt's work, and I still have a poster of "The Kiss," on the wall of our master bedroom.

My sister KK (Kerry) (Chapter 16) and her husband at the time, Bob Soderstrom, lived in Italy, and they were going to come up to Vienna to hang out with Molly and me. In 1999, I stayed at a nice hotel, but this time around, in 2000, I stayed on a raggedy mattress on the floor of Molly's living room. (Molly tried to give me her own bed, but I couldn't accept; I was bound and determined to rough it out.)

After my two days of pondering Klimt, KK and Bob arrived, and Molly took a couple of days off from work. It was time for Molly to show us the town! For KK and Molly's whole lives, I was a dominant figure in our family (older brother), but on this trip, I decided to let go of the controls. I decided that I was "on a boat." When we were deciding where to go next, coffee or beer, when we were deciding whether to turn left or right, they constantly asked my opinion, and I said, "I'm on a boat, you guys choose." It was a wonderful trip!

There was a philosophy behind my being "on a boat," and I shared it with them. I told them:

> *Metaphorically speaking, I spent years choosing the right river to be on. Some were too fast, and some too slow. Some too straight, and some too winding. But I always had the authority to choose the river that I am currently on. At this moment, I'm on the perfect river, and I don't want to do any rowing. I insist on paying for everything that we do, but I will not choose any of it. I'm going to follow your lead, so you guys decide what we are going to do, and where we are going to go, every day.*

After two fun-filled days with KK, Molly, and Bob, I went in to play the first qualifying session on Thursday October 5, 2000, and I advanced. There were 456 who started, and I reached the final 24. There were two more qualifiers (one Friday, and one Saturday morning), and then the 72 of us would play in the finals Saturday night. Since I was back at Molly's by 10:30 p.m., my family and I hit Vienna for a happy gathering!

On Friday evening, we found a big Picasso exhibition. And, at 7 p.m., the overseas travel, the traversing about Vienna, the poker, and the fun finally all caught up with me, and I excused myself.

My "boat" was being commandeered. I was exhausted, and I headed toward the old mattress on Molly's floor. I would sleep as much as I could over the next 20 hours. I had a big tournament that I needed to win on Saturday.

London Ali's Vision Becomes a Reality?!?

When KK, Molly, Bob, and I walked into the Casinos Austria at 5 p.m. on Saturday, I ran into European professional poker player, and well liked "London Ali" Sarkeshik. And my mind flashed back to the year before, in 1999, when London Ali told me, "I've had a vivid vision in which I saw you winning the Poker EM." I told London Ali, "Last year, you had a vivid vision that I won the Poker EM, but maybe you had the year wrong? I'm in the finals again!"

Eight hours later, I made the final table, and I must say that it was one of the loudest final tables that I had ever played on! First, it was 1:30 a.m., and most of the room had been drinking for hours, including KK, Molly, and Bob! Second, every time a pot was awarded, the Europeans were screaming for their friends, or their countryman, as if it were a soccer match. Third, KK, Molly, and Bob were every bit as loud as the Europeans; and I loved it! My sisters kept shouting "yer-da-brother, yer-da-brother, yer-da-brother" (to this day, I'm not sure what that means) and Bob was screaming every time I won a pot.

During play, every two hours or so, I would walk across the casino and tell London Ali, "Looks like your vision is coming to pass!" And then he would say, with great confidence, "You will win it, for sure. I have no doubt in my mind." And at 4 a.m., the title was mine! I had won the Poker EM, and $106,250! I found London Ali and thanked him for the support, and for relaying his vision to me. Then I celebrated with KK, Molly, and Bob until 7 a.m.! I had a flight out, seven hours later at 2 p.m., and I tried to sleep, but I always have trouble sleeping when I have won something big.

After a few broken hours of sleep, and a quick journey to the airport, I found myself on a connecting flight to London. Sitting next to me, completely covered, was a beautiful, massive, first place trophy, for winning the Poker EM. Had it really happened? Had I just won the biggest poker tournament in Europe? Or was I dreaming? I started crying, not a little bit, but a lot. In my mind, I chuckled, while I cried out loud, wondering if anyone on the plane could possibly imagine that I was crying tears of joy?

Hole Card Cameras in Wales?

I had heard the buzz about hole card cameras being used to broadcast No Limit Hold 'Em Tournaments on London television. They were saying that it would change the course of poker forever (they were right!). It was simple, the players put their two hole cards, face down, on piece of glass. Underneath the glass, there was a camera which recorded the hole cards, and showed them later, for all to see, on television. When I asked my European friends about it, I was soon put in touch with the producers of *Late-Night Poker*. And the producers invited me to play in *Late-Night Poker III*, December 12, 2000. I accepted their invitation, and thought, "Back to Europe I go." Although I wasn't even thinking about the tournament itself. Rather, I was fired up to watch the hole card cameras in action, and learn more about the technology. Were they using a technology that I could adopt?

They kept emailing me, asking me to wire in my entry fee. Oh yeah, that's right, it's a poker tournament! There were nine television shows that made up the series *Late-Night Poker III*, and 49 total players. Seven players would play in a heat (there were seven preliminary heats), and if you won your heat, then you advanced straight to the finals. If you finished second in your heat, then you would play in the semi-finals heat, where only one would advance to the finals. So, the final heat would be eight-handed: the seven winners, plus the winner of the semi-final heat.

For some reason, I didn't have a lot of confidence heading into *Late-Night Poker III* (sometimes this is duck soup for me). Maybe I thought it impossible for me to win two big tournaments in Europe within a few months? So, I decided to fly in, but I had a backup plan. If I didn't finish in the top two in my heat, then I would fly to Italy to hang out with my sister Kerry and her husband Bob.

I hadn't been great at sleeping on flights, even flights overseas, but I didn't expect what happened on this long trip to Wales. I brought the book *Hannibal* with me, and started it in the San Francisco International Airport; and I didn't sleep a wink! Not on the flight to London, not on the bus to Wales, and not in the taxi to my hotel. *Hannibal* was engaging, but my lack of sleep would certainly hurt my chances of advancing in my heat.

I arrived a few hours late, and, even as tired as I was, I could see that the producers of the show were visibly relieved. They said, "Hello Phil, it's 4 p.m. now, and your car over to the tournament leaves at 5:30." OK, then. No time for sleep... but time for a good workout.

I Jump Right in, and Win?

Working out had usually done wonders for me in the past, and I knew that a good workout would keep my mind strong for four or five hours. So there I was, watching the clock as I arrived at the studio. My workout had ended at 5 p.m., and I thought I might be fresh until 9 p.m., maybe 10 p.m. But they didn't start until 8 p.m. (that's televised poker). Bad for me!

I believe that in the last hand of my preliminary heat, when I made it down to heads up, that I put my chips into the pot in a bad spot, and got lucky. In any case, I won my heat, and now I could sleep for two days straight (sweet!). And be well rested for the final heat. The backup plan to Italy, although it would have been fun, was *not* as fun as winning my heat!

Two days later, I sat down in the finals, and I immediately recognized Paul Alterman, who had taken me out of the Poker EM in ninth place, in 1999. Paul had put an ugly bad beat on me then. What would happen this time? Barney Boatman, "Mad Marty" Wilson, and Mike Magee (I would duel with Mike six months later, in the 2001 WSOP main event) also made the finals.

When we made it down to three handed, Paul and I had all the chips. Paul limped in on the small blind, and I raised it up with A♠-A♣ in the big blind, Paul called. The flop was J♣-9♣-2♣, and Paul checked. I bet, Paul raised it up, and I moved all-in. Paul called quickly with Q♣-10♦. Paul had a strong holding, an open-ended straight draw, and a queen high flush draw. But I had the medicine for his hand: a pair of aces, with an ace-high flush draw. Paul would need to avoid a club *and* make a straight, two pair, or trips, to win the pot. The first card off was a club, and it was over. I won that massive pot and I went on to win the tournament and $65,000.

My first experience with the hole card cameras was a great one, a win! And as you will see in upcoming chapters, the hole card cameras changed the face of poker forever. The primary reason? Texas Hold 'Em is an easy game to learn, and the hole card cameras show that. In the past, when poker was on television, it was too confusing for people to watch No Limit Hold 'Em, and understand what they were watching, even with great commentators. But now, Hold 'Em was revealed to be a simple game. This classic line comes to mind: "Texas Hold 'Em takes five minutes to learn, but a lifetime to master." Now, the global public could watch on television, see how easy it is to play the game, and root for cards to come off the deck, or great players to make great bluffs, or great calls. You could be at home, shouting, "Call him, call him, he has nothing" and then watch your poker hero fold, no!

Meanwhile, these European poker tournaments were all right! Two big victories, in two months, yum, yum!

30

The Greatest Poker Player of All Time, Already?

My performance in the 2001 WSOP was spectacular! In the 23 WSOP tournaments held that year (and they were two-day-long tournaments), I had five final tables: a first place, a second, a fifth (main event), a sixth, and a ninth. Add to that, a 15th place, and another 15th for good measure.

A few months earlier, *Card Player* magazine had polled us professional poker players, and I was voted the "Best No Limit Hold 'Em Tournament Player in the World." And who was voted second best, and third best in the world? The up and coming Layne "Back-to-Back" Flack was voted second best, and the legendary T.J. Cloutier third best in the world.

Strange then (or was it), that on April 23, 2001, in the WSOP $2,000 buy-in No Limit Hold 'Em tournament, in a field of 441 players, Layne, T.J. and I made the final table. Nine of us would come back the next day to duke it out.

"Drunk Layne" Runs Us Over!

Let's go back a day, to the night before Day 1 of the WSOP $2,000 No Limit Hold 'Em tournament began. Layne went out drinking, all night long. So, Layne stumbled into Day 1 of the tournament completely hammered, and on zero sleep. Layne told me, "Phil, I breathed on someone at noon, and they almost fell over!" Fast forward 14 hours to 2 a.m. on Day 1, and Layne was so drunk he had trouble talking. The blinds were 1,000–2,000, there were 12 of us left, and nine made the final table. We would stop play for the day when there were nine players left.

I had 140,000 in chips, and I was at Layne's table (Layne had 110,000), and the other four guys at our table had 40,000, 28,000, 22,000, and 18,000 in chips. "Drunk Layne" made it 10,000 to go, every hand, in the dark! Without ever even looking at his hole cards.

I was at Layne's table, and we all folded, over, and over, and over, again. "Drunk Layne's" "making a big raise in the dark every hand" tactics were winning tactics. Because we all folded so often – no one wanted to make a stand and finish in 12th, 11th, or 10th place – Layne was accumulating chips at a rapid pace. Every time we folded, Layne won 4,800 (1,000 small blind plus 2,000 big blind plus 300 in antes × 6 = 4,800). For the rest of us, it was important to make the final table, because 40% of the money was in the top three spots. Thus, if Layne opened for 10,000 at our six-handed table, then these other players would have to commit all their chips, or fold. And it is hard, and takes a while, to find a hand that you want to go all-in with for your tournament life, especially when you know Layne will call you!

Meanwhile, I tried re-raising him with 9-9, and he moved all-in! I was hot! And I made sure that Layne noticed my anger, which he did, because he respected my play. My anger slowed Layne down a little bit the rest of the way, which was good for me, because then I could win a few pots as well, by pressuring the short stacks.

Coincidently, Layne and I were both being staked by Ted Forrest (we both had staking deals with Ted), and we were both staying at Ted's house. After Day 1 ended, I called Ted and I told him the good news: he had both Layne and me at the final table, and first place was $316,000! I also told Ted that Layne had been drinking for 36 hours, and that he should make sure to wake up Layne at 11 a.m.

Layne Doesn't Remember
He's at Final Table, and Makes a Bold Prediction!

In my bedroom, on the second floor of Ted Forrest's house, I woke up at 11 a.m. A few minutes later, I heard Ted waking Layne up. Layne says, "Dude, I'm way too tired and hungover to play today." Ted says, "Player (play-ahhh), you're at the final table." Layne, "Huh? Sweet!"

Some 45 minutes later, Layne, Ted, and I drive down to the Horseshoe together, and Layne asks who else is at the final table. I tell him that Stan Goldstein has the chip lead (I thought Stan was a tough player), and Layne says, "What? I'll destroy Stan in minutes." Sure enough, on the third hand, Layne has 9-7 on a 7♦-5♦-3♠ board and he's all-in vs. Stan's 6♦-2♦. Stan was a small favorite to win the pot, but Layne's pair of sevens held up. Nice prediction, Layne!

441 Players, and it's Down to the Three Best in the World!

When we hit the final three, it was Layne, T.J., and me. Who says there is no skill in poker? Our peers rank us first, second, and third in the world in No Limit Hold

'Em tournaments, and here we are, the last three standing out of 441 players! Layne finished third, T.J. finished second, and I won it. No deals, no saves, $316,550 for first, and more important to me, my seventh WSOP bracelet.

The 2001 WSOP Limit Omaha 8-or-Better

I was really feeling it, coming into the last few tournaments at the 2001 WSOP. I had bracelet number 7 in the bank, and I had come close to another bracelet four other times this trip. In the $5,000 WSOP Limit Omaha 8-or-Better (8/b), it came down to Bono (John Bonetti), Scotty Nguyen, and me. When Bono finished third, it was Scotty vs. Phil. Scotty wanted to make a save, and he was a better Omaha 8/b player than I was. It was $207,000 for first, and $103,000 for second. My only issue was that my make-up number, with Ted Forrest, including loans, was $140,000. In other words, if we took $30,000 apiece, and played for the other $43,000, then I wouldn't walk away with any cash. I wanted to make some money, and I had to clear my make-up number with Ted before I could collect cash. Scotty was insulted that I refused to make a deal, even after hearing my explanation.

In a matter of minutes, I had Scotty down to 140,000 in chips to my 395,000. And then, a weird hand came up. I had A♥-2♥-10♣-9♦ in my hand, and the flop came down Q♥-8♠-3♥. I flopped the nut-flush draw, the nut-low draw, and a straight draw. We put in 4-bets on the flop, 20,000 in chips, 5,000 at a time (it was a limit tourney). The turn card was the 4♦, and we put in another 40,000, four big bets, and the river was the 5♠. I made a wheel, Scotty checked, I bet, he raised, I re-raised (30,000 each), and he called. I flipped up my wheel, and he laughed and folded. I was like, "What a weird reaction. I think Scotty has to be drunk or something. He gave me way too many chips, he's down to 50,000, and I feel sorry for him." (Never feel sorry for anyone during competition, and never underestimate anyone!)

Scotty, Verbally Abusing Me?

Around 30 minutes into our match, Scotty began to abuse me verbally, like I've never been verbally abused before. Both of our wives were in the stands, and it wasn't a smart move on his part, because I had the goods on him! I could have destroyed him, in front of his wife, but I decided that I would take it like a man. What could he say about me? That I had a big ego? That I whined too much? I would take it, and crush him for bracelet number 8.

Scotty and I played for three hours, before we finally made a $30,000 save. After 90 more minutes, Scotty won the bracelet. I had given it everything that I had. I knew Scotty was a better Omaha 8/b player than I was, but I had him down to 50,000 to my 485,000! 10-to-1 chip lead for a bracelet, and I lost, sigh.

The 2001 Main Event, Scotty Apologizes

There were 613 players anteed up for the $10,000 WSOP main event in 2001. On Day 1, I was still upset with Scotty from a day or two earlier, so I found him in the middle of the main event, and I asked him to talk to me privately. There were so many people around that we went into a stairwell to talk. He gave me a heartfelt apology, I accepted, and now it was time to focus on the most important tournament of the year.

Day 2 of the 2001 WSOP Main,
One of the Best Pictures of Me, Ever!

On Day 2, Irishman Mike Magee raised it up to 1,500 to go in early position, sitting in the big blind, I re-raised it to 3,000 with the A♣-6♣. Mike called, and the flop came down A♠-10♦-6♦. I flopped two pair, what a sweet flop! I bet out 3,000 and Mike moved all-in. If I wanted to call, then I would have to put in my last 30,000 (we started with 10,000 in chips). In my mind, I thought that Mike could easily have a drawing hand: like a pair of aces and a flush draw (A♦-9♦ or A♦-J♦), or he could easily have a straight and a flush draw, like K♦-Q♦, or K♦-J♦. I sat there, studying, sitting up on the back of my chair, with a big smile on my face: that's when someone snapped a great photo of me (see photo section). Usually, especially in the WSOP main event, I was grumpy, intense, and jittery. And yet, here I am, put to the test for my WSOP main event life, and I'm, apparently, thoroughly enjoying the moment!

I decided to fold my hand, and showed it to the table as I folded it. I even said, "Nice hand, Mike." I never asked Mike what he had. I folded, and that was that. Then, out of nowhere, Mike says:

> I've never seen you handle yourself so well. I'm going to tell you what I had. I had the A♥-10♥. You were beat, and that was a great fold that you made! I actually thought you had flopped aces and sixes, and I moved all-in, because I knew you couldn't fold it!"

Whew, bullet dodged!

Day 3 of the WSOP Main Event

Late in Day 3, Daniel "Kid Poker" Negreanu, Mike "the Mouth" Matusow, and I flipped the chip lead, back and forth, for hours. And Phil Gordon folded pocket kings to my pocket aces, before the flop. But I think that it was an easy fold. The blinds were 2,000–4,000, Mike the Mouth opened for 20,000 (a huge over-sized raise) in first position, Phil Gordon made it 80,000 to go (another huge oversized raise) with K-K, and I made 520,000 to go with A-A! I believe that everyone in the room knew that I had pocket aces. Phil folded his kings (it's still impressive when someone folds kings before the flop), I showed my aces, and then I asked to see the flop. It was K-4-2, whew!

When we made the final table, National Public Radio (NPR) asked to interview me. I agreed. I was feeling my oats, because I told them, "Tomorrow, with a win, I will become the greatest poker player of all time! It would be bracelet number 8, another WSOP main event, and I've been crushing tournaments since 1989." (NPR was not impressed with my ego.)

Day 4 of the 2001 WSOP Main Event, a Huge Opportunity

For a couple of hours, late on Day 3, Phil Gordon had been playing a dangerous game with me. Every time I raised it up in late position, and he was in the blinds, he moved all-in for a massive amount of chips! That tactic had worked for him for hours, and I had folded a ton of hands, but the table was set for Day 4.

Two hours into Day 4, everyone else folded, and, on the button, I looked down at pocket nines. The script was written. I felt like I knew what was going to happen. I would raise, Phil Gordon would move all-in, and I would snap call his last 570,000. That's exactly what happened! Phil Gordon then showed his pocket sixes, and I was 4½-to-1 favorite to win the 1.14 million chip pot, and take a massive chip lead. I had waited hours to catch Phil Gordon, and now I was going to reap the rewards.

But, stunningly, the flop came down K-7-6! Surely, in the most important poker pot that I had played in, in ten years, I would find a way to win? Nope, an ace, and then an eight, hit the board. Wow. That was one of the worst bad beats of my life! At least I still had chips left in my stack.

K-10 Offsuit, the Hand I Never Played

An hour later, a hand came up that I have obsessed over, for years. I had K-10, Phil Gordon was in the big blind, and I was going to just call with my holdings. Then, Mike the Mouth called (he was sitting directly to my right). Mike was thinking what I was thinking, don't raise the amateurs (Phil Gordon) big blind, because he's likely to do something crazy. I had my calling chips lying in front of me, nearly in the pot. And then, a thought hit me hard, "I bet Mike has K-Q, or K-J, and has me in bad shape." So, I folded.

The flop was K-K-Q, and Phil Gordon bet out 60,000 with Q-J. Mike just called with K-J (I had been right, Mike had had what I thought he had!). On the turn, a ten hit and Phil checked, and then Mike checked. On the river, a four came off, and Phil bet out 200,000, and then Mike raised another 200,000. I was shocked to see that Phil had called the 200,000! What a horrible call in that spot. And I had "folder's remorse." All I could think about was how Mike and Phil would have paid off a ton of chips (to my full house), and I would have had the chip lead. Looking back now, I'm proud of the read that I made. How did I put Mike on exactly K-Q, or K-J?

I Expose My Hole Cards?!? What? My 2001 WSOP Bust Out

With five players left, I limped in with Q-10, and four of us took the flop, which was Q♣-9♠-6♠. Both players in the blind checked, and I bet out a smallish 40,000. Two players folded, and then Carlos Mortensen made it 150,000 to go. It got back to me then, and it suddenly hit me that either Carlos had flopped two pair, or he had exactly Q-J. I decided that if he had Q-J, then I could bluff him out. So, I moved all-in for over 600,000 in chips. Carlos said, "Count?" The dealer said, "Call." So I flipped my cards face up, and as I was flipping them up, Carlos said, "I didn't call." It happened so quickly. That's the only time in my entire life that I remember exposing my hole cards, when another player hadn't acted yet. I covered them with my hands, super quickly, and Carlos claims that he never actually saw my cards. Carlos took another two minutes to call my all-in bet, so perhaps he hadn't seen my exposed hole cards.

But I had a routine I was going to use, and this disrupted it, at the very least. My routine was this: If Carlos didn't call me instantly, then I was going to say, "Whew, you don't have two pair! Thank god!" And then I was going to fist pump. Carlos knew how tight I played, and that I never put my chips in weak, and that I rarely put them all-in on a drawing hand. I don't know what would have happened, if that dealer hadn't said, "Call." Perhaps my routine would have made Carlos fold his hand? It was a super tough call. Or perhaps Carlos would have called anyway.

In any case, Carlos did call 450,000 more. The turn card was a jack, which was great for me, even though it made Carlos two pair; because it gave me an open-ended straight draw (eight wins – four kings and four eights). Carlos shouted, "Yes!" And I said, "That was a great card for me!" Then Carlos said, "Oh, yeah." We were all tired after four grueling days of play in the main event.

The last card was a blank, and I busted out; and collected $303,750. After I busted, the young Benny Binion (the grandson of the Benny Binion who had started Horseshoe Hotel and Casino, and the WSOP), told me:

> Phil, I don't want to rub salt in your wounds, but if you had won it, it was decided that we would have put you into the Poker Hall of Fame, immediately. In essence, we would have publicly declared you the greatest poker player of all time.

Man, what a dream scenario that would have been for me! By the way, Carlos, who is an amazing poker player (and inductee to the 2016 Poker Hall of Fame), went on to win the 2001 WSOP main event.

Ted Forrest, and $550,000 in Cash...

Ted's share of my 2001 WSOP haul, including his make-up money (taken off the top), and his 50% of the profits, was over $500,000. I had tried to pay Ted his cash several times over the last two weeks, but one of us was always busy. So, finally, at the end of the WSOP, Ted and I went to the Horseshoe's cage. I opened my temporary box, which was filled with chips, and I counted out $550,000 for Ted. I asked the cashiers for a check, for my portion of the haul, but Ted asked for cash! And did they have some sort of a bag to put it in? Have you seen what $550,000 in cash looks like? It's like a small bale of hay!

The cashiers found a bag for Ted, like a cheap plastic gray duffle bag, and then Ted filled it with cash. And asked me, "Do you want a ride somewhere?" I said, "Sure." Then Ted walks across the street to the dingy, poorly lit, parking garage (in dangerous downtown Vegas). And as Ted is a bit absent-minded, he can't remember where his car is! I told Ted, before we left the casino, that we should hire a security guard from the Horseshoe to come with us; and that I wasn't going to get shot by a robber, defending his cash. If someone robbed us, I was hoofing it!

Did Ted take the duffel bag full of cash to a casino and secure it in his account, or a safety deposit box? No, he took it straight to his house!

Ted and I Conclude our Business, Quite Profitably!

Ted had started staking me in late 1999, and I immediately made him some money, and then I headed down, down, down, primarily in cash games. But during the time that Ted was staking me, I was afforded the luxury of taking a lot of time off from the poker world, and spending that time with my wife and kids. What was the sense of traveling around and playing $200-$400 limit mixed games, when my "make up" number was $220,000?

In the end, I made Ted $300,000 or more, I'm not sure what the exact amount is, but he had my back for 18 months (and loaned me money to pay my bills for nine months): Ted deserved every penny!

31

Kathy Has Had Enough!

One evening, in September 2001, Kathy informed me that she was leaving me, unless I did some major growing up, and quickly. And frankly, she said, she didn't think that that was possible for me to accomplish. She was sick and tired of being with a man who couldn't give her empathy. She had had enough of my self-centeredness. She had had enough of what she termed, "my subtle emotional abuse." Kathy was shocked at how little I had grown over the preceding 12 years! Kathy felt that she had given me more than enough time to grow up, and she was sick and tired of waiting. She wanted a man, not a boy.

I was completely devastated. I was brought to tears, both at that moment, and on every single day for weeks afterward. I was happy in our marriage. I was secure in our marriage. And Kathy was quite a catch! She was beautiful, brilliant, and supportive, a great mother, strong mentally and strong physically (a black belt at Kenpo Karate). And I was deeply, and desperately, in love with her. I knew everything that she said about me was true, and that scared me even more.

Thank goodness Kathy wasn't leaving me that day, or even that week. She knew that we would both benefit from seeking a couples therapist, whether we made it as a couple, or not. We would go into therapy, and we would choose a great therapist, not one that I could bamboozle with my celebrity, warmth, charm, and stunning personality.

But I wasn't going down without a fight! I would man up like I'd never manned up before. I would find a way to listen, deeply, to what Kathy had to say, and give her the empathy that she sought, and deserved. I would work hard toward becoming a better man. So we found a good couples therapist, and we went to work.

Desperation and Inspiration Often Lead to Great Things

One thing is certain. I have done great things in the poker world on the strength of inspiration and desperation. And the desperation that I was feeling over the potential loss of my beloved Kathy drove me to confront my demons, and my issues. This desperation caused me to take a long, hard look at myself, and to see my flaws. I wanted to give Kathy good empathy. I wanted to be a better man. I wanted to improve myself, one step at a time, but as quickly as possible.

On the plus side of the ledger for Kathy: I clearly loved her, I was loyal (never cheated on her), I was fun to be with (most of the time), I was successful, and I was prepared to work hard in therapy to improve myself.

I relished couples therapy. I loved the honest feedback, in a calm, neutral, environment. I took a long hard look at myself, and with Kathy's guidance and with our therapist's guidance, for the first time, I could clearly see my issues, and this was a big first step. I was ready to make big changes. Whether I could change enough in time to save our marriage wasn't clear, but I began to change, big time. I was in pain, and that's the perfect time to grow.

My Three Issues

Here are my three major issues, the ones that Kathy outlined, and that I began to tackle in couples therapy: I was yelling too much during our more intense arguments, with both her and the boys; I was self-centered and entitled, to the exclusion of other people's needs; and I took up too much space.

I Used to Yell Too Much

It's interesting for me to re-examine the yelling issue. If two people get married, and they both come from families where there was a lot of "loud" communication, then that seems to become their natural, normal way of communicating. I know of a few families who do this, and they seem unaware of the big impact that the yelling has on others, especially those who were raised in a quiet household. I was raised in a louder household, and I wasn't aware of the negative impact that my yelling was having on Kathy. When I was in high school, my father and I yelled at each other almost nightly (Chapter 2). So, that's what I was accustomed to.

With Kathy and me, don't get me wrong, I didn't scream at the top of my lungs in every argument, nor did Kathy accuse me of this. Rather, I would yell once or twice a week when we had an argument. As a child, I was not taught that yelling was bad. Now, I could see that yelling is bad.

This yelling issue was at the forefront of Kathy's three major complaints against me, because she felt that it had a negative impact on both her and our boys. Kathy said she was still bothered by some of our loud arguments. I needed to get this under control sooner, not later, and I was ready to resolve it. Within a few months, I cut my yelling down to once a month maximum, and within a couple of years, I got rid of it completely (maybe once a year I'll yell about something). And it's a good thing, too, because this new-found control may have saved our marriage. One nice thing about resolving my yelling tendency was that it augured well with poker. Showing less emotion in my primary relationship meant that I would show less emotion when I lost big hands. And so, at the poker tables I became calmer, and tilted far less often.

Great Logic, I'm Right, but What is This; I Still Lose?!?

In the heat of the moment, I seem able to retain my logic and my deductive reasoning. My many battles at poker tables had taught me the necessity of being less emotional, and more logical and reasoned. Because if you lose control of your logic and reasoning at the table, it could cost you a tournament, or at least a healthy stack of chips. Back then, Kathy didn't retain her logic and deductive reasoning when we fought, and thus, when we found ourselves in arguments where I was clearly right, I would press, press, press, and it became messy. When I pressed, Kathy felt as if I was beating her up.

It wasn't until the age of 48 (I was slow on this learning curve) that I learned that it doesn't matter who is right logically in an argument in your primary relationship. It's not about right and wrong. Especially if you're scarring your wife with your winning arguments, and blowing up your marriage in the process. By the way, the latest research shows that a single "eye roll" can have a profound impact on your spouse, or your primary relationship partner, for up to six months!

So, Kathy and I would have an argument, and she would list the points demonstrating why she was right. And then, like a skilled debater, I would attack her last, weakest, point. And then things would go sideways. Kathy may have been right in the actual overall argument, but I would be right about the last point. I used to joke that Kathy would argue that "one plus one does not equal two" when she was emotional.

The argument might go like this:

Kathy, "The Rolling Stones are the greatest rock band, ever."

Phil, "What about the Beatles? Why do you think the Stones are the best?"

Kathy, "First, they have the greatest number of number 1 hits of all time. Second, they have been doing it for 50 years. Third, they have the biggest brand in the rock and roll universe. Fourth, Mick Jagger is the best singer, ever."

Me, ready to pounce on the last, weakest point, "Mick Jagger isn't the best singer ever! You're just plain wrong. There are hundreds of better voices, like Whitney Houston's voice, and Prince's voice. Those two have better voices than Mick's, admit it." (I switch the point from singer to voice, but I do say "voice.")

Kathy, "I have good reasons for the claim that the Stones are the best band of all time."

Phil, "Admit that Mick's voice isn't the best voice ever!"

Kathy, "You're wrong!"

Phil, rolling his eyes (and causing more damage than he can imagine), "Admit that Mick's voice isn't the best voice, ever!"

Kathy, "You're wrong!"

Now, emotions are flying, I'm smug, I'm sure that I'm right, I roll my eyes (horrible for any relationship), and I continue to hammer my winning point home. Unbeknownst to me, the "hammering my points home" and the eye roll feel like subtle emotional abuse to Kathy. And, from my side of the coin, I'm truly upset that this argument continues when I'm so obviously right. How can Kathy not see that Mick Jagger's voice is not the best voice? Not even close?

What happened? I've managed to find the weakest point in Kathy's argument, and, if she weren't defensive, she would at least concede that point in a second. But because I've rolled my eyes, and sent her into a protective state, she is in no position to hear my logical argument. Me, pressing on, fighting with logic and deductive reasoning, she clinging to the original argument, feeling a small amount of abuse, and going into a defensive shell. This pattern can ruin a marriage! By the way, I actually agree with her that the Stones are the best band all time, but I couldn't help questioning her weakest point.

Obviously, I was way too obsessed with winning arguments, and to be fair, it is important in my profession both to win, and to clearly see logic, and deductive reasoning.

The 20-Second Response Rule, and the Stop Sign

Now, at the beginning of an argument, Kathy and I have learned to take 20 seconds before we respond to one another. It's amazing how many potential responses I can throw away, when I wait 20 seconds before responding to something that Kathy said! And, when things feel out of control, then one of us can give the other a "stop sign." We find these tools helpful for us.

Poker Brat

I Was Taking Up Too Much Space, 70% of the Box

Our therapist was particularly brilliant with the concept of Kathy and me "sharing a box." If our primary relationship was in a box, then what percentage of that box did I take up? Kathy and I both thought that I took up 70% of the box. Now, to be fair, I couldn't own 70% of the box without Kathy conceding too much ground, so this wasn't all on me. But we would have to figure this out. One thing we did immediately was to let Kathy choose (or a lot of times force her to choose) where we were going to eat every night. (I had been making most of our food choices for the last 12 years!)

I was the primary breadwinner in our family, and it was important that my head be right. Thus, Kathy and I constantly talked about my state of mind. If I was off, then I could lose way too much money, on any given day. So, you can see how it happened that I occupied 70% of the box.

Meanwhile, here Kathy was super successful, and she was taking up only 30% of the box. We have worked hard on this discrepancy for years, but it's not easy when I get global attention, when fans ask Kathy to take pictures of them with me, and when I'm the center of attention just about everywhere we go. Still, we have come a long way.

Offering Empathy, the Right Way

This would prove to be quite difficult for me. In 2001, I was so self-centered and had so much ADD, that I couldn't even listen to Kathy talk for more than three minutes. And when I did manage to listen for that meager three minutes, then I would always want to solve her issues (like us men tend to do) and tell her that everything would be OK. What Kathy really wanted was for me to see her predicament, to communicate clearly to her that I saw it, and to let her know that I understand why she felt bummed out. I know this now. I'm better at it now. It turns out that I saw her issues clearly most of the time, even back then, but that I would skip the "that sucks" part of the empathy process, and go straight to the "have you tried this?" or the "you will be OK" parts of the process.

But back then, when I was listening to Kathy with all my attention, and trying my hardest to give her empathy, my mind would wander too easily. My ADD had a big effect on us. One useful trick was for me to stare at Kathy as she talked. If I broke eye contact, then I risked losing track, or, even worse, and more disrespectful, switching subjects on her.

My ADD serves me well in the poker world. I seem to see everything at the poker tables. If we have nine players at the table, and one of the players does not ante, I always know who it is. I even have a routine for it: I will wait for the dealer to gather in the chips, and for someone else to say something. If no else notices, then I will ask the dealer, "Is the ante right?" No? [That's a shocker!] And then I will point out who owes the ante. If the guilty party argues, then I always offer to bet them $5,000; we can check the camera? The guilty party always declines, and throws their ante in quickly!

This hyperfocus thing may be great at the poker tables, but it is hell for primary relationships!

We Emerge from Couples Therapy Stronger than Ever, and Closer Than Ever

After 16 months of couples therapy, with the first few months being super intense, Kathy and I came out of the process as close as we had ever been as a couple. At that point, I told myself, and my friends, "Kathy has made me into a better man." I loved couples therapy, and when we stopped going, I missed it! I missed the growth. I could feel the growth, and I wanted more of *that*. Yes, I had grown, but I knew that I still had a lot more growing to do.

Bonetti Stunned, in Disbelief and in Tears as I Listen to Him

One night, nine months into couples therapy, I had a random conversation with John Bonetti. Suddenly, Bono starts crying! I'm like, "Are you OK?" Bono says, "Yes, I'm happy. It's the first time that you've ever listened to me. I feel like it's the first time that I feel like you've really heard me." Whoa. I realized then, that by improving my primary relationship, I would improve all my relationships. And, I had to smile, because it was the first time that I saw clear evidence that I had grown as a man. I was also sure that all of this growth would help my poker skills.

32

The 2002 WSOP, Chan vs. Hellmuth, and the Shaved Head

At the 2002 WSOP, I made one final table (in Limit Omaha), and had another deep, deep, run in the $2,500 Heads-Up No Limit Hold 'Em Tournament, but only 29 of us signed up. In the first round, I drew Mel Weiner, and the ace WSOP tournament director at the time, Matt Savage, had a lot of fun with that match up, saying it was "Weiner vs. whiner!" Ouch! I guess I deserved that needle. With eight players left, there was talk that the finals could end up Johnny Chan vs. me. And, in the semi-finals, I beat World Champion of Poker, Tom McEvoy, and Chan dispatched Diego Cordovez.

Chan vs. Hellmuth III, for a WSOP Bracelet!

WSOP history was at stake! I had a chance to win my eighth WSOP bracelet, and tie Doyle Brunson (poker legend; the late Johnny Moss has nine). At the same time, Johnny had a chance to win bracelet number 7 and tie me for second place in WSOP bracelet wins. Johnny was the all-time leading money winner at the WSOP, with over $3 million in earnings, and I was third on the list with about $2.8 million. (T.J. Cloutier was about $60,000 ahead of me. I had started the 2002 WSOP one month earlier, first on the list.)

The scheduling of matches during that WSOP Heads-Up Championship was wacky. Players were left on our own to determine when the matches would get under way, and some players would agree to a time, and then show up an hour late (not me!). Sometimes, when players were deep in the current WSOP tournament that they were playing, they didn't have time to play their matches. So, the heads-up tournament took two weeks to complete, and ran all the way into the finale, the WSOP main event.

I made a deep run in the WSOP main event that year, and, immediately upon busting, the WSOP staff said Johnny Chan and I needed to play our match. The press was there in full force by then, and it was determined that Johnny and I would play in the main casino, not the tournament area, in front of cameras. I was super tired after busting the main event, and I tried to put my foot down and insist that we play the next day. But the next day was the main event final (Day 4), on ESPN, and the WSOP staff told me I had to play that day. I agreed to play the match three hours hence, after I took a nap. After just busting in the WSOP main event, I couldn't nap.

By the way, before I whine about the timing of our match, let me point out that Johnny was in the zone! He had had a good 2002 WSOP, making four final tables: finishing second, third, fifth, and eighth, and I knew that he was in good form. Johnny started the match by playing super-fast. He raised, re-raised, and bet and bet, and I chose to slow-play my big hands. Basically, I never put in a raise. I let him win all the small pots, and then, when I had a big hand, I let him try to bluff me out, and then called him down.

One pot that came up during our session was when I called and didn't raise, with Q-Q. Johnny was playing fast, and I knew he would raise it up if I just called, and then I could re-raise. But Johnny surprised me, and checked. The flop came down K-K-9, Chan checked, and I checked. A seven came off, Chan checked, I bet, Chan raised, and I called. The last card was a six (K-K-9-7-6), and Chan bet out 12,000, a huge amount (we had started with 40,000 each in chips)! I studied for four minutes. Why so much? I had seen him make big bluffs before. Finally, I folded. I think it was a good fold, but there were no hole card cameras at the 2002 WSOP, so I'll never know.

After 45 minutes, Chan had won 65% of the pots, but I managed to hold a tiny chip lead. In general, he won the small pots, and I won the big pots. I could see that he was frustrated with his tactics, and he reset. I reset as well. I was going to try to play fast vs. Johnny. I had 28,000 to Johnny's 52,000, when the following hand came up: I opened for 700 on the button (the blinds were 100–200) with J-9. Johnny raised 1,500 more, to 2,200 total. I called that in the spirit of "it's time to play/outplay" this guy. It's not my usual style to play these kinds of hands for a big re-raise, but I was going to mess with Johnny a bit. The flop was K-J-9 rainbow (meaning no flush draws), and Johnny bet out 2,000. I had flopped two pair! Now I mulled over my options. I knew that Johnny would play all-in with me with K-Q, K-10, A-K, A-A, or maybe even with Q-Q. I studied Johnny, but he kept still and quiet (no read yet). Should I smooth call his 2,000 or raise right here? What to do?

I didn't think he would have re-raised me with K-J or K-9 or Q-10, so I could eliminate those hands. Unless he had trips, I felt like I had him beat. Finally, I raised 6,000, making it 8,000 to go. Johnny then moved all-in, and I called, for my last 18,000 in chips. Alas, Johnny had pocket kings. I was drawing dead, match over! I had lost way too many chips on that hand. My fault.

Meanwhile, the all-time bracelet race was heating up! Chan and I had seven bracelets each, and Doyle had eight (Johnny Moss had nine), as we battled for WSOP history. Over the next seven years, the active players bracelet lead went back and forth between the three of us!

If That Guy Wins, I'll Shave My Head!

On Day 3, as I have already mentioned, I had busted out of the main event, and then lost, heads up, to Johnny Chan. Busting the Main, and then losing a bracelet heads up; that's a bad day! The next day, the ESPN producers asked me to hop into the booth to comment on the WSOP main event final table with Gabe Kaplan. I agreed.

Some back story is in order. On Day 3 of the WSOP Main, Robert Varkonyi, a rank amateur from New York, beat me in a massive pot, and then a couple of hands later, he busted me. In the big pot, Robert had Q♦-10♦ and raised it up. I re-raised with A♥-K♥, and Robert moved all-in, for a mountain of chips. I correctly smelled weakness, and I called for most of my chips. When Robert flipped up Q♦-10♦, the whole table was like, "What in the world is this guy doing." You just didn't see players put in mountains (42 big blinds) with Q-10! All-in pots were usually like A-K vs. Q-Q. The door card (the first card that you can see when the dealer flops three cards) was an ace, but right behind it was a queen, and a ten: pretty sick!

So, when Varkonyi somehow made the final table, I felt like he would "blow up," and give the chips away. And, almost immediately, he massively overplayed his pocket jacks vs. pocket aces, and lost most of his chips. At that point, I told the producers that I was going to say, a few minutes before he blew his chips, and on air, "If Robert Varkonyi wins, then I'll shave my head." But now that he blew most of his chips, the statement lacked potency. But the producers said, "You should still say it." So, when they turned the cameras back on, I said it.

By the way, I could determine the moment when someone told Varkonyi what I had said, because he bristled in his chair! Shortly thereafter, Varkonyi doubled up, and then doubled up again. When they made it down to the final three players, someone told the assembled crowd (hundreds of people) what I had said, and they began chanting, "Shave Phil's head, shave Phil's head, shave Phil's head!" This chanting continued, on and off, until Varkonyi won the WSOP main event. At which point, I manned up, and I had my head shaved in front of the assembled crowd, the media, and ESPN. My head shaving made the ESPN show, and that moment is caught on YouTube.

What were the odds, seriously? Varkonyi was an amateur, and he was a short stack at an eight-handed table, when I officially told the world that he was so poor at poker, that I would shave my head if he won! And, if he didn't win, my comment would have become a cliff note. Instead, they show my head being shaved, for two minutes, on ESPN!

The World Poker Tour

As I check TheHendonMob.com website, it appears that I made ten more final tables in 2002, from June to December, including two final tables in the burgeoning WPT: first, at the Bicycle Club, where I finished in eighth place, and second, in San Francisco, where I finished in fourth place. I felt as if the WPT would make poker grow in a big way, and that's why I decided to write *Play Poker Like the Pros* (Chapter 34) ahead of the coming poker wave.

33

2003 WSOP: The Bracelet Race is on, and Forgiveness Pays!

I was scorching hot in poker tournaments in the first four years of the new millennium! At the website TheHendonMob.com, I count 51 final tables (11 wins!) from January 1, 2000, to December 31, 2003. But, I was still short of my lifetime goal of being the all-time WSOP bracelet winner, especially because Johnny Chan had won his seventh bracelet, heads up vs. me no less (Chapter 32), at the 2002 WSOP. At the beginning of the 2003 WSOP, the legendary Doyle Brunson had eight bracelets (poker great Johnny Moss had nine), and Chan and I had seven apiece.

The Bracelet Race Heats Up! Brunson vs. Chan vs. Hellmuth

At the 2003 WSOP, on April 23rd, I finished in 12th place in the fixed-limit HORSE (Hold 'Em, Omaha 8/b, Razz – Seven Stud Low, Seven Card Stud, and 8-or-Better Stud) tournament. World Champion of Poker, Doyle Brunson, won his ninth bracelet to tie Johnny Moss for the all-time bracelet lead! What a legend!

Just three days later, on April 26th, in the $2,500 WSOP Limit Hold 'Em, I won my eighth bracelet in a 194-player field. Bracelet count then: Moss nine, Doyle nine, me eight, and Chan seven. Johnny Chan, not to be outdone, won the $5,000 buy-in No Limit Hold 'Em tournament, with 127 players! Wow, in the first week of the WSOP, Doyle Brunson, Johnny Chan, and I all won bracelets, and we weren't done yet! Bracelet count: Moss 9, Doyle 9, Chan 8, me 8.

The very next day, I made the final table of the $1,500 Limit Omaha, but in my first attempt to tie for the all-time bracelet lead, I came up short and finished in third place. Then, on May 8th, Johnny Chan struck again! Johnny won the $5,000 Pot Limit Omaha tournament in a field of 94 players. The press was having a field day! WSOP bracelet count: Chan 9, Moss 9, Brunson 9, Hellmuth

8. Two days later, I made the final table of the $3,000 Limit Hold 'Em, but alas, another time knocking at the all-time door ended in sixth place.

Chan, Brunson, and I Win 5 WSOP Bracelets in 2003

On May 15th, in a field of 398 players, I brought home bracelet number 9! Finishing in third place, and in second place, respectively, were Erik Seidel and the up and coming Daniel "Kid Poker" Negreanu (Appendix 2 – also Daniel wrote the foreword for this book). What a final three: 398 players, and it comes down to the three of us? There is skill in poker, don't mess with us! The WSOP bracelet count at the end of the 2003 WSOP: Moss nine, Chan nine, Brunson nine, and Hellmuth nine. A four-way tie in a battle for WSOP history that would continue for the next seven years!

For good measure, two months later, Doyle won a WPT title at the Bicycle Club. That seems odd now, considering our ages, me winning the title at the Bike in 1988 (Chapter 13), and Doyle winning it in 2003. Time warp!

President Trump's US Poker Championships in Atlantic City

To finish off the year, I finished third in two major tournaments. First, Donald Trump (President Donald Trump, that is) held the US Poker Championships, and the main event was televised. It came down to Erik Seidel (he's always there!), Toto Leonidas, and me. I had the chip lead, but I folded A-K to Toto's A-Q. Toto raised, I re-raised big, and he moved all-in. I couldn't believe that Toto would put that much money in with A-Q! I thought he was stronger, but I was wrong. Although I folded, I did keep a healthy chip stack.

Later, when we hit three handed, I made a fold that I regret. Toto raised it up on the button, and Erik folded. I thought Toto was super weak, and I knew that he was super-aggressive, so I just called, to trap Toto. The flop was 8-7-2, I checked, Toto bet 70,000, and I called. The turn was a king (8-7-2-K), I checked, and Toto bet 200,000. I was rooting for no ace, and no king, on the turn. But still, my trap was coming together perfectly! And I could still beat 10-10, 9-9, and all bluffing hands. But I couldn't beat a king, as if for example Toto held K-Q, or K-J. I studied forever, and I folded! Toto then flipped up Q-J offsuit, sigh. A stone-cold bluff! That one really hurt.

When I did get my money, all-in vs. Toto an hour later, I had him in bad shape with my top pair to his bottom pair. I recall that he had hit his card, and I had fallen over backwards on a side stage. Television didn't capture that moment (that would have been great for the ratings!), but it is seared into my mind. With first place $388,000, second $223,146, third $116,424, and no deal. Third place really hurt!

Betrayal!

On Monday November 10, 2003, I received an odd phone call. Someone from the online poker site that I represented, UltimateBet.com (UB), (see Appendix 1), called me to tell me that there had been some unusual activity in an account that I had funded. Apparently, that account had played another account heads up and lost $28,000.

The unusual thing was that the $28,000 had been lost "chip dumping." Chip dumping is when one player plays another player heads up, and loses cash to him. Chip dumping started off innocently enough, when Player A wanted to lend Player B money online; Player A would intentionally lose money to Player B. So, I might call Huck Seed and ask him to lend me $5,000 at UB, so that I could fund my account. Then, we would play heads up, and Huck would lose $5,000 to me by folding his hand on the end, and I would pay him cash later, or send him a check.

I had been staking a known poker player, and loaning him money to support him and his loved ones. This player had done well for me online, and of the $28,000 he stole from me, $14,000 was his money! And he would have got away with it if he didn't try to save $3 a hand in rake. If he had played his opponent (apparently, it was his brother!) 40 or 50 hands, then no one would ever have known. But they wanted to save the $3 a hand in rake, while they stole my $14,000, and this left a trail. Apparently, the cash had already been taken off the site, thus couldn't be recovered. I felt so betrayed!

How to Handle the Betrayal?

I was stunned! I was upset and in disbelief. How could this player steal from me, especially when all he had to do was call me and ask, "Can I have $10,000, I really need the cash?" I called a close friend, and my friend said, "Fry him! Release all the evidence. This guy deserves pain!" Yes, I could do that. And then a long war on the internet would ensue for all to see, even though this guilty player had nothing on me, because I live my life at a high, high, level, both morally and ethically. Still, when you throw stones, you can get hurt, too.

After an hour of feeling tortured, I made a key decision. I would celebrate my life. At 7 p.m., I grabbed Kathy and told her:

> *Honey, we are going to the most expensive restaurant in the bay area, right now, and we are going to buy the most expensive bottle of Château d'Yquem that they have. Our lives are blessed, and I want to focus on that. I want to walk up any hallway in the world, and not have to turn left, or to turn right, when someone is walking toward me.*

I decided to forgive this player, not destroy him, but he would have to pay me back the $14,000. I called UB and said, "Bury this, there is no upside for me in going to war with this guy. I don't walk in his shoes. Maybe he had some sort of reason to steal from me? At least one that made sense to him." I called the guilty player and he was in tears, begging for forgiveness.

Forgiveness for the Win!

Kathy and I had studied Buddhism at a retreat in 1999, and I loved the concept of forgiveness. I don't forgive for the benefit of the guilty party, I forgive for my own benefit! The guilty party is *not* the one who *feels* negativity; that party probably doesn't even think of us very often. *We*, the wronged, feel negativity when we think of the guilty party. So, I forgive them, just so I don't have to feel the negativity.

So I hopped onto my own bed and closed my eyes, and meditated. I thought of the guilty party, and I sent waves and waves of love toward the guilty party. It's not easy to do, but once you send that love sincerely, it seems as if the negativity in your own mind fades. And while I was at it, I sent waves of love to all my family and friends. There is no downside to spending 30 minutes sending out waves of love!

Forgiveness Leads to What?!?

A few days later, on Thursday, I flew to the East Coast to play in Foxwoods WPT tournament. On Friday, while walking down a hallway at Foxwoods, I ran into the guilty party, who was visibly shaken. I admit that it was hard for me to shake his hand in that hallway, but I did. Three days later, I found myself at the final table of the Foxwoods WPT. I played well enough to win that thing three times over, but the cards didn't cooperate and I finished third, for... $281,700!

I forgive somebody for stealing from me, and then, within a week, I cash for ten times the amount that was stolen, weird! Can't make that up. But think about it. If I had gone public, then I would have spent that week fighting in online forums. I would have spent that week confirming to the other players in the WPT that yes, indeed, the guilty player had stolen cash from me. But instead, I forgave him, and continued living my blessed life. I won $281,700. And what of that guilty player? He paid me back in full, and he became a "protector" of mine (my wife pointed this out to me, years later, in 2010). She used the word "protector." And it's true! If we're at the same table and someone attacks me, he always defends me. Whenever he can, he defends me, and he always says nice things about me. That's why I'm a big believer in forgiveness. It keeps my energy clean. It eliminates hate, the kind that most people accumulate.

34

A *New York Times* Best Seller!

In 1987, I wrote down a list of "lifetime goals" (Chapter 10), and by 1990 I had achieved most of them! One lifetime goal that I had not knocked off my list by 2002 was to write a *New York Times* best-selling book. As time passed, and I dwelled on that goal, I felt as if my autobiography, this book, would give me the best chance to hit the prestigious *New York Times* best-seller list. (By the way, I started writing this book, on and off, in 1998.)

Hello, WPT; Golden Opportunity to Write a *New York Times* Best Seller?

In early 2002, it was announced that the WPT would be formed forthwith. This new WPT would consist of 12 poker tournaments, a series of 12 shows (12 six-handed final tables), and they would appear on the Travel Channel. Man, had I been waiting for this! I theorized that if people watched bowling, and were excited by its $10,000 first-place prizes, then poker, with its $1 million prize pools, should be huge! (By the way, I like bowling!)

So, still in early 2002, I decided to surf the upcoming poker wave. I would write a book ahead of the perceived wave. I decided that I was too young (I was 38 years old) to finish my memoirs, this book, but maybe I should, finally, write a poker strategy book? I had been planning on writing a "how to" book for years, knowing that Doyle Brunson had crushed it with his "how to" book *Super System*. I even had an outline prepared.

To maximize the audience for my "how to" book, I thought that I had to write the book primarily for beginners. After all, there were billions of beginners, and only a couple of thousand pros. I would write it for everyone, as opposed to writing it just for professional poker players, like most of the other poker authors had done. It would be for rank beginners and seasoned veterans, cover cash game strategy and tournament strategy, and cover every HORSE game. I knew I could sell a lot of copies, but for this book to become a *New York Times* best seller? That was more a distant dream of mine. But, I had a goal, and I thought, "Just put the book out there, for everyone, ahead of the upcoming poker wave, and who knows what could happen?"

Harper Collins Rosy Proposal, All Smoke?

So, my agent Sheree Bykofsky and I submitted a book proposal to Harper Collins. Harper sent us a rosy offer, detailing how they would push the book with posters in local book stores, and make sure that I was on big, national television shows, like *The Tonight Show*. Personally, I didn't care about the size of the cash advance and I wanted nothing. I wanted an annuity! (Harper Collins pays royalties twice a year.) And if the book were to do well, then it would be a big annuity. But, Sheree taught me that most books do not earn their advance. Harper Collins offered $35,000, which wasn't great, but both Sheree and I liked their rosy proposal.

We accepted Harper Collins' offer, and it was agreed upon that the manuscript would be due on January 30, 2003. The book was to come out during the 2003 WSOP. Matthew Benjamin, at Harper Collins, would be my point of communication, and straight off, he suggested a change in my outline.

Understand, I had a vision of exactly what I wanted the outline (the chapters, the appendixes, and the order of chapters and appendixes) to look like, and I didn't like his change. But it was small, and I agreed to it. A few months later, Matthew suggested another minor change to my outline, and I laughed when I saw it. Unbeknownst to Matthew, the chapter he suggested that I move in the preceding change, he now suggested that I move somewhere else, in fact, right back where it started. The book would look exactly as I had game planned it. It was my book, through and through.

Matthew also proposed that we call the book, *Play Poker Like the Pros*. I thought that that was a brilliant title, and I loved it right away!

Play Poker Like the Pros

Now that I had sold it (in April), I would have to write the thing! I kept my schedule clear for December and January, but as the months passed, I was getting nervous. Could I actually write a whole book? I knew the subject matter well, teaching basic and advanced strategies in all the HORSE games, but I was intimidated by the task of writing 100,000 words. Especially, 100,000 words in two months! In late October, I called a friend, professional writer Andy Glazer, and asked for his help. Andy agreed to help me, and he would get started right away. But sadly, Andy got sick for a couple months, and that left me writing the book by myself. So, on October 20, 2002, I dove in, head first!

My Player Types: Mouse, Jackal, Elephant, Lion, Eagle

One week into writing the book, I decided to scrap the first 5,000 words, and start over. I couldn't write a poker strategy book without writing about how strategies changed against certain "types" of players. So, the first thing I had to do was to outline these "player types." It seemed to me that it would feel easier for readers to remember those player types if I classified them as animals.

So, here are the basic animal types in *Play Poker Like the Pros*: a super loose player is a "jackal," a player that calls a lot is an "elephant," a player who plays super-tight is a "mouse," a player who does most things right is a "lion," and a player that is a top-50 player on the world stage is an "eagle." With that frame of reference established, I went back to work.

My "Writing Mode": Opening My Mind

When I'm writing a book, as I finish one chapter, I always begin another one or two chapters, before I knock off for the day. Why? I trust that part of my mind will work on the new chapters, either when I'm sleeping, or even during the rest of my active day. I trust that I will have fresh, relevant copy to write later, when I did sit down to write again. And that's exactly what seems to happen!

Writing Mode: Writing in Bed

While writing *Play Poker Like the Pros*, I would go to bed at night, and my mind would conjure up good changes to the chapters that I had worked on, and conjure up good material for the chapters that I was going to write next. At first, I would write these changes down (I kept a pen and paper next to my bed), but after a week or two, I decided to trust my mind to remember, and implement, the changes the next morning.

So, when I woke up, it was like, "Go!" I wouldn't talk to anyone, not Kathy, not the kids, and not the waiter at University Coffee Café after I rushed over there! Instead, I would throw open my laptop, and go to town implementing all the changes that I had come up with the night before. I had to get it all out immediately, before I forgot it!

"Writing Mode": I Can't Keep Track of Time!

The second thing about my "writing mode" is that I cannot keep track of time. After I did finally order breakfast at University Coffee Café, the pesky waiter would ask me if I wanted more food, and I would quickly answer, just to get rid of him, but politely, "No thanks." Then, shortly thereafter, at least it seemed to me, he would ask me if I wanted to pay the bill. Again, I would say no, just to get rid of him. Then he would come back and tell me that I had to pay him now, because he had to leave for the day. In my mind, I would be like, "What? Oh, I see, it's noon, and I came in at 8 a.m." So, I would apologize, pay the bill, tip a healthy amount of money (at least 30%), and then proceed to order lunch from the next waiter! Time flies for me when I'm sculpting every single word, and banging them out at a pace of 1,500 words a day.

Making the Deadline

After two months of writing, I had 98,000 words. I wrote about 88,000 of them, and Andy Glazer, who was feeling better by January, wrote roughly 10,000 words. Now it was time for me to hire an editor. I found Bill Carver on my own, and he makes my writing shine! (Thanks, Bill!) I especially love how Bill brought the word "auger" into use in *Play Poker Like the Pros*. (As in, "my writing augers well with Bill's editing.") In any case, I handed Bill 300 pages of clean-looking white paper, with a black typeface, and he handed me back 300 pages with red ink marks everywhere. So much red ink, that it looked like a one-year-old had got ahold of it: his red marker. Bill must have used four pounds of red on my first draft! Each word or phrase that he changed would have to be carefully examined by me, or the meaning of the poker tactics that I wrote about would subtly change. No one could do this for me, and it took 100 hours of my time. Painful!

All that red ink? Though I may be good at telling stories, and delivering good solid poker tactics, remember, I told you in Chapter 2 that I never did get a grade as good as a B in any of my English classes, or writing classes. I never did well in English, but I did manage to turn in my first book on time, before the deadline.

The Razz Tourney at 2004 WSOP: *Play Poker Like the Pros* is a Best Seller?!?

I remember well that when I received the call on my cell phone I was just outside the Loews Hotel in Santa Monica, in August 2004. It was Matthew Benjamin, and he said, "Where are you right now?" I said, "I'm at the Loews Hotel, in Santa Monica." Matthew said, "*Play Poker Like the Pros* just hit the *New York Times* best-seller list! We are sending a bottle of Dom Perignon to your room." I was stunned! And elated! Another lifetime goal (from my goal sheet in Chapter 10) realized! And a big one, at that. I walked around feeling a huge amount of energy, and satisfaction. I was walking on sunshine for a couple of weeks!

How Did *Play Poker Like the Pros* Hit the List?

It turned out that one of the players at the WSOP $1,500 buy-in Razz (Seven Card Low) final table, which was recorded, and then broadcast on ESPN a couple of months later, held *Play Poker Like the Pros* up to the camera, and said, "I didn't even know how to play Razz, but I read Phil Hellmuth's book on the plane out to Las Vegas, and now I'm at the final table." He didn't win life-changing money either; I believe it was $21,100. But, *Boom!* Book sales skyrocketed!

Harper Collins Smoke... Not Anymore!

And, now that *Play Poker Like the Pros* had hit the *New York Times* best-seller list, Harper Collins finally sprang into action! Roughly a year had passed since the book had been released, and now that it had hit the list, Harper sent out posters to hundreds of book stores all across America.

Meanwhile, on Amazon, which tracks up to the minute sales of every book on the planet, old and new, *Play Poker Like the Pros* hit as high as number 3! That's as high as I saw it, or as high as any of my friends saw it. I can't tell you how many times I clicked on that Amazon link to see where my book ranked! Andy was psyched for me when it hit number 988 on Amazon, never mind top 100, never mind top 10, never mind number 3!

Harper Collins then informed me that the book would be translated into French, German, and a bunch of other languages. I loved it! Poker was taking off across the globe!

A Spin-off Book: *Phil Hellmuth's Texas Hold 'Em*

A year or two later, Harper Collins asked if they could take the Texas Hold 'Em chapters, and turn them into a stand-alone paperback book, called *Phil Hellmuth's Texas Hold 'Em*. I agreed, with the caveat that I would write some new strategy chapters, for those who accidently bought this book, thinking it was different from *Play Poker Like the Pros*. Harper didn't love the idea, the new book was only $5.99, and they weren't worried about people who accidently bought it and *Play Poker Like the Pros*, but I said that it was a deal breaker. They agreed, and I wrote a cool new chapter on how to win a No Limit Texas Hold 'Em tournament.

Between the two books, and the different languages that they were translated into, we may have sold 1 million copies by now.

I'm Proud of *Play Poker Like the Pros*

I'm proud of *Play Poker Like the Pros*; I put my heart and soul into writing it. I shared, with the world, solid basic strategies for all the HORSE games. I also included advanced techniques, and tips and tactics, for No Limit Hold 'Em tournaments. And I did it in an entertaining, easy to read style. I used stories from actual hands to illustrate points, actual hands that I had played in, or that other great players had played.

I came up with my poker animals out of thin air, because I wanted to teach the best possible, and most accurate, poker tactics.

35

2004-2005: Tournament of Champions; NBC Heads Up

In the last couple of chapters I wrote about the WSOP bracelet race, and my book *Play Poker Like the Pros*. I mentioned that at the 2003 WSOP, the all-time WSOP bracelet lead exploded when Johnny Chan won two bracelets, Doyle Brunson won one, and I won two. We won five bracelets in one year! Entering the 2004 WSOP, the all-time bracelet count was: Johnny Moss nine, Chan nine, Brunson nine, Hellmuth nine. At the 2004 WSOP, the three of us won no bracelets, but I did make three final tables. But the most memorable thing for me, from the 2004 WSOP, was my line, "If it weren't for luck, I'd win 'em all."

I made that remark to my sister Kerry, innocently enough, during a break in the action, when I was at a WSOP final table. I said it while we were standing on the rail, during my 15-minute break. Honestly, I thought that the cameras were off. And I probably wouldn't even have remembered uttering that excellent line, except that when the show hit ESPN, the internet exploded!

I do remember the hand that I lost, the one that caused me to rattle off that line, one of my best lines ever. A player moved all-in with A♦-3♦, and I called with Q-Q. The board ran off: J♦-10♠-7♣-5♦-8♦, sigh. My opponent hit diamond, diamond, to make a flush. ESPN captured the hand, and then later, at the break, they captured my famous line.

The 2004 Tournament of Champions

On September 1, 2004, the WSOP (Harrah's owned the WSOP), in conjunction with ESPN, decided to have a Tournament of Champions (TOC), in which they invited the biggest names in the poker world. It would be invite only (ten players), with a first-place prize of $2 million. Harrah's and their partners were putting up the $2 million for the ten of us to play for, sweet! So, $2 million for first, but second place? Well, second place would be... nothing. And Harrah's would not allow us to make any deals. Understandably, Harrah's did not want us to split the prize money and take $200,000 each, and play for no cash. So, there it was, $2 million, or nothing. Cue up... Drama!

Invited to play were Doyle Brunson, Annie Duke, Howard Lederer (Annie's older brother), Johnny Chan, reigning World Champion of Poker Greg Raymer, Phil Ivey, Daniel Negreanu, David "Chip" Reese, T.J. Cloutier, and me. Some of the players were making saves with one another (trading 10% of Player A for 10% of Player B), and some were selling off pieces of themselves. On paper, each player had equity of roughly $200,000. So, the players could sell 10% of themselves to investors for $20,000, or 20% for $40,000. And most of them did sell, or trade pieces. And it seemed like a smart hedge to me. But, personally, I didn't sell even 1% of myself, and I didn't trade any pieces either. Not out of ego, but I think I was embarrassed to reach out and sell a piece of myself for something this specula- tive! What's more, I was busy traveling, making appearances, and attending book signings. I did give 5% to my new agent, Brian Balsbaugh, as a gift. Brian started Poker Royalty (to represent poker players), and was relocating to Las Vegas. It looked like he could use some cash, so it seemed like a cool gift to give him.

Hellmuth vs. Chan, Again, But Hellmuth Gets Lucky!

When we hit five-handed, I was all-in with 10-10 vs. Johnny Chan's K-K. Johnny was a 4½-to-1 favorite to bust me. The flop was A-2-2, and the turn card was a jack (A-2-2-J). Going into the last card, there were two tens left for me to win with, and 42 cards for Johnny to bust me with! I can't say that I was expecting a ten, but *boom!*, I smashed the ten of diamonds on the river! What an amazing card. Good thing too, because if I had busted at that point, then I was getting zero dollars.

Chan, Hellmuth, Lederer, and Duke Make a Save?

When we hit four-handed, a "save" was proposed. We would save $1 million, and play for $1 million. Based on chip stack size: I would get $340,000, Annie $300,000, Howard $240,000, and Johnny Chan $120,000, and we would play for $1 million for first place. Harrah's wasn't thrilled that we were talking, but if we were still playing for $1 million for first place, and we didn't tell anyone that we made a save for the next year (they wanted max drama on ESPN), then they were OK with it. After we agreed to the numbers, Howard Lederer had a change of heart. And at the last minute, he said, "No deal." (I heard later that Howard had sold off pieces to people, and wouldn't make much money if we made that deal.) OK, let's go, get the cards in the air! Shortly thereafter, Johnny Chan, who was the short stack, went broke.

Brother and Sister, Annie and Howard vs. Phil?!?

When Chan busted, shockingly, the three of us never even discussed making a save! No one said a word, and the cards were back in the air immediately. Normally, if I'm playing a brother and a sister in a three-handed game, I would be worried! Especially, when first place is $2 million, and second and third places combined receive zero dollars. But Annie Duke and Howard Lederer had reputations beyond reproach. Still, it was a lot of cash, and I would keep my eyes open for anything untoward. I knew that Annie and Howard had a heavy bias toward their sibling doing well, rather than me doing well. I also knew that they both had a heavier bias toward themselves doing well! I needn't have worried though, because Annie and Howard played so hard against each other that even I was shocked!

Couldn't Script It This Good: Great Drama in the TOC!

Annie and Howard were bombing each other, raise, re-raise, re-raise, all-in! The pace of play was insane. So, I sat back and waited. I was in no rush, I was in no hurry, I had enough chips (700,000 out of the 2 million in play) to sit back and see what happened between the two of them. And I thought that any time that I put a chip, voluntarily, into the pot, they would bomb me. Annie's and Howard's aggression level was high (way too high, in my opinion), and it seemed like any raise I made would be countered by a re-raise from one of them.

Before long, Annie had Howard all-in, her pocket 6-6s to Howard's pocket 7-7s. Howard was a 4½-to-1 favorite to win this pot, but if Annie somehow won the pot, then I would be heads up vs. Annie. On the flop of Q-Q-6, Annie smashed the biggest flop of her life! And yet, she put her head in her hands and looked disgusted. And overwhelmed. Can't blame her, can you? Imagine that you're about to outdraw your older brother, the guy who taught you how to play poker, the guy who invited you into the poker world, and you cost him at least $500,000! And send him home empty-handed! On the other hand, you're now about to play heads up, and in position to make at least a $500,000 save! Mind boggling. The board ran out 9-2, and Annie busted Howard in third place.

We Save $750,000!

After Annie was done consoling Howard, and apologizing for the bad beat that she had put on him, we looked at each other, and Annie said, "Let's take the microphones off and talk." Annie had 1.3 million in chips, to my 700,000, but she had a ton of respect for the way I played No Limit Hold 'Em. Annie offered a save at even (a generous offer), and eventually we agreed to take $750,000 apiece, and play for $500,000. Annie wanted to save $500,000, but I wanted to save $750,000, and it was agreed.

Thank You, Thank You, for that Sweet Ten of Diamonds!

Remember that ten of diamonds that I hit on Johnny Chan to stay alive? It was now worth at least $750,000! In a world where professional poker players remember too many bad beats, it's important to remember, and to give thanks, for the big cards that we did hit! Thank you, thank you, for that ten of diamonds.

Back to Annie vs. Phil: immediately, I took the chip lead when we both made trip fours on the turn card (10-8-4-4); my Q-4 to Annie's J-4. At this point, I thought the tournament was mine: 1.4 million for me, 600,000 for Annie. I was a little unlucky the rest of the way, but give credit where credit is due. Annie played great poker and won the TOC. Nice job, Annie!

I'm Over the Top in Defeat!

After I busted, I lurched into the only time in my life when I acted for the cameras. Sadly, all the other outbursts, the ones that have tens of millions of hits on YouTube, are me genuinely losing control. Don't get me wrong, I was smoking hot mad after I busted, but the $750,000 save had softened the blow. In any case, I exaggerated my usual tantrum, and it did make for good television. Harrah's appreciated my tantrum, and so did ESPN, because ratings for the 2004 TOC were off the hook!

The Inaugural NBC Heads-Up Poker Championships, 2005

On April 27, 2005, while I was running a super-busy schedule, I wasn't paying much attention to what was happening in the poker world. And when I saw the NBC Heads-Up Championships on my schedule for the following weekend, I was actually mad! I had planned on spending that weekend at home, with Kathy and the boys. Damn it! And what is this? The championship folks need me there the night before for a party; sigh.

Disrespected, and Out of Practice?

When I arrived, it seemed as if the players were disrespecting me with the betting line on who would win the thing. I wasn't listed as the favorite? Or in the top three picks? Were these guys on drugs! I had the best record in history, by a long shot, in No Limit Hold 'Em tournaments. I felt dissed, disrespected, and I was steaming. I had a chip on my shoulder heading into my first match!

Poker Brat

I showed up cold for my first match. I hadn't played any Hold 'Em in weeks, and I heard that the top pros had been practicing their heads up play. Everyone thought this would be a huge event in the poker world, and they wanted to be ready, and prepared, to play their best poker. Whatever. I didn't have high hopes; I hadn't thought about the NBC Heads-Up Championships at all. But when I saw the quality of the production, the draw party, the enthusiasm of everyone involved, and I realized that it was on network television, my level of enthusiasm changed. This really would be big!

I would play great poker, with a chip on my shoulder, no less, and see what happens. After I won my first two matches, rather easily, I remembered that I was pretty good at No Limit Hold 'Em tournaments.

Huck Seed, then Antonio "The Magician" Esfandiari

In the third round, my best friend, Huck Seed, was waiting for me. Huck was truly one of the best Hold 'Em players on the planet, and I knew it. I wouldn't take Huck for granted, that's for certain! I played my best, and Huck didn't play his best, which led to victory for me, and the right to face Antonio "The Magician" Esfandiari in the "elite eight."

Antonio and I had had an interesting relationship. I had hired him to do magic tricks for a party I had had at my house during the Bay 101 tournament in 2002. It was agreed that we would play heads-up No Limit Hold 'Em for his "fee." The fee was $500. We played, and I still recall that I had let Antonio run me over, until I had pocket aces. On a flop of K-2-2, Antonio hit a five (he had 5-5) on the turn to stack me. I was supposed to beat this kid, this magician, but he showed some grit and heart, and got lucky, and beat me. I was annoyed more than I should have been!

Antonio "Holds Over" Me, 2003–2011!

Then, in November 2002, in one of the first WPT tournaments ever held, Antonio made the final two tables with me. Antonio is a great poker player, now, and has been for years, but back in 2002 he was a megalomaniac at the poker tables! Moving all-in more than everyone else at our table combined, Antonio put himself low on chips (for no reason), with 14 left. He kept on playing crazy super-fast Hold 'Em, and I kept on waiting for him to bust. He was in my way! When someone is that "aggro" (super-aggressive), it is hard for the rest of the table to play many hands, unless you have "it" (a strong hand). Antonio, somehow, made the final six and busted me, and this started a long history of him crushing me in a super high percentage of the pots that we played. Much to my great annoyance,

Antonio "held over me" (was super lucky vs. me) for years! Including at a 2004 WSOP final table, when Antonio had Q-Q, to my K-K, and beat me on the river for a mountain of chips. (Antonio went on to win his first bracelet in that one.)

Antonio is well liked in the poker world now, but back then not so much. He once busted Phil Ivey in a WPT tournament in LA, and shouted at him, "Don't let the door hit you in the ass on the way out." Antonio was rough around the edges, and made quite a stir.

So now I'm matched up with a guy who is super lucky against me, and can bring out weird, negative talk. But I knew Antonio was good, and I wouldn't underestimate him! Early on, he tried his usual bluffing strategy vs. me, and he was almost rewarded. I had A-9, and he had 8-7 offsuit, and he bluffed on an A♥-5♥-2♦ board, then again on the 10♥ turn card. On the river, another heart hit, and his eight of hearts somehow turned into a flush, and he bet big. I called, and was disgusted when he said, "Flush." But then, much to my surprise, he showed only the 8♥, and I had trumped that with the 9♥! Hmmm... Maybe this time it would be different?

I hit a couple of big hands vs. Antonio, finally, and most of his chips went in when he was completely dead. That's the hope with a super-aggressive player, that you have them in bad shape for a huge pot. And it happens quite often. But they can inflict pain on you before you pick up those big hands.

In the NBC Heads-Up Championship "final four," vs. Poker Hall of Famer Lyle Berman, I picked up a lot of big hands, and he tried to bluff me when I had those strong hands. So, I was lucky vs. Lyle, and my timing was just fine. Onward, to the finals!

Chris "Jesus" Ferguson vs. Phil Hellmuth

The 2000 World Champion of Poker Chris Ferguson was waiting for me in the finals. It was now 2 a.m. at the Golden Nugget, and Chris and I had been playing 12 hours a day of intense poker, for the last two days. Fatigue could well be a factor! I knew Chris would be a tough match, but I also knew that he wasn't as experienced at No Limit Hold 'Em as I was. Chris may have been better at other poker games than I was, but not at No Limit Hold 'Em. Still, it was a bad time to underestimate anyone, so I assumed he would play amazing poker. I breezed through my first match vs. Chris, but the finals, and only the finals, was best two out of three.

I Stand Up to Thrust My Arms in the Air, And...

Our second match started with me winning the first two hands, and then it happened! I was expecting Chris to raise the third hand, and try to win it, and he did just that. I called with A♥-3♠. The flop was 9♦-5♥-2♥, Chris bet, and I called.

The turn was the 4♥, and I made a straight, with the nut-flush draw as a nice backup. The 4♥ was a huge card for me, but I couldn't beat a made flush. Chris checked, I bet 40,000, and Chris raised it to 120,000 to go.

It's rare to have so many chips out there already! And we weren't done yet. You see, we were deep, with tons of chips and tons of time to use those chips effectively. The NBC Heads-Up was designed to last a long time. Both of us started with 600,000 in chips, and the blinds were a relatively small 3,000–6,000. OK, I had a big hand, but could Chris beat a made straight? Did he have a flush, or a higher straight (6-3)? I considered moving all-in for roughly 600,000. If I did move all-in, and Chris had a flush, then I was in trouble, but I would still have outs (seven cards) to make a higher flush with my aces of hearts. I could fold this hand. I didn't have that many chips invested, and I could wait for a better spot. But something seemed wrong to me. I didn't think that Chris had it! So I moved all-in for that 600,000 total!

Now Chris began talking out loud... whew! He didn't have a flush, or a higher straight, or he would have called me immediately. I knew that I had the better hand. Then Chris said, "I think I have 11 or 12 outs." I thought, "11 or 12 outs, huh?" I was puzzled. And I knew that it couldn't possibly be true. I thought that perhaps he had K♠-K♥, had counted the nine hearts that he thought were left, and also had two kings. If he had that hand (K♠-K♥), then he was drawing dead! Finally, Chris said, "I call," and flipped up 9♥-2♠. Great! Chris had four wins to make a full house (two nines and two deuces), and I had 40 wins.

As the dealer turned the last card, I began to stand up and throw my arms into the air to celebrate, but a nine hit! The room exploded with wild cheering. Looking back at the video now, I see that as I was in the process of standing up, the dealer turned a nine, and halfway up I rerouted and fell to the floor. How cruel: 10-to-1 favorite to win NBC Heads-Up Championships, and then *this* card hits? I get Chris to put it all in *that* spot and lose?

A few minutes later, Chris finished my small stack off and won match number 2, and we were on to the rubber match. One match for the NBC Heads-Up Championships! At 3:30 a.m. I had Chris all-in with my 6-5 to his 2-2. I flopped a six, and the turn card was safe. With one card to come, Chris had two wins (a deuce), and I had 42 wins. This time, I did not stand up. I would wait. And I wouldn't be shocked if a deuce hit. Stunningly, the river was a deuce! And a deafening roar filled the room. I didn't react. There was no room for emotion, no room for anything but my best game. I paid Chris his chips, and counted down my chip stack. No need to show any emotion. I would have to keep my head down and play great poker, no matter how long it took, no matter what happened. Finally, at 4 a.m., the title was mine!

I told everyone in the room that I was buying them as much Dom Perignon as they could drink. I asked the owner of the Golden Nugget if they could give me fair price (might as well save a few dollars), and they brought every bottle of Dom in the casino. Fast forward to 5 a.m., and who was standing next to me helping me pour, with a smile on his face, but Chris Ferguson! Well handled, Chris. Classy until the end.

Jamie Horowitz Bets on Me!

With one major "featured table" on the NBC Heads-Up set, and a lot of matches under way simultaneously, NBC had to choose who they would put at the featured table. Jamie Horowitz, the big boss from NBC, who had had the idea to have the NBC Heads-Up Championships, decided that they were going to have me at the featured table all the way through. All the other producers tried to veto his decision. And apparently some of the players asked for the featured table, but Jamie stuck to his guns. And Jamie was rewarded when I won the whole thing.

The Bracelet Race Heats Up, Again, at the 2005 WSOP

After winning five WSOP bracelets between us, at the 2003 WSOP, and none at the 2004 WSOP, the late Johnny Moss had nine bracelets, Doyle Brunson had nine, Johnny Chan had nine, and I too had nine bracelets. That was about to change. On June 25th, Johnny Chan won the $2,500 Pot Limit Hold 'Em, with 425 players, to take the WSOP bracelet lead, by himself, for the first time in his life. The next day, I tried to respond to Chan's win with a win of my own, when I made the WSOP Pot Limit Omaha final table, but finished in eighth place.

But the great Doyle Brunson responded, and responded quickly! Doyle dug down deep, a mere four days after Chan won number 10, and on June 29th he won the WSOP $5,000 Six-Handed No Limit Hold 'Em tournament! With 301 players, Doyle showed us who he really is: a champion through and through! Bracelet count: Doyle 10, Chan 10, Moss 9, Hellmuth 9.

The 2005 WSOP Main Event: "I Can Dodge Bullets Baby!"

On Day 1 of the 2005 WSOP main event, I played like a wild man on the ESPN feature table! I successfully bluffed, and bluffed, and power bluffed some more. It felt like I played an absurd 50% of the hands at that table, and that I completely dominated play. I ran my starting stack of 10,000 chips, up to 40,000 in chips. Whereas the television coverage in the past made me look like I played poker super patiently (and this is an important gear to have), I just knew that the 2005

WSOP television coverage would show my wide open fast-paced domination of that table! ESPN would finally show the world all my beautiful moves! Not!

When I turned on the WSOP coverage on ESPN, they didn't show any of moves or my domination! Instead, they showed an amazing fold that I had made, where I had A♣-K♠, and I opened to 1,500, and a player behind me made it 3,000 to go. I sensed that something was wrong, but I called. The flop was A-4-4, I checked, and then my opponent checked. The turn was a queen, I checked, and then my opponent bet 10,000. Alarm bells as loud as church bells were going off in my head! I talked to my opponent, hoping that he would talk back; he did. He gave away more information, and I was sure that I was beat and I made up my mind to fold. For extra flourish (this was a wizardly fold), I flipped my cards face up as I said, "I am Phil Hellmuth!" The players around me were stunned; this play looked crazy to the world; to only lose 3,000 with A♣-K♣ in this spot was impossible. Then, my opponent showed A-A!

Inspired, I stood up, and said, "Honey, they were supposed to bust me this hand, but they forgot one thing: I can dodge bullets baby!" When this sequence hit ESPN, the internet exploded! First, many top poker players said that it was the best fold that they had ever seen. Second, and even bigger, was the line, "I can dodge bullets baby!" This became my most famous line ever, along with "If it weren't for luck, I'd win 'em all." (From earlier in this chapter.)

How Did Doyle, Johnny and Phil Get into the 2005 TOC?!?

The WSOP was having another TOC in November 2005, at Caesars Palace Hotel and Casino. But this time, it wouldn't be ten invited players. This time, players had to earn their way in, playing in WSOP Circuit Tournaments. But Doyle, Johnny, and I were too busy to play WSOP Circuit tourneys, so we didn't qualify. Because Harrah's was giving away $2 million, they reserved the right to invite whomever they wished to invite. As Harrah's examined the list of qualifiers in the TOC, they felt they needed some star power, players that the public knew. And so, it was announced to some fanfare, and a lot of whining (from the qualifiers), that Chan, Brunson, and Hellmuth would be invited to play in the 2005 TOC.

Phil Shows up for the TOC Five Hours Late; Hungover?

The night before the TOC, I had to MC a charity poker tourney in Phoenix for the Fallen Officers Foundation (Appendix 3). I had been hired to MC the charity poker tournament by the chief executive officer (CEO) of Taser, Rick Smith, and his brother Tom, head of sales for Taser. Back then, in 2005, I charged $10,000 a night for events, and in this case, I requested a private jet from Phoenix to Vegas after the charity event ended.

So it was that Rick Smith and I left Phoenix on his plane at midnight, and we started drinking on the plane. I've never been a huge drinker, volume-wise – and by the way, I don't recommend trying to "keep up" with any CEO! When we hit Vegas, I said to Rick, "Let's go to a club!" So, we shut down Tao Nightclub. And, I drank way too much, and went to bed at 8 a.m. The TOC started at noon. I was famous for showing up at least two hours late, so at least I could sleep in.

My Head is On Fire!

When I woke up, at 4 p.m., my head was on *fire*! The lyrics from Billy Joel's song *Big Shot* came to mind and I couldn't think straight. I knew I had to switch hotel rooms, didn't I? In my fog, I thought that it made sense to stay at Caesars Palace Hotel and Casino, where the TOC was being held, so that I could run to my room at dinner breaks, and just be closer to the action. But it was 4 p.m. already, and Harrah's had fought hard for me to play in the TOC. Best to get over there ASAP. Foggy and groggy, I rushed a shower, slammed water and coffee, and hightailed it to Caesars Palace. I sat down, with my head pounding, and my headphones on. I thought I could feel a little glare coming from the Harrah's folks (we get you in, and you show up five hours late with a hangover?), but I was too foggy to know for sure.

I was feeling miserable, and I felt like I couldn't even carry on a conversation. I had music on, and I wasn't taking those headphones off for anything. In this state, I felt as if I needed to play super patiently, and stay in there until I felt better and could play the game. It would be a shame to bust out when I was in this state, and then have regrets later (why did you drink so much...?). This super-tight gear kept me alive.

At dinner break, I had to taxi over to my hotel, and move my stuff to Caesars Palace. I arrived back at the tournament area, sweaty, still hung over, and still feeling awful. I stayed in that super-tight mode, and by midnight I had the chip lead, and I was 50% of my usual, talkative self.

Late Day 2 of the TOC, Chan and Brunson Deep

Fast forward to Day 2 and Doyle, Johnny, and I all made deep runs in the 2005 TOC. Johnny finished in 13th place, and Doyle in tenth place, the bubble (nine were paid, and Doyle finished tenth). But I flew into the final table, Day 3, third place in chips. At this point, I noticed that first place was $1 million, second was $325,000, and third was $250,000. I already knew that the winner would get a WSOP bracelet!

I was thinking:

> *Wouldn't it be sweet to win bracelet number 10 in this event? $1 million for first place, and three days of ESPN coverage; it was like I could say, "Hello, world! You just watched me win the NBC Heads-Up Championships and $500,000 on network television, and now bracelet number 10 and $1 million stood there on ESPN. Hello world, my name is Phil Hellmuth Junior."*

The night before the final table, I was flipping through the channels, and I saw poker legend and future Poker Hall of Famer Mike "the Mouth" Matusow playing poker. I thought, "Well, I might as well watch closely, because Mike is at the final table with me tomorrow, and maybe I'll pick up something watching him with the hole cards revealed." Indeed, I saw something when Mike bluffed, something that I could use against him at the TOC final table the next day.

Another Deal in Another TOC, or Not?

When we hit three handed, it was Mikey, Hoyt Corkins, and me. Hoyt was like Antonio Esfandiari (earlier in this chapter I commented on Antonio) to me, kryptonite. I knew, given time, that I would smash Hoyt, because he plays too many hands. And he plays those hands too aggressively. But that man has run really well against me for years. And to be fair, Hoyt is a tough opponent. If you give him room, he will take it, plus a lot more!

Three handed, I raised it up with A-8, Hoyt folded, and Mikey moved all-in. I wasn't paying attention to my raise sizing, and I did something a little bit differently. Mike perceived that as weakness, and whenever he sees weakness he moves all-in. I was pondering a call, and I counted the chips out to call. Here was my chance. I had studied Mikey the night before, and I saw the weakness then. (And I saw it now). I was thinking:

> *Mikey is weak. But, I have the chip lead, and I don't want to call off too many chips with A-8. Mikey could easily have A-J, and then I'm in bad shape. It may be a good opportunity, but surely a better opportunity will come along soon.*

I folded, and Mike showed 8-3 offsuit! Man! And then Hoyt said he had 8-3 offsuit, meaning that Mike had only two threes left in the deck to hit. Wow, I wished more than ever that I would have made that call!

An hour after that hand, Mike was all-in with A-Q to Hoyt's A-K. If Hoyt's hand held up, then I would be heads up with Hoyt for the bracelet, and the cash, and we could make a good save and lock into $500,000 apiece. But Mike won the pot. Then I picked up A-Q to Hoyt's A-A, sigh. And, after losing that pot, I was suddenly the short stack! I busted, without making a deal, for $250,000 for third place.

Still, it was a good day cash-wise for me, but I'm a history guy! I needed bracelet number 10, and my dad was there to watch me win it. One more note, the television coverage showed only one hand of the Mike vs. Hoyt heads-up match for the bracelet. I guess I'm pretty good television, win or lose, for better or worse.

36

President Bush, French Open and the 2006 WSOP, All in a Month

On June 6, 2006, I flew to Yorkshire, England, about 200 miles north of London, to give a paid speech ($65,000 plus first class airfare and hotel) at the Yorkshire International Business Convention (YIBC). Two days later, at 2 p.m., as I'm putting the finishing touches on my speech for the YIBC (I was staying at the beautiful Rudding Park Hotel and golf course), I received a phone call from the front desk inquiring whether it would be all right to have my suite searched, first by a dog, then by a team of policemen! I wasn't shocked, or was I? I had been warned that I would be thoroughly vetted, because President George Bush Sr. was going to be staying in the suite across the hallway from mine, so I immediately said, "Yes, send them up." (By the way, my wife doesn't know if I'm a Democrat, or a Republican, but I love both President George Bush Sr. and President Clinton, for their charity work.)

A couple of hours later, as I was walking into the hotel stairwell, I was suddenly aware of eyes on me (up a few flights of stairs, in the stairwell, someone was staring down at me). As I finished my climb and opened the door to my floor, I saw five secret service guys, and one of them says to me, "So it's true, you really are staying here, Phil." (I had fans in the secret service, cool!) I say, "Yep, and I'm looking forward to meeting President Bush." As I walked down the corridor, I noticed that the door to the three rooms in my private hallway was shut. And I don't think that door is ever shut!

Stared Down By an Agent Holding... What?!?

Beyond that closed door, at the end of that short private hallway, is a wall. Turn left at the wall, and the door to my suite is in front of you. Turn right at the wall, and you're in front of the door to President George Bush Sr.'s suite. As I continued toward my suite, I opened the door to the private hallway. And as I walked through the door, suddenly, I'm being intently stared down by a gentleman who proved to be a secret service agent! This agent was planted, with his back to the wall, and his eyes focused sternly on me. Immediately, I noticed that his right hand, in his suit, high up, next to his heart, was holding something, duh! He must be holding a gun! (Hadn't I read something recently about how the USA was on high alert? Something about a high-level terrorist killing...) I walked on a couple of steps, then noticed that the door to the third room, on the right, in the hallway, was open. I glanced casually into the third room, and noticed that that room was filled with what proved to be policemen. As I passed the third room, feeling sure that the secret service agent was holding a gun, I told myself: walk slowly, and be cool. No sudden moves!

As I approached the agent, he says, "Hi, Phil, nice to see you." OK, cool, situation defused... although I notice that he still has his hand in his jacket! As I opened my door, I decided that I should stay safely in my room for as long as I can. No need to go grab coffee or food anytime soon. Room service would do...

Helicopter Trip, and I Speak Before President Bush?

Before my speech, I recall that for the first time in a long time I was nervous. So, I flew by helicopter from Harrogate to Hull to give my speech, then flew back and gave it again. Hull has about 500 people. I have given decent motivational speeches. It's easy for me to be on stage, and tell stories, but the first person I ask about my speech says, "I hate gambling, so the minute you got up there I tuned out." OK, thanks for that! Then the next person tells me that I dropped too many names, and showed too much ego, and that I should take my hat and sunglasses off. I know the English hate ego, but (sigh)...

Stupidly, then, I tore up my speech while in the helicopter, and rewrote the thing, but this time I was to speak right before George Bush, and to 1,600 people! (I should have stuck to my guns!)

It happens that I have some cool "life tips and techniques" to share in my motivational speeches (Chapter 10), and some great stories, and shouldn't have been deterred by a few naysayers. (My second speech was delivered with too much doubt, and not enough conviction, but it was OK.) Thankfully, President Bush missed it.

President Bush Asked Me, "How Is Your Life?"

A few minutes after I finished speaking, President Bush strolled into the green room with a huge throng of press, police, and secret service. He saw me, and then walked straight up to me, and said, "You must be staying in the suite next to mine. It's a pleasure to meet you, I'm George Bush. How is your life?" What a great question! I talked for a minute, all positive, and then told him that I thought it was cool that he and President Clinton had been teaming up together to raise money for tsunami and hurricane relief. I thought it cool that former presidents from the two sides of the aisle, Democrat and Republican, could team up and work together for disaster relief.

I called him George at first, and then realized my mistake and apologized. It is "Mr. President" to us Americans! When I apologized, President Bush handled himself perfectly, gave me a warm and genuine smile, and told me to call him whatever I might want. In America, we revere our presidents, so "Mr. President" it was. I knew that a few of the secret service guys were fans of mine and I suspected that they told the President who I was, which helped garner interest from President Bush. After his speech, President Bush asked if I would like to grab a beer? Uh, yeah! But after four or five minutes together, left alone as we were by the gathering crowd, the crowd decided that that was enough, and they broke in. President Bush soon began to be mobbed, and I stepped back.

That night, President Bush, the other speakers, and I were taken to a black-tie party at the Queen of England's cousin's place (more like a mansion), and there, finally, I received some positive feedback from my speech!

Next Stop: Paris WPT

No rest for the weary! The next day, Saturday June 10, I flew off to Paris to play in the WPT-Paris. After landing, while riding to my hotel (the Marriot on Avenue des Champs Élysées), I saw French Open tennis posters everywhere, and quickly learned that the French Open final was to be held the next day (Sunday). And it was a classic: Federer vs. Nadal! So I popped over to the beautiful Aviation Club and asked club owner–manager Bruno Fitoussi if he had tickets.

Bruno is himself a European poker legend, who will soon be inducted into the Poker Hall of Fame. Bruno owned, and ran, the Aviation Club, one of the most beautiful cards rooms in the world. Bruno has done a lot for poker, and he has game! (Bruno continues to play in the biggest games in the world.) Bruno said, "Come with me," and we went to his office, where he called Patrick Bruel. In Paris, Patrick's nickname is "President Bruel," as he is the most famous person in France. But to me, Patrick was just a poker player, one that I had hit it off with. Yes, I knew that he was a French actor and singer, of some adored sort, but I knew Patrick better as a WSOP bracelet winner in Limit Hold 'Em, and I respected his Hold 'Em skills.

When Bruno called him, Patrick's assistant answered and said, "Patrick will call you back in one hour. He is on a movie set right now." It turned out that Patrick went from the movie set, to singing in a big concert, to playing poker at the Aviation Club late that night (rock star!). In between all of these, Patrick called my hotel room and left a message saying that a car would pick me up to take me to Roland Garros at 2 p.m. the next day. In his message, Patrick added that, "You'll be sitting in the Presidential Suite."

Roland Garros: Red Carpet, General Splendor

At 2 p.m. an official French Open car shows up! It was a white minivan, with a green sign on the side saying "French Open," and I asked the driver if he has ever picked up Andy Roddick? He says no, but he has picked up Nadal and Federer many times. It is only three miles from the Marriot to Roland Garros, but it takes 15 minutes as we pull through a gated security stop.

I'm asked if I have a ticket, I say no. I am asked again by another fellow, and I say no. There is a lot of French being spoken, quickly, but I'm not worried because I know that President Bruel has my back! Sure enough, I'm in. And I walk through a red carpet entrance with tons of press and other people lining up on both sides to see the celebrities. I have my black-and-white Gianni Versace shirt on (see photo section), a classic shirt for me, and it looks as if I'm someone, but I do not get recognized. No one snaps a picture. I was used to tons of attention, and I recall that I was a little surprised, and disappointed, that no one took a picture of me.

The red carpet led into a hall that is maybe 20 yards by 30 yards, and through that the Presidential Suite looms. The suite is actually a big section you might see had you walked into a football game. I walked straight through to the stadium section and see 18 rows by 14 seats, about half in front of me and half behind me. As I walk out into the hot sun, two things were apparent: it was really hot, and the whole stadium appeared to be staring at me! I suddenly realized that I'm the only one in the whole section who is outside at this point, because everyone else is enjoying cold drinks and sushi in the air-conditioned room behind me, and avoiding the extreme heat. As to everyone staring at me, it turns out that all the celebrities, athletes, and politicians will be sitting in this elite section, and they are staring at me just in case I'm someone famous, like, say, Jennifer Aniston.

Just then, Patrick finds me, hands me a fancy-looking ticket, makes sure I'm all right, and then talks to me for seven or eight minutes. I suddenly realize that this seven or eight minutes is above and beyond the call of duty for him (we have a nice rapport), as everyone in the known French world wants time to talk to him. I tell Patrick, "Thank you for everything," and he takes off. On my elegant white note-card-sized invitation (ticket) is written "Le President Christian Bimes... Monsieur Phil Helmutt" and a bunch of other cool stuff like the logo of

Fédération Française de Tennis, with a handwritten R 12, P M in the left-hand corner. R 12 I understand, P M turns out to be seat 11, go figure.

A few minutes later, everyone in my section starts making their way to their seats. I'm alone now, and it's OK with me, I'm just happy to be here at this classic tennis match, where Federer is trying to win all four majors (at one time!), and Nadal is trying to win his record 60th clay match in a row, and his second consecutive French Open. It would have been better for me had my friend Andy Roddick made it to the finals. Every tennis match I've been to in the last few years leading up to this one has been to watch Roddick play, and mostly win.

Just as I'm walking up the stairs to my seat, I look down at... Vince Vaughn! He looks up, recognition in his eyes, and says, "Phil, how are you doing?" I lean over and shake his hand, and right away I could tell that he wants to chat, and hang out, and that's cool with me.

Vince is jetting around Europe, with his movie star girlfriend Jennifer Aniston, promoting their new movie, *The Break Up*. I was a huge fan of Jennifer's, and now that I know how cool Vince is, I'm a Vince fan as well. When I watched Vince in *Wedding Crashers* I laughed so hard that I fell out of my chair at the movie theatre (a first for me)! We start chatting, and Vince asked me if I'd like to meet Jennifer, and I say "of course." So, Vince and I walked down to the third row, right behind the French Open trophy, to say hello to Jennifer. Having my wits about me, I suddenly remember (my wife has drilled this into my head) to introduce Patrick and his wife to Vince and Jennifer. It is the only proper thing to do.

It turned out that Patrick's wife often gets mistaken for Jennifer in Paris. I gave Patrick a star-quality introduction: I told Vince and Jennifer that Patrick is the biggest movie star and singer in France. Everyone but Jennifer, Vince, and I know that this is President Bruel (even my hotel concierge referred to him like that!). I went back to my seat, and Vince said, "We'll see you at the break" (in the air-conditioned room). Anyway, the day is getting better and better, and the tennis hasn't even started yet!

As the first set ended, I recall that I had sweat literally, dripping down my Versace shirt (my favorite shirt). So I hit the air-conditioned room for relief, water, and sushi. By then, I was aware that there were a lot of legends sitting around the Presidential Suite section, as every time one of them stood up, the folks in the stadium would shout out their names. When I walked into the refreshment room, I saw Vince and Jennifer chatting with another couple, but I didn't want to bother them; I know what it's like to get swamped by people. So I went to the bar, and then started watching the match on the television there.

Nadal looked absolutely flat in the first set, and I was like, "Why is Nadal such a big deal? I thought he is some sort of clay court phenom?" Just then Patrick walked by and said, "This thing will be over in four sets, Nadal will win easily." Huh? I thought Federer was the greatest, and indeed, he smashed Nadal in the first set. While I'm watching the second set on television, someone to my right says, "Phil, Nadal is the short stack, now he's starting to push!" I look back at Vince and say, "I didn't know you've been studying the game!" Nadal was doing exactly that. He was freewheeling it now, and dominating the first three games of the second set.

After the second set ended, I ran into Jen and Vince again, and this time we had 20 minutes to talk, while we were watching the match on TV. I meet a lot of celebrities, athletes, actors, and billionaires, and I usually hit it off well with them, but I'm not always impressed. Vince and Jennifer were impressive: smart, social, and fun to be with.

In the middle of the third set, Vince told me they had to leave, this minute, to go watch Team USA in a World Cup game in Germany. Huh? I gave Vince shit about having to leave the match early. I said, "I know you're busy, but c'mon. You going to leave the French Open final, Federer vs. Nadal, a classic, in the middle of the third set! That just doesn't seem right." Vince loved it! Then he said, "Yeah, but we get to go to the World Cup and watch Team USA." I said, "Federer vs. Nadal, a classic, with history on the line as Federer's going for the Federer slam (all four tennis major trophies at once)!" We had a laugh, and then Vince handed me his ticket for the French Open; seat upgrade!

The WPT-Paris

The next day, on Monday June 12, 2006, in my first European WPT, I made a deep run, well into Day 3. I was not all-in and called for the first two days, and that's a rare feat. When I hit 250,000 in chips, we started with 15,000 in chips. I made a mistake with J-J vs. 5-5, when I didn't raise on the turn on a board of A-4-2-10. And then I called on the river when a 3 hit. I didn't play my best poker, and I didn't finish well (just outside the money).

The 2006 WSOP

Entering the 2006 WSOP, the all-time bracelet count looked like this: Doyle Brunson ten, Johnny Chan ten, Johnny Moss nine, Phil Hellmuth nine. I had my eye on the big prize: WSOP bracelets. But there was another meaningful prize at the WSOP (starting in 2004): the WSOP Player of the Year Award. I didn't pay much attention to it, because bracelets trump all at the WSOP, but it's a cool award and a nice feather in your cap (if you can win it). If we had had that award starting back at the 1989 WSOP, then I would have picked up a few of them.

The Late 2006 WSOP Tournaments Count?

The year before, in 2005, for the first time the WSOP had tournaments after the main event started, but they didn't award bracelets for first place. No bracelets for first place, then who cares? So, in 2006, the WSOP announced that those late events would be bracelet events. The WSOP wanted to encourage the champions to play, as well as anyone else seeking bracelets.

Four WSOP 2006 Final Tables, with Huge Fields! And an All-Time Cash Lead

I had a monster 2006 WSOP! First, I passed Men "the Master" Nguyen for the all-time WSOP "cashes" (times in the money) lead, when I posted cash number 49. For the last ten years I have continued to build that lead up to my current 118 cashes (still number 1). Meanwhile, on July 6, 2006, in my third cash (number 51), in the $5,000 buy-in No Limit Hold 'Em tournament, with 622 players, I made it down to three-handed play with a massive chip lead.

I nearly had a chance to win the thing when I limped in with 5-5 on the button, and poker professional Jeff Cabanillas raised in the big blind. The flop was Q♦-J♦-9♠, he checked, and I bet out 60,000. He called, and the next card was the 6♥. Jeff checked, I bet out 80,000, and he raised 100,000 more. Something told me that I had the best hand, so I called. The last card was the 7♦ (the flush draw hit), and Jeff moved all-in for around 560,000. I couldn't beat much, so I folded, and he showed the A♣-K♣! If I had called him there I would have been heads up, with 2 million in chips against an opponent with 350,000! Man, I smelled something on the turn when I called with pocket fives, if only I could have made that call.

When Jeff and I hit heads-up play, it seemed the whole room was full of people watching us play. Many of them were there to see me make history (or fail to make history). The atmosphere was electric! Doyle Brunson and Johnny Chan were there, as well as the actress Shannon Elizabeth. And my friends Mike Matusow and John Bonetti were there. It was if there were a thousand people there watching, with standing room only, while ESPN taped the thing, in case I won my tenth bracelet. I recall how electric and festive it all was, along with the bad memory of losing the match, and failing to make history. My buddies Matusow and Bonetti shed tears for me later, which I really appreciated.

Not Done Yet!

Eleven days later, I fought my way through 352 players to reach another WSOP final table in Limit Omaha 8/b (High-Low Split, the O in HORSE), but I played badly and finished in sixth place. Eight days later, in a field of 754 players, and 1,600 rebuys, I made the final table in the $1,000 No Limit Hold 'Em with re-buys. And this time, under the bright lights, with ESPN recording, and with a huge audience watching, and my 16-year-old son Phillip watching (we snuck him in), I would not be denied! I won WSOP bracelet number 10! The all-time bracelet race looked like this: Johnny Chan ten, Doyle Brunson ten, Phil Hellmuth ten, and Johnny Moss nine.

Bracelets Number 10 and 11, and Player of the Year?

The rules for the 2006 WSOP Player of the Year were simple: most money won wins Player of the Year, excluding the main event. Going into the last WSOP tournament of the year, 494 players signed up for the $1,500 No Limit Hold 'Em tournament. At 3 a.m., when we hit the last 27, Doyle Brunson and I were chip leaders! Later that day (at 5 p.m.) the WSOP Final Table would be played, but what a story it would be if Doyle or I won WSOP bracelet number 11 at 7 a.m.! Doyle finished 21st, but I hit the final table with the chip lead. Eventually, I finished in third place, but my $53,945 pushed me over the top and I won the 2006 WSOP Player of the Year! Or did I? The press announced that Phil Hellmuth had won WSOP Player of the Year! But the WSOP said, "Hold the presses, the WSOP staff has to have a meeting to decide who the proper winner is." They had to decide whether I or Jeff Madsen was Player of the Year. Madsen was 22 years old, a newcomer, and he was a worthy candidate with two bracelets and two third-place finishes. But I had won by the rules they had posted! Finally, they de-cided to give it to Madsen, saying that the last tournaments, which began after the WSOP main event had started, although they did indeed count for bracelets, did not count for the Player of the Year race. Oh boy. I felt like 2006 WSOP Play-er of the Year had been taken away from me. But I would win a few Player of the Years in the years to come, right? Or would I finish second in the 2011 WSOP Player of the Year, and again, in 2012, to last-second charges by someone else?

37

My Biggest Loss, Ever: Nightmare in Monte Carlo

Because I have a substantial reputation, poker players will lend me any amount of money that I ask for. Anytime, anywhere. This can be a blessing, and a curse. The respect is nice, and sometimes it is helpful to borrow money when you didn't bring enough cash with you on any given day (especially in Europe). On the other side of the ledger, this borrowing power can allow me to lose way too much money, especially when I'm out of control. What's to stop me from losing my life savings in one night? Only my strong will and discipline will suffice. (I came close to losing it all in one night – see Chapter 26!)

The Good

On March 26, 2007, I was lucky enough to move into a beautiful suite overlooking the Ligurian Sea, at the world-class Hotel de Paris: Monte Carlo. On Tuesday March 27, 2007, I ran into Patrik Antonius and Phil Ivey in the lobby of the Hotel. At the time, Phil and Patrik were young guns who played in the biggest poker games in the world, both online and in the casinos, and they were crushing! These two were among the hottest three or four players in the world as far as money won, and in skill set.

The $12,000 Bottle of Champagne that I Didn't Buy!

On a previous trip to Monte Carlo, I saw a bottle of champagne on the menu at the Monte Carlo Bay Hotel for €8,000 (about $10,000) and I told myself, "If UltimateBet.com goes public, then I'm going to buy this bottle of champagne the next time I'm in here." By then, UB had gone public (Appendix 1) and the bottle was now listed at €9,500 ($12,000). For some reason, I was gun-shy and I didn't buy it! I feel like the "poker blood bath" that happened to me next happened because I didn't follow through on my promise to myself.

The Worst Loss of My Life!

Phil and Patrik were sitting in the lobby playing Chinese poker for $1,000 a point. In Chinese poker, you are dealt 13 cards, and you set them in three rows. Five at the bottom, five in the middle, and three at the top. The bottom row must beat the middle row, and the middle row must beat the top row. I joined their game, and started playing Chinese poker with them for $1,000 a point. And things went south quickly. The next thing you know, I was losing $83,000, and I decided to play for $2,000 a point. Patrik quit, and at that point I was losing $200,000. Shortly thereafter, I headed off to Ivey's suite for room service and criss-cross Chinese poker (where you play four hands, two vs. two). The skill factor in Chinese poker is small when you have two competent players, and I felt as if Ivey and I both play it at about the same level. In any case, things continued to get worse, and we kicked it up to $3,000 a point! The next thing you know I was an over $500,000 loser. Understand, mind you, that my biggest loss ever was $135,000 (about $105,000 of which was mine): I was freaked out, and shocked!

Finally, after an all-night session, we quit, at 10 a.m., and I had lost $536,000! Back then, the very reason that I avoided the big game at the Bellagio, my oft-stated reason was this: "I never want to have to lose $500,000 in one day." Thus, one of my worst fears in poker had come to pass.

Positivity! Might as Well Flip This Night on Its Head...

This was the biggest loss of my life, by far! I was distraught, and a thought hit my mind. If you're going to be this reckless, then you might as well do some good! I formed a plan, and immediately upon waking up at 5 p.m., I called my wife, and set it in motion. I said:

> *Honey, I stupidly lost $536,000! I need some positivity. I want to give money to charity, and pay down the mortgage, and I'm not getting off the phone with you until you have mailed off checks for another $464,000. Might as well make this a day to remember, and spend $1 million!*

My wife liked Doctors with Borders, so we donated $25,000 to them, and $25,000 to Habitat for Humanity, and paid down the mortgage, $414,000. I refused to get off the phone with my wife until the checks were in the mail.

Because I didn't buy that bottle of champagne, and lost $536,000, that night I spent $4,400 on a bottle of 1958 (I think) Château d'Yquem! But I still felt like I hadn't fulfilled my promise to myself.

The Ugly

I hopped into the European Poker Tour (EPT) Monte Carlo, ready to win my cash back (it was $1.8 million for first place). On Day 1, I ran my Q-Q into an opponent's A-A, but not for that many chips. Then I ran my K-K into their A-A, sigh. Then, on Day 2, I ran my K-K into their A-A, to go broke, and I thought, "What the hell is going on here? $536,000, then these three bad beats in the EPT? I'm a little superstitious, but something is telling me to get out of town!"

Get Out of Town, Now!

I acted on that "get out of town" impulse immediately! I went straight back to the hotel and tried to rent a helicopter to visit my sister in Bormio, Italy. No helicopters available? I was tired, and paranoid, and I thought, "Get out of Monte Carlo before something even worse happens to you!" After considering many possibilities, I hired a private driver to drive me, seven hours straight, to Bormio. We had started at 10 p.m. at night, and I arrived in Bormio 5 a.m.

I spent five days with my sister Kerry (Chapter 16) and her family, staying at the nearby Grand Hotel Bagni Nuovi, featuring old roman baths! I slept in, rested up, and recharged my battery. I was down, but not out. As I treated myself to massages, and roman baths, I was already looking forward to the 2007 WSOP...

38

Poker Hall of Fame; Magical WSOP Bracelet 11

One day before the 2007 WSOP started, on May 30, 2007, I decided to tour the WSOP tournament area at the Rio Hotel and Casino. Ty Stewart, now the commissioner of the WSOP, led my tour and told me, "Phil, keep it under your hat, because we haven't announced it to the press yet, but you're going to be inducted into the Poker Hall of Fame on July 6th." Sweet! I was so excited that I immediately called my wife and parents! I knew that I would make it into the Poker Hall of Fame eventually, and it almost happened in 2001: had I won the 2001 WSOP main event, instead of finishing in fifth place, then I was going in on the spot (Chapter 30). But it's one thing to know you're going in, and another when it becomes official. By the way, the WSOP bracelet count before the 2007 WSOP was: Johnny Chan ten, Doyle Brunson ten, Phil Hellmuth ten, and Johnny Moss nine.

Eleven, Eleven, Eleven, 11, 11, 11

On June 9, 2007, my sister Molly (Chapter 16) emailed me and wrote, "I know you're going to win bracelet number 11 on June 11th, because you're giving me bracelet number 11, and I was born on 11/11/1971." Molls had so much conviction in her tone! I loved the positivity, and thought that I might as well use that to my advantage. Why doubt it when I could possibly use it to my advantage?

Kathy and the Boys Help Me, as Usual

I entered the $1,500 No Limit Hold 'Em tournament on June 9th (2,624 players), but I had backup plans with Kathy and our boys. We bought four tickets for the show *Ka*, and the four of us had a sushi dinner (my sons love sushi) scheduled beforehand. So, I had one eye on the clock as I was playing in the tournament. And when a hand came up at 8:45 p.m., my family influenced my action. A player raised it up, and I called with pocket tens. Then a player in the blinds moved all-in, and the original raiser folded his hand. I was a top-ten chip stack, and the all-in player was as well.

As I made my decision, to call or to fold my 10-10, I couldn't help thinking:

> *This player has either A-K or a big pair. So, I'm either 4½-to-1 underdog vs. a big pair, or a coin flip (12-to-10 favorite) vs. A-K. Normally, I would fold, because I hold too many chips to call with pocket tens. But I'm going to call because I have a nice evening planned with Kathy and the kids. Either I'm going with them (the kids weren't in town too often during the WSOP), or I'm going to have tons of chips!*

I called, my opponent had A-K, I was 12-to-10 favorite to win, and I won the pot when the board ran out 9-8-5-2-8.

At midnight on Day 1, when I started struggling a bit, I told myself, "You missed a beautiful evening with Kathy and the boys to be here, don't play poorly now!" And that gave me extra energy to finish the day strong. I ended Day 1 with 72,000 in chips.

On Day 2, with this enormous field of 2,624 players, we played until 3 a.m. to trim the field down to the final table (final nine players). I made it to that final table with 1.48 million in chips.

Sequestered Final Table? Sushi Dinner!

It was the first year that a tournament was broadcast "live" (on a 30-minute delay) on the internet at the WSOP. And because they were showing our hole cards, the WSOP confiscated our phones and made us play in a tent in the middle of the WSOP tournament room. For that reason, it was the first year that the players – and one guest – were sequestered (completely cut off from the outside world).

At first, I was overwhelmingly whiny and negative at the final table (negative poker brat!), but I caught myself, and I was like, "What are you doing? Shut the hell up and be nice to the rest of the players!" Too negative is bad for me! It seems that when I'm too negative, I never seem to do well. A little "poker brat attitude" can be great for me, and for my results, but if there is too much negativity alongside, then it seems as if I can nosedive.

In any case, an old friend of mine, Morgan Machina, was at that final table, and told the tournament staff, "If you're going to sequester us, then we need great food for our dinner break." The players took our cue from Morgan, and we banded together and demanded sushi, and more good food, from the WSOP. The WSOP relented, and we deserved it, too, as we were putting on a good show for the WSOP, and we were putting up with being sequestered!

Normally, when you're at dinner break, you would be nowhere near your opponents, but in this case, we all ate dinner together. This was unheard of. The final table players were all friendly and nice to each other, but then we went to war!

I seemed to have the chip lead all day long, and without any major trouble, I won WSOP bracelet number 11, and $637,000! Johnny Chan and Doyle Brunson presented the bracelet to me in the WSOP tournament room, in front of a packed house. It was an incredible day for me, and I was pleased to see that my win made ESPN's Sports Center "top-ten plays" (number 9) that night. I finally had the WSOP bracelet lead all to myself. Some might think it strange, but I was rooting for Johnny and Doyle to win number 11, and tie me! I loved the competition, I loved the WSOP bracelet race, and I figured that we could drive each other toward new heights.

Being the Greatest

In 1993, I upgraded my "life goals" (end of Chapter 10) to include this big goal: I will become the greatest poker player of all time.

A big part of achieving this goal was to become the all-time leading WSOP bracelet winner. Now that I finally had it, I figured that the floodgates would open, and that I would win at least one more bracelet at the 2007 WSOP.

WSOP Record Final Table No. 39 and WSOP Bracelet No. 12

Seven days later, on June 18, 2007, I found myself at the final table of the WSOP $3,000 buy-in No Limit Hold 'Em tournament (827 players). When we stopped play for the day, someone told me that it was my record-tying 39th final table – I tied T.J. Cloutier. Another WSOP record, sweet! Or was it? The WSOP staff stopped us at ten-handed, which I had never heard of before. Hmmm... I wonder why? Because ESPN wanted me to be part of their show!

You see, ESPN was covering the tournament, and they told me that I'm great for the television ratings. Because I was a short stack, with ten of us left, they didn't want to play on and risk me busting in tenth place. So, they decided to bring ten of us back to the final table the next day. And in Texas Hold 'Em, nine is an official WSOP final table.

Controversial Fold? Then Next Hand, Stunningly, A-A!

On June 19, 2007, we resumed play under the lights of the ESPN cameras. Early on, with the blinds at 10,000–20,000, I raised it up to 50,000 to go with K-6 offsuit, and someone behind me re-raised. It came back to me, and I had only 70,000 in chips behind. The announcers, while broadcasting the tournament live on the internet, told the world that I would call. They said that I was "priced in." The pot held 220,000: my 50,000 plus that of my opponents: 120,000 (50,000 call plus 70,000 raise), plus 20,000 antes (2,000 a man), plus 30,000 in blinds (10,000 plus 20,000). I could win 220,000 if only I called 70,000; I was getting laid over 3-to-1. I thought that my opponent may have had pocket queens, which would make me 2½-to-1 underdog. So, a call here made sense. I knew it was close, and I always hated calling off my money with weak hands, when I could fold and wait, and maybe ladder up. Plus, I admit that I thought, "If I go out now, then I won't tie T.J. for most WSOP final tables." So, I folded, and everyone at the table told me I made a mistake. The very next hand I picked up pocket aces and doubled up! I told everyone at the table, "That's why I waited! I wanted to give myself a chance." Partly true. Although I won that pot, sadly, I went on to finish in sixth place...

Carl Westcott, "Martha, Please Pass the Peas"; PH the NASCAR Driver?

A few months before the 2007 WSOP began, I was talking to my attorney Dan Friedberg about all the companies that I represented or had a piece of that wanted me to wear a logo. When Dan said, "You're like a NASCAR [National Association for Stock Car Auto Racing] driver, logos everywhere!" And then I said, "Why not show up to the WSOP in a NASCAR driver's outfit, with all of the company logos patched onto my suit?" As my friend Carl Westcott says, "When most people have a great idea, they outline it at the dinner table to their family, and then they say, 'Martha, please pass the peas.' Most people, it seems, do not pursue their great ideas."

Carl Westcott is an amazing man whom I've been blessed to call a good friend since 2007. Carl was awarded the Horatio Alger Award for Distinguished Americans, a huge honor! Carl started with nothing, but enlisted in the 101st Airborne when he was 16 years old, and served in the air assault company, then became a used car salesman in Los Angeles, and eventually owned a string of car dealerships in multiple states. After that, Carl bought the telephone number for 1-800-FLOWERS, and took a piece of that company. Then Carl started Westcott Communications, and sold it to Kohlberg Kravis Roberts for $500 million, because he thought that this "internet thing" may cut into his business. He was right! One more time, Carl's timing was impeccable. Carl's wisdom and intellect have helped me more times than I could count, from how to raise my children to business decisions of every kind. Thanks Carl, I love you!

As per Carl's way of thinking, I was determined to pursue this idea (I wouldn't ask my wife to pass the peas!), and I wouldn't let it go until it was set in motion. I called John Bonetti and asked if his beloved granddaughter Natasha, who was college-aged at the time, would be interested in making a few dollars? Natasha said she would do it, and I ordered two NASCAR outfits (onesies) from her, one black and one gold (see the photo section for the black). The companies patched onto the NASCAR suit were: UB, Pro Player Endurance Formula (drink), iAmplify.com (where I had my poker course), Oasys Mobile (I had the number-one app for almost one full year: Phil Hellmuth's Texas Hold 'Em), Poker Royalty (the poker agency that represents me to this day), WSOP Xbox game, *Card Player* magazine and website, World Poker Store, and Ultimate Blackjack Tour.

My original idea was to debut the suits at the beginning of the WSOP, but fortunately for me, they didn't arrive until a few days before the main event. So, I would debut the NASCAR outfits at the main event. By then, UB (Appendix 1) had caught wind of my idea, and they asked if they could turn it into "a grand WSOP main event entrance." UB also wanted to shoot a television commercial around my entrance! I agreed.

I Crash the NASCAR Car During Filming! Publicity Stunt?

UB decided to film the television commercial in the parking lot, in the back of the Rio Hotel. When I showed up, they had an actual NASCAR car, repainted black and yellow (UB colors), with my face painted on the hood. I thought that was cool! The producers warned me that I would stall the car, like everyone else who had driven it, and that it was OK, because the car had a "racing clutch" (you had to really hit the gas hard as you let your foot off the clutch). But I had owned a car with a racing clutch (a midnight blue Porsche), so I said, "I won't stall this thing, trust me." Then I thought to myself, "I have a knack for this," and I started showing off, as I took off fast, nearly burning rubber.

The last thing I wanted to do was to hurt someone in this busy parking lot. Especially because the car didn't have a rearview mirror, or a seat belt. So I went super slow when there was any threat of a pedestrian. But when I hit open spaces, I wanted to test the limits of this car! So there I was, hurtling across the parking lot toward the cameras (man, this car had pickup!), and then slowing down to make a sharp right (between a curb and the side of a parked pickup truck), followed by another sharp right between the front of the pickup truck and another curb, and then as I took a third sharp right (on the other side of the pickup truck), I floored it! As I floored it I gained speed quickly and the car started fish tailing, and suddenly, coming up quickly, I saw... A cement post! Uh, oh.

Crash! And I'm Sports Center "Top-Ten" Highlight, Again!

I slammed on the brakes, and cranked the wheel left, but *wap!* I hit the cement barrier hard and totaled the car; and I was momentarily frozen. Then, I saw smoke, and thought, "Get out, now!" Time seemed to slow down, and I quickly jumped out of the window of the car. As my feet hit the pavement, my instincts were to jump again, and I did just that. And whoosh, right under my airborne right foot, there was at least 20 gallons of fuel flowing downhill (the car was ensconced on the side of a small incline). Somehow, I avoided getting even one drop of fuel on my shoes. Lucky. Then I ran toward the Rio Hotel, and the producers grabbed the film as fast as they could and zipped it off property (something to do about lawsuits, or legal issues).

I was a bit dazed, and then the right side of my shoulder, close to my neck, started hurting, and seemed to get worse with every passing minute. I was whisked away to a private room at the WSOP. As I walked through the WSOP tournament room toward the private room, I'm not sure why, but the WSOP staff announced on the loud speaker that I had just totaled a race car in the parking lot! To the players' "oohs and aahs," they also announced that I was not hurt. When I arrived at the private room, I called my wife, and asked her what to do. Was it ice, or hot water that I should use? Should I have a massage or no massage? She recommended ice, and no massage. With each passing hour, my wound continued to hurt more and more.

Within hours, the film of the crash went viral, and I found myself, again, as a "Top-Ten Highlight" on Sports Center on ESPN. Then a series of articles came out speculating that the whole thing was a publicity stunt! I didn't mind so much, but I assure you, the reader, that it wasn't.

My 2007 WSOP NASCAR Entrance; a Spectacle!

My official WSOP entrance on Monday June 9, 2007, had by then received a lot of press. (I was supposed to drive the car, but it was totaled!) UB hired 11 models to walk in with me, one for each of my WSOP wins, and each model had a WSOP Phil Hellmuth win date (and the event that I won) on her skimpy black onesie. My simple idea of wearing a NASCAR outfit at the beginning of the WSOP had morphed into a spectacle! Before coming over to the Rio, I called my agent, Brian Balsbaugh (Chapter 35), who told me that there were three camera crews and over 100 people waiting for me to show up. Huh?

I was more than a little shocked and embarrassed when I walked into the Rio, surrounded by camera crews and 11 models. They wanted me right in the center of the hallway, and I had to stop multiple times to let the camera crews catch up to me. Fans were shouting, "Phil, you're my favorite player," or "turn right" (so they could take a picture), or "sign this." Talk about the center of attention! The whole spectacle seemed way over the top, and more than a little bit absurd. I told myself that this was good for the poker world, and good for me, and I knew that it was true. Whenever anyone brings more eyeballs into the poker world, especially mainstream eyeballs, then it's good for poker.

Meanwhile, I was still in a lot of pain from the car crash, and I think this had a profound impact on my play in the 2007 WSOP main event. I didn't make it through Day 1, and the pain continued. After about five days, the pain switched from one side of my shoulder and neck to the other side! I thought this was strange, but I'm told that this happens a lot to the NASCAR guys. Finally, ten days later, the pain disappeared! Thank god! I was lucky, and there was a lesson here: I need to be careful when I drive.

39

12 Million Beer Cans; Deep Run 2008 WSOP

In early 2008, my agent Brian Balsbaugh (Chapter 35) called me to tell me that Miller Brewing Company wanted to put my picture, and some my best lines, on 12 million Milwaukee's Best beer cans. Was I interested? Uh, yeah! What an honor. There had been only a few people in history who had had their own can. I thought that it would be the coolest thing that had ever happened to me! As I told my friends about the deal, they all said, "The beast!" (Milwaukee's Best popular nickname.)

Strangely, the offer came from Harrah's Hotel and Casinos, not Miller Brewing Company (and so did the check!). Hmm... I was offered $70,000. I wonder what Harrah's, the owners of the WSOP, were being paid? $250,000, $400,000, maybe more? In any case, I would have paid *them* to have me on 12 million beer cans! So, I was delighted. I also asked for 500 empty beer cans, which I could sign and send to family and friends.

After I accepted Harrah's (Miller's) offer, I hired my personal designer to gin up a good version of the can. I wanted the PH Milwaukee's Best beer can to look as good as it possibly could, and spending $500 on my personal designer seemed like a no-brainer to me. I figured that her design would be terrific (she came up with my personal PH logo), and would be something to use if Miller's creative team couldn't do any better (her design established a minimum quality threshold).

A few months later, when the Miller folks showed me their design, I suggested that they add more gold coloring on the WSOP bracelet on my wrist, and the logo on my shirt (they added more gold). In the end, the can they showed me looked awesome! And there were several versions, with several of my lines, across three different brands: Milwaukee's Best, Milwaukee's Best Ice, and Milwaukee's Best Light. They used these lines: "I can dodge bullets, baby" and "If it weren't for luck I'd win 'em all" (Chapter 35), and "These people are trying to give their money to me" (see the PH beer cans in the photo section).

The PH Milwaukee's Best Beer Cans Roll off the Line!

On May 6, 2008, I was on the floor of the Miller Brewing Company (in Milwaukee) with my mom and some friends to watch the first PH Milwaukee's Best beer cans roll off the assembly line. Afterwards, my mom, my friends, a bunch of Miller's employees, and I had a party right at the factory. We drank Milwaukee's Best in the new PH beer can!

On the packaging for the beer cans, on the 12 packs and 24 packs, there was some cool signage for the "poker lesson" that I would give the winner of a contest that Miller was running. I still think that's one of the coolest things that has ever happened to me!

2008 WSOP: Going for WSOP Number 12!

In the 2008 WSOP, I had two good shots to win WSOP bracelet number 12, and go two bracelets up on Johnny Chan (number 10) and Doyle Brunson (number 10). First, I made a deep run in the $5,000 buy-in (with rebuys) Pot Limit Omaha tournament, making it to the final table, and then finishing in eighth place. Fifteen days later, I hopped into the $1,500 buy-in HORSE, and made it down to the final table. With 803 starting players, it would have been sweet to take this HORSE tournament down! Especially as I now had a reputation as a Texas Hold 'Em specialist, because all 11 of my WSOP bracelets had come from Texas Hold 'Em (I had WSOP bracelets in Limit Hold 'Em, No Limit Hold 'Em, and Pot Limit Hold 'Em).

I knew that I would win a non-Hold 'Em bracelet eventually (I had been at a bunch of non-Hold 'Em WSOP final tables), but it couldn't come soon enough! And it didn't come in the aforementioned HORSE tournament, as I faded down the stretch and finished in third place.

The 2008 WSOP Main Event Entrance – General Patton!

Last year's 2007 WSOP grand entrance as a NASCAR driver had tracked so well, that UB wanted to do another grand entrance for the 2008 WSOP. After some creative discussion, it was agreed that I would come in as General Patton (see the photo section). I would be driven up to the Rio Hotel and Casino in a military jeep, in full Patton regalia, and I would be escorted into the WSOP tournament area by 11 models (in soldier dress) and a couple of male "US Army troops" (my friends Mark "Poker Ho" Kroon and Wisco Murray). UB started shooting television commercials of me as General Patton, months in advance.

This time, I wouldn't let the spectacle get to me. I would not let the crowds, the cheering, and the ego rush of being the center of attention affect me. I was there to win the WSOP main event. As we marched into the WSOP tournament room, under the glare of tons of cameras, I was set down at the ESPN featured table next to the "baddest man on the planet": Ultimate Fighting Champion Chuck Liddell (see the picture of Chuck and me in photo section). Chuck was the best in the world at what he did; could I prove that I was the best in the world at what I did?

The 2008 WSOP Main Event:
Q-10 and 51 Times I Call Someone an Idiot!

I made a deep run and, just like in 2001, Q-10 hurt me again. And I went off on ESPN: I had a classic Phil Hellmuth meltdown! But that tirade was nothing compared to the one I had late on Day 5, when someone called 250,000 in chips with 10-4 offsuit. With about 100 players left (6,844 started), and history squarely in my sights, a player opened, I made a huge re-raise with A-K, and that player called with 10-4 offsuit! The flop was 10-9-8, I checked, he bet, and I folded. Then he showed 10-4, and I saw the absurdity of his play. Here I was, in the final 100 players of the WSOP main event, and someone was calling a raise with a 10-4 offsuit, to cost me 250,000 in chips, no less!

Someone filmed the tirade, and it appears that I called my opponent an "idiot" 51 times; not to his face, but you get the idea. It was the only time that I know of that ESPN pulled back and made me look better on television than I had actually looked in person. I'm not proud of these tirades. I understand the genesis of them (Chapter 14). I understand that the world thinks I'm a big baby when I act this way. In my defense, I will say that this was 20% of my chips, deep in the main event. Still, there are no excuses, and I really do strive to handle losing these pots better and better as time passes.

Phil Gets a Penalty?

Since that 10-4 hand was one of the last hands of Day 5, the staff at the WSOP had a meeting that night to decide whether they would give me a penalty at the start of Day 6. A penalty would cost me 35% of my chips and would have been devastating to my chances of winning! Did I deserve a penalty? Yes, and no. On the basis of the rules that they had in place at that time, no. And it's hard to let me act like that 24/7, never penalize me, and then suddenly penalize me for that offense. On the other hand, I had gone too far. After a few hours of discussion, the WSOP staff didn't give me a penalty; instead, the WSOP made me attend sensitivity training with the floor men before the 2009 WSOP.

Sensitivity Training Before the 2009 WSOP

At sensitivity training, before the 2009 WSOP started, I took the microphone and I asked the assembled floor people at the WSOP, "Raise your hand if you've seen me disrespect you, or any other dealer, ever." One guy raised his hand, out of 40 people, and I said:

> Steve, did you notice that you're the only one who raised his hand? That's because you screwed me in several rulings to prove you're a man, or because you're mad at me from something in the past, or something stupid like that. My point is this: I'm not here because I have issues with the dealers or the floor people. I'm here because I have work to do. Sometimes I lose it at the tables and, frankly, the producers of the WSOP and WPT encourage me to do it, because they say I'm good for ratings. And 100% of the time I apologize to whomever it is that I get upset at. But, I'm not asking for special treatment. If you see me cross the line, then give me a penalty.

And that was the end of my sensitivity training!

Hail, Caesar! Coaching Shulman

The 2009 preliminary WSOP was a bust for me: I had six cashes, and no final tables. On the plus side, I made a deep run in the main event (I lost when my A-A was beat to finish in 436th place), and my WSOP main event entrance was awesome! I came in as Caesar, with a great outfit (see the picture in the photo section), and 100 women dressed in togas (fun!). If you're interested, and my wife still teases me about it, there are great videos on youtube.com, where I'm actually carried in by four "Roman slaves." Coming in as Caesar is definitely my favorite Phil Hellmuth grand WSOP entrance.

Hail Caesar! My Chariot on Regent Street!

A couple of months later, on September 25th, we ratcheted up my Caesar entrance at the World Series of Poker Europe (WSOPE) main event in London, when I rode through the busy streets of London in a horse drawn chariot! To my knowledge, we didn't have permission to ride our chariot up Regent Street, where it merges with Piccadilly (one of the busiest parts of London), a couple of blocks from Leicester Square, so I was a bit paranoid as double-decker busses whizzed by, and the bemused people on the street took videos. Imagine this: we were moving at a snail's pace in our chariot as the traffic zoomed by on both sides. Would the police arrest us? And what did the pedestrians think? I'm sure they wondered, "Who is that guy, and what the heck is going on?" But it ended well at Leicester Square!

WSOP November Nine, Coaching Jeff Shulman

Jeff Shulman made the final table (final nine players) of the 2009 WSOP main event, and then he hired me to coach him. Since the final table was being played in November, even though it was reached July 11th, the WSOP was calling it the November Nine. As Jeff's coach, while I was contemplating his best strategy and tactics for the November Nine final table, I devised a new system of bet sizing. I suggested that Jeff open for 5x (five times) the size of the big blind when he entered a pot. So, if the blinds were 40,000–80,000, then Jeff would open for 400,000. Barry Shulman, Jeff's father, and recent winner of the WSOPE main event, loved that tactic, as did Jeff.

Back then, in 2009, the standard opening raise size was 2.5x. No one made 4x raises, never mind 5x raises; this tactic was way outside the box! And when Jeff made his first 5x raise at the November Nine final table, the players, announcers, and the press stared in disbelief. Did Jeff put in too many chips by accident? No one understood the tactic... But the players all folded their hands super quickly!

My reasoning for the 5x raise was simple. No one could take a flop for a 5x raise with a small pair. Thus, Jeff wouldn't lose his chips when someone flopped a set, because no one would call a 5x raise with a small pair. Jeff could not go broke when he had pocket queens to a 6-5-2 board, because his opponents couldn't have pocket sixes, fives, or deuces. I believed then (and I still believe now), that Jeff's best possible chance of making the final three would be to use this tactic. I also preached super-tight play. And Barry and Jeff heartily agreed. Starting a few weeks before the November Nine, we played simulation after simulation in Jeff's basement in Las Vegas.

The 2009 November Nine

The final table was live on ESPN, and the players were playing for $8.5 million for first place! Second was $5.2 million, and third was $3.5 million. Pressure! Jeff started out fourth place in chips, and played super-tight for hours, wisely biding his time. Finally, eight or nine hours into the final table, Jeff was all-in with A-K vs. his opponents A-Q (a 2½-to-1 favorite), and his hand held. With six players left, Jeff had 18 million in chips, and he was comfortable.

Brutal!! Not Again...

Twelve hours into this final table, Jeff opened for 1.75 million in first position with J-J, and Joe Cada moved all-in for 10.8 million in chips with 3-3. Jeff called, and found himself a 4½-to-1 favorite to bust Cada in sixth place, and have 29 million in chips; 29 million would give Jeff enough chips to play comfortably. But alas, the flop was 8-4-3! And "we" went on to lose that pot. Ouch... It pained me on so many levels to watch that hand! I felt so sorry for Jeff as I flashed back to 2000, where Jeff had had a massive chip lead at the WSOP main event final table and lost a pot with his 7-7, to Chris "Jesus" Ferguson's 6-6, all in before the flop. Back in 2000, had his pocket sevens held up, Jeff would have had a massive chip lead (over 60% of the chips in play) and a great chance to win.

Back to 2009 and the J-J vs. 3-3. Losing this pot left Jeff short, and he eventually fell in fifth place. But Jeff had played well enough to win! And as the final four players fell apart right before my eyes, as they recklessly tossed piles of chips around (I think 14 hours under the spotlight frazzled their minds), I couldn't help but think that Jeff would have been a big favorite to win the whole thing, if only his J-J had held. Personally, I was only getting paid if Jeff made the top three, so the three that Cada had hit cost me some serious money!

USO Tour and Black Friday

After only one final table at the 2010 WSOP (seventh place), I marched through my grand WSOP entrance as an mixed martial artist fighter, with a sharp black and yellow satin robe by Everlast (see the picture in the photo section). UltimateBet.com (UB; Appendix 1) pulled out all the stops again, setting up an entire stage in the Rio parking lot, with dancers and models. The models carried 11 Championship belts with my 11 WSOP wins listed on them. Bruce Buffer, the UFC's "official octagon announcer," announced my entrance. He said, "Let's get ready to rumble!" For my first three grand entrances (race car driver, General Patton, and Caesar), I was embarrassed. But for this, my last grand WSOP entrance, I was super comfortable.

Future Friends?

Right before the beginning of the 2010 WSOP main event began, I was eating dinner with my wife and kids at Bar Masa Restaurant at the beautiful Aria Hotel and Casino, when we were approached by a smiling, fun-looking group: Chamath Palihapitiya and his wife Brigette Lau, and Dave Goldberg and his wife Sheryl Sandberg. Chamath said, "We live in Palo Alto, and we have a regular No Limit Hold 'Em game, just $5-$10 blinds, but if you're interested in joining us sometime, you're more than welcome. And, here is a pair of lucky socks for you." My wife and I thought the socks thing was cute, but I still tease Chamath about it (only because he's embarrassed by it). The four of them seemed jovial and nice, and I exchanged email addresses with Chamath. Although $5-$10 was a small game, I thought it would be nice to have some poker friends in Palo Alto.

I Join the Game, and Whine Too Much, Like a Jerk!

The first time I played in Chamath's and Goldie's (Dave Goldberg) private game (we *never* played for cash, always checks), I lost almost $2,000 and whined way too much (poker brat!). I did have a good time, and the group was awesome. With too much whining comes a lot of apologizing. I hate that I couldn't control myself better in front of this new home game! But a sincere apology always goes a long way, and they could tell I was a good guy, despite all of my bluster.

Soon Chamath and I developed a healthy rivalry in the game, as we measured our wins and losses, and competed for who could win more money. I enjoyed that rivalry, and after eight months he was ahead $37,000 and I was losing $12,000. Then Chamath sold a fortune in Facebook stock, and he lost his ability to play for those modest stakes! Who could blame him? And I took the lead in the rivalry. Then he took it back. And so on.

USO Tour for the Troops!

For years, I had been waiting for an opportunity to support the troops. Democrat or Republican, we all support the troops. In some countries, military duty is mandatory. And I've always felt indebted to, and grateful for, the men and woman out there defending our borders. So when I had a chance to do an official United Service Organizations (USO) tour, I jumped at the chance! And so did Annie Duke and her brother Howard Lederer, Tom Dwan, and Huck Seed. The five of us would make up the first USO poker tour.

Camp Virginia and Camp Buehring in Kuwait, and Qatar?

In April 2010, the five of us had an itinerary that included Camp Virginia and Camp Buehring in Kuwait, and a stop at a base in Qatar. But as the dates grew closer, the USO canceled the Qatar segment of the trip because they thought it was too dangerous. So it was a short trip. I was surprised to learn that we would leave the USA to hit these far-flung places, and be back in the country within one week.

When we landed in Kuwait, it was weird, but someone at customs there told me that he was a fan of mine. Wasn't expecting that. After we cleared customs, we were picked up and driven around in a bus with an armed vehicle in front of us. Our first stop was a hotel in Kuwait City (it was 5 p.m. in Kuwait), and the USO advised us that we shouldn't leave the hotel. Uh, OK. So those of us who were married didn't leave the hotel, but Huck Seed and Tom Dwan ventured out to check out Kuwait City. The next morning we were driven in our bus to Camp Virginia in Kuwait. The first order of business was to meet the base commander.

So we sat around the table with the base commander, and his second and third in command, and we asked a lot of questions. We wanted to know how things worked. How was food brought in? What were the supply lines? Could the troops leave the base? And as we were leaving, the commander told us, "I've done hundreds of these with celebs, and no one has ever asked this many good questions before. I enjoyed it." Poker players aren't stupid!

Poker Tournament with the Troops!

The next stop was the USO building, where there were 50 poker tables set up to play a No Limit Hold 'Em tournament. I was MC and I had the microphone for the next six hours as we played down to a winner. Although I played in the tournament, my job was to MC: I rapped on the microphone (Jay Z!); called out big hands ("Huck has A-Q, and his opponent Sargent Lee has J-J, Sargent Lee is 13-to-10 favorite"); teased Huck, Annie, Howard, or Tom; and generally just put out big energy to get the room pumped up. Kind of like I do when I MC Tiger Jam or any other charity events (Appendix 3). At all of our stops, Tom and I put up $500 in cash apiece, so that there would be a prize pool at each stop. A little something for the troops to play for. We took hundreds of pictures at each stop, and signed hundreds of autographs. Then it was rinse-and-repeat at the other bases that we visited. After MCing four tournaments in five days I was exhausted, but I was super happy. All I could think was, "I showed up for the troops!"

April 15, 2010: Black Friday!

On the morning of Friday April 15th, the five of us landed back in the USA to devastating news. The US government would enforce the Unlawful Internet Gambling Enforcement Act (UIGEA; see Appendix 1), and had taken the extraordinary step of shutting down access to all internet poker sites, for everyone in the USA. Man! It felt like a personal betrayal. We do a USO tour, and then they shut down online poker.

The poker world called it Black Friday, and it really hurt me! I was about to sign a $30 million contract to represent Full Tilt Poker. When I say $30 million, I mean equity (to the extent legally possible), a healthy monthly salary from my equity and bonuses ($120,000 a month), and entrance into millions of dollars of poker tournaments, including a $500,000 buy-in tournament that was coming soon. I had completed my mission at UB, I helped build the site from scratch, and then when the players were cheated, I stayed until every penny was paid back (Appendix 1). And now Full Tilt Poker was moving all-in with me. And then it all fell apart.

When UIGEA passed in 2007, I lost $15 million worth of stock (Appendix 1), then Black Friday in 2010 cost me at least $30 million (over time). But I'm a silver lining guy, so that's OK, and on the plus side of the ledger, at the beginning of 2017 I'm the number 1 free agent in the world for a poker site, right next to the amazing Phil Ivey. Great things happen to me, it's on my bathroom mirror (Chapter 10), and I believe that something amazing will come along for me soon in the online poker space. So I'll stay positive regarding online poker.

Legalize Online Poker, Please!

I'm not happy that the US government took away online poker, and millions of poker-loving US citizens felt the sting. My English friend told me, "That could never happen in England, no one would dare take away our rights like that. You Americans! First, prohibition in the 1920s, and then the government takes away online poker. It just shows how young your country is!"

I hear that legalized sports betting is coming to the USA, and if that's the case, then poker should definitely be legalized. Sports betting is a not a game of skill, and poker is.

42

A Year of Seconds, an Amazing Gift!

Heading into the 2011 WSOP, for the first time in years, I was worried about money (because of Black Friday), and I didn't have enough cash to play comfortably in all the WSOP tournaments. It took about $250,000 in cash to play in them all. To be clear, my house was already worth $4 million, and I had stock in several different companies, and a SEPP fund. But the fact that we spent $65,000 a month, for years, didn't help the status of my savings account. Roughly $20,000 per month of that was spent on running companies like Poker Brat Clothing Company (PokerBrat.com), Poker Brat Publishing Company, Two Black Nines (a company that owns patents on games like Poker Jack), and websites like Phil Hellmuth.com. Also, we had two kids in college, an assistant, a chef, a maid coming in five days a week, and a full-time CEO who ran all my companies.

While I contemplated being staked, I wondered who I would ask. Almost everyone I asked would do it, and several good possibilities came to mind. Carl Westcott (Chapter 38) would do it for sure, but it felt like he wasn't as excited about it. For as long as I've been in the game (33 years), when I was staked or sold a piece of myself, I've lost money for only two people (less than $70,000 total), and made $4 million for everyone else. You see, if I lose for someone, then I always give them another chance to back me, and I've been a consistent winner for a long time.

Finally, I called Chamath (Chapters 41 and 48) and asked him to stake me. He was interested. I told him that he should stake me in a "make-up deal": he would put up cash for me to play with, and when I hit, he would get his cash back off the top, plus 33% of the profits. It was a no risk deal for him, assuming I was a winning player. I further told him that we could start with $60,000, but that sometimes I could go through $300,000 or more before hitting big. Chamath agreed.

Nick Graduates High School; I Find "The Zone"

I played in a couple of small events at the WSOP, and then I flew home the night before my son Nick's high school graduation, for our family graduation dinner (actual graduation day he was at a school party with the rest of the graduating seniors). While having dinner the next night with my wife and my parents, after Nick's graduation ceremony, this weird thing happened. I didn't want to talk! I didn't want to waste any energy talking to anyone, including my own parents (I love my parents). I knew what this meant, woo hoo! I was in the zone. I don't know why, but when I see talking as a burden, as an unnecessary use of my energy, and all I can think about is poker and saving every ounce of my energy for the tables, then I seem to be at the peak of my powers. All I could think about was flying back to Vegas after dinner and playing the WSOP $2,000 buy-in Limit Hold 'Em tournament that night. I apologized to my parents for not being able to talk, and went with the flow.

There was one problem though, Chamath had misunderstood our deal, and told me that he only wanted to risk $60,000, total. I explained again, the nature of a make-up deal, and how it was risk-free, but Chamath is strong-willed, and stuck to his guns. He would stop at $60,000 loser. Not wanting to burn up Chamath's cash, I had skipped a $25,000 buy-in heads-up tournament that was right up my alley. Because I couldn't justify risking such a high percentage of the $60,000 on one tournament.

WSOP No Limit Deuce-to-Seven Lowball

I flew back to Vegas, and I didn't do anything in the Limit Hold 'Em, but the very next day I hopped into the $10,000 No Limit Deuce-to-Seven Lowball tournament. And, suddenly, the game made perfect sense to me! Two days later, when we made it to heads-up play (126 started), I had a massive chip lead over John Juanda (a great poker player and a Poker Hall of Famer). After a five-hour battle, Juanda beat me (I won $226,000 for second place). It was a massive disappointment!

First, I have convinced myself that I will win a WSOP No Limit Deuce-to-Seven bracelet, and I had Billy Baxter all-in and drawing for a deuce bracelet in 1993 (Chapter 23). Against Billy, I had a pat ten, and he was drawing to an eight, so I was roughly 63% to win my deuce bracelet right then and there. Second, it was a chance to win my first non-Hold 'Em bracelet, and by then I was taking a lot of heat for being a "Hold 'Em specialist." Third, the whole poker world was watching closely! It had been a few years since I won a bracelet, and I was hearing whispers that I was overrated, that the younger generation was better than I was at poker, and that poker had passed me by. Great players were saying that the game had passed me by, in their blogs and interviews.

Seven Card Stud 8-or-Better (High-Low Split)

Nine days later, in the $10,000 buy-in WSOP Seven Card Stud 8-or-Better with 168 players, I was back at another final table. Again, I made it down to heads-up play, and again I finished in second place for $273,333. This time my disappointment was contained, as I never really had the chip lead. This one hurt, but not nearly as badly as the last one, or the next one...

The $50,000 WSOP Players Championship

There are only two tournaments at the very top of the poker mountain: the WSOP main event, and the WSOP Players Championship. In 1989 I won the WSOP main event (Chapter 17), and in 2011 I battled through four days of the best poker players in the world, to reach the final table of the Players. Once I doubled up at the final table, I dominated play for eight hours, and I was never even close to being all-in. Heads up vs. Brian Rast, I had four chances to win the tournament.

The first chance, Rast raised it up to 200,000 to go with K-K (he had 3.9 million in chips to my 15 million in chips), and I sensed super strength, so I just called with A-7 offsuit. The flop was 8-6-4, I checked, Rast bet, and I called. The turn was a five! *Boom!*, I made a straight. I checked, Rast checked. The river was the six of diamonds (8♣-6♠-4♦-5♦-6♦), I checked, Rast bet 600,000, and I called. What a disaster! If I had moved in pre-flop, then I would have won the tournament, although I hate that play. If I had bet on the turn (after the five hit), and then bet on the river, I may have won the tournament. And finally, if I move all-in on the river after Rast bet, which I should have done, then I may have won the tournament. But no matter, Rast had 2.1 million in chips, to my 17 million. The dream was coming true, right?

Two hands later, I called with 9♥-6♥, and Rast raised it up with A♦-K♣. The flop was 10♥-4♥-4♣, Rast bet 340,000, I moved him all-in, and Rast called. I was a favorite (about 53% chance) to win the Players Championship and shut up all the haters forever about my non-Hold 'Em abilities! But alas, I missed my heart (nine of those), my nine (three of those), and my six (three of those), and A-K high won the pot; Rast was up to 4.5 million.

A few hands later, Rast raised it up with K-7 offsuit, and I called with 10♣-8♣. The flop was K♣-J♣-4♦, and we went all-in again. I needed a club, or some sort of running two pair, trips, or straight; I was about 40% to win the Players Championship. But alas, I missed again.

A few hands later, I had 8♦-2♦, and Rast had K-Q, when the flop came down J♦-10♠-9♦. I had a straight draw, and a flush draw, and Rast flopped the nut straight. We went all-in again, and this time for 98% of the chips in the tournament, and I was 37% to basically win the tournament, but alas, I missed again! Second place again, but at least this time for $1.06 million.

A Bitter Pill to Swallow

In that moment, I was more disappointed that I have ever been! My chance to win the coveted Players Championship had been missed: 17 million in chips, a massive chip lead, and I finished second? I had regrets. My chance to be the undisputed greatest of all time had been missed. The chance to win my first non-Hold 'Em WSOP bracelet in the most coveted poker tournament in the world had been missed. Standing room only, with the global poker world watching my every move, and I finished second.

It was no consolation to me that the guys on the internet ran the math, and said I had had an 84% chance to win one of the three all-in pots, and thus an 84% chance to win the WSOP Players Championship. (Where's the flush card when you really need it?!?) I tried to handle my second-place finish with class, and I'm sure that I pulled it off, despite feeling awful. I handled it so well, that for the first time in my life my wife yelled at me about poker tactics, "What's wrong with you?!? How could you put it all-in drawing like that? This one was too important!" I was shocked. I recall that poker player Jean-Roberte Bellande (also on the show *Survivor*) came up to me and said, "Don't worry Phil, you have WSOP Player of the Year locked up. You have a massive point lead." From his mouth to God's ears, please.

Chamath's Amazing Gift to Me

Remember that Chamath had staked me in the 2011 WSOP, and he didn't even have to put any cash up! Before I had a chance to collect the $60,000 he was putting up for me to play with (I was using my own money), I had hit for $226,000 in the WSOP deuce. It got sweeter and sweeter for Chamath, as I finished second twice more for $1.33 million – a total haul of $1.56 million. After I finished second in the Players, Chamath and I went back to the Aria Hotel to have a few drinks, and he asked me, "Did you see the text that I sent you?" I opened my phone for the first time in four days, and said, "No, I have 203 new texts, and they're still pouring in. What's up?"

Chamath said, "I'm letting you hang on to $300,000 of the money you won for me." I said, "Wow, thank you!" A few days later, I asked, "Can I invest it in your Social Capital venture capital fund?" Chamath said, "Absolutely, I enjoyed watching you work for me, and now I hope that you enjoy watching me work for you." What an amazing gesture, so classy! And what an amazing gift, thanks Chamath.

Ben Lamb vs. Phil Hellmuth for WSOP Player of the Year

As the WSOP main event rolled on, the press reported that Ben Lamb could pass me for WSOP Player of the Year if only Ben could make the final table. And as the 6,865 players narrowed to hundreds, Ben took the chip lead. But even if Ben made the final table, I had the WSOPE in Cannes in October, to retake the lead. Sure enough, Ben made the final table and became a November Niner, and I would need to respond in Cannes to retake the points lead. And even if I responded at the WSOPE in October, then Ben could possibly take the lead back in November at the WSOP final table. The WSOP Player of the Year race was on!

Ben is in the Lead Until 2011 WSOPE

In October, in the €2,500 WSOPE Six Max No Limit Hold 'Em, I responded. I took the chip lead, but then played poorly and faded to seventh place, sigh. This seventh-place finish gave me the points lead, but to take back the lead, Ben only had to finish in eighth place or higher in the November Nine, and there were only nine players left. Had I won the WSOPE Six Max, then Ben would have had to win the WSOP main event to win WSOP Player of the Year. I simply did not put enough pressure on Ben.

2011 WSOP Main Event

After finishing in second place three times at the 2011 WSOP, I finished second in the 2011 WSOP Player of the Year. It really hurt, especially as I reflected on how I had won the 2006 WSOP Player of the Year, only to have the WSOP staff take it away from me! (Chapter 36) Well, at least I would never finish second in another WSOP Player of the Year race, right? Hah!

43

Hello WSOP Numbers 12 and 13!

Coming off three second-place finishes in the 2011 WSOP the year before (last chapter), I headed into the 2012 WSOP thinking, "If I can finish second in three WSOP tournaments in the modern era, then I can win three WSOP tournaments in the modern era!" After Chamath's amazing $300,000 gift (last chapter), I let him stake me again.

The 2012 WSOP

In the first week of the 2012 WSOP tournament, I finished in 61st place, then 52nd, and then 15th in WSOP tournaments. I was trending in the right direction! Then I entered the $2,500 buy-in Razz (Seven Card Low) with 309 players. Razz is the R in the HORSE mix, one of the five basic games that we have been playing forever. It is a game of great skill (as I proved over the next four years!), with gutsy betting, and reading abilities held at a premium. I recall that I had the chip lead after Day 1, and I started to fade a bit coming down the stretch, until I caught a break in a huge pot, and tripled up.

Brandon Cantu

I was joined at the final table by my good friend Brandon Cantu, who has won two WSOP bracelets, and one WPT title, and is the only player in the world that I share advanced poker strategies and tactics with. And it is quid pro quo, as he contributes heavily to the discussion. Cantu and I discuss complex hands and strategies across every game in poker, but mostly around Texas Hold 'Em. Cantu has a brilliant poker mind capable of considering any and all possible strategies. Cantu's not bound by mathematics, the latest theories, or logic, or reason. We once discussed why it would make sense to fold A-A pre-flop, which everyone else in the world thought was absurd. (We ruled against it, but in those days you could pick up a lot of chips bluffing with not much risk, so then why get them all-in only 4½-to-1 favorite?) And like me, Cantu has great reading abilities. As we both have strong reading abilities we can do things that others cannot do in the poker world. Sometimes we need to remind each other that "reads" can change any well-constructed mathematical strategy.

By the way, in the old days I used to share tactics with Mike "the Mouth" Matusow. Mike swore that he would never reveal what was discussed in our high-level talks about how to optimally play No Limit Hold 'Em tournaments, but then he would casually mention that another great player had called him to talk tactics. I guess I should have known that anyone with the nickname "the Mouth," couldn't keep a secret! I might tease Mikey, but he has a pure heart! I love Mikey, always have, always will.

Ivey Heads Up for WSOP Number 9 at same time I'm Heads Up for WSOP Number 12

OK, let's get this straight. At 10 p.m. on June 10, 2012, the legendary Phil Ivey (Appendix 2) was playing heads up with Andy Frankenberger for bracelet number 9 in No Limit Hold 'Em, while I was playing heads up for bracelet number 12 in Razz vs. Don Zewin. Additionally, I was going for my first bracelet in a non-Hold 'Em game, while Phil Ivey went for his first bracelet in a Hold 'Em game. Got it? So if I won, and Ivey lost, then it would be me, up 12-8. If Ivey won, and I lost then it would be me, but only 11-9. It was a big night for WSOP history, and the all-time bracelet race!

I won the Razz tournament before midnight (for $182,793), in front of my son Phillip (Phillip was also there when I won WSOP bracelet number 10). Finally, the monkey was off my back! My first non-Hold 'Em bracelet was on my wrist. Meanwhile, I kept track of Ivey's progress as I celebrated at a nightclub at the Aria Hotel, and he wound up finishing second place. All-time WSOP bracelet count: Hellmuth 12, Johnny Chan 10, Doyle Brunson 10, Johnny Moss 9, Phil Ivey 8.

Mori Eskandani, and More Bracelets at the 2012 WSOP?

Speaking of Phil Ivey, he and I made a WSOP final table together in the $10,000 buy-in WSOP HORSE tournament a few weeks later, on July 3, 2012, with 178 players. We had the poker press all riled up! But Ivey finished in fifth place, and I finished in fourth. Also at that final table was the uber talented Mori Eskandani, the man behind *Poker after Dark*, the NBC Heads-Up Championships, and for the last seven years, the WSOP coverage. Mori went from successful professional poker player (Mori was a Seven Card Stud player) to super successful television producer. Mori commands everyone's respect, and his intellect is second to none! He is the only television producer who manages to remain friends with the players, which is hard to do with the huge egos in poker, and the demands that the poker players have to get what they believe is their "fair share" of television time.

Mori was at dinner in 2012 with the NBC Sports bigwigs and the WSOP bigwigs when the subject of former Pittsburgh Steeler running back Jerome "the Bus" Bettis (I'm a fan) came up. Mori bet everyone at the table that at least 50% of the people in the room didn't know who Bettis was. The assembled table, mostly sports people, laughed at Mori, and they pulled their wallets out. When they polled the room, less than 20% of the people knew who Jerome Bettis was, and Mori collected $11,000 from the table. Don't mess with Mori!

The $1 Million Buy-in One Drop Charity Poker Tournament

At the 2012 WSOP I was hot, and it made sense for me to play in the $1 million buy-in Big One for One Drop. Chamath had made more money on me at the 2012 WSOP, and he wanted me to play, so we formulated a plan. By the way, you would expect a $1 million buy-in tournament not to sell too many spots! But Guy Laliberté, the founder of Cirque Du Soleil, brilliantly capped it at 48 players. It seems like people want something that is scarce, and in this case it seemed to drive players in. Once it was announced that Guy had 30 players signed up, then we knew it would sell out.

Three days before the One Drop, there was one more seat available, and I had an inside track to buying it. I would MC a One Drop seat giveaway at the luxurious Aria Hotel and Casino, the day before the One Drop began, and Chamath and I would approach the winner and see if he wanted me to play for him, in exchange for some cash, and a piece of me.

A One Drop Syndicate is Formed

Chamath and I had already secured investments from my friends Joe Lacob (Golden State Warriors primary owner), Vivek Ranadivé (now the Sacramento Kings primary owner), Bobby Baldwin (Chapter 32), Rick Salomon (from Paris Hilton sex tape), professional poker player Eddie Ting, and a couple of others. We bought the seat, and I was in. One problem: I was tired from MCing the $1 million giveaway all day long. So, I came in late – Chamath had bought in as well and was at my table – and I played horrendously! Here I was, in a $1 million buy-in poker tournament, by far the biggest poker tournament of my life (I played in one

$100,000 buy-in before that), and I'm going crazy raising, and re-raising, and jamming my chips around like a wild man. And Chamath, my main backer, was at the table to witness my super-fast play! If we didn't start with over 1,000 big blinds, I would have busted out. I recall losing nearly half of my stack for no good reason, that's 500 big blinds (1.5 million in chips)!

Absurd Bet Sizing!

Poker star Daniel Negreanu (Appendix 2) was at my table, and he picked that day to 3-bet me like a crazy man, and try to outplay me in tons of pots. He did outplay me, but I told him that one way or another I was going to smash him if he kept messing with me. Finally, I went bonkers trying to bluff Daniel with an inside straight draw. I had 5-3 offsuit on J-7-4 board, and I hit the 6 on the river! That turned it around for me, and when I hit 3 million in chips, a weird hand came up. With the blinds 3,000–6,000, Player A opened for a huge 5x raise to 30,000, and two players called. I peered down at A-A and I thought, "Why mess around here? I'll just end this pot right now." I made an absurd raise to 700,000 to go. Most of the young guys would have made it like 60,000 to go, and the veterans would make it 90,000 to go. The absurd 700,000 bet telegraphed that I had pocket aces, and it said, "Look at me, I'm making the biggest bet of the tournament, don't mess with me." I expected everyone to fold, and to fold quickly, but then Player A moved all-in! For 3 million in chips. Uh, OK, I call. Player A had K-K, and I was 4½-to-1 favorite to take the chip lead. My hand held. From tilting like a madman to the chip lead!

Day 2 of One Drop: $1.1 Million "Bubble!"

Late on Day 2, I moved all-in with 5-5, and I was called by A-K. It was the only time I was all-in, other than the aforementioned A-A, and luckily my hand held (I was 52% to win). Then we hit the money bubble. There were ten players left, and nine were to be paid. But what a bubble! Ninth place was $1.1 million, and tenth was nothing, nada, zilch. I dug in and prepared for a long battle. It could take hours as players patiently folded hand after hand and waited for the $1.1 million payday. I was expecting to play on the bubble for at least four hours. Wrong! One guy was all-in every other hand it seemed, and 35 minutes later it was over. Now we had another bubble, the television final table bubble. Nine of us were left, but only eight would come back for Day 3, with a chance to win $18.3 million for first, and to sit at a live final table on ESPN. Mike Sexton, the poker legend and full-time announcer for the WPT, bubbled the television coverage. Mike wasn't happy, but it was one million one hundred thousand times better than the cash bubble!

Day 3 of the One Drop

Two of my sisters, KK (Kerry) and Molls (Molly) (Chapter 16), decided to fly in for that final table. I am so lucky to have a great family! In the old days, KK and Molls could come hang out with me on the road a lot more often, before husbands and children entered their lives. So I was honored that they were both able to drop everything and come out and "sweat me" for the One Drop final table! Love you KK, love you Molls!

And what a sweat for my investors! Want to own a horse in the Kentucky Derby? How about a piece of me, playing for $18.3 million for first place, and you can watch for hours and hours, live on ESPN! And, one of the investors, Bobby Baldwin, made it to the final table as well.

I didn't pick up many hands, and on patience alone I made it down to the final four players. Sadly, I busted out in fourth place for $2.6 million, and headed to the legendary Aria Hotel's High-Limit Bar, which Michael Jordan, Charles Barkley, Dustin Johnson, Wayne Gretzky, and many other super stars frequent. Coach Jim Harbaugh and his sweet wife Sarah met my wife and me there for a few drinks. Jim is so much fun to hang out with! He had just watched the final table, and wanted to know why I played certain hands, and we discussed the cross over between coaching football and poker. It's all about tactics!

Hitting Europe Early, to be Well Rested

On September 15, 2012, I accepted an offer from Party Poker to fly to Malta and play in a WPT tournament. Basically, I accepted the offer (first class airfare, hotel, and buy-ins) because I wanted to adjust to European time, so that I was ready for the WSOPE in Cannes, France. I was sick of flying to Europe at the last minute, and then struggling with my schedule for days at a time while playing tired, uninspired poker. I wanted to be fresh for the WSOPE! And I liked Malta. I had been to Malta before (Chapter 15), in September 1988, but I never thought that I would be back. But after five days in Malta, it was time to move on, I had bigger fish to fry.

Cantu and Game Planning the WSOPE in Cannes

On September 20th, I flew to Cannes to play in seven WSOPE bracelet tournaments. Once there, my poker confidant Brandon Cantu and I started having serious discussions about No Limit Hold 'Em tactics. We decided that the younger generation in the poker world had merged their play so much that we could take advantage of it. The kids all played the exact same way! They were like robots. If they were playing a certain way, then we needed to figure out how to beat them using alternate strategies. We came up with the concept of making huge oversized raises. The kids weren't trained for it. They didn't know how to deal with the big bet sizing. And even better, they thought that we were bad players. They rolled their eyes when they didn't understand something, and went back to their forums to report how poorly Cantu and I were playing. When I was young, I would have never have made that mistake. I would have never underestimated any strategy or any player, especially the great ones! I would have watched and learned.

The WSOPE Cannes

On September 21st, in the first tournament, a €2,500 buy-in No Limit Hold 'Em, with 227 players, I finished in 24th place. On September 25th, I won my table in the €3,000 shootout tournament, and made Day 2 with 14 other players. I didn't play my best on Day 2, and I fell in 12th place. The next day was hugely disappointing! I entered the WSOPE €10,000 buy-in No Limit Hold 'Em Mixed Max, and when we hit the final 16 players, we had a redraw to play heads-up matches. With several players sitting on less than 30,000 in chips, I had over 200,000. I drew the chip leader, my friend and poker confidant Brandon Cantu, sigh. Man, if I had drawn a guy with 18,000 in chips, or one of the other short stacks, then I'm almost a lock to advance. Instead, I drew Cantu, and he had a massive chip lead of 500,000. Cantu wound up beating me. For those keeping track, that was three deep runs in six tournaments. I had some momentum going into the WSOPE main event.

Sergii Baranov (Who?!?) Says I'll Win WSOPE Main Event

The night before the main event began, a random poker player from the Ukraine played a few hands of Open Face poker with me, and when I quit he accosted me and said, "You will win the main event, and I will come in second." Huh? How strange. There were 420 players, and I had never heard anyone predict something quite like this before! First and second? At the end of Day 1, this guy found me again and said, "See? You are in the top ten and I'm in the top five in chips." At the end of Day 2, with 77 players left, this guy found me again, and said, "See? I'm the chip leader, and you're fourth in chips. You are going to win, and I'm going to finish in second place." By then I knew his name was Sergii Baranov, although I wasn't buying into his theory quite yet.

At the end of Day 3, the poker press started reporting that I had a chance to win the WSOP Player of the Year. Yeah, there it was again. In 2006, I felt like the WSOP took the Player of the Year away from me (Chapter 36), and in 2011, Ben Lamb passed me by making the WSOP main event final table (he still had to not finish in ninth place, Chapter 42). The press reports said that I needed to make the WSOPE main event final table to take the points lead in the 2012 Player of the Year. Now, with 24 players left, Sergii was in third place in the chip counts and I was in sixth place and he found me and said, "Phil, you will win this and I will finish in second place. Do you believe me now?" I smiled. I had heard him say that at least 20 times by now, but I didn't understand what was happening, and I didn't want to assume that I would win. I needed to play my best on Day 4 and make the final table. I needed to stay focused, and in the moment.

At the end of Day 4, with nine players remaining, I was stunned to see that I was leading the tournament with 3.4 million in chips, and Sergii was second in chips with 3.3 million! Huh? The next closest stack was the young talented professional poker player Joseph Cheong with 1.9 million in chips. In my mind, it was truly amazing that Sergii and I had both made it to the WSOPE Main Event final table! I was starting to believe, and starting to have an inkling of what might happen. Also, the press was reporting that if I won the WSOPE main event, then the only way I would lose the 2012 WSOP Player of the Year was if Greg Merson won the WSOP main event in November.

One of the reasons I did so well in Cannes was that I napped to the max. Every dinner break was long, and I napped through them. I walked a ton to tire myself out. And in the middle of the final table, because we had to play it streaming live globally, on television networks in Europe and the USA (ESPN), we had a two-hour break. Sweet! A 90-minute nap was a game changer for me.

The WSOPE Final Table; A Big Decision, Sergii vs. Me

I recall that I was in a real pickle vs. Sergii when he re-raised Stéphane Albertini to 200,000 to go from the small blind (I called from the big blind with J-J), then bet 275,000 on the 9-2-2 flop (I called), then bet 500,000 on the Q♦ turn (I called), and then Sergii bet 1 million in chips on the 10♥ river (9-2-2-Q-10). I tanked for five minutes, I couldn't beat any real hand that Sergii would bet on every street, but something didn't feel right. It felt like Sergii was bluffing, but if I called and I was wrong, then I would be the short stack. Still, it felt like he was bluffing, and I called. Sergii said, "You win." And I shouted, "Yes!" That pot gave me 5.8 million to Sergii's 3.3 million, while Joseph Cheong and Stéphane were hanging around with 1.5 million in chips.

As we passed midnight, the WSOPE staff told us, "By law, they must shut down the casino at 4 a.m., and we are not sure what we're going to do if this isn't over by then." Then Joseph Cheong busted, and there were three of us left, including Sergii and me with most of the chips. Is this real life? Too late to wonder about that now, stay focused. I had Stéphane all-in when we put 900,000 each in before the flop, with my 7-7 to his J-J. The board came down K-5-4-Q, and then, *boom!*, a seven!

Sergii vs. Phil for the WSOPE Main Event Title

Are you kidding me? Is this real life? Sergii had said all along that I would win and that he would finish second. And now it was down to the two of us. By now I believed him. I believed that I would win and he would finish second, and so he did. Before we played heads up, Sergii wanted to talk and make a "save." I had 9.5 million in chips to his 3 million in chips, and I was willing to talk, especially as he had seemed to will us both here! First place was €1 million and second was €632,000. We made a small save: I would get €150,000 if he won, and he would get €60,000 if I won. After 15 minutes, Sergii was all-in with his A-4 vs. my A-10. I was 2½-to-1 favorite to win the WSOPE main event, $1.2 million (I had 100% of myself except for the save), and bracelet number 13 in style! The board came down J-9-5-A, and with one card to come, Sergii had some cards that would tie me (three fives and three nines) and three fours to beat me. I couldn't bear to watch. I listened to the announcers call it, "And the river is... a three! Phil Hellmuth has won the WSOP main event and bracelet number 13!" (And it ended on schedule for the WSOPE staff, at 3:45 a.m.)

I was overwhelmed. It was the best poker tournament that I had ever played in my life, bar none! And just because I had played the best tournament of my life certainly didn't mean that I would win it. This is poker! In golf, if Tiger plays his best, then he wins by double digits. But in poker, you can get unlucky, or lose every flip. After I won, I was interviewed on global television, and I said, "I know you're not expecting to hear this, but I'm humbled. I'm thankful. I appreciate this one so much. Yes, I played one of the best tournaments of my life, but I've been around, and the fact that I won is a blessing." I tipped the WSOPE staff, and the WSOPE dealers $20,000! They said, "It's too much." But it felt right to me.

Then we went out to drink Dom Perignon (on the casino) across the street for a couple of hours. Next stop was my suite for cigars and more drinks, and then I took the people still celebrating with me out to the shoe store and bought them all two new pairs of shoes (hello Warren Lush!). On absolutely zero sleep, but with lots of wind in my sails, I embarked for the airport at 11 a.m., and off I went!

Player of the Year, Finally?

I took a big lead in the WSOP Player of the Year, and Greg Merson would have to win the main event in November to deny me that title, for the third time. Second in Player of the Year in 2006, second in 2011, but it looked good for me in 2012. I would finally win a Player of the Year, unless Merson made me finish in second for a third time.

Prologue: PH Mental Break Down

I left Cannes on cloud nine, but I left beyond exhausted. Five intense days in the WSOPE main event culminating in a win at 3:45 a.m., partying all night, no sleep, followed by an overseas flight to San Antonio. And sadly, it got worse, much worse. I left Cannes on Friday at 1 p.m., and I landed in San Antonio on Friday to MC Eva Longoria's charity poker tournament. Eva, the woman who was voted (several times) the "world's most beautiful woman," sent a limo for me and I was whisked away to my hotel. I tried to rest up, because I knew that I would have the microphone for eight hours on Saturday night MCing "Eva's Heroes Celebrity Casino Night" (Appendix 3).

Eva in San Antonio to
John Legend and President Clinton in LA

Saturday night I MCed Eva's charity poker night; eight hours on the microphone, over $700,000 raised. Then Sunday morning I had to get up early and fly to LA to give rock star John Legend a private lesson at his house, and then MC President Clinton's charity poker tournament (we raised $2 million) (Appendix 3). I didn't have much sleep on Saturday night, and I was running on fumes in the middle of President Clinton's charity poker tournament on Sunday night, but I made it through another eight hours on the mic. Exhausted just reading this yet?

After one day (Monday) to rest up in LA, my wife and I flew to Chicago on Tuesday and hopped into a private poker game with J.B. Pritzker (Chapter 44) and the Chicago crew. Fun, but no rest for the weary. And on Wednesday I had the microphone for another eight hours as I MCed the Chicago Poker Challenge (Appendix 3) and raised over $1.2 million in one night. Then we went out to the Chicago nightclubs until 2 a.m. It was right after that that I hit the wall. I was totaled!

I was exhausted three cities ago (a mere five days earlier) coming out of Cannes. Then eight hours on the microphone in San Antonio on Saturday, private lesson to John Legend in LA on Sunday afternoon, then eight hours on the microphone on Sunday evening ($2 million for Clinton Foundation), then a poker game in Chicago on Tuesday evening, eight hours on the microphone in Chicago on Wednesday (made $1.2 million for Teaching Tolerance Charity), and then a nightclub midnight on Wednesday. Hello wall!

The Wall! Never Go There!

It was all about stress for me then! For some reason, if my wife misspoke, then my mind would leap to me saying something, then her getting mad, and I would get super-stressed before I even corrected her. I think of the words, "stress sandwich." I couldn't think straight, and the preponderance of stress that would appear out of nowhere, and for the smallest things, was maddening. I felt so much stress that I was almost shaking. I told my wife what I was feeling, and she gave me a wide berth. I told her that we needed to cancel our flights and stay in Chicago until I could recover to at least 80%. From the top of the world only one week before, to this? We spent an extra three days in Chicago chilling, and that seemed to bring me back to at least 75% of my full power, and that was good enough to fly home. (For the record, I will never jump city to city to city again like that.)

Can Greg Merson Win the WSOP Main Event and Player of the Year?

I was going to win Player of the Year, or Merson was going to win the main event and Player of the Year. I should have been there in Las Vegas, I guess. Not anti-sweating Merson (I don't root against players) but observing the action. It was a big moment for me! Instead, I was in New York City watching the coverage, all night long, on ESPN. It was then that I decided that I should always be at the WSOP final table, every year, to support the game of poker. Had I let the haters, the ones that say "Phil is just there stealing the spotlight" affect me too much? Yep. That night, I thought that the poker world needed me, and I needed it, and I decided that I would never miss another WSOP main event final table.

Greg Plays Beautifully

As I watched the hands unfold from afar, I loved the way that Greg was playing! And there was only one time, when he was all-in with his A-K vs. their K-Q, that I could have won Player of the Year. Yes, Greggy was a 2½-to-1 favorite to win that pot, but if he lost, then I was Player of the Year. But his hand held up, and he played so beautifully that he was never all-in again. Greg defied the current theories of the day, and just called on the button in quite a few hands. The vast majority of players would have raised it up in all of those hands on the button. I'm a fan of calling on the button, when I have the right opponents. Greg took a page out of my book. Because real poker players know how to play after the flop, on the turn, and on the river. Greg was making his opponents play after the flop poker, and he won it all. Greg Merson won the WSOP main event, and he won Player of the Year.

For the third time in less than ten years, I finished second in Player of the Year. For the second year in a row, someone passed me by making the WSOP main event final table! And this time, if Greg didn't win the WSOP main event then I would have won Player of the Year, ouch. But give credit where credit is due: well played, Greggy.

44

2013: NBC Heads-Up Success and WSOP Failure

On December 29, 2012, I landed in the Bahamas with the intent of staying with my friend J.B. Pritzker, his wife M.K., and their two kids until Jan 4th, and then playing in PokerStars Caribbean Adventure (PCA) tournaments. I first met J.B. when he reached out to me in 2010 to MC his charity poker tournament the Chicago Poker Challenge for Teaching Tolerance Charity, and we have raised over $10 million (Appendix 3), so far.

J.B. is an amazing guy and a legendary businessman. J.B. and his wife M.K are great people who have their values in perfect alignment: family first. J.B. manages to be on the board of at least six charities, and gives heavily of himself, his time, and his money to support many wonderful causes (not just Teaching Tolerance). Their two kids are terrific and well balanced, and I don't know how they do it, but J.B. and M.K. seem to have no ego, and they are thankful for everything they have. J.B. and M.K. are authentic and genuine, and they care about other people. My favorite M.K. line is her lucky tub line that goes like this, "My butt has landed in this lucky tub, and I know it, and I'm grateful for it."

J.B.'s father started Hyatt Hotels, and J.B. inherited well over $1 billion, but what he has done with it tells the story of his business acumen. In the 1990s he was criticized because he started investing in this weird thing called "the internet." Well, I guess that that worked out well for him! And J.B. continues to crush it with The Pritzker Group, as a venture capitalist, early stage investor, and stock market investor. He has invested in Facebook, Dollar Shave Club, and Playdom, to name a few.

When J.B. found out that I was going to the PCA, he invited me to stay with his family in the Bahamas. I accepted his invitation. Now, I'm not sure that M.K. was completely onboard with me staying at the house with them for six days;

she didn't know me at the time. And to be fair, it was family time for them: J.B., M.K., their two children. I imagine that she thought, "You invited a random professional poker player to stay with the four of us?" But we all hit it off swimmingly! As the oldest of five, I have always enjoyed hanging out with kids. We played tennis and basketball, we swam and relaxed, and at night we played poker for no stakes and Mario Kart (J.B. and I had a rivalry there; he was better than me, but neither of us could beat the kids!). Late at night, J.B., M.K., and I would have a drink, and J.B. and I would smoke a cigar. I must say that J.B. and M.K. are terrific parents, and a blast to be with.

The NBC Heads-Up Championships

The NBC Heads-Up Championship was held 2005–2011 (I won it in 2005 – Chapter 35), and in 2012 it was canceled. The death of online poker in the USA was the reason it was canceled. But on January 20, 2013, the NBC Heads-Up Championship was brought back, to much fanfare. Remember that the NBC Heads-Up is a bracket tournament, with 32 heads-up matches where winners advance to the "sweet 16," then 16 matches where winners advance to the "elite eight", then the "final four" and so on.

With a new ever-expanding crop of young internet wizards, many who specialized in heads-up No Limit Hold 'Em, the press said that it was the year outdated old-school players weren't supposed to be around at the end. Not! As I marched through my matches, I looked up at the other side of the bracket and noticed that Mike "the Mouth" Matusow was still in there. With eight left, we had three old-school players in there: John Hennigan, Mike, and me. When it came down to Mikey and me for the whole ball of wax (the old school might not be as elegant mathematically as the young guns, but we have "reads"!), we knew that the ratings would be good. With two old-school "talkers" with huge personalities, NBC was thrilled!

Mikey vs. Me

I was thrilled that J.B. was in Las Vegas to watch the final match! In any case, every match was one round, until the finals, where it was best two out of three. In a packed house in Caesars Palace Hotel and Casino, Mike took down the first match, and I took down the second.

After spewing off a few chips, I was finally "locked in" in the third match, when the following hand came up. Mike raised it up to 32,000 with 8♦-4♦, and I called with K-10. The flop was K♦-J♠-2♦, I checked, Mike bet 30,000, and I called. The turn card was the 6♠, I checked, and Mike bet 105,000. Watching a video of the hand now on the internet, I say, "I have a bad feeling about this hand. Mike, what will you do if I move all-in for 357,000?" As I studied Mike, I felt more and more weakness, then I said, "I might make the worst fold of my life. Well actually, I have to go with my instincts, I'm all-in for 357,000." Mike hesitated and I instantly said, "Yes! I have the best hand, he would have called immediately if he had my hand beat." (True.)

The video doesn't show that I baited Mikey into calling me. When Mikey was folding, I said, "It's your chance to win. You may not get another chance. I may have a pair of deuces." Then Mikey stopped, pondered for a minute or two, and said, "I'm going for the win, I call!" Everyone on the planet, including Mike, knew that he had an easy fold. He had nine wins, I had 35 wins. He was almost 4-to-1 underdog, and had to call 252,000 to win 586,000. The math wasn't there. But it was a chance to win, and to be fair, I might not have given him another chance. I might have just rolled him over and won it. So going to the river, Mike needed a diamond, and the dealer turn the Q♦. Mikey started celebrating, but the cameras stayed on me as I muttered to J.B., "That's why I'm the best in the world." First place was $750,000, second was $300,000, but Mikey had made a $100,000 save, so I walked out of Caesars with $400,000. Also, on the plus side, J.B. and I had some good time to hang out, and we had some 75-year-old Macallan at the Aria High-Limit Bar.

The Barren 2013 WSOP and M.J.: My Ego Soars

I made a deep run in the WSOP $10,000 buy-in heads-up tournament (bracket style), making it down to the elite eight and then busting. After I busted, I was exhausted and I went back to the beautiful Aria Hotel and ordered from Javiar's Mexican Restaurant. It was the only place that room service wouldn't pick up from, so I had to go pick up my "to go order." Oddly, before I left my room to pick up my food, I told my wife, "I think I'm going to run into Michael Jordan." What a weird thing to think. (I knew he was in town and staying at the Aria, but still.)

I walked to Javiar's and grabbed my food, and I did ask if M.J. was in the restaurant, but he wasn't. With food in hand, I quickly decided to take the route to my room that involved an escalator, instead of walking by the High-Limit Bar to the elevator. At the top of the escalator I turned left toward the Sky Suite elevators, and *boom!*, M.J. was about 15 yards ahead of me, walking super slow (with his 80-year-old friend). I always walk super-fast in Vegas, so I was walking up quickly on him, when I thought, "Just leave M.J. alone," and I walked even faster and slammed my sunglasses on. As I flew past M.J., I nodded a quick hello, and after 15 yards, I turned left and walked 15 more yards to the door that led to the VIP elevators. As I opened the door with my Sky Suite key, I glanced behind me, to see if I could hold the door open for anyone (Midwestern manners), when M.J. came flying up behind me.

M.J. should have just been turning the corner, but there he was, and he said, "Hello Phil, how are you?" I said, "Great, congrats on your wedding." He said, "Thanks. How are you doing in poker?" I said, "I won two more WSOP bracelets last year, but I'm not in a great mood as I just made the elite eight and busted in the WSOP heads-up tourney." M.J. and I talked for a while on the elevator, and I was feeling puffed up like a peacock. M.J. had hustled to catch up with me! I was cool. I was a bad ass.

Mind Blown, Hello Hellmuthian Ego!

The next morning I woke up, and I read an email from a friend in the bay area that said, "I was with President Obama last night and we talked about you. He was asking how you are doing at the WSOP." Huh!?! Obama knows who I am? And he was asking about me? I'm a bad ass. I'm so cool. And sadly, my ego seemed to hit escape velocity. My mind was blown. For the next week, I wanted to tell all my friends about M.J. hustling to catch up with me and Obama asking about me, and those useless egotistical thoughts dominated my mind. I knew something was wrong with me, I knew I wasn't handling this well, and I thought, "This is the WSOP man, snap out of it!" But I didn't, and for 12 days I didn't even come close to cashing.

Late 2013 Cutbacks

After a dry 2013 WSOP, I realized that we couldn't spend $65,000 a month anymore. For the first time in years, or ever, it was time to cut some fat. My wife and I sat down and reviewed our spending habits. I thought that we could cut about $20,000 a month by getting rid of the full-time CEO of Poker Brat Companies, an assistant, and whatever else made sense. And we did exactly that, we cut $20,000 a month. We still spend $45,000 a month, but that seems easily manageable.

WSOP Close Call and Phil has Health Issues

Traditionally, every time I've suffered through a bad WSOP I seem to crush the very next year. And the 2013 WSOP had been a bad one for me! So I was expecting great things at the 2014 WSOP and, right away, in a field of 352 players, I made a final table in the WSOP $1,500 buy-in Razz (Seven Card Low), with the chip lead. Joining me there was my poker confidant Brandon Cantu. Sound familiar? Cantu and I had made the Razz final table together two years earlier, in 2012, when I won bracelet number 12 (Chapter 43). In 2012, Cantu finished in third place, and this time Cantu busted in fifth.

Eventually, I found myself heads up with Ted Forrest, and I had massive respect for his Razz game. Ted is the player who I had declared in my *New York Times* best-selling book *Play Poker Like the Pros* to be the best Razz player in the world. Still, I wasn't afraid. I had played a lot of poker with Teddy, I had a nice chip lead, and I had won the WSOP Razz two years earlier. By the way, there was a good measure of history on the line. Teddy was going for his WSOP record second Razz bracelet, as was I. The winner could lay claim to being the best Razz tournament player in the world. Teddy and I played heads up for five intense hours. Ted is great at Razz, but I fought him tooth and nail until the bitter end. But Ted eventually claimed his second Razz bracelet; his sixth WSOP bracelet. I liked the way that I played, other than a couple of hands, and it could have gone either way. Congrats on the win, Teddy.

WSOP Continues, Phil Blows One, Stud Lessons

I had six more cashes at the 2014 WSOP, including a super-disappointing eighth place finish in the WSOP $3,000 buy-in No Limit Hold 'Em Six Max tournament. I busted out of that one with a lot of regret. I had the chip lead, and I should have finished stronger. I faltered down the stretch. I should have either kept up my super-aggressive play, or I should have gone to super-patient play. Instead, my ego entered the picture, and I was caught in a verbal battle as I took my eye off the ball. I didn't finish with my usual flourish. I should have shut my mouth, and finished the right way!

WSOP Seven Card Stud – Lessons

When the $10,000 buy-in Stud (Seven Card Stud) tournament came along, I decided to skip it based on my dry record in stud tournaments since 2004. But the temptation to play was too strong, so I called up Ted Forrest for lessons. Ted gave me great information about starting with the best hand, and I used it to make the final table. I played wonderfully for two days to make it down to the final table, but again I blew it. I fell apart at the final table and finished in sixth place. I lost a big pot with a strong hand, but I could have finished a lot stronger. I lost my patience.

Health Issues?

In October 2014, I was having some trouble breathing. It felt like my nose area was clogged up a bit, so that I had to make a bigger effort to draw a normal breath. I have a concierge doctor, someone I pay $300 a month whether I need him or not, but when I need him, then I have amazing service. My doctor hadn't been earning his cash, as I called him twice a year, but boy did that change! I saw at least five doctors while trying to get the bottom of my issues. From a heart doctor, to an ear, nose, and throat doctor, to a stomach doctor, and more that I can't recall.

Also, I was battling panic attacks, and they are nasty! A panic attack might start for me when I thought that I might have a heart attack and die, and then my level of paranoia would spike up. During one panic attack, I recall falling to the floor, sweating profusely, while I was unable to move, and wondering if I was going to die. The problem is that once you have one panic attack, then it is easier to have another. And this can go on for months. In 2007, I recall having five or six panic attacks in one month! So, while having mini-panic attacks I rushed from specialist to specialist, and really struggled with my mysterious health issues. I was in this negatively charged state for weeks, and I made my wife miserable! I called her constantly, always worried that something was seriously wrong with me.

Finally a Diagnosis: GERD

Finally, I was diagnosed with gastroesophageal reflux disease (GERD), which is commonly diagnosed in people when they turn 50 years old. Like me, President Obama was diagnosed with it when he turned 50 years old. GERD basically means that a latch in your stomach can open for two reasons: when you eat too much fatty food, and when you eat too much food. Well, OK, I would need to avoid fatty foods and big meals. That was a lot to go through for such a simple thing as GERD.

Hello Australia, Hello WSOP-APAC

On the heels of my diagnosis, while still battling panic attacks, I hopped a flight to Australia to play in the WSOP Asia-Pacific (WSOP-APAC). I was worried that I would have a panic attack on the flight, but I wasn't going to miss a chance to win WSOP bracelets! I slowly found sure footing in Melbourne, and I had a shot at another bracelet in the WSOP-APAC A$2,200 buy-in No Limit Hold 'Em Six Max, with a field of 243 players. This time I didn't blow the Six Max, like I had done at the 2014 WSOP (see earlier in this chapter). But sadly, I lost some key pots and finished in fourth place.

December 2014, Wife Too Emotional

In December, Kathy was near the end of a brutally long stretch of work. She was working tons of hours, for ten weeks straight, and she seemed to lose it quite often when she was at home in the evenings. I was very patient, especially because I had been such a drag on her for a month straight in October. I simply had to be patient and put up with her losing it emotionally in arguments far too often, because I know how hard it can be to put up with me. I put up with it and handled it like a champion, but I knew I wasn't happy the whole month of December. And, unbeknownst to me, the month of December took a big toll on me.

In retrospect, December 2014, made me question whether Kathy was choosing me or work? I was convinced that she was choosing work over me, and it hurt! And it led to a crack in our relationship. A crack that grew bigger and bigger in 2015 (the next chapter).

46

We Lose Goldie; Phil Almost Leaves Kathy

In 2001, Kathy had some very good reasons to leave me, as I was unable to give her the empathy that she desired, was too immature, was self-centered to the exclusion of others, and took up too much space in our relationship (see Chapter 31). Fair enough. But rather than leave me, she gave me a chance to address my issues, and make some wholesale changes. Under the threat of losing my beloved Kathy, and the accompanying pain that I felt, I found a path to growth. And I worked hard to address (to some degree), my issues. Or, put another way, Kathy made me, not for the first time, into a better man!

Dave Goldberg; We Lost a Great One

On May 1, 2015, Dave Goldberg died of a cardiac arrhythmia caused by coronary heart disease. Goldie had been the glue that held our regular poker game together (Chapter 41). By then, the group had been playing genial poker together for five years. And Goldie was always late, because he wanted to put his kids to bed before he came over. That's roughly once a week, where we spent six hours together laughing, joking, teasing each other, competing against each other, giving each other intimate advice, and having fun. Our spouses told us that we should treasure our poker game, and that precious time together! The group bonded, and we formed a tight-knit group. And Goldie, the best of us, was beloved by everyone in our regular game. He was humble, reasonable, generous, and always there to offer friendly advice. I recall saying, "I'll be in Santa Monica next week, staying at the Loews Hotel." Then Goldie said, "You're welcome to stay in my apartment in Santa Monica. It's nice."

And he had the most modest ego of anyone in our group, which was amazing, because he was a giant in the real world. Along with his wife, Sheryl Sandberg

– chief operating officer (COO) of Facebook, author of *Lean In*, and founder of the Lean In Movement – the two of them were considered the most powerful tech couple in the world! Goldie was CEO of Survey Monkey, Sheryl COO of Facebook.

At Goldie's funeral, a hastily planned event held in an auditorium on Stanford's Campus, thousands of seats were filled, and President Obama sent his best. Over the next few weeks I heard tribute after tribute to Goldie. Goldie, Chamath, and I had been scheduled to speak together on stage at Founders Conference the following Wednesday. I would have enjoyed that, deeply. I would have gone after Chamath on stage, and showed Goldie nothing but respect and admiration. There was nothing to tease him about. He handled himself with effortless class.

The following week, I went to Founders Conference, and the participants shared story after story about the great Goldie, and all the help that he had given so many. Ryan Smith, founder and CEO of Qualtrics (Survey Monkey's direct competitor) sought me out and told me a story about Goldie, whose company Survey Monkey was in position to acquire Qualtrics. But Goldie told Ryan, "Don't sell Qualtrics to me if it's your dream to run it." Ryan reminded me that most powerful CEOs would have pushed young Ryan into a sale, but not Goldie. And when Ryan decided not to sell, Goldie took him out to lunch! A few days before Goldie passed, he was at lunch with Ryan, helping him with an issue that he had. Who helps their biggest competitor like that? Goldie, that's who. It was extraordinary and unprecedented that for a full week after Goldie passed, Qualtrics had the following message up on the front page of their website, "We are all monkeys this week."

The 2015 WSOP: Bracelet Number 14, I'm Giving it to...

Bracelet number 13 went to Chamath. Bracelet number 14 was going to my friend Bill Lee (Chapter 48). Bracelet number 15 was going to Goldie. Early in the 2015 WSOP, I made the final table of the $10,000 buy-in Razz tournament. Sound familiar? I had finished in first place in a WSOP Razz in 2012 (Chapter 43), second in 2014 (to Ted Forrest, Chapter 45), and now I was at another WSOP Razz final table. I was playing for some great history as well. If I could win it, then I would be the only person in history with two Razz bracelets and a second-place finish. When I woke up, on the morning of the Razz final table, June 8, 2015, I called Chamath and said, "I can't stop thinking about Goldie. If I win this thing, I'm going to give the bracelet to Sheryl and the kids." Chamath said, "OK, but don't bring up Sheryl's name unless you win it." I called Bill Lee (Chapter 48) and said, "Bill, you're my boy, and I promised you bracelet number 14. But if I win today, then I will feel compelled to give it to Sheryl and the kids." Bill understood completely.

I did win it! And Sheryl and the kids have it. The fact that it was record-setting bracelet number 14 was stunning, and awesome, but to me it felt overshadowed by the loss of Goldie. I love you, Goldie.

Golden State Warriors vs. Cleveland Cavaliers, Game 5

I won the Razz on Monday June 8, 2015, and on Sunday June 14th, per Golden State Warriors primary owner Joe Lacob's amazing invitation, I was going to Game 5 of the NBA Finals. I like the photo of me sitting on the floor (it's on my Twitter account), with Bill Lee on my left, Floyd Mayweather over to the far left, while LeBron James goes up for a three and Klay Thompson is up in his face attempting to block it. Bill Lee has been amazing to me, and I was happy to invite him to Game 5. Bill said, "Those tickets are worth $38,000 each. Are you sure you want to bring me?" Yes, of course!

As excited as I was to attend the game, I didn't immediately accept the invitation. Although I thought it would be the best game ever, and I'm a passionate Warriors fan (and attend roughly ten games per year), I had to skip a bunch of WSOP tournaments to be there. And I had already missed some cool stuff so as to stay in Las Vegas and play WSOP tournaments. In 2007, a big-league company had offered me $35,000, a private jet to Bandon Dunes, two rounds at Bandon, and a jet back to Vegas. My job was to MC a poker tournament for their clients (a job I actually enjoy!). Alongside MCing charity poker tournaments (Appendix 3), I have MCed poker tournaments for many big companies, including the Bank of America, Samsung, Bain Capital, Microsoft, Netflix, and Pacific Crest. I also shot a Super Bowl commercial for Diet Pepsi in 2004, and one of my favorites is the television commercial that I shot for Carl's Jr. (Google that one!)

In any case, I accepted Joe Lacob's amazing offer within two hours, and my friends told me I was an idiot for questioning, even 1%, whether I should attend the game or not! After all, it was LeBron James, Steph Curry, and the others, and the series was tied up at two games apiece. The Warriors really needed a win, especially because Game 6 was in Cleveland, and anything can happen on one's home court. I flew in from the WSOP in Vegas on Sunday afternoon, and flew right back that evening. It was the best game that I have ever been to! Thank you, thank you, Joe Lacob and Nicole Curran! And we won Game 5 to take a 3-2 lead.

By Thursday night, the Warriors were in Vegas at the Aria Hotel celebrating their NBA Championship! And I was there with Chamath Palihapitiya, Bill Lee, and the Elon Musk, celebrating with the team. Respect to the Warriors for the accomplishment, and respect because this team is a genuine, authentic, and "nice guy" team.

Back to the WSOP; One Drop

A few weeks later, in the $111,111 buy-in One Drop, I took the chip lead to the final table. At one point, I had 10 million in chips, almost one-third of the chips in play. But I fell apart a bit, not a lot, and it was enough to cost me. Playing my best game would have translated into at least a top three finish (and at least $1.5 million). And I would have enjoyed playing Dan Colman heads up for that bracelet. I believe that if I had made it down to heads up, then Dan would have made it as well. It seems like when I make it down to heads up, then I always face a great player! But this time, neither Dan nor I finished. But I look forward to a few showdowns with the top young guns in future!

WSOP Messes Me Up!

Kathy has noticed that I'm tough to be with, as a primary relationship partner, post-WSOP. At the WSOP, I'm President of the United States! It feels like all eyes are on me for seven weeks straight. Every day, I'm besieged with autograph requests, selfie requests, people telling me how great I am and that they are my biggest fan, and the press looking for interviews. It is a very unnatural state to be in. Then, after seven weeks of this craziness, I try to come home and fit into the role of husband and father.

In order to bridge the gap between the WSOP craziness and the normalcy of my everyday life, Kathy and I have decided that I need a week off, somewhere else, anywhere else, before I come home.

Hello, Temptation!

In 2015, after the WSOP ended, the temptation to be with a specific woman (no names here) was overwhelming as I was traveling down south and clearing my mind. Why was I so tempted to be with someone else? Sure, the other woman was brilliant, beautiful, interesting, cool, and fun. And yes, I was still messed up mentally from the 2015 WSOP. And the grass is always greener on the other side.

But in the moment I never figured out the real reasons – other than the obvious – why the temptation was almost overwhelming. I just knew that I couldn't act on it! To me, it is fundamental to my life that I have strong ethics and morals.

I believe that these ethics and morals allow me to achieve great things in life. When I'm deep in a poker tournament, I never waver because I'm an alcoholic, or an abusive spouse or father, and prone to do bad things. So I just focus 100% of my energy on winning. Why not me? Why shouldn't I be the greatest of all time? I live my life at a high level, I help others out, I've raised $44 million for charity, I'm loyal and true, and I inspire tens of millions of people through televised poker tournaments. People watch me play poker like Michael Jordan played basketball. I like to think that I inspire people when I fold hands that they couldn't imagine folding, or make calls that they couldn't imagine making. It is inspiring to watch the best in the world at the top of his or her game.

I have a lot of excuses to win. (I do not need an excuse to lose!) And not being loyal to Kathy could end up being an excuse to lose. So I avoided the temptation for days, while informing Kathy what was happening (that I was drawn to another woman). Even though nothing physical happened, Kathy was crushed, Kathy was in tears, and I didn't seem to have the proper level of empathy for her. In fact, I had no empathy at all. Why?

What is Really Going On?!?

Your beloved is crushed, and in tears, and you don't seem to care? While I examined this not caring issue closely over a few days (with temptation close by), it occurred to me that I thought that Kathy deserved this. First, if I was that important to Kathy, and she knew this massive temptation was ongoing, then why hadn't she hopped a flight to save us? Second, it occurred to me that I was really hurt by Kathy, and hurt usually turns to anger. So, this was it? I was angry at Kathy? Yep, and that's why I was having trouble feeling any empathy for her.

This wasn't about another woman, it was about Kathy and me. And why was I so mad at Kathy? Upon reflection, over the next week, I figured out that I was angry at Kathy over three issues. And I needed her to address those issues, and make some changes. In 2001, Kathy threatened to leave me unless I made some changes, and now the shoe was on the other foot.

First, I was upset with Kathy about the way she had conducted herself throughout the whole month of December 2014 (last chapter). Second, she was working way too many hours; I needed to know that she wasn't choosing work over me. And third, I needed her to resist work during the WSOP.

December 2014, Kathy Pushed to the Limit

As to the first issue of how Kathy conducted herself in December 2014, I'll start by saying that in October 2014, I struggled for a whole month with health issues

(Chapter 45). I wondered if they were serious health issues, and my constant, intense worrying was a huge energy drag on Kathy. I called her every day, worried about breathing, panic attacks, and much more. I stretched her to the limit while she worked an intense schedule. And as a result, I believe that Kathy was dreading my daily calls to her at her workplace, and I didn't blame her.

So when December rolled around, at the tail end of a brutal ten-week-long stretch of working for Kathy, she couldn't control herself emotionally when we quarreled. She would come home at 7 p.m. with no energy left, and then let it go when we had an argument. By the way, under normal conditions, she controls herself really well. So, she would become a bit too emotional (and I would perceive her losing it as a lack of effort). I would perceive this lack of control as Kathy choosing work over me, and I thought, "If she didn't work so many hours, she wouldn't be so exhausted, and she would have better emotional control! She is choosing work over me."

I knew that I wasn't happy in December 2014. I knew that I was disappointed in Kathy's conduct, but I couldn't fully connect with the pain that I was feeling. I managed to be the good guy all month, the one who pulled us back from the emotional cliff night after night, because Kathy deserved my best effort. Especially when she was this tired and overworked. But, unbeknownst to me, it was taking a big toll on me!

Working Too Many Hours, and Working During the WSOP

The other two complaints I had against Kathy were also related to her work. First, we had an understanding that she wasn't supposed to work during the WSOP. But to be fair, we made that deal in the 1990s when the WSOP lasted only a couple of weeks, and now the WSOP lasts almost seven weeks! And second, I felt she was working way too many hours, and choosing work over me. Over time, these issues, combined with the sting of December 2014, drove me away from Kathy and toward temptation.

Kathy or...?

I was smart enough, and strong enough, to resist falling into temptation, and it's a good thing, because eventually I figured out that I was mad at Kathy. I needed Kathy to address these three issues. And the pain that Kathy was feeling, when it looked like I might leave her, drove her to improve rapidly. And when I saw her in that pain, then I knew that she loved me, and that she wanted to be with me. And it didn't take long before I realized that I loved her, and I knew that I wanted to be with her.

In Chapter 31, when Kathy demanded that I grow up, give healthier empathy, and make changes, I wrote, "Kathy has made me into a better man." I'd like to think that I made her into a better woman, as well. And I believe that Kathy and I will go along together, hand in hand, for many more years, always fighting to improve ourselves, and to strengthen our relationship.

The Question, Founders, and my Partner Companies

In November 2015, I stopped by Antonio Garcia's place in Chicago for a drink. Antonio is cut from different cloth! While he was in law school at the University of Chicago, Antonio bought three (3!) companies! The big one he purchased was Electronic Plating Service (EPS) for $5 million (cash in). Right after buying the company, located in LA, he went to the factory floor and asked, "What is the slowest part of the assembly line?" The employees told him that it was the nickel bath, the first metal that they deposited on the parts (of several metals) that EPS was producing, and it was slowing the whole assembly line down. EPS had 120 employees, and it turned out that by listening to the people on the floor, Antonio learned that if he hired one more employee he would be able to increase production and revenue 200%. (Hello, triple revenues!)

A little more background on Antonio: he was the first institutional investor in Tesla, back in 2005, and is still the lead director there. He is also on the board of SpaceX and Solar City, and he owns over 300 Little Caesars and almost 50 Dunkin' Donuts restaurants. Oh, and he is founder, principal owner, and CEO of the private equity and venture capital firm Valor Equity Partners. Antonio has a well-earned reputation as a CEO whisperer.

The Question

When I sat down with Antonio, he handed me a Kimo Sabe Mezcal (I represent Kimo Sabe), and asked, "Tell me what's going on with you?" And I began talking, authentically and truthfully. I talked about how I struggled with temptation a few months earlier (last chapter). I talked about the WSOP, and my neighborhood game (next chapter). After five minutes, Antonio asked me, "How many WSOP bracelets would you have without your wife?" I snap answered, "Well, maybe a few more?" Antonio looked unconvinced, and I realized the truth; I would have less, and maybe a lot less. I said, "Ten?" Antonio said, "Maybe you would have eight or nine?" Man. Antonio was right. If I didn't have Kathy, and the stability and love that she brings into our marriage, life would look much different for me. At the very minimum, I would have had to look for another woman, and who knows what that process would have looked like. Would I hit the clubs more often? Would I find an unstable woman for a partner for a while? Or would I find someone, fall in love, and then have her break my heart?

"I" Did It; No, "We" Did It!

In that moment, for the first time, I attributed my successes to someone other than myself. I went from, "I am the greatest poker player in the world, I am amazing, I do great things like writing *New York Times* best-selling books, I am the man," to "we have done it all together." It was a profound moment for me. I had heard that Antonio had helped out Elon Musk (CEO of SpaceX, Tesla, and Solar City, and he's sending the human race to Mars!) and my boy David Sacks (CEO of Zenefits, next chapter) in the past, and a few months later I sent my technologist friend Diego Berdakin (a CEO, a professor at the University of Southern California, and a regular in the Masters of the Universe poker game, next chapter) to him, and he helped Diego out as well (CEO whisperer!).

I have been watching the "majors" in golf, and I have noticed that young Jordan Spieth uses "we" a lot. Now, there is the "royal we," which seems to mean God, and there is just "we." Does it matter? Probably not. In any case, Jordan uses "we" when he describes his wins and losses, and I think that helps him. It is much harder to imagine yourself a god of golf, or a god of poker, and much more inflammatory for your ego. When it is you and someone else, then the ego seems more controlled. Now, in 2017, Antonio emailed me this:

> In recognizing your gratitude for Kathy, you were able to free yourself from the parts of your ego that were hurting you, while still enjoying the parts that propel you forward. You freed yourself, to experience the happiness that comes with all you have achieved. As I always say; there is no happiness without gratitude!!

Well said, Antonio, and thank you for the help.

Back in November 2015, Antonio's question launched me into a huge winning streak! I didn't do great in the 2016 WSOP, but I finished in fourth place in the $300,000 Super High Roller Bowl, and I've been crushing the cash games for 15 months straight.

The Super High Roller Bowl – the Syndicate

So I told my partners at Poker Central that I would play in their $300,000 buy-in Super High Roller Bowl (SHRB) on May 27, 2016. (I just needed to raise the money!) In early April, I decided that I needed to reach out to my friends in the Masters of the Universe poker game (next chapter), and raise $541,000. I decided to start a syndicate and charge $54,000 for 9%. I would take a 10% free roll, and invest the first $54,000 myself. Thus, I would invest $54,000 and retain 20% for myself. I was going to use the cash to play in the $300,000 buy-in SHRB, the $111,111 WSOP One Drop, a $100,000 buy-in cash game with the colorful energy trader Bill Perkins in Florida, the $10,000 WSOP No Limit Deuce-to-Seven with one rebuy for $10,000, and the WSOP $10,000 Seven Card Stud tournament.

My thinking was that five events (four tournaments and one cash game) would spread the risk, and I told the group up front that it was a high-risk bet. I also told them that if I went deep in the SHRB, they could watch me live on television, for up to eight hours a day! You wanna piece of a horse, and a great sweat, then this deal put the Kentucky Derby to shame! You could have the best horse in the world, and watch him play your money for days, and first place was $5 million! Just in case there was serious interest, I included wiring instructions. I didn't know what would happen. I have never tried to raise $541,111 by myself before; although Chamath helped me raise $1 million in 2012 for One Drop (Chapter 43). It was first come, first serve, and within 20 hours I had sold out! (And a couple of people were mad at me for not giving them more time.)

So I went to Florida and lost the first $100,000, most of it to Bill Perkins (well played, Bill!). Then I entered the $300,000 SHRB. It was a beautiful event, with lots of tough players. I played great poker to double up, and then fell apart for a while and played poorly. But I was never all-in and made it to Day 2. At the end of Day 2, live on television, I felt a little pinned down. Poker pro and young gun Dan Smith was on my right, playing well, and the new poker sensation (based on "high roller" results) Fedor Holz was on my left, playing well. They all seemed to have a good read on me, and I was sick of it! It was time to get crazy!

I'm on a Rampage!

I announced to the table (on live television), "I'm on a rampage!" And I started raising every hand! It must have looked bad to my investors, 9-2 offsuit, raise! 7-4 offsuit, raise! J-3 offsuit, raise! And I kept repeating, "I'm on a rampage." Fedor and Dan knew that I was telling the truth. They knew that I was on a rampage, just going crazy. But they didn't know how far I would go. If they re-raised me with A-5, then would I just slam my stack all-in on them? They wisely stayed out of my way. After 20 minutes of my act, Dan moved 700,000 all-in from the small blind with 10♦-9♦, and I picked up Q-Q in the big blind and called. My queens won (K-4-4-7-Q) and *boom!*, I had 1.4 million in chips! I also had some emails from my investors saying stuff like, "Stay patient" and "Don't lose control." Lol! They didn't know that there was method to my madness.

Final Table

I made the final day, and was in complete control of my game, when I went card dead for hours. By then, we were down to four players, fourth place was $1.6 million, third was $2.4 million, second was $3.5 million, and first was $5 million. I was trying to win, but I was also trying to wait out Erik Seidel to pick up that extra $800,000 pay-bump! When I finally picked up A-9 in the small blind, my opponent picked up A-Q in the big blind; sigh. When I finally picked up 6-6 on the button, my opponent in the small blind picked up Q-Q; sigh. At least I didn't go broke. Some 95% of the players in that tournament would have moved all-in with those pocket sixes on the button and busted out, but I survived. Meanwhile, Erik hung in there for hours with a super short stack, and he finally outlasted me. It hurt: at least I had picked up $1.6 million for my investors, but it seems as if I should have won at least $800,000 more! Still, I enjoyed making my investors, and myself, over $1 million.

The 2016 WSOP

With the momentum of the SHRB, played just one day earlier, and the fact that I was working out every day, I expected a *huge* 2016 WSOP. But somehow, I had a bad WSOP; with just three cashes, and only one final table. Weirdly, the working out thing backfired! And not for the first time; at the 2013 WSOP, I worked out almost every day, and had my worst WSOP ever. Then in 2016, I was working out almost every day, and had my second worst WSOP. But I couldn't believe that my working out was hurting me. That's why I kept it up for the whole 2016 WSOP. I wish I could say that I understand it, but I don't. Maybe I would have had a bad WSOP whether I was working out or not?

Kimo Sabe Mezcal – Sharp Company Founder!

Jim Walsh approached me to represent a new app called The Signal, which determines whether you're lucky at any given second. The Signal is based on quantum physics, and has some complex science behind it. It would make sense that you would come to a professional poker player for such an app, and as we talked, Jim brought out a bottle of Kimo Sabe Mezcal. I loved the Kimo Sabe! I also loved Jim, and he has since helped me out with his wisdom, and his ability to see the world clearly. After a couple of meetings, Jim signed me to represent both Kimo Sabe Mezcal and The Signal!

Kimo Sabe Joven Wins Gold Medals!

Kimo Sabe was a triple gold-medal winner and named Best of Class International Specialty Spirit by the American Distilling Institute Spirits competition! It was the first time that a mezcal has taken this honor. Kimo Sabe Joven beat out all tequilas and mezcals against 645 entrants, with 28 judges, to take best of class and best of category for all agave and imported spirits.

Working with Jim and his daughter Ashley has been a pleasure, and we have something big going on here. (Mezcal is the fastest-growing alcohol category in the world, and Kimo Sabe is spreading quickly.)

Muzik Headphones, Jason Hardi

In June, during the 2016 WSOP, while I was being pitched by businessman Dan Goodstat from Collide (a video-streaming platform, which I eventually agreed to provide content for), my eyes were drawn to these super-sharp-looking headphones, and I asked Dan about them. He told me these were "smart headphones." And it turns out that they are packed with technology to enhance all third party apps and control all connected devices. These "game changers" were designed by Jason Hardi, the founder & CEO of Muzik, and hit the market in October 2016. The Muzik smart headphones are designed beautifully, with high end metal finishes and upgraded materials.

I asked if I could be introduced to Jason, to explore working together. Clearly Jason was disrupting the headphone game! Jason called me that night, and we hit it off on so many levels and must have talked for 90 minutes on FaceTime where Jason showed me how he was going to change the headphone experience forever, and was looking to partner with myself and some of the guys that I play poker with from my Masters of the Universe poker game (next chapter). Jason and I are both strong believers in positivity, and leaving our mark on the world. Jason told me that he wants to collaborate with the best of the best, whether NBA players, rappers, or movie stars.

"Jason, Doing Both Hardware and Software is Impossible!"

In 2013, Jason pitched one of my venture capital friends about investing in Muzik. My friend met with Jason and listened to his vision, reviewed his deck, brought in some very experienced partners to vet him, then proceeded to put his arm around Jason and tell him, "I like you, I can feel your passion, but your vision is huge, and it's almost impossible to create a software and hardware company out of the gate. Only Steve Job and Elon Musk can do that." Jason recalls his vision:

> I knew that the only way to create the most amazing smart hardware, that would change the headphone forever, was to design it from the ground up with state of the art components. And have it powered by an intelligent custom operating system that would connect the dots between hardware, third party apps, connected devices, and everything in between, compatible with any platform, creating game changing experiences to connect culture.

Uh Jason, that is a grand vision!

And guess what: he did it! Muzik headphones were designed from scratch by him, and his team of geniuses, and Jason created both the hardware and software, and won five CES Innovation Awards in the process!

Muzik App, Camera, and Raising Capital

After we talked for a while on the phone in June, Jason thought that I might be able to help him with Muzik in two ways: I could wear the headphones, and I could help him raise cash from some of the guys who I play poker with, from my Masters of the Universe poker game (next chapter). As to wearing the Muzik headphones, the next version has a camera, and Muzik already has a deal with Facebook Live! Facebook Live is embedded in the app for the headphones, and Twitch is an investor. Imagine that I'm wearing the headphone and I say, "Siri, turn on Facebook Live." Imagine that I'm playing poker in a WSOP tournament and I turn the camera on, and Twitch it out to the world! Millions of fans could see my hole cards, see my opponents' faces, watch the moves that I make, watch the fold that I make, and gain phenomenal insight into how I win No Limit Hold 'Em tournaments.

Celebrity Endorsers, No!
Meet the Dream Team of Muzik Investors

Jason met an artist at the beginning who wanted to connect the world through his music and had many creative ideas. He actually named the platform Connect, which is still used today on the iOS store. At that time Drake wasn't the top artist yet, he joined Muzik early on to help create the most connected and best sounding headphones in the world. Together they created a connected technology platform to allow artists, fans, and brands to connect in groups and listen to music together like never before. They call it Connected Content. Next Drake brought CP3 (NBA star Chris Paul), Kevin Hart and Travis Barker onboard. After they joined the company, so did NFL stars Von Miller, Demaryius Thomas, Pat Patterson, Trent Williams, and Golden Tate. Next Olympic gold medalists Paul George, Kyle Lowry joined as well. Then one of the greatest baseball players of all-time, Derek Jeter, and top tennis star, Novak Djokovic, joined, and many other top leaders on the field and in the boardroom joined.

I've never seen anything like this where so many leaders at what they do came together to connect the world! I am so excited to be working alongside a group of visionaries and disruptors who all share Jason's vision of creating products that bring us all closer together with technology, are simple to use, and connect us all like never before.

We are going to launch Muzik One soon, then later Muzik Live. We will do this with some of the biggest strategic partners across the globe. I'm looking forward to seeing how we change the headphone forever! Like Jobs did to the phone, and Elon to the car and rocket ships.

Random Meeting, Was It Meant to Be?

One day in August 2016, after I hadn't spoken to Jason for two months, I picked up the phone and called him. I wasn't involved with Muzik yet, but I wanted to be. Jason said, "Hey, my guys are at this show at the Wynn Hotel, go talk to them, I'll let them know you're coming." I said, "I'm in Palo Alto." He said, "I land there in two hours. Come to dinner with me and the head of Intel Capital." I said, "I'm in. Come to my house before the meeting." The timing seemed strangely wonderful to me.

Jason was looking for the perfect strategic investors, but he was also looking for a connection to Tesla (Jason had heard rumors that Tesla might be doing headphones), and the next day, I took Jason and his head of sales to Bill Lee's house. Bill (next chapter) is one of the best investors in the world, a huge investor in Tesla, and he loved the headphones. From Bill's house, we went to a meeting with Antonio Garcia in San Francisco. In one day, I had Jason meeting with Antonio, who has his own venture capital firm (above), and who is the lead director on the board of Tesla. I delivered Jason's wish list, and I delivered it quickly! A few weeks later, I was honored to join the advisory board for Muzik. (Check out http://MuzikConnect.com to see how cutting-edge Muzik headphones are!)

Poker Central and Cary Katz

When I found out that Cary Katz was starting Poker Central, a new 24/7 poker network, I asked my agent Brian Balsbaugh to find out if I could come onboard. A few years earlier, another group was attempting to start a poker network, and that group had given me 3% of the company. That project didn't make it, but I didn't want to miss out when someone finally built a successful poker network! Golf Channel is worth $2 billion! And 3% of $2 billion is $60 million.

Brian called the president of Poker Central, and they said no. I was surprised. I felt like I could add so much value, with content, raising money, and much more. Did they know I owned the concept television show *College Poker Showdown*? Did they know I had hosted a bunch of television shows like *Celebrity Poker Showdown* and *Best Damn Poker Show*? Did they know I was close friends with the biggest venture capitalists on the planet?

Two months later, I told Brian that I wanted to call Cary, personally. I left this message for Cary, "Arnold Palmer helped Mark McCormack build IMG [International Management Group], and I can help you build Poker Central. Every time I have signed with a company, I have added more value than they thought I would. I am a good partner." A few weeks later, Cary and I met for lunch, and we began talking about what it would look like if I worked for Poker Central. Cary was convinced, and we started talking about a deal. I was so sure that I would add value that when we were talking later about equity, I told him (through my agent), "I'm happy to leave Option A and Option B open, and in one year, you can decide." Cary said, "OK, we'll do it like that." So if I added a ton of value, then I would receive the bigger amount of equity. I was confident that I would deliver! But then the next day Cary called back with a counter offer. I chuckled, and I was happy, because I could see that Cary truly believed that I would add value to Poker Central. I was happy that he had confidence in me, and we accepted his counter offer. And I'm pleased to be a part of the Poker Central team. Let's run it up!

Cary Katz is already a business baller! In 1999, he founded College Loan Corporation, and was CEO for 15 years. Under his leadership, the company became the seventh largest student loan company in the USA, providing $19 billion in loans. After Cary retired, he sat on the sidelines for 18 months, and played a fair amount of poker (he is an excellent poker player with over $10 million in tournament cashes!). Then he had a vision for Poker Central. I share his vision, and I believe in Cary. In 2016, we decided to change course and launch Poker Central as a digital network following the successful business models of the UFC and World Wrestling Entertainment. Cary also signed Daniel Negreanu and Antonio Esfandiari. Boys, let's build Poker Central together.

Poker Night in America and Todd Anderson

Way back in 2004, Todd Anderson tried to reach out to me. He was starting the Heartland Poker Tour (HPT), and he wanted to give me a piece of HPT in exchange for me joining his advisory board. But he couldn't get to me! Too many buffers. My agent takes a long look at each deal, and most of the time I never find out what was offered, and by whom. Meanwhile, dozens of other poker tours were launched, and they all went out of business. Except the HPT. Todd made it by being fiscally responsible, and by his sheer force of will!

Fast forward to 2011, and Todd sold HPT for $4 million. After a few weeks on the sidelines, Todd launched *Poker Night in America* (PNIA) on CBS Sports Net. Todd started *PNIA* to "bring the fun back to poker." *PNIA* films No Limit Hold 'Em cash games, and brings some of the best (and some of the most entertaining players) in the world to the poker tables. Guys like Daniel "Kid Poker" Negreanu, Antonio "the Magician" Esfandiari, Jennifer Tilly (actress, entertainer, and tough poker player), and entertainers like comedian Brad Garrett (from *I Love Raymond*). And we have some great, super-entertaining shows!

Todd approached me about getting involved with *PNIA*, both as an advisor to and star of the show. Todd felt like I could help him bring sponsorships, help the ratings by playing on the show myself, and bring him top poker players and celebrities. (We had Jim Harbaugh ready to play on one show, and the casino said no! Compliance with the National Collegiate Athletic Association (NCAA) was OK because Jim would have been playing for charity, but the casino said no because Jim was an active NCAA football coach. Role reversal! Weird.) I wanted equity, and we made a deal. And now, Kimo Sabe Mezcal has partnered up with *PNIA*. Jim Walsh (above) and Todd Anderson, good people, great partners!

Brett Richey and BlitzPick

I've always believed that anyone who could make it in the poker world for five years as a professional player could make a fortune in business. Brett Richey is one of those! Brett played professional poker successfully for years, and then he decided to create an app. Brett believed in the future of daily fantasy sports

(DFS), and with DraftKings and FanDuel crushing in 2017, it looks like he is right. So Brett started BlitzPick, an app that supports DFS players by giving them proprietary information from the sports world. BlitzPick gives pure and valuable information for the PGA tour, NFL teams, NBA teams, National Hockey League teams, and their players. Which NFL teams do well in Seattle? How do the 49ers do when it rains? How do the Golden State Warriors do in back-to-back road games? Who is injured? Who matches up well with who in the playoffs? How does Eli Manning perform when the temperature is 2 degrees? All the above correlations, and one thousand more, paint a picture for a smart bettor. And BlitzPick delivers that information in a clean and easy to decipher manner. And with legalized sports betting around the corner, this information is even more valuable.

In February 2017, Brett convinced me to buy points at a $3 million pre-money valuation, and to join his advisory board. I hope that I can help him spread the word: BlitzPick is truly the best sports information app out there. I hope that I can introduce Brett to some other key investors. I hope that sports betting is legalized like it is in England, and most other countries!

3Bet Poker Clothing

I watched my boys Phillip and Nick buy skateboard clothing when they were young, and I watched some of those clothing companies that we bought clothing from blow up to $100 million valuations. I thought, "that could happen to poker clothing brands," and I started Poker Brat Clothing Company with the grand hope of selling millions of shirts and hats to poker players and aspiring poker players. After spending years on Poker Brat Clothing to smallish results (I still sell PH hats and a few shirts at PokerBrat.com), I decided to approach 3Bet Poker Clothing to talk about a sponsorship. I loved the clothing at 3Bet.com, and I could see myself wearing it all the time (love those the gray hoodies). Also I believed that 3Bet had a chance to hit a $100 million valuation, because their clothes are that good!

3Bet was happy to hear from me, saying, "We were saving 6% equity in the company for one more poker player, and we only had two players in mind that we could give that equity to, and you're one of them." I was happy to hear that, and a couple of days later I happily signed with 3Bet. A few months after that, 3Bet created a cool shirt, one that I've always wanted, that said, "What would Phil do?" It is black and yellow, and catchy. My friends have been telling me for years that they would buy a "What would Phil do?" shirt, and now we have one. Next time you catch me on television I'll most likely be wearing my favorite gray 3Bet hoodie. (My wife loves it on me!)

Deck of Dice and Tom Donelan

In 2014 Tom Donelan approached me about a new product called Deck of Dice. Essentially it is playing cards on dice! There are nine dice, which have 54 total surfaces, which is enough to fit all 52 cards plus two jokers. A great concept. Shortly after our meeting, I joined the advisory board, and now we are creating a new platform for gaming; from gambling games to board games. My first move as a company advisor was to bring Tom and his team to meet with Bill Lee (Chapter 48). Bill was an angel investor in and on the board of Big Fish Games. Thus, Bill had years of experience in creating new games, building new games, and overseeing revenue models for games, and had seen everything in that space. Bill's advice was invaluable! Bill thought that what makes dice great is that they are physical things. So that when we designed our new games, we needed to design games that could be played electronically or physically. One should be able to play the game with the actual dice from Deck of Dice, and on a smart phone, tablet, or computer.

Tom could have given up, but he persevered. He raised money in small amounts, and kept extending the runway for Deck of Dice, and thanks to his efforts and perseverance, we have deals for our games with Sci Games, and a bright future!

The Aria Hotel – My Primary Sponsor

In 2009, during the six-week-long WSOP, I was staying in a beautiful two-story suite, at the Golden Nugget, right above the swimming pools. The Golden Nugget wanted me there, and gave me free room, food and beverages; I liked my suite and the Golden Nugget. Then I had a few drinks with Bill McBeath, the president of the swanky Aria Hotel and Casino. Bill recruited me to MC some "high roller giveaways" for Aria. He proposed that when the Aria had a poker tournament where they gave away $500,000 or $1 million, I would come in and MC the tournament. Bill knew that when I had MCed tournaments the customers liked it. I added energy and enthusiasm, and I was accessible to the customers for conversations, pictures, and autographs. At that point, I was charging $50,000 a night to various companies to MC their poker tournaments.

As Bill and I sipped our drinks, we discussed the terms of a potential deal. Then, before we finished, Bill said, "Come with me." And we went upstairs to an amazing suite at the Aria. Bill said, "Do you want to stay at the Golden Nugget, or do you want to stay here in this magnificent room on the cutting edge of technology?" Bill told me that the Aria was green (great for the environment), they had spent $1.2 billion to build it, and it was the best hotel in Las Vegas. The hotel was brand new. The suite was truly awesome, and the Aria Hotel is swanky.

Bill and I went back downstairs and continued our negotiations, and after another drink, we had a deal! I would receive a locker at Shadow Creek (an amazing perk), wear an Aria logo, stay at the Aria for free, receive some cash, and MC Aria's big giveaways, and if they needed me for another event, then I would be there for them.

This was a nice deal for me, and I could tell that Bill was happy as well: win, win. I was happy at Aria from Day 1, but in 2011, when online poker disappeared (my monthly salary vanished in November 2010), I was deeply grateful for my Aria deal. And I'm still grateful. The staff at Aria are wonderful, from Bobby Baldwin and Bill Cramsey to the valet staff, to the limo drivers, to the room service folks, to the maids. Thanks for having me!

48

Great Friendships and Masters of the Universe Poker Game

It's a weird thing for me to contemplate. I found my best friends in a small-stakes poker game in Palo Alto! I guess it's fitting. From the moment that I sat down in Chamath and Goldie's poker game in 2010 (Chapter 41), I spent more and more time with the players from that game, both together and individually. Our regular game is filled with good guys, family guys, with generosity and class. And they all believe that they can do great things in life, because they have already scaled many mountains in the business world. And when it comes to being smart, the combined intelligence of our group is off the scale. I've put this out there in the press before, and I have called the players in our poker game Masters of the Universe.

Masters of the Universe Poker Game

We never bring cash with us. We keep a ledger, and we settle by check or wire transfer at the end of the year. The game used to be $5-$10 blind No-Limit Hold 'Em, and in time we kicked up to $25-$50 blinds. By 2012, I realized that I couldn't make a living in the game. I was actually playing poker purely for the comradery and social aspects! Which is a strange thing for a professional poker player to do. For most pros, the last thing we want to do is spend our free time playing low-stakes poker! In 2015 I lost money for the whole year (my ledger balance was negative at the end of the year), and no one in our game lets me forget that! In 2016, we kicked the game up to $100-$200 blinds No-Limit Hold 'Em, and now it feels like a big game to me! (I'll be talking about some of our regular players.)

JCal First

Most regular poker games have an antagonist, and in our game the antagonist is Jason Calacanis (JCal). JCal has a talent for making fun of everyone in the game. His wit and ability to find the truth and the stuff that hurts the most, and then throw it out there on the table, is unparalleled. And JCal's "whippings" are good for all of us! In moderation... JCal goes after Bill Lee (below) about the fact that he doesn't have a full-time job. (He goes after me for my annoying ego!)

JCal's No Limit Hold 'Em game at the beginning of 2016 was sorely lacking, but by the end of 2016 he was playing beautifully. Chamath and Sky Dayton used to bluff JCal at will, but I guess all that uber "paper money" has made JCal's fear of losing depart!

JCal's book *Angel* is out right now. And his reality show *The Incubator* will merge in 2017. JCal made $100 million by "angel investing" in Uber, and is the Voice of Tech. His show *This Week in Startups* has been cruising for years. JCal is a regular on CNBC, *Squawk Box*, and most every other financial show that exists.

Roger Sippl

Roger Sippl is an old timer, his last name is Sippl, but we call him "Shippl," because of his propensity to move all-in (he "ships" all of his the chips into the pot). Shippl took three companies public that he founded or co-founded, Informix, Vantive, and Visigenic software, pioneering database servers, application software and application servers in the process. Three IPOs is something special, and as an inventor and angel investor he has participated in 25 companies as a board member, six of them public companies.

Roger could have had any of several careers. He did creative writing in both fiction and poetry while an undergraduate pre-medical student, but got stage IIIB Hodgkin's Lymphoma when he was nineteen. He was still going to apply to medical schools, but was warned that with only a twenty percent chance of survival he just wasn't going to get in, and he would never be told why. So he switched majors to computer science (UC Berkeley), and built enough of a fortune to spend the rest of his life living well. Like Sky Dayton (below) he flies his own plane, and enjoys boating and SCUBA diving. And Shippl is getting back to creative writing.

Roger wrote a poem for a couple in our Masters of the Universe poker game:

Lifelong Couples

Couples who touch each other while they sleep
live longer and enjoy
twenty-eight percent greater happiness,
according to university researchers.

Without knowing this he touched her in three or four places
through the night,
innocent touching and holding,
a hand holding an arm,
toes warming her toes,
or a knee inserted in the back of her knee
so that physical warmth is shared
from the thigh to the ankle,
each night some touching
all night long.

When not there, no touching,
she sleeps alone,
in the unwrinkled sheets, a turn
of the pillow until –
in the unmeasured time of the dark,
sneaking in from the poker game,
his clothes form a path on the floor
from the door to the bed
so as not to rustle sounds in the dark.

She wakes with a lack of touch,
unknowingly seeks him, primordially wanting
to know he is there in the black cave with her.

Adoration and charm,
commitment with no thought of it,
whether the end of life is near
or still too far to picture,
all is in these touches
that last through the night,
through the lives
of the one touching
and the one who is touched.

Poker Brat

Roger has put this poem into his *Mating for Life* series in his *Real Nature* poetry chapbook, available on Amazon and elsewhere. He has also written a mystery novel about Silicon Valley, with a beautiful woman and a proper murder, called *Rebreathing*, and has a new chapbook of poems out that anchor on his eight-and-a-half seconds of death, flat-lined heartbeat, and what he saw during his recovery from open heart surgery ten years ago. That is a quick and very rewarding read called *Heavenly Whispers*.

Rick Thompson

Rick Thompson (RickyT) used to be a Chinese chef, who had the goal of starting his own Chinese restaurant chain. Rick shadowed Francis Tong (Chef Tong), doing everything that he did, including following him to the poker tables. Eventually, Rick learned that Chef Tong was on work release (Rick didn't follow him to prison!), and Rick gave up that dream. Instead, Rick pivoted, and became a professional poker player. After a couple of years of grinding, Rick opened his eyes for other paths. With his eyes wide open, Rick was himself recruited by someone sitting right at the poker table. Rick's new job was writing software, and when that company sold, Rick decided to start his own. His next move was to start Flycast, and to build it up from scratch. Despite several close calls, where Flycast almost went under, Rick hung in there and sold it for $2.5 billion.

These days, Rick is at venture capital firm Signia Venture. Rick convinced our boy Chamath (see below) to invest his own money in Playdom, which was later sold for $763 million. Chamath gives Rick credit for jump starting his venture capital career.

At the poker table, Rick is fearless! I've watched him make some impressive calls, and win huge pots with weak hands, because he knew his opponent was bluffing. Somehow, you have the feeling that Rick cannot be bluffed, as Sky and Chamath have found out, repeatedly. Rick will also bet big when he has a drawing hand, and that makes him difficult to read. (Does he have a hand, or a draw?)

Sky Dayton

Sky Dayton is universally loved in the game, and manages to play regularly in our Palo Alto based game, even though he lives in Oregon. Sky is calm, reasonable, and quick-witted, and loves to laugh. But he always wants to know what hand you had! Whenever someone folds their cards face down, Sky will dependably ask what hand they held. And Chamath drives Sky crazy by lying to him after the hand! Sky has his own plane, and loves to surf, so he'll just fly in somewhere on the west coast, and surf for a couple of hours (baller!).

When Sky was 19 years old, he started a coffee house on Melrose Avenue in LA and called it Café Mocha. The place had lines out the door, and was a smashing success. When Sky was 21, he started a computer graphics company, and one day in 1993, when he was 23 years old, and couldn't get service on the internet, he said, "What's up with this?" Then Sky messed around with the settings on his computer and became convinced that a simple, user-friendly internet service provider was a good play. So, Sky founded EarthLink. It wasn't long before he had 5 million customers, and EarthLink went public in 1997. Then Sky co-founded JAMDAT, a cell phone games company that went public in 2004, and founded Boingo, a wi-fi service provider he took public in 2011. Sky is building five companies right now, and some of them are really cool. He's chairman of the largest online education company for kids, ABCmouse, and a board member of a start-up creating an all-electric airplane that takes off and lands vertically. Crazy!

Bill Gurley

Gurley won VC of the Year in 2015 at the ninth annual Tech Crunchies, beating out our boy Chamath Palihapitiya, who finished second, and Gurley should have won it! He is at the venture capital firm Benchmark Capital Partners, and they have a fund that has both Uber and Snapchat. Uber has traded at $71 billion, and at one point Benchmark had 18% (I believe that they have roughly 10% now)! Snapchat traded at $25 billion recently, and Benchmark itself has roughly 10%. Not bad for a fund that started at $350 million. You do the numbers.

Gurley is another beloved member of the game. The only person who even teases him hard is JCal. And Gurley is a competitor – he played Division 1 basketball at the University of Florida – and for all his successes, he remains humble (so far). In the venture capital business, a big ego can be the kiss of death, but Gurley has managed to keep his feet firmly on the ground. Over the years, Chamath has had Gurley's number at poker, but Chamath, who throws compliments around like manhole covers, admits Gurley is a better venture capitalist, for now!

David Sacks

David Sacks is the founding COO of PayPal and is a member of the legendary PayPal mafia. PayPal was sold to eBay for $1.5 billion in 2002. Then Sacks founded Yammer, which invented social networking for enterprises, and sold that to Microsoft for $1.2 billion in 2012. Sacks tried his hand in Hollywood when he produced, from start to finish, *Thank You for Smoking*. When the movie became a huge hit and Sacks broke even, he decided to give up on Hollywood!

Sacks, like his brother-in-law Bill Lee (below), has crushed it as an angel (early stage) investor, getting early money into Facebook, Uber, Airbnb, Slack, Palantir, and Houzz. In December 2014, after a couple of years off, Sacks made a major investment in Zenefits, and then took on a job as COO of the company (JCal made fun of him for being "only a COO"). When Zenefits ran into legal issues and almost cratered, Sacks took over as CEO and saved the company. (By the way, Sacks's wife, Jacqueline, is the most powerful woman in San Francisco, serving on the boards of the top school, hospital, and art museum!)

Sacks is another beloved member of our game. He is always laughing at the table, and he has no fear! He's not afraid to move all-in on a drawing hand. He reasons that he has two ways to win: he bluffs you, or he hits his hand. Sacks can be a quiet guy, but he's so smart he sees between the lines, and then has a way of making fun of you, that even you laugh at. Jovial is the perfect word to describe Sacks. For a couple of years now, he seems to have had my number at No Limit Hold 'Em, and he has crushed me at Pineapple Poker (Open-Face Chinese). I played Sacks on our Pineapple app (Bill Lee built it, see below; I'm "PhilHellmuth" on the app, find me at http://www.playpineapple.com/pokerbrat) for $50 a point, and lost $27,000 to him. Then I quit. I played him again for $20 a point, and lost $14,000 to him, and quit once again. Sacks is truly one of the best Pineapple players in the world, and beats the top pros regularly. He holds his own with Barry Greenstein, a professional poker player and Pineapple genius.

Bill Lee

Bill Lee is one of my best friends, and I love to go over to his house and hang out with Bill and his family. His partner Nat (Natalee) is like a ray of sunshine, their six-year-old son "Lil P" (Preston) is a warm-hearted boy, and their three-year-old daughter Valentina is cute, strong-willed, and energetic. And Bill is one of the smartest guys I know. Bill is a standup, straight up, all-round good guy. Bill likes everyone, so if he doesn't like you, then you have given him good reason! Bill and I always manage to have fun, whether watching NBA games on television, chilling in his backyard and watching his kids run around, grabbing a cigar, or going for a walk.

I love Bill's lifestyle choices. Bill made enough money to make choices, and he has wisdom well beyond his years to help him implement those choices. Bill sold the company Remarq for $300 million in 2000, then went to Costa Rica and taught people how to surf for two years. He was giving surfing lessons at a hotel in Costa Rica, making around $10 a lesson, but meanwhile he had a nice room in the hotel! For the last seven years, Bill has chosen to work fewer hours than everyone else. And yet, amazing deals find their way to Bill's door! He has "deal flow"

– great deals come to him. He is in SpaceX, Tesla, Yammer (sold to Microsoft for $1.2 billion), and Twitter. David Sacks, Elon Musk, Jeff Skoll, Chamath, and Antonio Garcia all look to Bill when they have an interesting investment opportunity. Why? Because Bill adds value. Bill sees the lines, both hidden and subtle.

Bill chooses to spend most of his time with his young family. This causes some of the guys in our poker game (JCal) to tease Bill constantly about his "open schedule." (I think they're jealous!) One thing they don't tease him about is his close friendship with Elon Musk. In the 1990s, Bill rolled around with Elon and Jeff Skoll (co-founder of eBay). (By the way, I find it remarkable that Elon doesn't seem to have any ego! He is down to earth, and a pleasure to hang out with.) Three CEOs and company founders that hadn't hit it big yet. In 2008, when Elon needed help, Bill and Jeff had his back, with their cash, and with their full support. That Tesla and SpaceX thing turned out all right for Elon, Jeff, and Bill.

Bill doesn't work, he is a genius, he is close friends with Elon, and Bill is easy to hang out with. All that keeps Elon inviting Bill to go with him, just the two of them, to climate conferences, jaunts around Europe doing Tesla and SpaceX business, and more. When Elon needs help, Bill is there for him.

One evening, when Bill and I were drinking a nice whiskey at his man cave in the city (San Francisco), Bill came up with the idea to do an app for Pineapple Chinese Poker. I loved the idea, and wanted to get involved, and a few months later Bill gave me 10% of the project. A very generous gift (especially considering we raised money from our friends at a multi-million-dollar valuation). Now the Pineapple app has thousands of players on it every day, because Pineapple is so much fun to play! But also because it's the best Pineapple app out there, by far. Thanks, Bill. (By the time you read this, I'm hoping that I have won WSOP bracelet number 15, and given it to Bill!)

Chamath Palihapitiya

Chamath Palihapitiya is my best friend, and the biggest winner in the poker game over the last six years. (Yo bestie, I'm coming for the "biggest winner in the game" title!) Chamath enjoys being a bad winner in the game (when he smashes you in a big pot, expect a verbal attack!), but he's a perfect loser. And we all love it! By the way, I guess I'm the opposite (poker brat!). Maybe that's another reason why we get along so well? Chamath is capable of playing super-fast poker, and then suddenly, when it looks like he never has a hand, he slows down, plays very few hands, and shows you pocket kings. Chamath bets big when he has it, when he has a drawing hand, and when he has nothing. He puts massive pressure on you, and he is very hard to play against!

I am impressed with Chamath because he keeps his family first. Maybe it helps that he is Canadian? Almost every Canadian I know is nice. In any case, Chamath does a great job with his wife Bridgette Lau and their three young children. It's clear to me that his family grounds him, and that's good, because with the success Chamath has had it would be easy to float away. There is no doubt that his amazing wife Brig will rein him in from time to time (much like my wife reins me in). Sometimes, Brig will clip his wings, but that is exactly what Chamath needs. A strong woman by his side.

Even though Chamath has made a fortune, crushes it as a venture capitalist, and has a big-league reputation all over the world, he handles himself well everywhere he goes. He is not afraid to tease people when they need to be teased, to challenge someone when they need to be challenged, or to give empathy when a friend needs it. Chamath started the growth department at Facebook, and boy oh boy, did Facebook grow! After he left Facebook, Chamath and Brig started Social Capital, their own venture capital firm, with some of their own money and with big investments from some high-profile investors like Li Ka-shing, the Mayo Clinic, and Peter Thiel, to name a few. In 2015, Chamath finished in second place in the Tech Crunchies VC of the Year Award (Bill Gurley, see above, won it).

In 2013, I gave Chamath my 13th WSOP bracelet (he gave me a great gift, discussed in Chapter 42), the one I won in the WSOPE main event in 2012. I look forward to our Hold 'Em games, and to our heads-up Pineapple Poker matches for the next 20 years (Chamath beat me for a lot of money in Pineapple in 2016, but I'm ready to mount my comeback).

Can Doctor Allan Mishra Cure Cancer?

[Allan doesn't play in the Masters of the Universe poker game.] My friend Allan Mishra (pictured with coach Jim Harbaugh and me in the photo section) is a busy orthopedic surgeon, who in his spare time cured tennis elbow! Allan pioneered the clinical use of platelet rich plasma (PRP) for a variety of sports medicine applications. Basically, Dr. Mishra takes a vial of your blood and spins it down in a centrifuge until he can capture the PRP. He can then use your PRP to treat your tennis elbow or other sports-related injuries. He has studied PRP extensively for more than a decade, and has published several articles in elite medical journals. He has also shown that PRP may be helpful in the treatment of heart attacks, and continues to investigate its potential value. The growth factors and other proteins in PRP help to heal damaged tissue at an accelerated rate.

What can PRP be used for? Tennis elbow? Yes. Post heart attacks? Yes. Alzheimer's? Maybe. Cancer? Allan hopes so, because he originally set out to try to cure cancer. That's a big goal. And he looked inside of us. Imagine all those people searching mountain tops, searching the rain forest, while looking for a miracle plant or insect that might cure diseases. And Allan decided to look inside our own blood! Yes, my friend Allan set out to cure cancer, and it wouldn't surprise me a whole lot if he managed to do it.

In 2003, I was there to pump Allan up when he needed it the most. He had thought that he could cure cancer by 2020, and I believed him. I watched another friend tell me that his old beat-up notebook would turn into a huge online website. He pulled it off, although his company Hungry Minds didn't make it past the internet bubble. I'm a believer in people with grand vision, and I started visualizing Allan winning a Nobel Prize for curing cancer. I believed Allan could pull it off then, and I believe it now. Go get 'em Allan, the whole world is rooting for you!

Can Joe Lacob Win an NBA Title?

[Joe doesn't play in the Masters of the Universe poker game.] When my friend Joe Lacob (picture of Joe and me with the NBA Championship trophy in the middle of the book) bought the Golden State Warriors, I had a good feeling. But that good a feeling—an NBA title, another close call (Game Seven of the NBA Finals in 2016), and the favorites in 2017, within six years? Nope. I knew that Joe knew a lot about basketball: I attend Stanford basketball games with Joe and his son Kirk (Kirk won a title as GM in the "D League"), and I thought that I knew a lot about basketball, until I heard Joe and Kirk break down Stanford games! I also knew that Joe would bring an intelligent, and a sophisticated approach to assembling a team. I love that they hired Jerry West as a consultant, Bob Myers as the GM (he's crushing!), and Kirk Lacob as assistant GM. Kirk is a winner, and smart, and he always sits with Jerry and Bob, learning from the masters.

When the Warriors traded Monta Ellis for Andrew Bogut (according to Joe at the time, the third best center in the league), I applauded the move, but Joe was roasted for it, and roasted publicly! In fact, the press crucified him, and the bay area fans booed him loudly at a ceremony a few weeks later. Of course, I called Joe the next day and said, "Well, I was booed loudly by 250,000 people at a NASCAR event, at least you'll be universally loved when this thing turns around."

Joe basically started his career at the best VC firm in the world throughout the 1980s and 1990s; KPCB (Kleiner Perkins Caufield & Byers). While Joe was there, KPCB invested in Google, Amazon, Juniper Networks, and EA (Electronic Arts) to name a few. After all those hits, when a young couple came into his office in the early 2000s to pitch invisible braces, some red flags were there for Joe to pass. First off, they pitched as a couple, second, they had pitched about every other VC firm in the bay area, and third, they weren't asking for enough money to interest the mighty KPCB. But Joe saw something, and KP funded "Align Technology" (Invisalign braces) with a $2 million investment. Align is now doing $1.3 billion a year in revenue, and is valued at $9 billion!

After making more than $1 billion in business, Joe's crowning achievement is the Golden State Warriors. Joe bought them in 2010 for $450 million, then the highest price paid for an NBA team, and completely turned the team around both on and off the court. They are the first team to win 65 games three years in a row, and now the team is building a new stadium in San Francisco with no public money. And no capital call for his investors (quite a trick!). Forbes just valued the Golden State Warriors at $2.6 billion! Joe got in trouble last year in the *New York Times Magazine* for saying that the Warriors "were light years ahead of other NBA teams." Joe told me recently, "Clearly I was using hyperbole, kind of like you Phil!" But hyperbole or not, it does seem like Joe is light years ahead!

Nicole Curran, Joe's long-term girlfriend, has helped in the Warrior team building process as well (but those stories are for another book). In any case, Nicole put together a charity poker tournament for the Warriors Foundation (I MC it, Appendix 3), and in three years we have raised $3.5 million! There's a nice picture of Steph Curry playing in the charity tournament in the middle of this book. The Warriors Foundation; for the kids...

Great Friendships

I didn't understand what it meant to have great friendships, and I wasn't ready to have great friends for most of my life. Thanks to the folks mentioned above, I now understand the value of friendships.

49

The Future, Love, and Goals, Goals, Goals

I spent decades of my life devoted to poker and family. I didn't have time for close friends, and I didn't understand the value of a close friendship. I'm sure that I was too self-centered, and traveled too often to maintain a close friendship. I wasn't quite ready for close friends until my late forties. For decades, my friends were poker players whom I would see on again off again, but never on a consistent basis. I would invite my poker friends in, but they couldn't connect with me that deeply. On the other side of the coin, my ego was too demanding to listen deeply to my poker friends and their issues. And then, it happened. I found friends with whom I could share my innermost thoughts, and vice versa. I found friends that I could invite in. I found friends who would invite me in.

Sharing the "Real"

When you share your deepest thoughts with someone else, or you reveal your deepest pain, or you reveal your deepest problems, then you are sharing the "real." This is the deepest possible connection! And it causes positivity in both directions: because it is an honor to have someone share with you; and it a blessing to be able to share with someone else that cares. Sharing the "real" binds people together as you let down your guard and let them in to comfort you, and they let down their guard and let you in to comfort them. Having great friends requires some time and effort, but man oh man, is it worth it!

I am blessed to have Bill Lee and Chamath as my greatest friends. I'm lucky that they see through my occasional poker brat behavior in our Masters of the Universe poker game (when I lose a big pot at the table now, I'm happy that the whole crew enjoys the "Poker Brat meltdown" show!). I'm lucky that I have a group of friends that can say to themselves, "I love Phil, and when he loses it at the table, it is something that I can laugh at, and truly enjoy. Phil can't help himself because he is a warrior and hates losing that much! I enjoy Phil's absurdity, and that's the way I feel sometimes as well when I lose a big pot to a thin draw." It's nice to have friends that can fully accept you for who you are; both the good and the bad.

My "Life Goals" – Checking In

My life goals (Chapter 10) from March 1988;

Life Goals
1. Win the "big one" (the main event) at the WSOP – Check, 1989
2. Meet and marry a wonderful woman, one who can abide me – Check, 1989 - present
3. Write a *New York Times* best-selling book – Check, 2004 (and 2017 and 2018?)
4. Buy a beautiful house – Check, 1989 and 1995
5. Buy a beautiful car – Check
6. Win tons of big poker tournaments – Check, 1988 - 2017

In 1993, I added:
Become the greatest poker player of all-time – Check, sort of. I have a record 14 WSOP Bracelets, but I still have a lot of work to do! And I still have a lot of pursuers, and there are other players that could lay claim to that throne. Guys like Doyle Brunson, who has 10 WSOP Bracelets, and has crushed the biggest poker cash games in the world for 60 years! Guys like Phil Ivey, who has 10 WSOP Bracelets, and has crushed the biggest cash games both online, and in the real world, for 15 years (and who knows how many more bracelets Ivey will win?).

My "Yearly Goals"

Although I have achieved all my original "Life goals" from 1988, over the years I have added more goals, and since 2005 I have listed them as "Yearly goals." I write goals that are super hard to achieve, but I like to think big! My yearly list always includes "Win three WSOP bracelets," and I haven't done that since 1993 (great year – Chapter 23). A list of my goals for the year 2017, written in February 2017:

2017 Goals

1. Win three World Series of Poker Bracelets
2. Write my next book *#POSITIVITY Phil's Top 5 Life Tips*
3. Get good time with Kathy, Phillip, Nick
4. Make my autobiography *Poker Brat* hit the *New York Times* Best Seller list
5. Win two World Poker Tour tournaments
6. Get good time with Chamath and Bill, and their families
7. Walk 10,000 steps a day
8. Sign a few big contracts!

The difference between my goals then and now is this: I have added friendship goals to the list. As I get older, I understand the importance of having a good friendship, and maintaining it!

Writing *#POSITIVITY*

I am also super excited about goal number 2: writing my next book, titled *#POSITIVITY Phil's Top Five Life Tips*. In fact, the reason that I sold *Poker Brat* when I did was this: I wanted to clear the decks for my "How to achieve great things in life" book. I have long felt like I can inspire, and help, tens of millions of people with my book *#POSITIVITY*! I have wanted to put pen to paper since 2010, and share with the world the tips and techniques that have propelled me onwards and upwards. The tips and techniques that have helped me think bigger, be stronger, and accomplish more. For example, I can't wait to share the first chapter of *#POSITIVITY* with the world: Hate Hurts You. Hate Hurts You teaches a three-step technique for getting rid of hate in your life. Simple, and hugely impactful.

The Future is Bright!

As I eye the future, and my future goals, I look forward to helping raise $100 million for charities, and I'm almost halfway home (Appendix 3). I look forward to sitting on the floor at Golden State Warriors games with Joe and Nicole. I look forward to hosting the WSOP Main Event coverage on ESPN, or better yet, winning the WSOP Main Event. I look forward to hosting at least two or three television shows over the next twenty years. I look forward to playing poker in our Masters of the Universe poker game once a week. I look forward to playing full court basketball at Bill's house with friends. I look forward to having this book (*Poker Brat*) inspire millions of people and hit the *New York Times* Best Seller list.

I look forward to having my next book *#POSITIVITY* help millions of people and hit the *New York Times* Best Seller list. I look forward to hanging out with Chamath and Bill, with their wives Brigette and Nat (and my wife Kathy), and their kids, for years to come. I look forward to winning at least five WPT Championships. I look forward to winning WSOP bracelets numbers 15, 16, 17, 18, 19, 20, 21, 22, 23, and 24 (and more than that!). I look forward to a beautiful future with my cherished wife Kathy, and with our sons Phillip and Nick.

Appendix I

UltimateBet.com, Start to Finish

[Disclaimer: These are the facts, as I remember them. I don't know all the facts, and some of this stuff happened 17 years ago, so please bear with me.]

In September 1998, David "Porkchop" Wight and I tried to start, quite unsuccessfully, our own online poker site. Porkchop had been a successful poker player in LA who transitioned to business. His business, which involved renting essential equipment for conferences (his employees drove a truck all over the country), included renting out laptops (sometimes at $500 a day), setting up conference space and booths, and more. And his business was booming!

Porkchop constantly told me how hard poker was and how easy business was. I had a theory. If you could make it in poker, you could make it anywhere. And many successful poker players have made that transition, to great success! (Guys like David "Doc" Sands, Mark Teltscher, CEO of Matchbook, and Tony Guoga, who won a seat in the European Parliament). Don't get me wrong, I didn't want to quit my day job, but having a piece of a good business, one that might generate some good cash flow, sounded sweet to me!

As Porkchop and I watched the internet site PlanetPoker.com crack 100 simultaneous players, then more, we wanted in! And we knew that it was good to be the "house." If you wanted to be the house in the real world, then you would have to buy or rent space, open your own poker room, supervise employees, make sure the doors were open and shut, and have tons of other small obligations, and even then you might not make it. When it came to online poker, we imagined that the barrier to entry was much lower, and thought, "Build software, and then collect a massive rake for the rest of your life." Nice model! Plus, there was no limit on the upside. Who knows how big an online poker room could get? The internet isn't limited by any physical space, like walls.

Our own online poker site project failed miserably, and we lost our invest-ment, because Porkchop and I didn't take control of our team of software engi-neers. We paid them, and then left them to their own devices. This caused delay after delay. In retrospect, we should have had milestones and penalties in place, for when the software team fell short of any stated goal. I believe that people perform better under pressure, thus putting a deadline in place is a good idea.

Failure, and Knowing Thyself

As for my own limitations, I knew by then that I could never be a CEO. First, I couldn't get up in the mornings! Secondly, the folks in my family tree that were super successful businessmen all seemed to die young; which is why my father was content as an assistant dean at the UW (Dad eventually advanced way up-ward, but without the stress his peers faced). Thirdly, in the parlance of the early 2000s, I wasn't an "animal" (someone who could work 16 hour days, seven days a week), and I believed that if I did work those kinds of hours, then I wouldn't live very long. And my last reason that I couldn't be a CEO is that I needed at least ten hours of sleep every night. So the bottom line is this: Porkchop and I were onto something, but we didn't have the wherewithal to pull it off.

Greg Pierson

In April 2000, a fellow named Greg Pierson called and asked if I would be inter-ested in getting involved in an online poker site. I was already a believer, and I jumped at the chance! Greg was putting together a nice package for someone else to potentially run: great software, and some big poker names to represent the site. I was interested, and I flew up to Portland, Oregon, to meet with Greg.

Greg was about six feet tall, with light hair, and a confident, patient way about him. If you didn't understand something, then Greg could patiently and clearly ex-plain it you. Greg had crushed everything that he had ever touched! From school, to working at the prestigious Anderson Consulting, to building his own house! With no contractor experience at all, he built his first house, from scratch. When Greg presented me with a beautiful (full color) 100-page business plan, detailing every small step that we would need to accomplish along the way, I was impressed. Greg was making a lot of money, and he was willing to quit his job and take the leap into being full-time CEO of a new company. Greg would build the thing from scratch. I knew that Greg had a lot to lose, and I believed that he could get it done. It was ob-vious to me that Greg had special business qualities, and a huge drive to succeed.

Since there were legal issues surrounding running an online poker site from the USA, we started a software company and called it ieLogic. The idea was to license software to offshore operators; ieLogic would build the software and someone else would run it.

After a few months of negotiations, it came down to this. I would invest $60,000 for 7% of the company, represent their first customer (UB), wear their logo, play poker on the site for at least ten hours a week, shoot commercials for the site, and be the face of the site. In exchange for that, I would receive a starting salary of $5,000 a month.

eWorld Will Run UB

In September 2000, ieLogic signed a software licensing agreement with eWorld, the owner-operator of UB. In the first few years there was a lot of pressure on the young UB to become profitable and to stop spewing money. And there was a lot of pressure on Greg. I mean, Greg took on money from family and close friends! And we almost went out of business many times. It was a struggle, and there was a lot of sacrifice. When the project got under way, I don't think that the team had any idea how hard it would be, and how much competition we would face. For years, we struggled with no money, on the edge of going under. Finally, three years in, a television show blew us up!

UB Becomes Number 1, and Then Drops the Ball!

On April 9, 2003, the UB Aruba Classic WPT aired on the Travel Channel, and the UB site was blown up! Within hours, tens of thousands of new downloads were requested, and the site began crashing. And the crashes went on for months afterwards! Players would be in the middle of a tournament, and whoops, UB crashes. They would be in the middle of a cash game, and whoops, the site crashes! It seemed that the site crashed once a day for months. That's a lot of crashes, and that's a lot of angry customers emailing the site to find out what reparations UB would make. And UB customer support completely dropped the ball.

Clearly, UB should have hired dozens of new people in their Costa Rica office to handle the mass of new customers, and the issues that a crashing site brought on. And even though the customers were remarkably patient, because they understood that this was the beginning of an industry, they could take just so much! UB had dropped the ball, big time.

But despite dropping the ball, UB became the biggest online poker site on the planet, overnight! After years of trying to build up players, and putting fishing poles into many marketing ponds (like China), suddenly *all* the fish jumped into the UB boat! And the UB boat sank under the weight of it all. Some said that UB had a great problem: we had too many new customers!

Partypoker.com is Number 1

On June 3, 2003, the partypoker Millions WPT television episode came out on Travel Channel, and PartyPoker.com took back the mantle of "world's biggest online poker site." And they were ready for it. Party saw UB's struggles after the WPT aired, and they had a few months to prepare for their own customer rush. Party was ready to handle 100,000 new customers. You have to give Party credit. They had excellent customer support in place by then, and their site rarely crashed. They were so good that a couple of years later, on June 27, 2005, PartyPoker.com went public for $8 billion on the London Stock Exchange. (For more on that terrific story, check out the book *Life's a Gamble* by Mike Sexton.)

Excapsa Acquires ieLogic and Takes eWorld Holdings and UB as Customer

With the intent of going public, Jim Ryan started a company called Excapsa. On April 24, 2004, he acquired ieLogic and took on their customers, including eWorld Holdings and UB. And boy oh boy were we excited! If Party was floating at $8 billion, and we were 25% the size of Party, would we float at $2 billion? 1% of $2 billion is $20 million, and I had almost six points, sweet! As lawyers explored whether Excapsa could indeed go public, steps were simultaneously being explored regarding Excapsa buying eWorld Holdings. Ideally, Excapsa would buy eWorld Holdings, go public in London, and hit a $2 billion valuation. Jim Ryan did a great job of pulling all of this off.

FullTiltPoker.com

In June 2004, Full Tilt Poker (FTP; www.fulltilt.com) launched, with a great product, and a great tagline: "Full Tilt Poker is built by poker players for poker players." My poker compatriots Chris Ferguson and Howard Lederer founded it, and they brought a ton of famous poker players on board, like Phil Ivey, Mike "the Mouth" Matusow, Jennifer Harman, Eli Elezra, and many more. From the moment that FTP launched, these aces carved into UB's players. They had their dozen or so pro poker players slowly convince the players at UB to switch sites and play on FTP. If you wanted to play in a big game on FTP, then their players (and FTP) would lend you money to play there. For a year or two, UB owned the biggest games on the internet: the $80-$160 games, and most of the high-limit action, until the FTP machine came along and persuaded players to switch to their site.

And FTP was brilliant when it came to marketing! The FTP television ads that were running in the USA were stunning. I marveled at them (there are currently a bunch of those ads floating around on youtube.com). FTP clearly had the best marketing in the online poker industry, and should have won awards for their television commercials!

Excapsa Goes Public; and then UIGEA

In February 2006, Excapsa went public on the London Stock Exchange for roughly $360 million. I took $5 million in cash off the table (roughly 28% of my holdings). Percentage wise, I took a higher percentage than anyone else. The UB insiders were all drinking the Cool Aid! They saw Party floating at $9 billion, and they reasoned that UB was worth $1 billion. My advisors told me to take it all off the table! I live in Silicon Valley, and my friends and had seen $100 million in equity in a company destroyed overnight. Remember February 2000?

The shareholders were under a "lock up" (they could not sell their shares) for one year. In February 2007, they could sell their shares. Excapsa floated around $360 million for months, until October 13, 2006, when the Senate unanimously passed a bill called the Unlawful Internet Gambling Enforcement Act (UIGEA). This was a small rider thrown onto the Port Security Act. Most Senators didn't even notice it. It was the last day of business for the Senate!

Excapsa in the Process of Being Sold for $750 Million to Party Poker

After the UIGEA bill passed in the US Senate, the internet poker stocks trading in London lost 90% of their value, overnight! Even worse for me, the Excapsa CEO Jim Ryan was in Germany selling UB for $750 million to Party Poker. One more day. I needed just one more day where nothing passed in the Senate, and I would have collected $28 million in cash and Party Poker stock. Now UB had to make a quick decision. It was now illegal to accept US customers' money (one interpretation of UIGEA), and that made up roughly 70% of the UB customer base. No one wanted to violate any laws. Thus, a sale had to be made, and had to be made quickly.

Another Change in Ownership to Tokwiro

Tokwiro, the guys who owned the online poker site AbsolutePoker.com (AP) weren't afraid to accept US customers. One of these is true: they had a theory that it wasn't illegal, or they thought it was illegal but they were willing to take the risk. In any case, Tokwiro agreed to buy UB for $10 million in cash and $120 million in deferred payments (fire sale!). At this point UB had $53 million in cash along with the $10 million that the AP guys had given to UB. This cash was to be disbursed immediately to the shareholders. But that didn't happen. Instead, around $30 million was disbursed ($1.4 million for me). And the rest lingered for a long time.

Trambopoline Reaches Out

In early 2008, I was playing online poker at UB, when a player at the table, with the account named Trambopoline asked if he could talk with me about a serious matter. I scoffed! Here is another guy that wants to borrow money from me! Or maybe he wants a signed picture, or an autograph sent to his house. The next day, Trambopoline was there again asking if he could talk to me about a serious matter, and this time he told me that some of my friends had told him to reach out to me. Trambopoline told me that the account nionio was cheating. Somehow nionio was winning an absurd amount of money while playing like 60% of the hands in No Limit Hold'Em. Also, the online poker forums were posting convincing data proving that this mysterious account had to be cheating.

The Investigation Begins

I thought, "Damn it! There probably isn't any cheating going on, but UB will lose tons of customers over this. UB better launch an investigation immediately, get to the bottom of this, and clear the air." I called the lead attorney at UB and asked for an investigation into the account nionio. Initially I was rebuffed when it turned out that the account that I called into question belonged to a certain powerful individual, who I will not name. I had given Trambopoline my cell phone number, so that I could communicate through him with the online poker forums, and when I told him that I was rebuffed, he convinced me that the investigation needed to be launched. So, I only had one move left. I threatened to quit UB if the investigation was not launched immediately. It was a little risky, as I was getting paid $60,000 a month in salary by then, but I knew that PhilHellmuth. com was pulling in at least that much for UB (in new customers). I was confident that my threat would get UB's attention. I mean, how hard was it to investigate the accounts?

"God Mode"

Apparently, a tool that was originally created by ieLogic to prevent cheating, which allowed site officials to look at hands after they were played, had been turned into a device that could be used to cheat. Initially, the tool was on a five-minute delay. I can see the need for having the tool on five-minute delay (to protect players from cheating by collusion), but somewhere along the way the delay was made variable. So now, in the wrong hands, the tool could be used to see all the hole cards for the players at the table in real time. Apparently, someone had been using that tool to cheat players. When news of what had happened hit the internet, the online poker forums called it "God Mode."

To this day, ieLogic and Excapsa insiders insist that God Mode was decommissioned in the transition from ieLogic to Excapsa in 2004. Either this wasn't done correctly or it was later put back in.

An Investigation by Paul Leggett: Cheating is Confirmed

Paul Leggett led a six-month-long investigation into the cheating claims, and he confirmed that the cheating had occurred, but it took Paul many months to come up with a list of the damages. Eventually, a list was put together, and one time, after Paul Leggett was promoted to CEO, I saw the list, when Paul showed it to me during UB's annual player party in Aruba in October 2008, and I recall that the total amount that was owed back to the players was well north of $20 million.

Now the AP guys were upset that they had purchased tainted goods, and they went back to Excapsa and said, "We know that you guys still have the Excapsa shareholders' money still locked up in Canada, and we need $25 million dollars of that cash, so that we can pay back the accounts that were cheated." Excapsa complied and gave up $25 million of the shareholders' cash (over $1 million of that money was mine). This cash was supposed to be disbursed to the shareholders the year before, but it was still lingering in the Canadian financial system.

By the way, when Paul handed me the list in Aruba, I said, "That's poker pro and universally loved Prahlad Friedman near the top of the list, and he's downstairs in the tournament right now." I took Paul downstairs and we told Prahlad that he was getting a refund, in the neighborhood of $1 million. I recall that Prahlad stood up from his chair in the tournament and did a jig!

Was I Involved? Hell No!
Evidence Exists Now That Clears Me, Finally!

For months in 2008, huge stories broke about the UB cheating scandal, and I had been representing UB since Day 1. I thought, "Oh my god, I am proud of the way that I have lived my life, with perfect ethics and morals, and now, my reputation is going to be destroyed over nothing?" Wow. That was a tough one for me. But after one week of feeling sorry for myself, I thought, "I didn't have anything to do with this, and I will not suffer. In fact, I will walk around with my head held up high in the air, because I am proud of the person that I am." I knew that the insiders in the poker world knew that I was innocent, as by then they had watched me live a pure life for 20 years. But my reputation took a big hit anyway, and there was nothing I could do about it. I suffered when online poker players came up to me and insulted me, right in public. But what could I do? I was innocent and I understood that they didn't know that. But it still hurt, and it wasn't until one of the Travis Makar tapes came out, in May 2013, that I was completely vindicated. That was a great day for me, and I did my own jig! You can listen to those tapes online anytime, or check out twoplustwo.com.

Why Did I Stay with UB?

Critics said, "Phil is staying with UB so he can get paid." Uh, well actually I could have made more money if I left UB and went to FTP (Chapter 41)! This criticism hurt me the most. But if I had I left UB, then they would have said, "Why did Phil leave?" Either way, I was going to get massacred by the haters. But the reasons I stayed were simple, and obvious: I had equity in UB (though I could have left UB and had equity in Full Tilt), and, more importantly, I wanted to make sure that the players were paid back 100% of the money they had been cheated out of. I didn't want anyone to be hurt. And if I had left UB then, the whole site might have collapsed.

Starting in 2003, I watched Doyle Brunson get hounded, for years, over an online poker site that he had been with when it collapsed. They all felt that Doyle owed them their money because he had represented the site. This site collapse had nothing to do with Doyle, but he was hounded nonetheless. I didn't want people coming up to me for years afterwards saying, "Phil, you owe me money. You represented the site, and they stole my money, and I went there because of you. Will you pay me back the cash I lost?" The site Doyle represented eventually paid the customers back every single penny, but I saw how he was hounded.

I'm proud of the fact that I stayed. I initiated the investigation at UB, and I stayed until everyone was paid back every penny in question. Over $20 million dollars!

The End of My Run with UB

In November 2010, my mission with UB was over. I had done my job. I had built the site up from scratch, and when the UB scandal hit, I stayed until the players were paid back every penny. UB was happy to hire Prahlad Friedman in my place, and I was happy to talk to my friends at FTP. I already knew FullTiltPoker. com would go all-in for me. The FTP guys came up with me in good times and bad, and they knew I was honorable and a great poker player, and they did not underestimate my value to a poker site. I officially left UB on November 1, 2010 (that's when they stopped paying me).

Black Friday

Six months later, the poker world was rocked by "Black Friday" (Chapter 41)! Black Friday hit on April 15, 2011, and it destroyed poker. All the sponsorship money coming into the players, the networks like NBC and ESPN, and the marketing campaigns that fueled the growth of poker globally, dried up. The money faucet had been going full blast, and now it slowed to a trickle.

I had just landed from my USO Tour (Chapter 41), and the following week I was going to sign a $30 million contract with FTP, with a $2 million signing bonus! I was going to be making at least $120,000 a month, every month, forever, but that disappeared. Man, did that hurt! At least I wouldn't be hounded for the rest of my life by customers from any online poker site, because by then I had been gone from UB for five months. The press wrote a few articles saying that my timing was so good that I must have known that Black Friday was coming (not!). The reality was that my agent and I were slow playing FTP, because we wanted the best deal possible. We knew FTP was drooling, and I was drooling to be with those guys.

Not Enough Funds at FTP and UB to Pay the Players Back

FullTiltPoker.com and UB couldn't pay their customers; at least this time my head wasn't on the chopping block. I had been through a lot of pain because of UB, which I didn't deserve. I felt bad for the UB customers. By the way, one major reason these two sites couldn't pay their customers was that a few transaction processors allegedly stole hundreds of millions of dollars from the sites. And the government confiscated a pile of cash as well. UB tried to stay in business with the "rest of the world" traffic, but losing all their US business was too much of a strain.

On January 23, 2014, it was announced that FTP customers would be paid back in full, through the US Government, specifically through the Department of Justice (DOJ). On April 11, 2017, the DOJ announced that AP/UB players would be repaid as well, a stunning development that no one saw coming. Apparently, according to the Poker Players Association (PPA), the PPA suggested to the DOJ that the extra unclaimed funds from FTP should be treated as a single pot of money to reimburse all players whose money was frozen on Black Friday. So the pooled money is now being used to reimburse AP/UB players in full. I must say that the PPA has been great for the poker players, and the poker world.

Greg Pierson Gets Persecuted; Wrongly?

Personally, I never thought that Greg Pierson was part of the cheating scandal. But when the scandal broke, his name was all over the online poker forums. As the creator of the software behind UB, claims ranged from "he must have known," to "he must have been involved in some way." As CEO of ieLogic, was Greg ultimately responsible for developing software that was ultimately used to cheat? Yes. Do I believe he may have dropped the ball in transitioning ieLogic to Excapsa as he rushed off to start his next company? Yes. But I'm almost positive that he was unaware of any cheating until the scandal broke. You see, on the day Excapsa went public, Greg's stock was worth $86 million! He could have sold it all, but instead he allowed his stock to be locked up for a year. He bet over 95% of his net worth on the future of Excapsa, and there's just no way someone would do this if they even suspected there was something going on that could kill the value of their stock.

Nevada Gaming Commission Licenses Greg Pierson

In 2014, Greg applied for a gaming license in the State of Nevada. In addition to allowing his new company iovation to do business in Nevada, I'm sure he also saw this as an opportunity to clear his name. I can tell you this much: the Nevada Gaming Commission did its highest-level investigation on Greg, and everyone who knows about this will tell you that it's the toughest and most exhaustive investigation possible. Tougher than an FBI investigation. They searched his home and his office, they took computers and cell phones, they looked at phone records, they poured over his taxes and every aspect of his finances, they spent months talking to everyone they could, they grilled him and his partners. In the end, they found absolutely no evidence that he was involved or benefited in any way, and the Nevada Gaming Commission unanimously granted him a license to do business in Nevada with his new company iovation, an authentication and fraud management company. They protect billions of transactions for hundreds of organizations around the world and stop 500,000 online fraud attempts every day.

But there are a bunch of people out there (internet trolls who accused me of doing things that I didn't do) who have been telling the world how guilty Greg is. And, man oh man, if Greg is as innocent as I suspect he is, then these haters better hope that the Buddha was wrong about the concept of bad karma! I hope the haters don't get punished, but persecuting an innocent man seems like an egregious thing to do.

Forgiveness, My Secret Weapon!

Speaking of people who persecute the innocent, I forgive all the people who maliciously attacked me, even though they were 100% wrong, and even though some of those guys were brutal. They were wrong, and I hope that they don't condemn any more innocent people. Forgiving others has led to beautiful rewards for me (Chapter 33).

WSOP Bracelet Number 12

Starting in 2007, I promised Greg Pierson that I would give him my twelfth WSOP bracelet. When I won it in 2012, many haters hassled me regarding my giving that bracelet to Greg. They said he was a cheater and the devil, and went public against me giving bracelet number 12 to Greg. Now, it is 2017, and I am still holding onto that bracelet. I have given away all my other bracelets to family and friends: my best friend Chamath has bracelet number 13 (WSOPE main event), and Sheryl Sandberg and her kids have bracelet number 14 (given to them because I loved her late husband, Dave Goldberg). Greg has always maintained his innocence, and I always keep my promises. I have decided to give WSOP bracelet number 12 to Greg in March, 2017. I'm going with my heart...

Appendix 2

Poker Aces

There are great players in cash games, and there are great players in poker tournaments. In this chapter, I'm going to talk about some of the best poker tournament players in the world. Guys that have done it for over 15 years: Phil Ivey, Daniel "Kid Poker" Negreanu, Johnny Chan, Doyle Brunson, and Erik Seidel; and a few of the young guns. But first I need to mention some of the best players in the world in cash games, guys that are winning all the money, but you have never heard of them, because they are under the radar.

The Best Cash Game Players in the World

A list of the best cash games players in the world includes: Phil Ivey, David Oppenheim, Phil Galfond, Billy Baxter, Andrew Robl, Bobby Buckler, Patrik Antonius, Johnny Chan, Abe Mosseri, John Hennigan, Chau Giang, Brian Rast, David Grey, Bobby Baldwin, Ray Dehkharghani, Antonio Esfandiari, Ted Forrest, Jimmy Cha, Jennifer Harman, Sam Trickett, Eli Elezra, Tom Dwan, Nick Schulman, John Monnette, Alex Kostritsyn, Mike Glick, Timofey Kuznetsov, and Doyle Brunson. These guys consistently play in the biggest mixed games in the world, oftentimes $2,000-$4,000 limit ($300-$600 blinds No Limit Hold 'Em), at the Aria Hotel and Casino and Bellagio Hotel and Casino. In a game like that, you can win or lose $500,000 in one night! These poker studs all started with nothing, and slowly climbed the poker mountain. They all started in small-stakes cash games, and found that they had a knack for poker. Now, they are winning all the cash!

Johnny Chan

Johnny Chan has all but retired from poker tournaments, because the high-limit cash games in Macau are too lucrative for him to resist! I'm sure Johnny would have kept winning WSOP titles had he put in full effort, and I believe that he would be pushing me higher and higher as well. Johnny has ten WSOP titles, and he has dominated in both tournaments and cash games since 1986 (he won his first WSOP bracelet in 1985). He won the 1987 and 1988 WSOP main events, and then finished second to me in the 1989 main event. This feat is considered one of the best in poker history, but it is much better than that! He also won the 1988 and the 1989 Hall of Fame Poker Classic main events; that's four of the biggest poker majors over a two-year span!

Everyone who plays poker with Johnny Chan knows how good he is. He is steady, consistent, and has probably won over $50 million at the tables over his illustrious career. And Johnny plays every poker game at a world-class level, from all forms of Hold 'Em, to Pot Limit Omaha, to Badugi. Johnny often laughs at the table, and he will continue to laugh, all the way to the bank! (For more on Johnny Chan, buy the book *Deal Me In* at philhellmuth.com.)

Doyle Brunson

What can you say about the biggest legend in poker? Doyle Brunson has been crushing since the 1950s! I'm hoping that I'm cut from the same cloth as Doyle; he still plays in the biggest poker games in the world (at Bellagio and Aria), and continues to crush at age 84! Like Johnny Chan, Doyle has all but retired from tournament poker (also with ten WSOP bracelets), and I'm sure that had he continued playing WSOP tournaments and focused on them more in the 1980s and 1990s, that I would be chasing him for the all-time WSOP bracelet lead.

Doyle wrote a book called *Super System* that many consider to be the bible of poker. Doyle will still come out and play on television in high buy-in No Limit Hold 'Em poker games, and he has an amazing record of wins there as well. Doyle has been married for well over 50 years. We all look up to Doyle, and I'm sure he will continue winning money in his 90s! (For more on Doyle Brunson, buy the book *Deal Me In* at philhellmuth.com.)

Phil Ivey

Most of the poker world thinks that Phil Ivey is the best poker player in the world: both in cash games and in tournaments! High praise indeed. And Ivey is my biggest threat in the bracelet race. Ivey is 40 years old and has ten WSOP bracelets, I'm 52 years old and have 14 WSOP bracelets. (Phil, I'll race you to 24!) Ivey has missed most of the 2015 and 2016 WSOPs, because the high-stakes cash games in Macau have been *that* good! I wouldn't be surprised to find out that Ivey has won well over $50 million. He is smart, and invests his cash well. And Ivey maintains a terrific lifestyle, including private jets, baller hotel suites, beautiful women, the best tables at the hottest clubs in the world, and more! Most upcoming poker players aspire to live like Phil Ivey, he is an aspirational brand! (I hope that a few aspire to live like me.)

There are two or three guys on the planet that have "held over" me (have been extraordinarily lucky against me in tons of poker hands), and Ivey is one of them! Once, in a televised cash game, Ivey raised it up, and I called with 10-10, and the flop came down 10♣-9♣-7♦. Ivey bet, and I called. A deuce on the turn (10♣-9♣-7♦-2♥), and I moved all-in ($86,000 apiece), and Ivey showed me 8-6, and busted me. Another time, in a televised cash game, I made a jack-high flush when Ivey made a king-high flush, after we jammed the 7♦-6♦-4♠ flop with me holding J♦-5♦ (I had no way out!). Finally, in the WPT's LA Poker Classic, with seven players left, we were playing down to six-handed and coming back the next day, I picked up A♥-K♥ in late position (the cutoff), and he picked up A-A on the button. I had 4.3 million before the pot, and Ivey had 2 million, ouch! Afterwards, he had 4 million and I had 2.3 million. And in 2007, I incurred the biggest loss of my life when I lost $536,000 to Ivey in Monte Carlo (Chapter 37). I'm sure that I will have my big wins vs. Ivey in the future, and I look forward to our battle for poker history! (For more on Ivey, buy the book *Deal Me In* at philhellmuth.com.)

Erik Seidel

Erik has eight WSOP bracelets, and he's moving up! Erik has one of the best records in the world in high roller tournaments over the last 12 years, if not the best record. He continues to stay relevant and to crush it. And Erik has been doing it for decades! Erik and I first played heads up for a title at the Bicycle Club's Diamond Jim Brady Tournament in 1988, he won (Chapter 13). And again, we played heads up, this time for a WSOP bracelet in 1992, and he won. Erik and I must have played at the same final table a dozen times.

Erik also has something that I don't have, a WPT title! He won his WPT title in 2008 at Foxwoods. And we share this: we both have a first-place and a second-place finish in the prestigious NBC Heads-Up Championship: he finished second in 2010 to his good friend Annie Duke, then he won it in 2011. And we have both been married over 25 years! Erik has also been a consistent winner in cash games over decades, specifically in No Limit Hold 'Em and Pot Limit Omaha.

He is also a world-class backgammon player. In the biggest No Limit Hold 'Em tournaments, Erik always seems to be there! (For more on Erik Seidel, buy the book *Deal Me In* at philhellmuth.com.)

Daniel Negreanu

Daniel "Kid Poker" Negreanu has an amazing reading ability (reads!), and he is the most popular poker player in the world. Daniel is fun to watch! And he signs more autographs, and takes more pictures than anyone else. I thought that I was good with the fans, but Daniel signs all day long *during* poker tournaments! Daniel has six WSOP bracelets, two WPT titles, and a terrific, positive attitude! Daniel isn't afraid to learn new tricks, and he studies all the elegant new theories developed by the kids. These theories are enhanced by his terrific reads.

Daniel is a thought leader as well, and teaches classes in emotional enlightenment at Choice Center. And Daniel isn't afraid to speak his mind! Occasionally it gets him into trouble, but he is sincere and authentic. I have been playing poker with Daniel since 1998, and he is tough as nails. Look for Daniel to win at least 15 WSOP bracelets over his illustrious career! (For more on Daniel Negreanu, buy the book *Deal Me In* at philhellmuth.com.)

The Next Generation

When I think of the greatest young poker tournament players, I look at the ones who are winning titles, like Brian Rast, Jason Mercier, Shaun Deeb, Byron Kaverman, Jake Schindler, Nick Schulman, Vanessa Selbst, Scott Seiver, Stephen Chidwick, Conan Drinan, Sam Trickett, Justin Bonomo, Mike McDonald, Igor Kurganov, Joe McKeehan, Brian Hastings, David Peters, Nick Petrangelo, Dan Smith, Fedor Holz (22 years old!), and Dan Colman. Which of these players will emerge as the greatest poker player of their generation? It won't be the one who wins the most in the cash games. Cash games are subjective. If you win $100 million vs. weak competition is that a measure of poker greatness, or your ability to schmooze and get invited back? It will be the one who keeps grinding WSOP tournaments (it's not easy!), and not the juicy, super-tempting, high-stakes cash games that occur at the WSOP. It will be the one who plays for history!

Appendix 3

Charity Poker Tournaments: $40 Million Raised to Date!

My goal is to raise $100 million for charity. I started using poker tournaments to raise money for charity back in 1998, when I raised $6,000 for Addison School (kindergarten – 5th grade) in Palo Alto.

- $4 million for Math for America (2003, 2004), Manhattan
- $400,000 for La Riata, for Cancer Research (2005, 2006), Dallas
- $4 million for Ante Up for Africa (2007, 2008, 2009, 2010), Vegas
- $2 million for Eva's Heroes (2008, 2009, 2011, 2012), San Antonio
- $400,000 for Fallen Officer Foundation (2005, 2006, 2007, 2009, 2011), Phoenix, Vegas
- $400,000 for Boys & Girls Clubs of Miami (2006), with Arod and Jay Z
- $9 million for Children's Hospital of Philadelphia (2008–2016), Manhattan
- $3 million for Clinton Foundation (2012, 2015), San Francisco, LA
- $10 million for Teaching Tolerance Charity Holocaust Museum (2010–2016), Chicago
- $500,000 for Derby Poker Championships UN Climate Fund, Blessings in a Backpack (2007–2016), Louisville
- $75,000 for Starkey Hearing Foundation (2011), co-hosts Larry Fitzgerald, Adrian Petersen
- $135,000 for Tipping Point (2011), with Bay Area Sports Team Owners and me

- $2.5 million for Eastern Congo Initiative and Lean In (2011, 2012, 2014)
- $80,000 for Adventures of the Mind (2011), Manhattan, with Amy Tan and Annie Duke
- $4 million for Golden State Warriors Foundation (2014, 2015, 2016, 2017), San Francisco
- $4 million for Tiger Woods (2012–2016), Las Vegas
- $150,000 for Michael Finley Foundation (2017), Dallas

My Part of The Process

Before I take too much credit, let me explain that I charge $25,000 (my corporate rate is $50,000) to come in and MC for the night. And someone else does the hard work of scouting out locations, setting the tournament up, setting up a great sound system, finding good food and beverages, and much more. For my part, the charities use my name in advertisements, billboards, television, and radio spots, to recruit players, and to create a buzz. And then I fly in, play a bit, and MC all night long. I also teach the charities, whether they hire me or not, to raise maximum dollars for their charity. And, if they want me to come in, I will not do it unless they are trying to raise at least $500,000. I cannot MC an event, charge $25,000, and then have them make only $125,000. I wouldn't feel right taking 20% of the money raised.

The Hold 'Em Learning Curve, the Energy, and the Drama in the Room!

When I'm on the microphone, I sing rap songs (like Jay Z, Nelly, or Wiz Khalifa), I tease the celebrity players – or big sponsors – who might be in the tournament, and I call out chip counts, big hands in progress, and the big hands at the final table. My MC job is to add energy and excitement, and generally to pump up the room!

I'm told that amateurs learn the game very quickly when I'm calling out the hands. One famous saying is this, "Texas Hold 'Em takes five minutes to learn, but a lifetime to master." I believe that I throw out a lot of information quickly, and that my listeners at the charity tourneys learn Hold 'Em at an accelerated rate. Most final tables at these charity tournaments have big audiences, who watch the action, learn something new about No Limit Hold 'Em, perhaps have a few drinks, and just generally chill out.

An example of me on the microphone, at the final table of Teaching Tolerance

Charity Poker Tourney in Chicago (when the players are all-in, and the hands are face up):

> J.B. Pritzker is all-in with pocket kings, and his opponent, Greg Carlin, has pocket queens. J.B. is a 4½-to-1 favorite to win the pot. The flop is J-10-8, and now Greg needs a nine for a straight, there are four of those, or a queen for trips, there are two of those. The turn card is a deuce, and now Greg has six outs (four nines and two queens), with one card to come, to J.B.'s 38 outs. J.B. is over a 6-to-1 favorite to win the pot. The river is a deuce and J.B. doubles up and takes the chip lead!

Another example, in New York: at the Children's Hospital of Philadelphia's All In for Kids Charity Poker Tournament, I might say:

> Dan Shak is all-in with A-K against Joel Friedman's pocket nines. Joel's nines are about a 6-to-5 favorite to win the pot. The flop is Q-10-7, and now Dan needs an ace; there are three of those; a king, there are three of those; or a jack, there are four of those; so ten wins for Dan, who is about 40% to win the pot. The turn is a four, and Dan has ten outs, an ace, a king, or a jack, going to the last card, and Joel has 34 outs. The river is a jack, Dan makes a straight!

If that hand comes up at the final table, then there will be a lot of shouting and excitement! The natural drama in poker emerges.

In 2013 at Tiger Jam, I said, "Some wrote Tiger Woods off, but how stupid were they? How short-sighted? How about Tiger Woods, he has never, before 2013, won three tournaments before May 15th! Great start, Tiger!" Later, at Tiger Jam, I rapped lyrics from "U Can't Touch This," to MC Hammer.

My Cameo on Showtime Hit Show *Billions* as Charity MC

I have been MCing charity poker tournaments for so long, that when I made a cameo on the Showtime hit show *Billions*, out February 2017, and played myself, I did *not* play myself as a poker player, but as a charity poker MC!

I love using poker to help all of these worthy charities, and I'll be MCing charity poker tourneys for the rest of my active life!

Appendix 4

All My Cashes

Date	Event	Tournament	Location	Place	Prize
1987	$1,000 + 40 No Limit Hold'em	1987 Pot of Gold	Reno	5th	$1,980
1988	$300 Pot Limit Omaha	Cajan Cup 1988	Las Vegas	10th	$1,775
1988	$200 No Limit Hold'em	1988 Pot of Gold	Reno	1st	$17,550
1988	$1,500 Seven-Card Stud Split	19th World Series of Poker	Las Vegas	5th	$15,450
1988	$10,000 No Limit Hold'em World Championship	19th World Series of Poker	Las Vegas	33rd	$7,500
1988	$10,000 No Limit Hold'em	4th Annual Diamond Jim Brady	Los Angeles	1st	$125,000
1988	$1,000 No Limit Hold'em	4th Annual Diamond Jim Brady	Los Angeles	2nd	$72,000
1998	$300 + 30 Limit Omaha Hi/Lo	Super Stars of Poker	Tahoe	1st	$17,685
1989	$2,500 Omaha Pot Limit	20th World Series of Poker	Las Vegas	5th	$25,300
1989	$500 No Limit Hold'em	Cajan Cup 1989	Unknown	1st	$48,306
1989	$300 Ace to Five Lowball	Cajan Cup 1989	Unknown	1st	$20,520
1989	$1,500 Limit Ace to Five Draw	20th World Series of Poker	Las Vegas	14th	$2,985
1989	$10,000 No Limit Hold'em World Championship	20th World Series of Poker	Las Vegas	1st	$775,000
1989	Pot Limit Omaha	All England No Limit Hold'em Grand Prix	London	2nd	$9,291
1989	5 Card Stud	All England No Limit Hold'em Grand Prix	London	2nd	$7,742

Date	Event	Tournament	Location	Place	Prize
1989	5 Card Stud	All England No Limit Hold'em Grand Prix	London	3rd	$6,155
1989	$10,000 No Limit Hold'em	7th Annual America's Cup	Las Vegas	2nd	$40,000
1989	$10,000 No Limit Hold'em	5th Annual Diamond Jim Brady	Los Angeles	3rd	$78,000
1989	$1,500 1/2 Lowball, 1/2 Hold'em	5th Annual Diamond Jim Brady	Los Angeles	5th	$10,980
1989	$2,000 + 50 No Limit 2-7 Lowball	Hall of Fame Poker Classic 1989	Las Vegas	2nd	$33,000
1989	$1,500 + 50 Limit Omaha	Hall of Fame Poker Classic 1989	Las Vegas	5th	$7,875
1990	$1,500 + 50 No Limit Hold'em	Amarillo Slim's Superbowl of Poker	Las Vegas	17th	$2,175
1990	$2,500 No Limit Hold'em	21st World Series of Poker	Las Vegas	5th	$32,500
1990	$300 + 30 Pot Limit Omaha	US Open	Las Vegas	7th	$2,424
1990	$500 + 30 No Limit Hold'em	US Open	Las Vegas	4th	$5,200
1990	$500 + 30 No Limit Hold'em	National Finals	Las Vegas	8th	$1,785
1990	$1,500 + 50 Limit 7 Card Stud	Hall of Fame Poker Classic 1990	Las Vegas	6th	$9,960
1990	$2,500 + 50 Limit Omaha	Hall of Fame Poker Classic 1990	Las Vegas	5th	$12,750
1991	$500 + 30 Hold'em	7th Annual Diamond Jim Brady	Las Vegas	6th	$5,380
1991	$1,500 + 60 Limit Ace to Five Draw Lowball	Hall of Fame Poker Classic 1991	Las Vegas	3rd	$12,420
1991	$2,500 + 60 No Limit Deuce to Seven Draw	Hall of Fame Poker Classic 1991	Las Vegas	4th	$14,000
1991	$1,500 + 60 Pot Limit Hold'em	Hall of Fame Poker Classic 1991	Las Vegas	1st	$80,400
1991	$2,500 + 60 Pot Limit Omaha	Hall of Fame Poker Classic 1991	Las Vegas	4th	$19,950
1992	$300 + 30 Hold'em Shootout	1992 Winnin' o' The Green	Los Angeles	6th	$2,160
1992	$1,500 No Limit Hold'em	23rd World Series of Poker	Las Vegas	9th	$5,715
1992	$5,000 No Limit Deuce to Seven Draw	23rd World Series of Poker	Las Vegas	4th	$26,500

Date	Event	Tournament	Location	Place	Prize
1992	$2,500 Limit Hold'em	23rd World Series of Poker	Las Vegas	2nd	$84,000
1992	$2,500 Hold'em Pot Limit	23rd World Series of Poker	Las Vegas	8th	$6,700
1992	$5,000 Limit Hold'em	23rd World Series of Poker	Las Vegas	1st	$168,000
1992	$2,500 Deuce to Seven No Limit	LA Poker Classic	Los Angeles	1st	$27,500
1992	$1,500 + 50 No Limit Hold'em	Jim Brady Tournament	Los Angeles	2nd	$45,000
1993	$1,500 No Limit Hold'em	24th World Series of Poker	Las Vegas	1st	$161,400
1993	$5,000 No Limit Deuce to Seven Draw	24th World Series of Poker	Las Vegas	2nd	$72,500
1993	$2,500 No Limit Hold'em	24th World Series of Poker	Las Vegas	1st	$173,000
1993	$5,000 Limit Hold'em	24th World Series of Poker	Las Vegas	1st	$138,000
1993	$1,000 + 50 Omaha Hi/Lo	Jim Brady Month	Los Angeles	1st	$50,000
1994	$300 + 30 No Limit Hold'em	LA Poker Classic III-1994	Los Angeles	3rd	$10,470
1994	$1,500 No Limit Hold'em	25th World Series of Poker	Las Vegas	2nd	$93,900
1994	$1,00 Hold'em	10th Annual Diamond Jim Brady	Oceanside	4th	$5,390
1994	$1,000 + 50 Deuce to Seven Lowball	Queens Poker Classic Summer Edition	Las Vegas	3rd	$9,525
1994	$1,000 + 50 Limit Hold'em	Queens Poker Classic Summer Edition	Las Vegas	1st	$42,400
1995	$2,500 + 60 Deuce to Seven Draw	Queens Poker Classic V	Las Vegas	4th	$12,500
1995	$1,000 + 50 Seven Card Stud	LA Poker Classic IV	Los Angeles	5th	$3,660
1995	$1,000 + 50 Deuce to Seven Draw	LA Poker Classic IV	Los Angeles	2nd	$19,050
1995	$500 + 35 Deuce to Seven Draw	Queens Poker Classic Summer Edition	Las Vegas	1st	$18,450
1995	$2,000 + 55 Pot Limit Hold'em	1995 Legends of Poker	Los Angeles	1st	$48,000
1995	$1,000 Deuce to Seven	1995 Four Queens Poker Classic	Las Vegas	2nd	$7,000

Poker Brat

Date	Event	Tournament	Location	Place	Prize
1995	$1,500 + 60 Limit Hold'em	Hall of Fame Poker Classic 1995	Las Vegas	1st	$117,000
1995	$5,000 + 80 Hall of Fame Championship	Hall of Fame Poker Classic 1995	Las Vegas	1st	$236,000
1996	$500 + 40 Pot Limit Omaha	Amarillo Slim's Superbowl of Poker	Los Angeles	1st	$14,850
1996	$1,000 + 50 No Limit Hold'em	1996 LA Poker Classic	Los Angeles	4th	$7,350
1996	$2,500 Omaha 8 or Better	27th World Series of Poker	Las Vegas	6th	$12,375
1996	$535 Limit Hold'em	1996 Four Queens Poker Classic	Las Vegas	1st	$38,600
1996	$7,500 + 100 No Limit Hold'em Championship Event	1996 US Poker Championship	Atlantic City	3rd	$63,000
1996	$6,000 7 Card Stud	1996 World Poker Finals	Mashan-tucket	4th	$9,600
1997	$1,000 + 60 No Limit Hold'em	Shooting Star	San Jose	7th	$3,920
1997	$3,000 Hold'em Pot Limit	28th World Series of Poker	Las Vegas	1st	$204,000
1997	$10,000 No Limit Hold'em World Championship	28th World Series of Poker	Las Vegas	21st	$21,200
1997	$1,000 + 60 Limit Hold'em	Hall of Fame Poker Classic 1997	Las Vegas	11th	$2,340
1997	$1,000 + 60 No Limit Hold'em	Hall of Fame Poker Classic 1997	Las Vegas	8th	$2,640
1998	$1,500 + 70 Limit Hold'em	Carnivale of Poker	Las Vegas	1st	$78,000
1998	$5,000 + 80 Championship Event - No Limit Hold'em	Carnivale of Poker	Las Vegas	2nd	$153,000
1998	$1,000 + 60 No Limit Hold'em	1998 L.A. Poker Classic	Los Angeles	1st	$50,400
1998	$1,000 + 60 Limit Hold'em	1998 Four Queens Poker Classic	Las Vegas	1st	$22,000
1998	$1,500 Omaha Pot Limit	29th World Series of Poker	Las Vegas	16th	$3,870
1998	$2,000 Omaha 8 or Better	29th World Series of Poker	Las Vegas	14th	$4,080
1998	$120 No Limit Hold'em	1998 Orleans Open	Las Vegas	5th	$2,670
1999	$500 + 40 Pot-Limit Hold'em	Carnivale of Poker II	Las Vegas	9th	$2,552
1999	$1,500 + 70 Limit Hold'em	Carnivale of Poker II	Las Vegas	7th	$6,552

Date	Event	Tournament	Location	Place	Prize
1999	$500 + 40 Pot Limit Hold'em	LA Poker Classic VIII	Los Angeles	6th	$5,130
1999	$2,500 No Limit Hold'em	30th World Series of Poker	Las Vegas	12th	$9,210
1999	$2,500 Omaha 8 or Better	30th World Series of Poker	Las Vegas	5th	$20,925
1999	$300 + 30 No Limit Hold'em	California State Poker Championship 1999	Los Angeles	2nd	$10,260
1999	$300 + 30 Lowball	1999 Legends of Poker	Los Angeles	5th	$1,755
1999	$500 + 40 7 Card Stud	1999 Legends of Poker	Los Angeles	4th	$3,120
1999	$1,000 + 60 Omaha Hi-Lo	1999 Legends of Poker	Los Angeles	8th	$1,675
2000	$500 + 40 7 Card Stud	Carnivale of Poker III	Las Vegas	7th	$3,765
2000	$1,500 + 70 No Limit Hold'em	Carnivale of Poker III	Las Vegas	6th	$10,657
2000	$5,000 + 80 Championship Event No Limit Hold'em	Carnivale of Poker III	Las Vegas	3rd	$100,700
2000	$1,000 + 60 Omaha Hi-Lo Split	2000 LA Poker Classic	Los Angeles	3rd	$8,040
2000	$500 + 40 Limit Omaha Hi/Lo	The First Annual Jack Binion World Poker Open	Tunica	24th	$658
2000	$1,000 + 60 No Limit Hold'em	The First Annual Jack Binion World Poker Open	Tunica	1st	$53,932
2000	$1,500 + 70 Pot Limit Omaha	The First Annual Jack Binion World Poker Open	Tunica	3rd	$13,968
2000	$2,000 + 70 Pot Limit Hold'em	31st World Series of Poker	Las Vegas	6th	$16,450
2000	$2,500 + 80 Pot Limit Omaha	31st World Series of Poker	Las Vegas	4th	$29,250
2000	$300 + 30 No Limit Hold'em Championship Event	2000 Peppermill Summer Tournament	Reno	7th	$755
2000	$100 Limit Hold'em	2000 Summer Pot of Gold	Reno	6th	$1,229
2000	$500 + 40 Half Pot Limit Hold'em & Half Pot Limit Omaha	Global Pot Limit No Limit Open	Los Angeles	1st	$9,225

Date	Event	Tournament	Location	Place	Prize
2000	$2,500 +80 Global Championship Cup - No Limit Hold'em	Global Pot Limit No Limit Open	Los Angeles	5th	$3,000
2000	$100 + 20 No Limit Hold'em	Fall Pot of Gold	Reno	1st	$8,092
2000	$250 Limit 7 Card Stud	Poker EM 2000	Baden	1st	$106,250
2000	$1,000 + 60 Seven Card Stud	2000 US Poker Championship	Atlantic City	9th	$1,575
2000	$1,000 + 60 No Limit Hold'em	2000 US Poker Championship	Atlantic City	12th	$1,352
2000	$1,000 + 60 Omaha Hi-Lo Split	2000 US Poker Championship	Atlantic City	8th	$2,175
2000	No Limit Hold'em - Grand Final	Late Night Poker Series 3	Cardiff	1st	$64,973
2001	$500 + 40 Limit Hold'em	2001 LA Poker Classic	Los Angeles	17th	$987
2001	$500 Omaha Hi-Lo	2001 Shooting Stars	San Jose	1st	$13,875
2001	$2,000 + 100 Texas Hold'em (No Limit)	32nd World Series of Poker	Las Vegas	1st	$316,550
2001	$1,500 + 90 Seven Card Stud Hi-Lo Split Eight or Better	32nd World Series of Poker	Las Vegas	9th	$4,685
2001	$3,000 + 120 Texas Hold'em (Limit)	32nd World Series of Poker	Las Vegas	6th	$19,555
2001	$2,500 + 100 Omaha (pot limit)	32nd World Series of Poker	Las Vegas	15th	$4,910
2001	$1,500 + 90 Limit Ace to Five Draw	32nd World Series of Poker	Las Vegas	15th	$1,850
2001	$5,000 + 150 Omaha Hi-Lo Split Eight or Better	32nd World Series of Poker	Las Vegas	2nd	$103,785
2001	$10,000 Championship Event - No Limit Hold'em	32nd World Series of Poker	Las Vegas	5th	$303,705
2001	ATS 34,400 + 1,650 World Heads Up Poker Championships Finals	Austrian Masters 2001	Vienna Simmering	33rd	$429
2001	ATS 10,000 + 500 World Heads Up Poker Championships	Austrian Masters 2001	Vienna Simmering	3rd	$1,999
2001	ATS 10,000 + 500 No Limit Hold'em	Austrian Masters 2001	Vienna Simmering	1st	$18,482
2001	$500 + 40 Omaha Hi Lo Split	California State Poker Championship 2001	Los Angeles	5th	$2,200

Date	Event	Tournament	Location	Place	Prize
2001	$200 + 20 Limit Hold'em	California State Poker Championship 2001	Los Angeles	9th	$1,721
2001	$2,000 Championship Event	Tournament of Champions	Las Vegas	19th	$6,000
2001	$1,000 + 60 7 Card Stud	2001 Legends of Poker	Los Angeles	2nd	$12,650
2001	$1,000 + 60 No Limit Hold'em	2001 US Poker Championship	Atlantic City	12th	$1,352
2002	$1,000 + 60 No Limit Texas Hold'em	The Third Annual Jack Binion World Poker Open	Tunica	8th	$3,841
2002	$300 + 30 Limit Texas Hold'em	The Third Annual Jack Binion World Poker Open	Tunica	2nd	$28,087
2002	$10,000 No Limit Texas Hold'em Championship	The Third Annual Jack Binion World Poker Open	Tunica	17th	$10,864
2002	$300 + 30 Pot Limit Hold'em	2002 LA Poker Classic	Los Angeles	10th	$1,213
2002	$1,000 + 60 H.O.S.E.	2002 LA Poker Classic	Los Angeles	2nd	$25,600
2002	$8,000 Limit Hold'em - Final Results	Party Poker Million	Cruise	3rd	$62,400
2002	$1,500 Limit Omaha	33rd World Series of Poker	Las Vegas	8th	$3,640
2002	$2,500 No Limit Hold'em - Gold Bracelet Match Play	33rd World Series of Poker	Las Vegas	2nd	$17,000
2002	$3,000 + 50 No Limit Hold'em	Larry Flynt Grand Slam of Poker	Gardena	3rd	$33,840
2002	$100 + 20 Limit Hold'em	2002 Legends of Poker	Los Angeles	6th	$1,255
2002	$300 + 30 Limit Hold'em	2002 Legends of Poker	Los Angeles	7th	$4,120
2002	$5,000 + 80 No Limit Hold'em Championship - WPT	2002 Legends of Poker	Los Angeles	8th	$12,900
2002	$300 + 35 Limit Hold'em	2002 Caribbean Poker Classic	Palm Beach	3rd	$1,220
2002	$200 + 20 Seven Card Stud	3rd Annual 49'er Gold Rush Bonanza	San Francisco	8th	$500
2002	$3,000 + 150 No Limit Hold'em - Main WPT Event	3rd Annual 49'er Gold Rush Bonanza	San Francisco	4th	$34,000

Date	Event	Tournament	Location	Place	Prize
2002	$1,000 + 60 Pot Limit Hold'em	Bellagio Five Diamond Poker Classic -2002	Las Vegas	3rd	$13,386
2002	$1,500 + 70 Pot Limit Omaha	Bellagio Five Diamond Poker Classic - 2002	Las Vegas	2nd	$29,449
2002	No Limit Hold'em	2002 US Poker Championship	Atlantic City	8th	$1,975
2003	$10,000 + 100 No Limit Hold'em Championship - WTP	The Fourth Annual Jack Binion World Poker Open	Tunica	10th	$18,324
2003	$1,000 + 60 Omaha Hi/Lo	2003 LA Poker Classic	Los Angeles	1st	$55,485
2003	$25,000 WPT Championship - No Limit Hold'em	2003 Bellagio Five-Star World Poker Classic WPT Championship	Las Vegas	20th	$15,999
2003	$2,000 H.O.R.S.E.	34th World Series of Poker	Las Vegas	12th	$3,160
2003	$2,500 Limit Hold'em	34th World Series of Poker	Las Vegas	1st	$171,400
2003	$1,500 Limit Omaha	34th World Series of Poker	Las Vegas	3rd	$15,800
2003	$3,000 Limit Hold'em	34th World Series of Poker	Las Vegas	6th	$15,040
2003	$3,000 No Limit Hold'em	34th World Series of Poker	Las Vegas	1st	$410,860
2003	$10,000 World Championship Event	34th World Series of Poker	Las Vegas	27th	$45,000
2003	$1,500 + 70 Pot Limit Omaha	Festa al Lago	Las Vegas	4th	$8,585
2003	$9,800 + 200 No Limit Hold'em Main Event	2003 U.S. Poker Championship	Atlantic City	3rd	$116,424
2003	$1,000 + 70 No Limit Hold'em	2003 Four Queens Poker Classic	Las Vegas	7th	$3,055
2003	$10,000 + 200 No Limit Hold'em WPT Event	2003 World Poker Finals	Mashantucket	3rd	$281,700
2004	$1,500 Omaha Hi-Lo Split	35th World Series of Poker	Las Vegas	17th	$4,120
2004	$2,500 Limit Hold'em	35th World Series of Poker	Las Vegas	26th	$3,280
2004	$2,000 Omaha Hi-Lo Split	35th World Series of Poker	Las Vegas	21st	$2,580

Date	Event	Tournament	Location	Place	Prize
2004	$2,000 Pot Limit Hold'em	35th World Series of Poker	Las Vegas	6th	$29,800
2004	$3,000 Pot Limit Hold'em	35th World Series of Poker	Las Vegas	7th	$34,880
2004	$15,000 + 300 World Poker Tour Championship - No Limit Hold'em	Five-Diamond World Poker Classic	Las Vegas	41st	$21,781
2005	Heads-Up No Limit Hold'em	2005 National Heads-Up Poker Championship	Las Vegas	1st	$500,000
2005	$1,500 No Limit Hold'em	36th World Series of Poker	Las Vegas	24th	$15,905
2005	$1,500 Limit Hold'em	36th World Series of Poker	Las Vegas	42nd	$4,200
2005	$1,500 Pot Limit Omaha	36th World Series of Poker	Las Vegas	10th	$5,080
2005	$5,000 Pot Limit Omaha	36th World Series of Poker	Las Vegas	8th	$70,625
2005	Tournament of Champions-No Limit Hold'em	2005 WSOP Tournament of Champions	Las Vegas	3rd	$250,000
2006	$25,000 + 500 WPT Championship - No Limit Hold'em	Fourth Annual Five-Star World Poker Classic	Las Vegas	50th	$58,585
2006	€10,000 WPT Grand Prix de Paris - No Limit Hold'em	Rendez Vous a Paris 2006	Paris	16th	$22,915
2006	$1,500 No Limit Hold'em	37th World Series of Poker	Las Vegas	67th	$7,578
2006	$3,000 Limit Hold'em	37th World Series of Poker	Las Vegas	13th	$10,309
2006	$5,000 No Limit Hold'em	37th World Series of Poker	Las Vegas	2nd	$423,893
2006	$3,000 Omaha Hi/Lo	37th World Series of Poker	Las Vegas	6th	$48,576
2006	$5,000 Short Handed No Limit Hold'em	37th World Series of Poker	Las Vegas	44th	$8,340
2006	$1,000 No Limit Hold'em	37th World Series of Poker	Las Vegas	1st	$631,863
2006	$1,500 No Limit Hold'em	37th World Series of Poker	Las Vegas	44th	$5,498
2006	$1,500 No Limit Hold'em	37th World Series of Poker	Las Vegas	3rd	$53,945

Poker Brat

Date	Event	Tournament	Location	Place	Prize
2007	Group 1 Match	Partypoker.com Premier League Poker	Maidstone	1st	$8,000
2007	Group Match 3	Partypoker.com Premier League Poker	Maidstone	1st	$8,000
2007	Group Match 4	Partypoker.com Premier League Poker	Maidstone	1st	$8,000
2007	Group Match 7	Partypoker.com Premier League Poker	Maidstone	1st	$8,000
2007	Group Match 10	Partypoker.com Premier League Poker	Maidstone	3rd	$3,000
2007	No Limit Hold'em - Finals	Partypoker.com Premier League Poker	Maidstone	3rd	$30,000
2007	$25,000 + 500 WPT - No Limit Hold'em Championship	Fifth Annual Five Star World Poker Classic	Las Vegas	18th	$123,760
2007	$2,000 No Limit Hold'em	38th World Series of Poker	Las Vegas	104th	$3,901
2007	$1,500 No Limit Hold'em	38th World Series of Poker	Las Vegas	1st	$637,254
2007	$3,000 No Limit Hold'em	38th World Series of Poker	Las Vegas	6th	$76,464
2007	$3,000 Limit Hold'em	38th World Series of Poker	Las Vegas	25th	$7,761
2007	$5,000 No Limit Hold'em - Six Handed	38th World Series of Poker	Las Vegas	31st	$13,344
2007	$1,000 No Limit Hold'em	38th World Series of Poker	Las Vegas	95th	$4,840
2008	$20,000 Week 1 - "Dream Table"	Poker After Dark III	Las Vegas	1st	$120,000
2008	$20,000 Week 3 - "Hecklers"	Poker After Dark III	Las Vegas	1st	$120,000
2008	Heat 1	PartyPoker.com Premier League Poker II	London	4th	$4,000
2008	Heat 4	PartyPoker.com Premier League Poker II	London	4th	$4,000
2008	Heat 5	PartyPoker.com Premier League Poker II	London	5th	$2,000
2008	Heat 12	PartyPoker.com Premier League Poker II	London	3rd	$6,000

Appendix 4 - All My Cashes

Date	Event	Tournament	Location	Place	Prize
2008	$9,900 + 100 No Limit Hold'em - Championship Event	2008 LA Poker Classic	Los Angeles	6th	$229,820
2008	$5,000 Pot Limit Omaha	39th World Series of Poker	Las Vegas	8th	$100,292
2008	$1,500 No Limit Hold'em	39th World Series of Poker	Las Vegas	71st	$6,604
2008	$1,500 Seven Card Stud Hi/Lo	39th World Series of Poker	Las Vegas	33rd	$2,895
2008	$1,500 H.O.R.S.E.	39th World Series of Poker	Las Vegas	3rd	$93,168
2008	$5,000 Ante Up For Africa Charity Event	39th World Series of Poker	Las Vegas	4th	$38,491
2008	$10,000 World Championship No Limit Hold'em	39th World Series of Poker	Las Vegas	45th	$154,400
2008	$50,000 Week 3 - Heads up Challenge	Poker After Dark IV	Las Vegas	1st	$200,000
2008	€2,500 + 150 Limit H.O.R.S.E.	2008 World Series of Poker	Europe, London	12th	$11,254
2008	Heat 3	PartyPoker.com Premier League Poker III	London	4th	$6,000
2008	Heat 6	PartyPoker.com Premier League Poker III	London	1st	$20,000
2008	Heat 9	PartyPoker.com Premier League Poker III	London	2nd	$12,000
2008	Heat 11	PartyPoker.com Premier League Poker III	London	5th	$4,000
2008	$15,000 + 400 No Limit Hold'em - Doyle Brunson Classic	2008 Doyle Brunson Five Diamond World Poker Classic	Las Vegas	93rd	$21,620
2009	$20,000 No Limit Hold'em	NBC National Heads-Up Championship 2009	Las Vegas	5th	$75,000
2009	C$5,000 No Limit Hold'em - Heads Up	Canadian Open Poker Championship	Calgary	5th	$15,035
2009	$2,000 No Limit Hold'em	40th World Series of Poker	Las Vegas	29th	$12,761

Poker Brat

Date	Event	Tournament	Location	Place	Prize
2009	$1,500 No Limit Hold'em	40th World Series of Poker	Las Vegas	113th	$3,231
2009	$2,000 Limit Hold'em	40th World Series of Poker	Las Vegas	17th	$8,019
2009	$1,500 Pot Limit Omaha Hi/Lo	40th World Series of Poker	Las Vegas	14th	$11,347
2009	$5,000 No Limit Hold'em - Six Handed	40th World Series of Poker	Las Vegas	24th	$26,823
2009	$10,000 World Championship No Limit Hold'em	40th World Series of Poker	Las Vegas	436th	$25,027
2010	Heat 2	Party Poker Premier League IV	Las Vegas	6th	$6,000
2010	Heat 3	Party Poker Premier League IV	Las Vegas	6th	$6,000
2010	Heat 5	Party Poker Premier League IV	Las Vegas	7th	$4,000
2010	Heat 6	Party Poker Premier League IV	Las Vegas	2nd	$22,000
2010	$9,600 + 400 No Limit Hold'em - Championship Event	Bay 101 Shooting Stars	San Jose	6th	$117,000
2010	$25,000 + 500 No Limit Hold'em - Championship Event	Eighth Annual Five Star World Poker Classic	Las Vegas	7th	$152,856
2010	$500 + 50 No Limit Hold'em	Derby Poker Championship 2010-Celebrity Charity Event	Louisville	4th	$4,272
2010	$1,500 No Limit Hold'em	41st World Series of Poker	Las Vegas	15th	$25,472
2010	$5,000 No Limit Hold'em	41st World Series of Poker	Las Vegas	50th	$14,517
2010	$1,500 Pot Limit Omaha Hi/ Lo 8	41st World Series of Poker	Las Vegas	7th	$30,633
2010	$10,000 Pot Limit Omaha Championship	41st World Series of Poker	Las Vegas	15th	$39,906
2010	$50,000 No Limit Hold'em - Qualifying Match 15	FullTiltPoker.com-Doubles Poker Championship	Las Vegas	1st	$5,000
2011	$5,000 + 170 No Limit Hold'em - Main Event	2011 Wynn Classic	Las Vegas	19th	$7,712

Date	Event	Tournament	Location	Place	Prize
2011	$10,000 No Limit Deuce to Seven Draw World Championship	42nd World Series of Poker	Las Vegas	2nd	$226,907
2011	$10,000 Seven Card Stud Hi/ Lo Championship	42nd World Series of Poker	Las Vegas	2nd	$273,233
2011	$5,000 No Limit Hold'em - Six Handed	42nd World Series of Poker	Las Vegas	36th	$17,270
2011	$1,000 No Limit Hold'em	42nd World Series of Poker	Las Vegas	28th	$10,560
2011	$50,000 The Poker Players Championship - 8 Game	42nd World Series of Poker	Las Vegas	2nd	$1,063,034
2011	$1,500 No Limit Hold'em - Pro-Am Event	2011-12 Epic Poker League - Event 2	Las Vegas	3rd	$20,000
2011	$200 + 40 No Limit Hold'em - Charity Event	2011-12 Epic Poker League - Event 2	Las Vegas	2nd	$1,500
2011	€2,500 + 180 6-Max No Limit Hold'em	2011 World Series of Poker	Europe, Cannes	7th	$32,305
2012	$2,080 Eight Game Mix	2012 LA Poker Classic	Los Angeles	1st	$22,630
2012	€3,200 + 300 No Limit Hold'em - Main Event	PaddyPower Irish Open 2012	Dublin	33rd	$12,384
2012	$1,500 No Limit Hold'em (Event #2)	43rd World Series of Poker	Las Vegas	61st	$7,204
2012	$1,500 Omaha Hi/Lo (Event #8)	43rd World Series of Poker	Las Vegas	52nd	$4,817
2012	$5,000 Seven Card Stud Hi/ Lo (Event #15)	43rd World Series of Poker	Las Vegas	15th	$11,637
2012	$2,500 Seven Card Razz (Event #18)	43rd World Series of Poker	Las Vegas	1st	$182,793
2012	$10,000 H.O.R.S.E (Event #32)	43rd World Series of Poker	Las Vegas	4th	$134,056
2012	$1,000,000 The Big One for One Drop (Event #55)	43rd World Series of Poker	Las Vegas	4th	$2,645,333
2012	€2,5000 + 200 No Limit Hold'em - Six Handed (Event #1)	2012 World Series of Poker	Europe, Cannes	24th	$6,376
2012	€3,000 + 250 No Limit Hold'em - Shootout (Event #4)	2012 World Series of Poker	Europe, Cannes	12th	$7,082
2012	€10,000 + 450 No Limit Hold'em - Mixed Max (Event #5)	2012 World Series of Poker	Europe, Cannes	12th	$26,671

Date	Event	Tournament	Location	Place	Prize
2012	€10,000 + 450 No Limit Hold'em - Main Event (Event #7)	2012 World Series of Poker	Europe, Cannes	1st	$1,333,841
2013	$5,000 + 300 Pot Limit Omaha (Event #15)	PCA - 2013	Paradise Island	4th	$33,180
2013	$20,000 No Limit Hold'em - Heads Up	NBC Heads-Up Championship	Las Vegas	2nd	$300,000
2013	$125,000 No Limit Hold'em	Partypoker.com Premier League Poker VI	London	11th	$42,000
2013	A$1,100 No Limit Hold'em - Accumulator	World Series of Poker Asia-Pacific	Melbourne	20th	$9,470
2013	$10,000 No Limit Hold'em - Heads-Up (Event #16)	44th World Series of Poker	Las Vegas	8th	$54,024
2013	$3,000 Pot Limit Omaha (Event #35)	44th World Series of Poker	Las Vegas	26th	$11,915
2013	$1,500 Seven Card Stud Hi/Lo (Event #39)	44th World Series of Poker	Las Vegas	42nd	$3,246
2013	€2,000 + 200 Open Face Chinese	EPT - 10 - UKIPT - 4 - London	London	1st	$25,618
2013	€2,000 + 200 No Limit Hold'em (Event #4)	2013 World Series of Poker	Europe, Enghien-les-Bains	29th	$5,685
2014	$2,140 Commerce 8 Game Mix	WPT - LA Poker Classic	Los Angeles	4th	$11,180
2014	$1,500 Seven Card Razz (Event #7)	45th World Series of Poker	Las Vegas	2nd	$74,848
2014	$3,000 No Limit Hold'em - Six Handed (Event #15)	45th World Series of Poker	Las Vegas	8th	$45,022
2014	$1,500 No Limit Hold'em (Event #26)	45th World Series of Poker	Las Vegas	29th	$9,877
2014	$1,500 No Limit 2-7 Draw Lowball (Event #36)	45th World Series of Poker	Las Vegas	18th	$3,471
2014	$1,500 No Limit Hold'em - Ante-Up (Event # 47)	45th World Series of Poker	Las Vegas	30th	$5,397
2014	$5,000 No Limit Hold'em (Event #49)	45th World Series of Poker	Las Vegas	35th	$18,318
2014	$10,000 Seven Card Stud (Event #61)	45th World Series of Poker	Las Vegas	6th	$46,885
2014	A$ 2,200 No Limit Hold'em 6 Max	World Series of Poker Asia-Pacific	Melbourne	4th	$34,192

Date	Event	Tournament	Location	Place	Prize
2014	$1,000 + 100 No Limit Hold'em - Championship Main Event Final Day #39	2014 Pittsburgh Poker Open	Pittsburgh	1st	$54,414
2015	$1,675 No Limit Hold'em Main Event #10	World Series of Poker Circuit	Baltimore	50th	$3,357
2015	$250 No Limit Hold'em	$100K Guaranteed Poker Showdown	Philadelphia	36th	$810
2015	$10,000 Seven Card Razz Championship (Event #17)	46th World Series of Poker	Las Vegas	1st	$271,105
2015	$1,500 H.O.R.S.E. (Event #24)	46th World Series of Poker	Las Vegas	31st	$5,388
2015	$1,500 Ten Game Mix Six Handed (Event #39)	46th World Series of Poker	Las Vegas	17th	$5,360
2015	$2,500 No Limit Hold'em (Event #47)	46th World Series of Poker	Las Vegas	16th	$20,263
2015	$111,111 No Limit Hold'em High Roller for One-Drop (Event #58)	46th World Series of Poker	Las Vegas	6th	$696,821
2015	$10,000 No Limit Hold'em Main Event (Event #68)	46th World Series of Poker	Las Vegas	417th	$21,786
2015	€550 No Limit Hold'em - The Oktoberfest #2	2015 World Series of Poker	Europe, Berlin	61st	$2,863
2016	$300,000 No Limit Hold'em	Super High Roller Bowl with 888poker	Las Vegas	4th	$1,600,000
2016	$3,000 H.O.R.S.E. (Event #18)	47th World Series of Poker	Las Vegas	45th	$5,081
2016	$10,000 Seven Card Razz Championship (Event #20)	47th World Series of Poker	Las Vegas	15th	$15,464
2016	$5,000 No Limit Hold'em (30-minute Levels) (Event #48)	47th World Series of Poker	Las Vegas	8th	$46,553
2016	$340 + 60 No Limit Hold'em - PH	2016 Aria Resort & Casino Recurring Tournaments	Las Vegas	6th	$2,148

Poker Brat

Appendix 5

All My WSOP Final Tables

Date	Event	Tournament	# of Players	Location	Place	Prize
1988	$1,500 Seven-Card Stud Split	19th World Series of Poker	206	Las Vegas	5th	$15,450
1989	$2,500 Omaha Pot Limit	20th World Series of Poker	99	Las Vegas	5th	$25,300
1989	$10,000 No Limit Hold'em World Championship	20th World Series of Poker	178	Las Vegas	1st	$775,000
1990	$2,500 No Limit Hold'em	21st World Series of Poker	268	Las Vegas	5th	$32,500
1992	$1,500 No Limit Hold'em	23rd World Series of Poker	254	Las Vegas	9th	$5,715
1992	$5,000 No Limit Deuce to Seven Draw	23rd World Series of Poker	30	Las Vegas	4th	$26,500
1992	$2,500 Limit Hold'em	23rd World Series of Poker	168	Las Vegas	2nd	$84,000
1992	$2,500 Hold'em Pot Limit	23rd World Series of Poker	134	Las Vegas	8th	$6,700
1992	$5,000 Limit Hold'em	23rd World Series of Poker	84	Las Vegas	1st	$168,000
1993	$1,500 No Limit Hold'em	24th World Series of Poker	284	Las Vegas	1st	$161,400
1993	$5,000 No Limit Deuce to Seven Draw	24th World Series of Poker	30	Las Vegas	2nd	$72,500
1993	$2,500 No Limit Hold'em	24th World Series of Poker	173	Las Vegas	1st	$173,000

Date	Event	Tournament	# of Players	Location	Place	Prize
1993	$5,000 Limit Hold'em	24th World Series of Poker	69	Las Vegas	1st	$138,000
1994	$1,500 No Limit Hold'em	25th World Series of Poker	328	Las Vegas	2nd	$93,900
1996	$2,500 Omaha 8 or Better	27th World Series of Poker	110	Las Vegas	6th	$12,375
1997	$3,000 Hold'em Pot Limit	28th World Series of Poker	170	Las Vegas	1st	$204,000
1999	$2,500 Omaha 8 or Better	30th World Series of Poker	186	Las Vegas	5th	$20,925
2000	$2,000 + 70 Pot Limit Hold'em	31st World Series of Poker	235	Las Vegas	6th	$16,450
2000	$2,500 + 80 Pot Limit Omaha	31st World Series of Poker	100	Las Vegas	4th	$29,250
2001	$2,000 + 100 Texas Hold'em (No Limit)	32nd World Series of Poker	441	Las Vegas	1st	$316,550
2001	$3,000 + 120 Texas Hold'em (Limit)	32nd World Series of Poker	192	Las Vegas	6th	$19,555
2001	$5,000 + 150 Omaha Hi-Lo Split 8 or Better	32nd World Series of Poker	107	Las Vegas	2nd	$103,785
2001	$10,000 Championship Event - No Limit Hold'em	32nd World Series of Poker	613	Las Vegas	5th	$303,705
2002	$1,500 Limit Omaha	33rd World Series of Poker	130	Las Vegas	8th	$3,640
2002	$2,500 No Limit Hold'em - Gold Bracelet Match Play	33rd World Series of Poker	29	Las Vegas	2nd	$17,000
2003	$2,500 Limit Hold'em	34th World Series of Poker	194	Las Vegas	1st	$171,400
2003	$1,500 Limit Omaha	34th World Series of Poker	120	Las Vegas	3rd	$15,800
2003	$3,000 Limit Hold'em	34th World Series of Poker	154	Las Vegas	6th	$15,040
2003	$3,000 No Limit Hold'em	34th World Series of Poker	398	Las Vegas	1st	$410,860
2004	$2,000 Pot Limit Hold'em	35th World Series of Poker	324	Las Vegas	6th	$29,800
2004	$3,000 Pot Limit Hold'em	35th World Series of Poker	316	Las Vegas	7th	$34,880

Poker Brat

Date	Event	Tournament	# of Players	Location	Place	Prize
2004	No Limit Hold'em - Tournament of Champions	WSOP Tournament of Champions	10	Las Vegas	2nd	$750,000
2005	$5,000 Pot Limit Omaha	36th World Series of Poker	134	Las Vegas	8th	$70,625
2005	Tournament of Champions - No Limit Hold'em	WSOP Tournament of Champions	114	Las Vegas	3rd	$250,000
2006	$5,000 No Limit Hold'em	37th World Series of Poker	622	Las Vegas	2nd	$423,893
2006	$3,000 Omaha Hi/Lo	37th World Series of Poker	352	Las Vegas	6th	$48,576
2006	$1,000 No Limit Hold'em	37th World Series of Poker	754	Las Vegas	1st	$631,863
2006	$1,500 No Limit Hold'em	37th World Series of Poker	494	Las Vegas	3rd	$53,945
2007	$1,500 No Limit Hold'em	38th World Series of Poker	2628	Las Vegas	1st	$637,254
2007	$3,000 No Limit Hold'em	38th World Series of Poker	827	Las Vegas	6th	$76,464
2008	$5,000 Pot Limit Omaha	39th World Series of Poker	152	Las Vegas	8th	$100,292
2008	$1,5000 H.O.R.S.E.	39th World Series of Poker	803	Las Vegas	3rd	$93,168
2008	$5,000 Ante Up For Africa Charity Event	39th World Series of Poker	88	Las Vegas	4th	$38,491
2010	$1,500 Pot Limit Omaha Hi/Lo 8	41st World Series of Poker	847	Las Vegas	7th	$30,633
2011	$10,000 No Limit Deuce to Seven Draw World Championship	42nd World Series of Poker	126	Las Vegas	2nd	$226,907
2011	$10,000 Seven Card Stud Hi/Lo Championship	42nd World Series of Poker	168	Las Vegas	2nd	$273,233
2011	$50,000 The Poker Players Championship - 8 Game	42nd World Series of Poker	128	Las Vegas	2nd	$1,063,034
2011	€2,500 + 800 6-Max No Limit Hold'em	2011 World Series of Poker	360	Europe, Cannes	7th	$32,302
2012	$2,500 Seven Card Razz	43rd World Series of Poker	309	Las Vegas	1st	$182,793

Date	Event	Tournament	# of Players	Location	Place	Prize
2012	$10,000 H.O.R.S.E	43rd World Series of Poker	178	Las Vegas	4th	$134,056
2012	$1,000,000 The Big One for One Drop	43rd World Series of Poker	48	Las Vegas	4th	$2,645,333
2012	€10,000 + 450 Limit Hold'em - Main Event	2012 World Series of Poker	420	Europe, Cannes	1st	$1,333,841
2013	$10,000 No Limit Hold'em - Heads-Up	44th World Series of Poker	162	Las Vegas	8th	$54,024
2014	$1,500 Seven Card Razz	45th World Series of Poker	352	Las Vegas	2nd	$74,848
2014	$3,000 No Limit Hold'em - Six Handed	45th World Series of Poker	810	Las Vegas	8th	$45,022
2014	$10,000 Seven Card Stud	45th World Series of Poker	102	Las Vegas	6th	$46,885
2014	A$2,200 No Limit Hold'em 6 Max	World Series of Poker Asia-Pacific	243	Melbourne	4th	$34,192
2015	$10,000 Seven Card Razz Championship	46th World Series of Poker	103	Las Vegas	1st	$271,105
2015	$111,111 No Limit Hold'em High Roller for One-Drop	46th World Series of Poker	135	Las Vegas	6th	$696,821
2016	$5,000 No Limit Hold'em (30-minute Levels)	47th World Series of Poker	524	Las Vegas	8th	$46,553

Index

Friedman, Prahlad 348
FTP (Full Tilt Poker) 284, 345–6, 349, 350
Furlong, Noel 122, 124, 125, 126, 128–9

G
Galfond, Phil 353
game theory 41
Garcia, Antonio 316–17, 323
Garrett, Brad 324
Giang, Chau 353
Gladden, Rose 23–4
Glazer, Andy 241, 242
Glick, Mike 353
God Mode online tool 347–8
Goldberg, Dave 282–3, 309–11, 328, 352
Golden Nugget Hotel and Casino 121, 151, 250–2, 326
Golden State Warriors *185*
Golden State warriors vs. Cleveland Cavaliers 311–12
Goldstein, Stan 218
Goodstat, Dan 320
Gordon, Jeff *189*
Gordon, Phil 221–2
Grand Hotel Bagni Nuovi 267
Grassy, Richard 16, 17, 21
The Great White Ninja 13
Green Bay Packers 205–6
Green, Draymond *184*, *185*
Green, Perry 73
Greenstein, Barry 333
Grey, David 353
Grizzle, Sam 106–7
Gurley, Bill 332

H
Hall of Fame Championships 103–5, 106, 154, 169, 174, 175–6, 200, 268

Hall of Fame Watch 164, 175
Haller, Kai 32–3, 40
Harbaugh, Jim *185*, *189*, 295, 324
Harbaugh, Sarah 295
Hardi, Jason 320–3
Hardie, George "Diamond Jim Brady" 124
Harman, Jennifer 345, 353
Haromy, Tuli (Patrick) 36–8, 39, 40, 41–2, 43–4, 45, 47, 53, 54, 126–7, *179*
Harper Collins 240, 243
Harrah's Hotel and Casino 209, 245–6, 253, 275
Hastings, Brian 356
Havenor, J.P. 76
hedge funds 207
Heimowitz, Jay 125
Hellmuth, Ann (sister of PH) 13, 18, 24, 142, *177*, *178*
Hellmuth, Dave (brother of PH) 13, 24, 27, 95–6, 104, 110, 120, 121, 140, 141, 156, *177*, *178*, *179*
Hellmuth, George (grandfather of PH) 25, 27–8
Hellmuth, George Jr. (aunt of PH) 28
Hellmuth, George Jr. (uncle of PH) 28
Hellmuth, Kathy (wife of PH) 15, 69, 141–5, 149–64, 168, 170, 172, 174, 175, 176, 195, 200, 204, 208–9, 212, 225–30, 237–8, 308, 312–15, 316–17
Hellmuth, Kerry (sister of PH) 13, 24, 110–11, *177*, *178*, *180*, 213, 214, 245, 267, 295
Hellmuth, Lynn (mother of PH) 9–10, 12, 15, 17, 24–5, 146, 168, 171, *177*, *178*, *180*, 195
Hellmuth, Molly (sister of PH) 13, 24, 113–15, 142–3, *177*, *178*, *180*, 212–13, 214, 268, 295